AI Innovation in Services Marketing

Ricardo Correia
Instituto Politécnico de Bragança, Portugal & CiTUR, Portugal

Dominyka Venciute
ISM University of Management and Economics, Lithuania

A volume in the Advances in Marketing, Customer Relationship Management, and E-Services (AMCRMES) Book Series

IGI Global
PUBLISHER of TIMELY KNOWLEDGE

Published in the United States of America by
IGI Global
Business Science Reference (an imprint of IGI Global)
701 E. Chocolate Avenue
Hershey PA, USA 17033
Tel: 717-533-8845
Fax: 717-533-8661
E-mail: cust@igi-global.com
Web site: http://www.igi-global.com

Library of Congress Cataloging-in-Publication Data

Names: Correia, Ricardo Fontes, 1978- editor. | Venciute, Dominyka, 1990- editor.
Title: AI innovation in services marketing / edited by Ricardo Correia, Dominyka Venciute.
Description: Hershey, PA : Business Science Reference, [2024] | Includes bibliographical references and index. | Summary: "This book explores the profound implications of AI for the services industry and its impact on consumer behavior. As AI continues to reshape the way services are delivered, experienced, and optimized, understanding the evolving role of services marketing is essential for businesses, academics, and practitioners alike"-- Provided by publisher.
Identifiers: LCCN 2024010194 (print) | LCCN 2024010195 (ebook) | ISBN 9798369321539 (hardcover) | ISBN 9798369344750 (paperback) | ISBN 9798369321546 (ebook)
Subjects: LCSH: Service industries--Technological innovations. | Service industries--Marketing. | Artificial intelligence--Industrial applications.
Classification: LCC HD9980.5 .A388 2024 (print) | LCC HD9980.5 (ebook) | DDC 338.4--dc23/eng/20240313
LC record available at https://lccn.loc.gov/2024010194
LC ebook record available at https://lccn.loc.gov/2024010195

This book is published in the IGI Global book series Advances in Marketing, Customer Relationship Management, and E-Services (AMCRMES) (ISSN: 2327-5502; eISSN: 2327-5529)

British Cataloguing in Publication Data
A Cataloguing in Publication record for this book is available from the British Library.

For electronic access to this publication, please contact: eresources@igi-global.com.

Advances in Marketing, Customer Relationship Management, and E-Services (AMCRMES) Book Series

ISSN:2327-5502
EISSN:2327-5529

Editor-in-Chief: Eldon Y. Li, National Chengchi University, Taiwan & California Polytechnic State University, USA

MISSION

Business processes, services, and communications are important factors in the management of good customer relationship, which is the foundation of any well organized business. Technology continues to play a vital role in the organization and automation of business processes for marketing, sales, and customer service. These features aid in the attraction of new clients and maintaining existing relationships.

The Advances in Marketing, Customer Relationship Management, and E-Services (AMCRMES) Book Series

addresses success factors for customer relationship management, marketing, and electronic services and its performance outcomes. This collection of reference source covers aspects of consumer behavior and marketing business strategies aiming towards researchers, scholars, and practitioners in the fields of marketing management.

COVERAGE

- Text Mining and Marketing
- Data mining and marketing
- Web Mining and Marketing
- Mobile CRM
- CRM and customer trust
- Cases on Electronic Services
- CRM in financial services
- Ethical Considerations in E-Marketing
- Customer Retention
- Relationship Marketing

IGI Global is currently accepting manuscripts for publication within this series. To submit a proposal for a volume in this series, please contact our Acquisition Editors at Acquisitions@igi-global.com or visit: http://www.igi-global.com/publish/.

The Advances in Marketing, Customer Relationship Management, and E-Services (AMCRMES) Book Series (ISSN 2327-5502) is published by IGI Global, 701 E. Chocolate Avenue, Hershey, PA 17033-1240, USA, www.igi-global.com. This series is composed of titles available for purchase individually; each title is edited to be contextually exclusive from any other title within the series. For pricing and ordering information please visit http://www.igi-global.com/book-series/advances-marketing-customer-relationship-management/37150. Postmaster: Send all address changes to above address.

Titles in this Series

For a list of additional titles in this series, please visit:
http://www.igi-global.com/book-series/advances-marketing-customer-relationship-management/37150

Impact of Teleworking and Remote Work on Business Productivity, Retention, Advancement, and Bottom Line
Harish Chandra Chandan (Independent Researcher, USA)
Business Science Reference • copyright 2024 • 311pp • H/C (ISBN: 9798369313145) • US $290.00 (our price)

AI-Driven Marketing Research and Data Analytics
Reason Masengu (Middle East College, Oman) Option Takunda Chiwaridzo (University of Science and Technology Beijing, Beijing, China) Mercy Dube (Midlands State University, Zimbabwe) and Benson Ruzive (Modern College of Business and Science, Oman)
Business Science Reference • copyright 2024 • 490pp • H/C (ISBN: 9798369321652) • US $290.00 (our price)

Marketing Innovation Strategies and Consumer Behavior
Belem Barbosa (University of Porto, Portugal)
Business Science Reference • copyright 2024 • 469pp • H/C (ISBN: 9798369341957) • US $325.00 (our price)

Corporate Governance and CSR Strategies for Sustainability
Maja Pucelj (Faculty of Organisation Studies, University of Novo Mesto, Slovenia) and Rado Bohinc (Scientific Research Centre Koper, Slovenia)
Information Science Reference • copyright 2024 • 368pp • H/C (ISBN: 9798369358634) • US $290.00 (our price)

Balancing Automation and Human Interaction in Modern Marketing
Arjun J. Nair (St. Lawrence College, Canada) Sridhar Manohar (Chitkara Business School, Chitkara University, India) Amit Mittal (Chitkara Business School, Chitkara University, India) and Wasim Ahmed (University of Hull, UK)

For an entire list of titles in this series, please visit:
http://www.igi-global.com/book-series/advances-marketing-customer-relationship-management/37150

IGI Global
PUBLISHER of TIMELY KNOWLEDGE

701 East Chocolate Avenue, Hershey, PA 17033, USA
Tel: 717-533-8845 x100 • Fax: 717-533-8661
E-Mail: cust@igi-global.com • www.igi-global.com

Table of Contents

Detailed Table of Contents

The widespread adoption of artificial intelligence (AI) has ignited transformative changes across diverse domains, including business and marketing. Consequently, this study immerses itself in the initiatives undertaken by Invest Lithuania, a non-profit foreign direct investment development agency, which orchestrated an inventive marketing campaign through the synergy of account-based marketing (ABM), storytelling, and artificial intelligence (AI) techniques. The campaign's overarching goal was to effectively engage target contacts and increase business opportunities in the game development sector. In this dynamic environment, innovative marketing approaches, like those explored in this study, can help build long-term relationships and promote sustainable business growth. The results showed that the potential is there.

Technological evolution has impelled companies to adopt innovative solutions supported by technologies. In a particular way, brands have been migrating from traditional marketing to digital marketing, with the vanguard of emerging technologies allowing them to obtain competitive advantages. Nowadays, artificial intelligence promises to transform the area of marketing, considering that machine learning, natural language processing, and predictive analytics are revolutionizing the way

Preface

In the ever-accelerating realm of business, the fusion of artificial intelligence (AI) with services marketing has surged to unprecedented levels. The dynamic landscape of AI is reshaping how services are conceptualized, delivered, and experienced. Welcome to *AI Innovation in Services Marketing*, a meticulously curated exploration into the transformative potential of AI within the services industry.

As editors, we are thrilled to present this compendium that delves deep into the profound implications of AI for services marketing and its profound impact on consumer behavior. This book is a testament to the evolving nature of marketing, where AI stands as a pivotal force driving innovation and disruption.

Our primary aim is to provide readers with a comprehensive understanding of AI's role in revolutionizing services marketing. Through a diverse array of real-world examples and case studies, we elucidate how AI amplifies productivity and enriches customer experiences. Moreover, we conscientiously navigate the ethical considerations surrounding AI adoption in services marketing, recognizing the importance of responsible innovation.

This book is a valuable resource tailored for a diverse audience. Whether you are a marketing scholar, educator, student, researcher, or industry practitioner, our aim is to equip you with the knowledge and insights needed to navigate the AI-powered landscape of services marketing.

Throughout these pages, you will encounter a rich tapestry of topics ranging from the convergence of services and AI to the ethical dimensions of AI-enhanced marketing. Our curated collection spans from foundational concepts to cutting-edge trends, ensuring relevance and applicability in today's dynamic marketplace.

Chapter 1 delves into the transformative potential of artificial intelligence (AI) within marketing, particularly through the lens of an inventive campaign orchestrated by Invest Lithuania. By synergizing Account-Based Marketing (ABM), storytelling, and AI techniques, the campaign aimed to engage target contacts and bolster business opportunities in the game development sector. The study reveals how innovative marketing approaches can cultivate long-term relationships and foster sustainable business growth, showcasing the promising prospects that lie ahead.

In Chapter 2, the focus shifts to the technological evolution propelling companies towards innovative solutions supported by AI. This chapter contextualizes AI within organizations, elucidating its potential for empowering brands in the digital marketing realm. By exploring machine learning, natural language processing, and predictive analytics, the chapter demonstrates how AI enables personalized experiences and data-driven decisions. Additionally, it presents a conceptual model for streamlining digital marketing functions, offering insights into its practical applications.

Chapter 3 undertakes an empirical analysis to uncover factors contributing to increased customer engagement in digital marketing campaigns. Through qualitative research methods and semi-structured interviews, the study identifies key tactics that shape user behavior and foster active engagement with digital ads. By leveraging insights from the research, managerial recommendations are provided using the RACE framework, offering a strategic roadmap for enhancing customer engagement across different phases of digital marketing campaigns.

The focus of Chapter 4 is on the intersection of information and communication technology (ICT) with preventive health, exploring how AI technologies can revolutionize healthcare marketing. By harnessing web and mobile applications, AI facilitates the storage and interpretation of medical data, thereby promoting preventive healthcare practices. This chapter examines the potential of AI to enhance patient care, optimize hospital operations, and foster a proactive approach to healthcare management.

Chapter 5 delves into the effects of AI on job performance among Tunisian employees, with a focus on gender and experience as moderating and mediating variables, respectively. Through empirical analysis, the study examines the relationship between AI and job performance, shedding light on the nuanced dynamics at play. While the direct impact of AI on job performance is found to be negligible, the study highlights the significant influence of employee experience on performance outcomes.

The profound influence of AI on advertising is explored in Chapter 6, tracing its historical evolution and current trends. From predictive analytics to hyper-personalization and conversational AI, the chapter illuminates how AI-driven strategies enhance user experience and target advertising efforts. Ethical considerations surrounding privacy and data security are also addressed, underscoring the transformative impact of AI on advertising practices.

Chapter 7 examines the integration of AI into service marketing in India, forecasting its significant impact on marketing strategies and economic dynamics. Through personalization, automation, predictive analytics, and chatbots, AI is poised to enhance customer engagement, streamline operations, and drive business growth. While concerns about job displacement persist, the chapter emphasizes the potential for AI-driven marketing to foster a technology-driven ecosystem in India, spurring innovation and entrepreneurship.

Chapter 8 emphasizes the need for innovation in service industries, particularly in developing robust business models that incorporate non-technical components. By synthesizing organizational, strategic, and marketing innovations, this chapter advocates for a holistic approach to service innovation. Various new business models are discussed, highlighting the importance of customer engagement and experience management in service-based firms.

In Chapter 9, the far-reaching impact of AI on the Indian service sector is explored, with a focus on consumer attitudes and perceptions. Through qualitative survey data, the chapter provides valuable insights into Indian consumers' views on AI adoption, addressing concerns about job displacement and workforce upskilling. Ethical dilemmas and future possibilities surrounding AI in the service industry are also examined, offering a comprehensive understanding of its implications in the Indian market.

We invite you to embark on this journey with us, as we traverse the intricate intersections of AI and services marketing. Together, let us explore, analyze, and envision the future of marketing innovation in the AI era.

Ricardo Correia
Instituto Politécnico de Bragança, Portugal & CiTUR, Portugal

Dominyka Venciute
ISM University of Management and Economics, Lithuania

Chapter 1
Where AI Meets Captivating Storytelling:
A Case Study of Invest Lithuania

Monika Belhaj
https://orcid.org/0000-0002-8946-8069
Mykolas Romeris University, Lithuania

ABSTRACT

The widespread adoption of artificial intelligence (AI) has ignited transformative changes across diverse domains, including business and marketing. Consequently, this study immerses itself in the initiatives undertaken by Invest Lithuania, a non-profit foreign direct investment development agency, which orchestrated an inventive marketing campaign through the synergy of account-based marketing (ABM), storytelling, and artificial intelligence (AI) techniques. The campaign's overarching goal was to effectively engage target contacts and increase business opportunities in the game development sector. In this dynamic environment, innovative marketing approaches, like those explored in this study, can help build long-term relationships and promote sustainable business growth. The results showed that the potential is there.

INTRODUCTION

Artificial Intelligence (AI) has recently experienced widespread adoption across various sectors, including marketing. Leading companies such as Google and Spotify have utilized AI to enhance operational efficiency (Jarek & Mazurek, 2019; Vlačić et al., 2021). However, AI's role extends beyond mere operations. According to

DOI: 10.4018/979-8-3693-2153-9.ch001

Haleem et al. (2022), strategically employing AI can be a vital asset for marketers, facilitating the development of innovative strategies and targeted marketing campaigns tailored to specific audiences.

Given this context and with a focus on B2B, innovative marketing strategies such as Account-Based Marketing (ABM) can assist in achieving that goal. ABM empowers marketers to customize initiatives to engage and influence key decision-makers within targeted companies or accounts (Burgess & Munn, 2021). When ABM is coupled with AI capabilities and compelling storytelling techniques, marketing efforts can be elevated to new heights, enhancing customer experiences and deeper connections (Spanos, 2021; Vidrih & Mayahi, 2023), potentially shaping future actions. This chapter is dedicated to delving into the dynamics of such transformative strategies.

The current study explores the synergy between ABM, storytelling, and AI, using a case study of Invest Lithuania, a non-profit agency that promotes foreign direct investment (FDI) in Lithuania. Considering challenges such as the global disruption caused by the COVID-19 pandemic to conventional marketing approaches (He & Harris, 2020), the organization implemented innovative strategies. Among these strategies was a One-to-Few ABM campaign (Mullen et al., 2022), designed to engage ten selected game development companies by involving storytelling and AI techniques.

The methodology of this study follows a qualitative interpretative approach. The chapter is divided into sections on the theoretical background, methodology, Invest Lithuania case study, conclusions, and recommendations for further research. Through this structured approach, the chapter endeavors to provide valuable insights that inform both academic discourse and practical applications in the field of marketing.

THEORETICAL BACKGROUND

A critical approach to marketing proves essential, as it plays a pivotal role in effectively connecting with target audiences and driving business expansion (Burgess & Munn, 2021). Given that, this section focuses on an emerging B2B strategy, account-based marketing, which is examined in conjunction with storytelling and AI. This fusion will be thoroughly explored, uncovering its transformative impact on reshaping marketing strategies and nurturing deeper connections with target audiences.

Account-Based Marketing

According to Vajre (2016), “The essential definition of account-based marketing is *focused* B2B marketing” (p. 10). It integrates by concentrating on specific, best-fit prospects. ABM treats these prospects, such as target companies or accounts, as distinct entities, tailoring personalized tactical initiatives that significantly impact key decision-makers (Burgess & Munn, 2021). This approach significantly diverges from conventional B2B marketing. As a result, ABM has garnered attention from researchers (Burgess & Munn, 2021) and practitioners (Vajre, 2016) for its substantial impact on business performance.

As Burgess and Munn (2021) highlighted, "there are some powerful economic, technological and social trends that are driving the need to incorporate ABM" (p. 6) into business strategies. These trends include competitive disruption, globalization and increasing complexity, evolving buyer expectations, and the growing emphasis on customization and personalization. Consequently, strategically minded businesses have acknowledged its potential and contemplated its adoption, considering its numerous benefits.

For example, ABM's personalized and targeted approach allows businesses to enhance customer engagement and improve conversion rates significantly (Upadhyay & McCormick, 2018). Furthermore, the alignment of sales and marketing teams, a fundamental aspect of ABM, has been recognized by academics like Golec et al. (2019) as a strategy that leads to higher revenue growth and improved overall business performance. ABM's ability to foster strong, long-term customer relationships translates into increased customer loyalty and higher customer lifetime value, further contributing to sustained business success (Bacon, 2021). Hence, empirical evidence highlights ABM as a robust strategy for enhancing customer experience and elevating business performance, thanks to its customer-centric and relationship-focused nature. However, a crucial inquiry emerges: What tools can effectively complement and bolster this approach? An intriguing response to this query emerges in the form of storytelling.

The Power of Storytelling

Storytelling, a fundamental and ancient form of communication, has been recognized as a potent tool for conveying information and shaping perceptions (Shivajirao & Verma, 2022). Scholars like Polkinghorne (1995) and Kreiswirth (2000) have emphasized the narrative structure inherent in human cognition and its role in constructing meaning. From a business perspective, storytelling possesses a unique ability to humanize and personalize the interactions between businesses and their customers (Lubis et al., 2023). It transcends the traditional transactional approach by creating emotional connections and fostering engagement. This tool enables organizations to communicate their values, mission, and brand identity compellingly and relatably (Denning, 2005). Moreover, as indicated by research such as that of Crespo et al. (2023), storytelling in marketing has been shown to elicit emotional responses and influence consumer behavior, serving as a pivotal factor in driving sales and nurturing brand loyalty.

In the context of ABM, integrating storytelling can be a strategic choice to make personalized outreach even more impactful. As Burgess and Munn (2021) suggest, integrating compelling narratives into communication with high-value accounts allows businesses to forge deeper connections, effectively convey their value propositions, and fortify relationships with target customers. However, this integration must be consistently implemented across all offline and online channels and stages, spanning from awareness to retention (Andersen et al., 2017), to ensure the attainment of strategic objectives.

It is worth noting that storytelling has evolved in tandem with technological advancements (Ellington, 2014). Thus, its synergy with AI software represents an innovative avenue with substantial potential. Subsequent sections will discuss this further.

Blending AI Software With the Art of Storytelling

There are numerous AI software applications available across various domains and industries. These applications range from general-purpose AI platforms (Li & Zhang, 2023) to specialized software tailored for specific tasks such as natural language processing (Marmolejo-Ramos et al., 2023), image recognition (Wu & Chen, 2015), speech recognition (Alhawiti, 2015), data analysis (Elish & Boyd, 2018), and more. The benefits of AI software vary depending on the application but generally include enhanced accuracy in data analysis, improved personalization leading to enhanced customer engagement, cost savings through optimized operations, scalability to manage extensive data volumes, and stimulation of innovation through novel possibilities and solutions, among other advantages (Elish & Boyd, 2018; Li & Zhang, 2023; Marmolejo-Ramos et al., 2023; Wu & Chen, 2015).

The question is, in what ways could storytelling contribute to enhancing AI processes within marketing activities? Combining storytelling with AI's capabilities, described by Spanos (2021) as a potent force in contemporary marketing strategies, yields effective communication and personalization. Drawing from Moin & Moin (2020), when stories are well-crafted and resonate with the audience's experiences and aspirations, they could evoke a range of emotions. On the other hand, the emergence of AI-driven personalization systems has revolutionized how stories are delivered and consumed (Haleem et al., 2022). These systems leverage vast data to understand individual preferences, behaviors, and interests. Thus, AI-driven personalization systems can adapt stories to suit individual preferences, delivering content that captures the recipient's attention and engagement (Brynjolfsson & McAfee, 2014).

As technology continues to advance, this convergence is likely to play an increasingly pivotal role in shaping the future of content creation and communication.

Therefore, expanding upon the symbiotic relationship between storytelling and AI, it is essential to recognize their collective potential in creating visual data, including images, which can convey diverse narratives and strategies. As LeCun and Bengio (2015) have highlighted, AI has made significant strides in image generation and interpretation, enabling visual content to align seamlessly with storytelling objectives. Through deep learning and computer vision, AI can craft images that complement narratives, visually narrating complex ideas and emotions (Patel & Thakkar, 2020). For instance, AI-powered image recognition can interpret user-generated content, allowing businesses to curate visuals that resonate with their audience and enhance storytelling efforts (Tahoun, 2020). This integration of storytelling and AI in visual data creation empowers organizations to communicate their brand stories effectively, leveraging the emotive power of images to leave a lasting impression and engage their customers on a deeper level.

Despite the myriad benefits, organizations undoubtedly encounter adverse consequences of AI implementation. One such challenge is effectively executing AI strategies while often neglecting to address the impact on the human workforce (Cheng et al., 2022). This oversight can lead to job displacement, changes in roles and responsibilities, and potential resistance to technological adoption among employees (Çolak, 2023). However, as emphasized by Tasheva and Karpovich (2024), AI can also complement human capabilities in the workforce, leading to more significant innovation, efficiency, and productivity.

This convergence of AI software and storytelling represents a new paradigm, allowing businesses to leverage narratives with precision and scalability (Vidrih & Mayahi, 2023). This approach facilitates stronger connections with audiences, amplifies customer engagement, and drives increased sales, especially when incorporated within an ABM strategy. The present study will further explore this perspective.

The Integration of Storytelling and AI Within an ABM Strategy

The fusion of storytelling and AI in an ABM strategy represents a formidable alliance that can redefine the landscape of customer engagement and business performance (Burgess et al., 2018). With its personalized approach, ABM establishes the groundwork for precise and targeted outreach, tailoring messages and strategies to individual accounts (Golec et al., 2019). In parallel, storytelling serves to humanize these interactions, weaving narratives that resonate with the audience emotionally, thus fostering deeper connections and engagement (Denning, 2005; Crespo et al., 2023). The inclusion of AI in this context significantly amplifies its potential by crafting narratives that evoke emotions, simplify intricate concepts, and reinforce brand identity (LeCun & Bengio, 2015). Such fusion enriches the overall narrative experience, enabling businesses to convey their messages visually, compellingly, and impactfully. Whether it involves generating customized images or dynamic content, AI allows businesses to engage their audience on a profoundly resonating visual level.

Additionally, AI-driven personalization, as discussed by Vidrih and Mayahi (2023), takes storytelling to the next level. Businesses gain insights into individual preferences, behaviors, and past interactions through AI's analytical prowess. Armed with this knowledge, they can tailor their stories to connect with each recipient on a profoundly personal level that helps to better respond to customer demands. Consequently, personalization captures the audience's attention and cultivates loyalty (Abraham et al., 2017), as prospect contacts perceive a genuine understanding and appreciation. This way, including AI in the strategic equation is a powerful catalyst for enhancing engagement and nurturing enduring customer relationships.

The convergence of ABM strategy, storytelling, and AI equips businesses with the capability to craft narratives that are profoundly personalized, emotionally evocative, and visually captivating. These narratives extend beyond mere influence on perceptions; they have the power to cultivate enduring relationships (Crespo et al., 2023). According to Burgess et al. (2018), this synergistic trio reshapes the essence of a customer-centric approach, propelling business performance to unprecedented heights and enabling brands to forge authentic connections with their audience, leaving indelible impressions.

While this concept shows potential, the forthcoming case study aims to provide deeper insight into its effectiveness. This study seeks to enhance comprehension of the intricate dynamics between these components and their potential impact on individuals' perceptions and decision-making processes in real-world contexts.

STUDY METHODOLOGY AND DESIGN

It is widely acknowledged that researchers employ diverse approaches and methodologies tailored to their unique perspectives, research objectives, and the nature of their inquiries. The selection of an approach is contingent upon the researcher's philosophical stance, research problem and aim, and the study's overarching framework, as Silverman (2013) emphasized. Consequently, it is imperative to provide a concise overview of the philosophical paradigms that underpin the approach adopted in this study.

Following Tracy (2019), the philosophical assumptions and beliefs underpin four distinct paradigms: positivist and post-positivist, interpretive and constructivist, critical, and postmodern and post-structural. Among these paradigms, the distinctions between positivist and interpretive stances have garnered significant attention (Bell & Bryman, 2022; Travers, 2001). To elaborate further, positivists aim to explain human behavior, whereas interpretivists are primarily concerned with comprehending it (Bryman, 2016).

Positivism is a philosophical approach that aims to formulate and test hypotheses to explain phenomena and develop laws. Researchers collect data to contribute to knowledge and facilitate generalization; all achieved through an objective lens (Richards, 2021; Tracy, 2019). In contrast, interpretivists adopt a holistic approach, seeking to understand how individuals perceive and make sense of the world around them. These researchers immerse themselves in individuals' experiences, actions, and contexts, striving to understand the world from their unique perspectives.

Acknowledging the ongoing debate, this study's methodology aligns with the interpretive paradigm, reflecting the researcher's philosophical stance and the study's goals. This approach facilitates the exploration of diverse, socially constructed realities in the intricate world (Goodson & Phillimore, 2004). It involves challenging the researcher's assumptions through participant perspectives (Denny, 2007) and exploring diverse, sometimes contradictory viewpoints on specific marketing campaign experiences. This decision is pivotal as the study seeks to comprehend different stakeholder perspectives and experiences related to the marketing campaign, each offering a unique subjective reality.

Furthermore, the researcher employs a qualitative research approach, aligning with the interpretive paradigm's emphasis on knowledge acquisition and co-creation within the natural world (Denzin & Lincoln, 2011; Mason, 2017). The nature of this research is exploratory, grounded in existing theories and knowledge while remaining open to the potential discovery of new phenomena or relationships. Consistent with Flick's (2018) concept of creating a new "version of a world", this research aims to contribute to existing theory by adding fresh insights to the field.

The Case Study as a Research Approach

This study aligns with Gummesson's (2005) argument that a case study approach can effectively achieve the conceptualization, understanding of phenomena, and theory development. The case study approach is widely used in the social sciences and is gaining increasing recognition. According to Yin (1984), a case study is an empirical inquiry that: investigates a contemporary phenomenon within its real-life context; when the boundaries between phenomenon and context are not clearly evident; and in which multiple sources of evidence are used (Yin, 1984, p. 23).

The case study design is particularly fitting for addressing "how" and "why" questions, with a significant focus on providing explanatory insights. It does not provide control over behavioral events but concentrates on thoroughly examining contextual conditions (Yin, 2003). While marketing research endorses case studies (Bonoma, 1985; Riege, 2003), some scholars have voiced concerns about its suitability in marketing contexts (Gummesson, 2005; Zainal, 2007). Despite being a widely employed research approach, it lacks comprehensive methodological guidelines (Yin, 2011, p. xix). Nonetheless, Stake (2005) argues that case study research's unique and human qualities can be attributed to the researcher rather than the methods themselves.

The case study approach is widely regarded as a valuable and distinctive research method, possessing unique characteristics that make it well-suited for various investigations (Tellis, 1997). It offers an excellent platform for in-depth exploration and comprehension of complex issues within specific contexts (Schell, 1992; Zainal, 2007). Additionally, according to Hartley (2004), the case study can yield rich and insightful information about organizational behavior and the dynamic interplay between behavior or processes and the contextual factors, where both influence each other.

Case study research is pivotal in refining and extending organizational theory, a central endeavor within organizational research (Eisenhardt, 1989). Therefore, the utilization of the case study approach in this study is well-justified. It stems from the belief that a thorough understanding of this phenomenon and its context can only be attained through a comprehensive examination using this approach.

A Single Case Study

Case research serves various purposes, from theoretical to practical (Stake, 2013). Cases can vary in complexity and scope, covering individuals, organizations, behaviors, events, or social phenomena (Yin, 2011). Case study research can be a single-case or multiple-case design, depending on the research issue (Gustafsson, 2017). Stake (2013) categorizes case studies as intrinsic, instrumental, or collective. Intrinsic cases focus solely on understanding the case itself. Instrumental cases aim to deepen comprehension of phenomena, using the case as a tool. Collective cases involve gathering and coordinating data from multiple cases.

In this study, the emphasis aligns with instrumental case study research. The researcher seeks a deep understanding of a marketing campaign to comprehensively describe, generate knowledge, and contribute to theory development (Gustafsson, 2017). Consistent with Eisenhardt's (1989) viewpoint, this approach aligns itself with the interpretivist perspective and supports the development of theories in areas where existing theory or empirical evidence may be insufficient.

DATA COLLECTION WITHIN THE CASE STUDY APPROACH

As Blandford (2013) highlights, research approaches vary, and researchers have flexibility in data collection and validation methods. While triangulation is often discussed as an alternative (Decrop, 1999; Denzin & Lincoln, 2011; Flick, 2018), Mason (2017) proposes *facet methodology* as a more flexible and insightful approach. Unlike triangulation, which can risk bypassing a thorough engagement with the chosen methodology, facet methodology fosters creativity and intuition, prioritizing insights over comprehensive knowledge (Mason, 2017). Considering this study's qualitative approach and interpretive stance, facet methodology is deemed suitable. It allows for a deeper exploration of the case study organization, offering insight into multiple socially co-constructed realities, knowledge, and interactions within a natural setting from diverse perspectives.

Furthermore, in qualitative research, Stake (2013) and Yin (2011) outline six sources of evidence in case studies: interviews, direct observation, participant observation, documents, archival records, and physical artefacts. These sources aid researchers in accessing organizational resources, planning data collection, and preparing for unexpected events (Tellis, 1997). Despite this, Krueger and Casey (2015) emphasize that research methods vary in effectiveness based on their situational use, the researcher's competence, and the research environment. In this study, the primary data collection method involves the responses from target contacts, complemented by the examination of secondary sources before the marketing campaign.

An ABM campaign was implemented to engage with ten selected companies operating in the game development sector. The campaign targeted four specific individuals in each company, making a total of 40 contacts. The aim was to personalize the communication to encourage engagement, collect feedback, and pave the way for potential future business prospects. Paper postcards were sent to the target contacts in various European countries, which included France, Germany, Sweden, Finland, Malta, and the United Kingdom. The postcards were dispatched to C-level contacts, from CEOs to business development directors. These individuals were chosen for their influential decision-making roles and involvement in developing and managing business strategies. An interval of three to four days was maintained between each mailing. This study also incorporated secondary data sources besides physical artefacts, such as postcards.

Secondary Data Sources

According to Coffey (2014), "most qualitative research takes place in settings that are 'documented' in various ways" (p. 367). For instance, organizations document themselves, and many methodological opportunities exist to explore their documentary realities. What can be included as a "document" involves a broad range of textual materials, for example, organizational documents, notes, cards, case records, email threads and reports, as well as various technological, digital, and social media materials, such as websites, social networking sites, and visual or sound materials (Coffey, 2014; Tight, 2019). Documentary research can be considered secondary data research (Tight, 2019) because the researcher does not directly collect or produce such secondary data. This study considered various internal organizational documents.

Internal Organizational Documents

Organizational documents are data or evidence of how an organization represents and accounts for itself (Coffey, 2014). Therefore, internal organizational documents, such as business and marketing plans, research reports, and other additional documents related to Invest Lithuania's business management, were analyzed. Internal documents are essential in business research because they help describe an organization and its history (Cassell & Symon, 2004). They further provide organizational value structures (Kabanoff et al., 1995) or help generate new business models for creating shared value (Michelini & Fiorentino, 2012).

ANALYSIS OF PRIMARY DATA

In this study, data analysis was conducted using NVivo 12 Pro, a software package developed by QSR International. It is worth noting that no single industry-leading data analysis program exists (Bell et al., 2022). The choice of software primarily depends on its alignment with the research methodology, the researcher's experience, and its effectiveness in facilitating the analysis process (Silver & Lewins, 2007). NVivo 12 Pro was selected for its extensive features, including the ability to hierarchically create and organize nodes, seamlessly open or initiate projects, user-friendly navigation, robust search functionality, and support for importing various formats of materials (Bell et al., 2022).

Creswell and Báez (2020) point out that text data are dense and time-consuming to analyze and interpret. However, the coding process is a crucial step in making sense of such data, and NVivo 12 Pro was employed to aid the researcher in this endeavor. A set of codes was established before the analysis to streamline the coding process. These codes were formulated based on the research objectives and critical factors identified in the literature review.

During the analysis process, a structure of themes emerged. The themes were as follows: positive feedback, exploring collaboration, future opportunities, interest in game development studios, positive impressions of Vilnius and geographic limitations.

(A detailed description can be found in the analysis section.) In this regard, NVivo proved invaluable for storing and managing data and ideas, visualizing thematic patterns as they unfolded, and facilitating comparisons and in-depth analysis. It is important to acknowledge that human involvement remains essential, and software cannot replace the role of the researcher in data analysis (Jackson & Bazeley, 2019).

Analysis of Secondary Data

Secondary data analysis was performed using content analysis within NVivo, a technique with a history spanning more than 60 years that has found applications in various fields, including business (Neuendorf, 2017). Krippendorff (2018), a recognized authority in the field, defines *content analysis* as a method for drawing replicable and valid inferences from texts or other meaningful materials within their contexts of use. Content analysis is not limited to written text; it can encompass verbal, textual, visual, sound, print, and electronic forms (Bryman, 2016), including images (Bell et al., 2022).

When conducting a case study of an organization, content analysis primarily aims to scrutinize media items, various texts, and documents that are either produced by the organization, such as annual reports, or written about it, like articles in the business press (Bell et al., 2022). In this context, the researcher examined diverse content generated by Invest Lithuania, namely internal documents and reports related to previous marketing campaigns and their outcomes. Both sources are conceptually rich and offer valuable insights into the organization's description, historical evolution, and the development and management of its core concepts.

LIMITATIONS

The qualitative research approach has its limitations. According to Goulding (2002), qualitative research is often criticized for being purely descriptive, needing a more structured and straightforward procedure, and potentially producing subjective data that may not meet rigorous standards. Furthermore, concerns are raised about the need for more transparency in the evolving procedures and processes adopted during the research (Miles & Huberman, 1994). Additionally, as Denzin and Lincoln (2011) pointed out, the criteria for evaluating and interpreting qualitative research can be problematic and may lead to misinterpretation. This chapter addresses these limitations by explaining the rationale for selecting methods such as content analysis and detailing how they were employed. The utilization of Computer-Assisted Qualitative Data Analysis Software (CAQDAS) has supported the qualitative data analysis process, ensuring that the research procedures are well-documented and enabling readers to examine all the methods employed by the researcher.

Employing a single case study methodology may also be perceived as a limitation. Despite the drawbacks of alternative methods, such as conducting multiple case studies and facilitating data comparison (Gustafsson, 2017), the single case study approach remains a credible choice. Dyer Jr. and Wilkins (1991) argue that a single case study can yield more prosperous and nuanced theoretical insights. Moreover, it allows the researcher to thoroughly examine a single case over an extended period. Therefore, a single case study is the most suitable choice when the research objective is to study a specific organization (Yin, 2003).

Additionally, specific risks are involved when using postal services to send postcards for a marketing campaign. The delivery process is partially within the control of the campaign implementers. Also, the addresses sourced from company websites could not be accurate, and the selected target individuals may have left their respective companies. As such, it is crucial to exercise due diligence and carefully consider these potential risks before implementing such campaigns. Despite these challenges, Valenti et al. (2023) have found that direct mail effectively drives customer acquisition in the offline channel.

ETHICAL CONSIDERATIONS

Several ethical concerns merit consideration in this context. One crucial issue pertains to confidentiality (Bryman, 2016), explicitly safeguarding the security of participants' responses (Robson, 2002). It is essential to emphasize that this study rigorously upholds a commitment to safeguarding the companies' confidentiality. Also, despite the researcher's access to potentially sensitive business practices and information, all matters of confidentiality were diligently managed following the mutual agreement established with representatives from Invest Lithuania. Any documents designated as commercially confidential were deliberately excluded from the analysis.

Regarding participants' responses, strict measures were implemented to ensure anonymity and prevent identification. Each participant was assigned a unique code, for example, G1, and their job positions were anonymized using a generic term, "strategic-level manager", to avoid any potential identification.

ANALYSIS OF THE INVEST LITHUANIA CASE STUDY

After a thorough review of internal documents and reports related to the company's strategy, including past marketing campaigns and their outcomes, it became apparent that there is a lack of knowledge and know-how in identifying the most effective marketing tools, channels, and potential target lists. There was also a noticeable absence of constructive collaboration between the marketing and sales teams, an essential element for the successful execution of campaigns and overall organizational performance. According to Vajre (2016), "marketing must play a part in sales acceleration, and sales must play a part in marketing" (p. 41). Despite this, Invest Lithuania's marketing and sales teams have continuously executed campaigns within their target industries in recent years. These initiatives involved testing various channels, tools, and strategies and adapting and modifying strategic KPIs while exploring automation options via customer relationship management (CRM) systems.

In response to these evolving circumstances and the insights gained from past endeavors, it was determined that Invest Lithuania's marketing and sales teams should embrace a new approach. As a result, the decision was made to implement ABM, a personalized B2B marketing strategy to target specific companies. This strategic shift aims to enhance engagement with target foreign investors by tailoring content to their specific needs and preferences (Burgess & Munn, 2021). The expectation is that the personalized approach inherent in ABM can facilitate smoother communication and lead to increased sales opportunities.

The decision to implement the One-to-Few ABM campaign was deliberate and well-considered. This approach was selected for its suitability when targeting a specific subset of potential clients within the broader target audience (Agaba, 2021). By focusing on a select group, the campaign aimed to create more personalized and tailored interactions by optimizing the chance of engaging these specific prospects effectively. This strategic choice aligns with the campaign's core objectives, enhancing its impact and success.

Given this, the imperative strategic decision to utilize AI tools for creating a more captivating marketing campaign emerged. This choice was particularly significant considering the characteristics of the target contacts. It is well-established that an extraordinary effort is required to truly captivate game developers, embodying creativity and delivering the element of surprise (Brynjolfsson & McAfee, 2014). It is essential to acknowledge that this undertaking goes beyond traditional marketing methods. The aim is to establish an emotional connection and evoke a sense of awe, with the overarching objective of leaving a remarkable and enduring impression on the target audience.

The ABM campaign ran from January to March 2023. As discussed earlier, it revolved around ten carefully chosen game development companies, emphasizing pinpointing their most iconic game characters. After these game characters were identified, the researcher started the process of AI-powered image creation (Figure 1). DALL-E 2 software was selected for this purpose due to its remarkable ability to generate lifelike images and artwork from natural language descriptions (Liu et al., 2022).

As depicted in Figure 1, the postcards generated by the researcher using AI portrayed game characters embarking on a business trip to Vilnius, Lithuania's capital. These characters, acting as virtual Vilnius "ambassadors", sent four postcards (from left to right) to the target contacts. The first image depicted the arrival in Vilnius and the game character's mission initiation. The second image introduced the landscape of Vilnius, its inhabitants, and noteworthy places to explore. The third one provided an overview of the city's infrastructure. Lastly, the fourth image delved into the potential within the game development ecosystem and detailed their departure from Vilnius. (A visualization of these texts is shown in Figure 2.)

With guidance from a marketing team to a creative agency regarding the campaign's concept and tone of voice of the game characters, artfully designed narratives were employed on the postcards. These narratives effectively communicated the journey, immersing recipients in their fictional adventure and providing an engaging glimpse into Vilnius and its potential for future game development collaborations. This innovative approach aligns with the research conducted by Brynjolfsson and McAfee (2014) on AI-driven personalization, which enhances engagement and fosters a deeper connection. It is worth emphasizing that each card included a QR code (see Figure 2) that directed individuals to the game development landing page on the Invest Lithuania website when scanned. Furthermore, each postcard incorporated symbolic details associated with the game character to elevate the sense of personalization, for example, the inclusion of bird-foot prints. According to Upadhyay and McCormick

Figure 1. A set of images "Angry Birds Business Trip in Vilnius" (the front side)
Source: Images generated by the author using AI software, 2023

(2018), "personalized messaging is proven to have two times the engagement rate from targeted prospects" (p. 94), which was the aim of this campaign.

After all the postcards had been prepared and printed, they were dispatched sequentially, every three to four days, to the target contacts via courier using the envelopes displayed below (Figure 3).

These envelopes were also given a "gamified" touch, with pixelated postage stamps on the front side and a heart-shaped pixelated image along with the hashtag #LITHUANIA LOVES GAMEDEV on the back side. In alignment with the viewpoint Barnard and Parker (2012) presented, it is imperative to maintain consistency across all communication facets of the campaign. This study includes visuals, text, tone of voice, packaging, digital tools, and channels, such as QR codes and landing pages. Maintaining consistency is vital for creating an elevated experience and receiving positive feedback.

Proactive communication from the sales team was also crucial to enhance the campaign's effectiveness (Vajre, 2016). They utilized semi-personalized texts and aligned their "follow-up" actions with the narrative conveyed in the postcards, yielding evident results.

The Results of the ABM Campaign

The representatives from eight of the ten target companies who received the postcards responded positively after receiving the sales team's first or second follow-up message. It is crucial to highlight that due to postage issues, not all recipients received postcards; in fact, some postcards were returned. This situation influenced the overall response rate. However, in B2B marketing, especially within niche sectors like game development, even a few meaningful engagements can hold significant value (Taylor, 2017). From an account-based perspective, 80% of the target companies responded positively, indicating that the campaign resonated effectively with its

Figure 2. A set of images "Angry Birds Business Trip in Vilnius" (the back side)
Source: Courtesy of Invest Lithuania, 2023

Figure 3. A customized envelope with gamification elements
Source: Pictures taken by the author, 2023

intended audience. This level of engagement is especially promising, given the competitive nature of the tech and gaming industry landscape.

Several notable patterns and experiences were observed from the responses that were collected. The most prominent theme in most responses was the positive feedback about the marketing campaign. Respondents appreciated the campaign's creativity, originality, and the meticulous planning and execution that was put into it. Strategic-level managers were impressed with the campaign. Here are a few noteworthy examples of their feedback:

I got to say that your campaign was well thought out & original! Big kudos to the team who thought about that! (G1)

[…] very clever move with the envelopes as well, I enjoyed it. (G7)

Following on from that, many of the respondents expressed interest in exploring potential future opportunities. For instance, G4 stated: "Thanks for the messages. Can you tell me more about what you would like to discuss?". Additionally, some acknowledged that the current environment may be challenging for technology companies, including gaming, but remained open to the possibility of future collaborations or discussions:

As you know, the current context is pretty tough for Tech companies in general and gaming in particular, but who knows. Future is full of opportunities (G2).

Expanding on this, a few individuals conveyed their intentions to initiate discussions regarding the campaign and potential collaborations with their respective management or relevant teams. For example, G7 expressed keen interest, stating, "I'd love to hear more [...]. Let me talk to my Management Team and get back to you". Similarly, other responses included statements such as, "I will share this cool experience with my peers internally in charge of business development" (G2) and "I can forward your information to some colleagues" (G8). These responses indicate a willingness to explore further engagement with the Vilnius gaming ecosystem.

Of particular interest is the response from one of the target contacts who expressed a desire to receive information about game development studios in the area. Their statement, "If you have a deck with the interesting game development studios in your area, I'll be happy to have a look" (G3), suggests a potential inclination towards exploring partnerships or collaborations within the gaming industry. In line with Burgess and Shercliff (2022), this response hints at the campaign's ability to generate immediate interest and pave the way for future collaborations and business opportunities. Furthermore, G5 expressed, "I have no doubt Vilnius offers great opportunities for not only Gaming companies […]", thus demonstrating a comprehensive grasp of Vilnius' ecosystem.

A notable aspect of the responses was the expression of positive impressions about Vilnius as a city. Several individuals appreciated Vilnius, which can be considered a potential advantage in future discussions or collaborations. The favorable views of the city, such as "I love Vilnius:)" (G6) and "I've been to Vilnius once, for a football tournament for my oldest son, I really enjoyed the city!" (G7), indicate that the campaign not only piqued their professional interest but also rekindled their positive memories of Vilnius as a destination. This positive sentiment may be a foundation for building rapport and fostering future collaborations (Souiden et al., 2016). It suggests that beyond the specific marketing campaign, it effectively displayed Vilnius as an attractive and appealing location for potential business endeavors within the gaming industry.

Lastly, several people mentioned they were not looking to expand their studios geographically. Such positioning indicates that while they appreciated the campaign, they might not actively seek new locations now. For example, G5 mentioned:

We highly appreciate your interest in [us] and in case such opportunity arises I will reach out. All the best!

Additionally, G8 expressed their position as follows:

I think at this point we are not looking to expand our own studio geographically […], but I appreciate you reaching out and inviting us. I wish you all the success and fortune, and for an amazing eco-system of flourishing gaming companies to emerge in Lithuania! Looking forward to see how things develop.

Nurturing ongoing relationships with these contacts presents the chance to reconnect in the future despite a lack of immediate interest. The ever-changing business landscape offers opportunities to revisit and explore potential collaborations when the timing is more favorable. This recommendation is especially pertinent for the Invest Lithuania marketing and sales teams.

Summary

The marketing campaign conducted by Invest Lithuania, combining ABM, storytelling, and AI-powered image creation, yielded positive feedback from recipients within the game development industry. Respondents expressed appreciation for the campaign's creativity and originality. While the quantitative response may seem modest, the qualitative impact and the potential for future opportunities are substantial. The positive impressions of Vilnius as a city and the interest in the gaming industry in the region provide a strong foundation for future collaborations. Additionally, even if immediate collaborations did not materialize, as some companies may not be actively expanding geographically now, maintaining close connections with these contacts allows for future re-engagement as the dynamic business environment evolves.

Despite encountering certain limitations, such as undeliverable postcards to some target contacts, which were beyond the control of the campaign implementers, the overall campaign can be deemed a success in accomplishing its primary objective. The campaign actively engaged with its target contacts, eliciting their interest and enhancing the appeal of Vilnius as a noteworthy destination. Furthermore, it effectively facilitated the initiation of prospective collaborations within the game development sector in Vilnius. This outcome is particularly significant considering the challenges the competitive tech and gaming industry landscape poses. Building relationships in the business world often takes time, and these responses lay the groundwork for possible future interactions and partnerships.

CONCLUSIONS AND RECOMMENDATIONS

This research has delved into the interactive synergy among the ABM strategy, storytelling, and AI within the scope of effectively engaging with target contacts in the game development sector. By utilizing AI-powered image creation and crafting immersive narratives, this ABM campaign aimed to leave a memorable impression on the target audience, offering a personalized and emotionally resonant experience to stimulate further discussions and potential business opportunities with Invest Lithuania. Following Spanos (2021), integrating these elements has the potential to redefine customer-centric approaches, driving business performance to new heights. As a result, the campaign was successful not only by reaching target contacts and getting their positive reaction but also by enhancing the collaboration between departments internally, enabling the adoption of better practices for future implementations.

The implications of this research are significant and suggest several valuable outcomes. For example, businesses can use AI-powered image creation and immersive storytelling to create personalized experiences that lead to meaningful interactions with their target audience. Moreover, the campaign's success achieved its immediate goals and led to adopting improved practices within the organization (Taylor, 2017). Therefore, the lessons from this research can be applied in future marketing endeavors, resulting in continued business growth and success. However, the real-world efficacy of this approach must be further elucidated through empirical research and data analysis. Critical recommendations for future research in this domain could encompass:

1. **In-depth Case Studies:** Conducting comprehensive case studies across various industries would provide invaluable insights into the impact and effectiveness of AI-enhanced storytelling within marketing campaigns. These studies can highlight how AI-driven narratives influence customer engagement, brand perception, and business outcomes. By examining success stories and potential limitations, researchers can create a nuanced understanding of the practical implications of AI in marketing.
2. **Emotional Engagement in ABM:** The role of emotional engagement in ABM strategies is an area ripe for exploration. Understanding how emotional resonance shapes customer perceptions, loyalty, and decision-making within ABM campaigns can uncover new avenues for strategy development. Researchers can investigate the emotions elicited by AI-driven narratives and their impact on customer behavior, helping businesses refine their storytelling approaches.
3. **Marketing and Sales Synergy:** Future research should explore various aspects of collaboration and communication between the marketing and sales teams. Understanding how these factors impact target contacts' experiences and other critical outcomes is essential for businesses aiming to optimize customer engagement strategies and drive long-term success.
4. **Scalability and Cost-effectiveness:** Assessing the scalability and cost-effectiveness of AI-driven content creation is crucial, especially for businesses of varying sizes and industries. Future research can delve into small and large enterprises' scalability challenges, identifying cost-effective AI solutions that

align with their goals. By comparing the costs and benefits of AI-powered marketing campaigns, researchers can provide valuable guidance for businesses seeking to adopt these technologies.

5. **Longitudinal Studies:** Longitudinal studies tracking the impact of AI-enhanced ABM campaigns over extended periods can offer insights into the sustainability of customer relationships and business performance. Researchers can investigate how AI-driven narratives evolve and adapt to changing customer needs, market dynamics, and competitive landscapes. Longitudinal studies can also reveal trends and patterns in customer engagement and loyalty, helping businesses refine their marketing strategies over time.

Overall, the intersection of ABM strategy, storytelling, and AI represents a promising frontier in reshaping marketing practices and establishing meaningful connections with target audiences. Ongoing research in this domain will continue to yield invaluable insights for businesses looking to harness these innovative techniques to foster sustainable growth and enhance customer engagement. As the business landscape evolves, staying at the forefront of such strategies will be crucial for organizations aiming to remain competitive and relevant in the ever-changing marketing world.

REFERENCES

Abraham, M., Mitchelmore, S., Collins, S., Maness, J., Kistulinec, M., Khodabandeh, S., & Visser, J. (2017). *Profiting from personalization.* Boston Consulting Group.

Agaba, M. (2021). *Account-based Marketing in B2B-Marketing.* Academic Press.

Alhawiti, K. M. (2015). Advances in artificial intelligence using speech recognition. *International Journal of Computer and Information Engineering*, *9*(6), 1432–1435.

Andersen, P., Archacki, R., De Bellefonds, N., & Ratajczak, D. (2017). How digital leaders are transforming B2B marketing. *BCG Insights.*

Bacon, A. (2021). Strategic account-based marketing: How to tame this beast. In *B2B Marketing: A Guidebook for the Classroom to the Boardroom* (pp. 419–435). Springer International Publishing. doi:10.1007/978-3-030-54292-4_17

Barnard, A., & Parker, C. (2012). *Campaign it!: Achieving success through communication.* Kogan Page Publishers.

Bell, E., Bryman, A., & Harley, B. (2022). *Business research methods* (6th ed.). Oxford University Press. doi:10.1093/hebz/9780198869443.001.0001

Blandford, A. E. (2013). *Semi-structured qualitative studies*. Interaction Design Foundation.

Bonoma, T. V. (1985). Case research in marketing: Opportunities, problems, and a process. *JMR, Journal of Marketing Research, 22*(2), 199–208. doi:10.1177/002224378502200209

Bryman, A. (2016). *Social research methods* (5th ed.). Oxford University Press.

Brynjolfsson, E., & McAfee, A. (2014). *The second machine age: Work, progress, and prosperity in a time of brilliant technologies*. WW Norton & Company.

Burgess, B., & Munn, D. (2021). *A Practitioner's Guide to Account-Based Marketing: Accelerating Growth in Strategic Accounts*. Kogan Page Publishers.

Burgess, B., Schwartz, J., & Leavitt, R. (2018). Raising the Game with ABM: 2018 ABM Benchmark Study. October). The Companies That Will Grow Your Revenue. In Lighting Design and Application: L.D. and A, 50.

Burgess, B., & Shercliff, T. (2022). *Account-based Growth: Unlocking Sustainable Value Through Extraordinary Customer Focus*. Kogan Page Publishers.

Cassell, C., & Symon, G. (Eds.). (2004). *Essential guide to qualitative methods in organizational research*. Sage publications. doi:10.4135/9781446280119

Cheng, X., Lin, X., Shen, X. L., Zarifis, A., & Mou, J. (2022). The dark sides of AI. *Electronic Markets, 32*(1), 11–15. doi:10.1007/s12525-022-00531-5 PMID:35600917

Coffey, A. (2014). Analysing documents. In U. Flick (Ed.), *The SAGE handbook of qualitative data analysis* (pp. 367–380). SAGE Publications. doi:10.4135/9781446282243.n25

Çolak, O. (2023). The impact of artificial intelligence on the employment structure of the tourism industry: An interview with ChatGPT. *İktisadi İdari ve Siyasal Araştırmalar Dergisi, 8*(22), 919-939.

Crespo, C. F., Ferreira, A. G., & Cardoso, R. M. (2023). The influence of storytelling on the consumer–brand relationship experience. *Journal of Marketing Analytics, 11*(1), 41–56. doi:10.1057/s41270-021-00149-0

Creswell, J. W., & Báez, J. C. (2020). *30 essential skills for the qualitative researcher*. Sage Publications.

Cun, Y., Bengio, Y., & Hinton, G. (2015). Deep learning. *Nature, 521*(7553), 436-444.

Decrop, A. (1999). Triangulation in qualitative tourism research. *Tourism Management, 20*(1), 157–161. doi:10.1016/S0261-5177(98)00102-2

Denning, S. (2005). *The leader's guide to storytelling: Mastering the art and discipline of business narrative*. John Wiley & Sons.

Denny, R. M. (2006). Pushing the boundaries of ethnography in the practice of market research. Handbook of qualitative research methods in marketing, 430.

Denzin, N. K., & Lincoln, Y. S. (Eds.). (2011). *The Sage handbook of qualitative research*. Sage Publications.

Dyer, W. G. Jr, & Wilkins, A. L. (1991). Better stories, not better constructs, to generate better theory: A rejoinder to Eisenhardt. *Academy of Management Review, 16*(3), 613–619. doi:10.2307/258920

Eisenhardt, K. M. (1989). Building theories from case study research. *Academy of Management Review, 14*(4), 532–550. doi:10.2307/258557

Elish, M. C., & Boyd, D. (2018). Situating methods in the magic of Big Data and AI. *Communication Monographs, 85*(1), 57–80. doi:10.1080/03637751.2017.1375130

Ellington, L. (2014). Technology: impact on the practice of storytelling. In *Handbook of Research on Education and Technology in a Changing Society* (pp. 104–115). IGI Global. doi:10.4018/978-1-4666-6046-5.ch008

Golec, C., Isaacson, P., & Fewless, J. (2019). *Account-based marketing: how to target and engage the companies that will grow your revenue*. John Wiley & Sons.

Goodson, L., & Phillimore, J. (2004). The inquiry paradigm in qualitative tourism research. In *Qualitative research in tourism* (pp. 48–63). Routledge. doi:10.4324/9780203642986

Goulding, C. (2002). Grounded theory: A practical guide for management, business and market researchers. *Grounded Theory*, 1-186.

Gummesson, E. (2005). Qualitative research in marketing: Road-map for a wilderness of complexity and unpredictability. *European Journal of Marketing, 39*(3/4), 309–327. doi:10.1108/03090560510581791

Gustafsson, J. (2017). *Single case studies vs. multiple case studies: A comparative study*. Academic Press.

Haleem, A., Javaid, M., Qadri, M. A., Singh, R. P., & Suman, R. (2022). Artificial intelligence (A.I.) applications for marketing: A literature-based study. *International Journal of Intelligent Networks*.

Hartley, J. (2004). What is a case study? *Essential guide to qualitative methods in organizational research*, 323-333.

He, H., & Harris, L. (2020). The impact of Covid-19 pandemic on corporate social responsibility and marketing philosophy. *Journal of Business Research*, *116*, 176–182. doi:10.1016/j.jbusres.2020.05.030 PMID:32457556

Jackson, K., & Bazeley, P. (2019). *Qualitative data analysis with NVivo* (3rd ed.). Sage publications.

Jarek, K., & Mazurek, G. (2019). Marketing and Artificial Intelligence. *Central European Business Review, 8*(2).

Kabanoff, B., Waldersee, R., & Cohen, M. (1995). Espoused values and organizational change themes. *Academy of Management Journal*, *38*(4), 1075–1104. doi:10.2307/256621

Kreiswirth, M. (2000). Merely telling stories? Narrative and knowledge in the human sciences. *Poetics Today*, *21*(2), 293–318. doi:10.1215/03335372-21-2-293

Krippendorff, K. (2018). *Content analysis: An introduction to its methodology*. Sage Publications.

Krueger, R. A., & Casey, M. A. (2014). *Focus groups: A practical guide for applied research*. Sage publications.

Li, C. Y., & Zhang, J. T. (2023). Chatbots or me? Consumers' switching between human agents and conversational agents. *Journal of Retailing and Consumer Services*, *72*, 103264. doi:10.1016/j.jretconser.2023.103264

Liu, N., Li, S., Du, Y., Torralba, A., & Tenenbaum, J. B. (2022, October). Compositional visual generation with composable diffusion models. In *European Conference on Computer Vision* (pp. 423-439). Cham: Springer Nature Switzerland. 10.1007/978-3-031-19790-1_26

Lubis, A., Purike, E., Stiadi, M., Judijanto, L., & Tobing, F. (2023). The Triad of Marketing Success: Product Innovation, Customer Engagement, and Market Penetration. *International Journal of Economic Literature*, *1*(3), 245–257.

Marmolejo-Ramos, F., Workman, T., Walker, C., Lenihan, D., Moulds, S., Correa, J. C., & Sonna, B. (2022). AI-powered narrative building for facilitating public participation and engagement. *Discover Artificial Intelligence*, *2*(1), 7. doi:10.1007/s44163-022-00023-7

Mason, J. (2017). Qualitative researching. Qualitative researching, 1-288.

Michelini, L., & Fiorentino, D. (2012). New business models for creating shared value. *Social Responsibility Journal, 8*(4), 561–577. doi:10.1108/17471111211272129

Miles, M. B., & Huberman, A. M. (1994). *Qualitative data analysis: An expanded sourcebook.* Sage Publications.

Moin, S. M. A., & Moin, S. M. A. (2020). Conclusion: The Future of Storytelling. *Brand Storytelling in the Digital Age: Theories, Practice and Application*, 89-96.

Mullen, A., Marcos Cuevas, J., & Theoharakis, V. (n.d.). *The anatomy of account-based marketing-a conceptualisation of strategic dimensions.* American Marketing Association.

Neuendorf, K. A. (2017). *The content analysis guidebook.* Sage Publications. doi:10.4135/9781071802878

Patel, P., & Thakkar, A. (2020). The upsurge of deep learning for computer vision applications. *Iranian Journal of Electrical and Computer Engineering, 10*(1), 538. doi:10.11591/ijece.v10i1.pp538-548

Polkinghorne, D. E. (1995). Narrative configuration in qualitative analysis. *International Journal of Qualitative Studies in Education : QSE, 8*(1), 5–23. doi:10.1080/0951839950080103

Richards, L. (2020). Handling qualitative data: A practical guide. *Handling Qualitative Data*, 1-336.

Riege, A. M. (2003). Validity and reliability tests in case study research: A literature review with "hands-on" applications for each research phase. *Qualitative Market Research, 6*(2), 75–86. doi:10.1108/13522750310470055

Robson, C. (2002). *Real-world research: A resource for social scientists and practitioner-researchers* (2nd ed.). Blackwell Publishers.

Schell, C. (1992). The value of the case study as a research strategy. Manchester Business School, 2(1), 1-15.

Shivajirao, S. K. D. M. P., & Verma, R. (2022). Examining the Impact of Storytelling in Content Marketing on Consumer Engagement and Brand Loyalty. *African Diaspora Journal of Mathematics, 25*(6), 121-130.

Silver, C., & Lewins, A. (2007). *Using software in qualitative research: A step-by-step guide.* Sage.

Silverman, D. (2013). *Doing qualitative research* (4th ed.).

Souiden, N., Ladhari, R., & Chiadmi, N. E. (2017). Destination personality and destination image. *Journal of Hospitality and Tourism Management, 32*, 54–70. doi:10.1016/j.jhtm.2017.04.003

Spanos, M. (2021). Brand storytelling in the age of artificial intelligence. *Journal of Brand Strategy, 10*(1), 6–13.

Stake, R. E. (2005). Qualitative case studies. In N. K. Denzin & Y. S. Lincoln (Eds.), *The SAGE handbook of qualitative research* (3rd ed., pp. 443–466). SAGE Publications.

Stake, R. E. (2013). *Multiple case study analysis*. Guilford press.

Tahoun, N. (2020). *The utilization of artificial intelligence in online advertising and its perceived effectiveness*. Academic Press.

Tasheva, Z., & Karpovich, V. (2024). Supercharge human potential through ai to increase productivity the workforce in the companies. *American Journal of Applied Science and Technology, 4*(02), 24–29. doi:10.37547/ajast/Volume04Issue02-05

Taylor, H. (2017). *B2B marketing strategy: differentiate, develop and deliver lasting customer engagement*. Kogan Page Publishers.

Tellis, W. (1997). Introduction to case study. *The qualitative report, 3*(2), 1–14.

Tight, M. (2019). Documentary research in the social sciences. *Documentary Research in the Social Sciences*, 1-232.

Tracy, S. J. (2019). *Qualitative research methods: Collecting evidence, crafting analysis, communicating impact*. John Wiley & Sons.

Travers, M. (2001). Qualitative research through case studies. *Qualitative research through case studies*, 1-208.

Upadhyay, S., & McCormick, K. (2018). *The Revenue Acceleration Rules: Supercharge Sales and Marketing Through Artificial Intelligence, Predictive Technologies and Account-Based Strategies*. John Wiley & Sons.

Vajre, S. (2016). *Account-based marketing for dummies*. John Wiley & Sons.

Valenti, A., Srinivasan, S., Yildirim, G., & Pauwels, K. (2023). Direct mail to prospects and email to current customers? Modeling and field-testing multichannel marketing. *Journal of the Academy of Marketing Science*, 1–20. doi:10.1007/s11747-023-00962-2

Vidrih, M., & Mayahi, S. (2023). Generative AI-Driven Storytelling: A New Era for Marketing. *arXiv preprint arXiv:2309.09048.*

Vlačić, B., Corbo, L., Silva, S. C., & Dabić, M. (2021). The evolving role of artificial intelligence in marketing: A review and research agenda. *Journal of Business Research, 128*, 187–203. doi:10.1016/j.jbusres.2021.01.055

Wu, M., & Chen, L. (2015, November). Image recognition based on deep learning. In *2015 Chinese automation congress (CAC)* (pp. 542-546). IEEE.

Yin, R. K. (1984). *Case Study Research: Design and Methods*. Sage Publications.

Yin, R. K. (2003). Designing case studies. *Qualitative Research Methods, 5*(14), 359-386.

Yin, R. K. (2011). *Applications of case study research*. Sage Publications.

Zainal, Z. (2007). Case study as a research method. *Jurnal kemanusiaan, 5*(1).

KEY TERMS AND DEFINITIONS

Account-Based Marketing: Is a highly targeted marketing strategy that focuses on tailors and customizes marketing efforts to specific individual accounts or a select group of high-value accounts rather than targeting a broad audience.

Artificial Intelligence: Is the simulation of human intelligence in machines, allowing them to perform various tasks.

Case Study: Is a research method that involves an in-depth examination and analysis of a particular individual, group, event, or situation.

Coherent Communication: Is the act of conveying information, ideas, or messages in a clear, logical, and organized manner to ensure that the recipient can easily understand and follow the intended message.

Invest Lithuania: Is the national agency responsible for attracting foreign investment to Lithuania and supporting businesses in the country.

Personalization: Is the practice of tailoring products, services, content, or experiences to individual preferences, needs, or characteristics.

Storytelling: Is the art of conveying a message or information through a narrative, often involving characters and emotions, to engage an audience.

Synergy: Refers to the combined or cooperative interaction of multiple elements, where the result is more significant or effective than each element's individual contributions or efforts on its own.

Chapter 2
The Role of Artificial Intelligence to Empower and Leverage Brands

Carlos R. Cunha
https://orcid.org/0000-0003-3085-1562
Research Centre in Digitalization and Intelligent Robotics (CeDRI), Laboratório para a Sustentabilidade e Tecnologia em Regiões de Montanha (SusTEC), Instituto Politécnico de Bragança, Bragança, Portugal

João Pedro Gomes
https://orcid.org/0000-0001-9308-0027
Instituto Politécnico de Bragança, Portugal

Vítor Mendonça
UNIAG, Instituto Politécnico de Bragança, Bragança, Portugal

ABSTRACT

Technological evolution has impelled companies to adopt innovative solutions supported by technologies. In a particular way, brands have been migrating from traditional marketing to digital marketing, with the vanguard of emerging technologies allowing them to obtain competitive advantages. Nowadays, artificial intelligence promises to transform the area of marketing, considering that machine learning, natural language processing, and predictive analytics are revolutionizing the way brands interact with their consumers, personalize experiences, and make informed data-driven decisions. This chapter, after contextualizing artificial intelligence within organizations and the competitive advantages it can represent, discusses AI as an automatic pilot for brand empowerment and proposes a conceptual model that, using artificial intelligence, allows companies to be trained and streamline digital marketing functions to empower brands. Finally, the authors also present some scenarios in which the proposed model can be applied.
DOI: 10.4018/979-8-3693-2153-9.ch002

INTRODUCTION

In a society that reveals itself to be a massive data producing system, the ability to process data and generate information and knowledge is currently inaccessible to human processing capacity. In this scenario, brand management is now a very demanding and extremely complex time-to-market exercise. However, if brands see in this reality an over-information, they will be making a big mistake – there is no such thing as an over-information. Not when we have Artificial Intelligence (AI).

AI and its derivative technologies (e.g., Machine Learning and Deep Learning), combined with the increase in computational capacity to process data, have demonstrated unique capabilities to analyze massive amounts of data and, from these, detect patterns, which allow characterizing realities and trends, anticipate scenarios and even detect week insights. In this context AI is driving the change in the way brands and customers interact with one another.

Business is strongly influenced by AI, being a good example the sales cycle, consumers habits and costumers support activities (Trawnih et al., 2022). Additionally, and according (Davenport et al., 2020), AI and its algorithms is capable of processing massive amounts of data, if almost no human interaction, and from multiple data sources. This process is also capable of extracting important insights that will support the prediction and anticipation of consumers-behaviors, int real time.

There is however a challenge to combine this capability of AI to analyze data and detect patterns and the relational nature that exists between brands and consumers (Aaker et al., 2004). Indeed, being able to understand and anticipate trends might be extremely helpful for brands to remain meaningful in an era where the consumer has several alternatives as never before.

This research discusses the role that Generative AI has and will increasingly play in empowering and leveraging brands, allowing them not only to better manage how they relate to their customers, but also to strategically create new brands that can meet the demand of their customers or niche markets that are being formed still in an embryonic stage – generating competitive advantages against competing brands. We also explore the concept of using AI as an autopilot for brands – that is, the strategy and its actions are guided, shaped and redefined in real time by AI. In a future that will in all probability be much more data producing (e.g., what exists today will be the tip of the iceberg of tomorrow) AI will be an indispensable tool for brands, with the AI algorithms used being the differentiating factors of the competitive brands-capacity.

In terms of organization, this work, after an introduction to the topic of AI and its role in the context of business and brand management, discusses in chapter 2 the importance of brands as a factor in creating value. Then in chapter 3, it contextualizes the role that AI has on organizations. In chapter 4, the potential of AI to be an automatic pilot for brands is explored. In chapter 5, some tools are presented that use AI to help perform a set of tasks related to marketing professionals. In chapter 6, a conceptual model is proposed that demonstrates the vision of using generative AI to automate the creation and management of brands, design and development of new products, customer relationship management and the empowerment of marketers and decision-makers. In chapter 7, the proposed conceptual model is discussed through the use of some scenarios. Finally, chapter 8 presents a conclusion to the work.

A BRAND AS A VALUE CREATION FACTOR

In the contemporary world, brands are almost omnipresent, becoming part of our daily lives. Their influence can be observed across multiple industries, cultural sector and even as a mechanism for affirmation of territories.

The brand concept can be defined as: "marketing-related intangible asset including, but not limited to, names, terms, signs, symbols, logos and designs, or a combination of these, intended to identify goods, services or entities, or a combination of these, creating distinctive images and associations in the minds of stakeholders, thereby generating economic benefits/values" (ISO 10668:2010).

For any company, brands are the intangible asset most valuable (Keller & Lehmann, 2003). However, the concept of brand is multifaceted and relatively complex, both from the point of view of companies that provide services or create goods under their own brand, and from the point of view of consumers who perceive that brand. The reality is that the brand image desired and projected by the organization does not always coincide with the brand's perception by customers. Additionally, brands are under the influence of changes constantly, in marketing and the external environment, requiring constant adaptation to market trends and consumer demand.

Presently, technological advances have led to a highly interconnected global landscape, necessitating a new evaluation in the field of branding research from the standpoints of businesses, customers, and the community. According to Swaminathan et al. (2020), the hyperconnectivity has enabled established brands to expand their geographic reach and social influence, while new types of brand entities (such as ideas, people, places, and organizational brands) are further expanding the brand landscape.

A brand brings together a set of attributes, benefits, symbols and experiences that identify and differentiate a product, service, company or person from its competitors. Brands have the power to influence consumers' perceptions, preferences, attitudes and behaviors, generating loyalty, trust, satisfaction and recommendation.

According to Kononenko (2021), brands are a combination of several tangible and intangible elements, which can be grouped into three categories:

- **Visual design elements**, such as: name, logo, graphics, typographic fonts, corporate colors, packaging, shapes, slogan;
- **Distinctive characteristics of products**, such as: aroma, flavor, quality;
- **Intangible aspects of customer interaction**, such as: reputation, service quality.

Thus, these various elements combined around brands facilitate brands to be a crucial element in creating value for both companies and consumers. They serve as a cognitive shortcut, allowing consumers to make informed purchasing choices without having to spend time and energy evaluating each product individually. Especially in consumer markets, brands play a crucial role as businesses strive to foster consumer trust, loyalty and preferences.

According to Kapferer, brands have different functions in terms of the value perceived by consumers (Kapferer, 2008), among which we highlight: identification, practicality, assurance, optimization, continuity and ethic.

In the context of these functions, there are several benefits for consumers, such as: the brand can be seen clearly and be quickly identified and associated with the product; allows time and energy savings, allowing the brand to be purchased again, due to brand loyalty; the consumer is guaranteed to find the same standard of quality, no matter where or when the product or service is purchased; guarantee of purchasing the best product in its category, the best performance for a given purpose; satisfaction caused by existing intimacy and familiarity with the brand; satisfaction linked to the brand's responsible social behavior towards its external environment.

The brand' value stems from its capability to create an exceptional, positive, and noteworthy significance in the consumer's perception. The value perceived by the customer is the main factor that allows the brand to ensure that customers will be comfortable to pay more for the brand's products and services.

The different approaches to brand equity show that different authors establish different ways for a brand to create value (Kapferer, 2008; Keller & Kotler, 2012; Oliveira et al., 2023), that we highlight: Financial perspective – the financial perspective regards brand equity as the extra financial worth that a brand contributes to a product or service. For instance, it explains why customers are available to pay a higher-price for a product from a reputable brand as opposed to a generic one; Consumer perspective - the consumer perspective centers on the consumer's perception and interaction with the brand. This encompasses brand recognition, consumer's emotional connection with the brand, brand loyalty, and perceived excellence; Furthermore, a combined perspective respects both financial value and consumer perception.

A successful brand is generally based on several key principles, which according to Kotler and Keller highlight five Branding principles (Keller & Kotler, 2012):

- **Consistency** is one of the fundamental principles of Branding for any organization. To become consistent, organizations must adopt holistic approaches that include products or brands, as well as all points of interaction between the organization and its stakeholders
- **Clarity** is crucial to making a brand more understandable and tangible. It is based on an organization's vision, mission, values and core competencies. These elements must be simple to communicate and also to understand, allowing that stakeholders can set a position of the brand's relevance in their mindset.
- **Continuity** is a fundamental principle for developing Brand Equity and long-term trust. People must trust that the brand delivers on everything it promises, based on past experiences. Therefore, continuity is essential to maintain customer trust and loyalty.
- **Visibility** is important for increasing brand-exposure and also to develop the brand awareness among consumers.
- **Authenticity** is a crucial aspect of a brand. The goal of brand authenticity is to create a unique feeling for the customer of owning a unique product or service. This helps to differentiate the brand in the market and establish a deeper connection with customers.

A brand cannot just be merely a symbol for a company or a product, it must represent the organization's most precious resource, fostering robust principles, values and emotions with customers to establish a deep connection between them and the brand.

Thus, we can say that a strong brand promotes the creation of significant value for a company through its ability to shape customer perceptions and preferences, differentiating products or services from competitors, and building long-term customer relationships.

THE CONTEXT OF ARTIFICIAL INTELLIGENCE IN ORGANIZATIONS

Organizations have always sought to increase their competitiveness. If in the past this aim was essentially achieved through the pursuit of improvements in the machinery supporting its businesses, it has progressively come to be achieved due to the ability to use data in a useful way, generate information and knowledge and, in recent years, in the ability of understanding what the data "does not reveal to the naked eye" and which allows organizations to preview the future – to anticipate problems and opportunities. In this field, Artificial Intelligence (AI) and its subsystems, such as Machine Learning and Deep Learning are the tip of the spear. According to Cunha (2023), insight-based knowledge, powered by AI, appears to be an ongoing reengineering within organizations.

AI plays an irreplaceable role in the era of the digital economy, providing a vital opportunity for organizations that wish to increase their performance and competitiveness (Li et al., 2024). According to Lee et al. (2023), who carried out a systematic review of the literature, the majority of AI implementations are motivated by process improvement and production efficiency. Also Mikalef et al. (2023) emphasizes that AI skills must be seen as management skills that go beyond the technical aspect, and used in a creative way to add value to the organization, proposing that these skills be considered central, not just secondary.

AI is transforming decision-making processes in organizations by taking over decision-making responsibilities previously assigned only to humans. AI self-learning capacity improves the quality of decisions, marking a fundamental change (Vincent, 2021). One of the examples is, according to Chatterjee et al. (2021), the integration of AI into Customer Relationship Management (CRM) systems that is transforming the analysis of large volumes of customer data in organizations where, to efficiently deal with the resulting opportunities and challenges, organizations are developing skills and processes that enhance their agility, aligning with artificial intelligence-powered customer service.

Research conducted by Sullivan & Fosso Wamba 2024) on AI and adaptation to market changes, revealed significant interactions between environmental-hostility and also dynamism in the relationships between AI-powered capabilities and the Adaptive Response to Market Changes (ARMC), as well as ARMC being observed to positively influence company' innovation and performance.

Regarding the role of AI in branding, according to Musaiqer & Hamdan (2023), AI has become a powerful tool for organizations to improve their strategy and brand-building efforts. Also, according to (Rahman et al., 2023), luxury brands in the fashion sector have been adopting AI-powered digital assistance to enhance the online shopping experience and influence customer engagement. In a study conducted by Ho & Chow (2023), on the role of AI in Hong Kong brand preference for retail banks, AI-driven marketing efforts showed a significant positive effect on brand preference, influencing customer repurchase intention. This suggests that AI marketing efforts should not only be seen as improving the customer experience, but also as an essential tool in building brand image, supporting (Godey et al., 2016).

However, despite the enormous potential of AI, according to Olan et al. (2022), organizations often have difficulties in integrating existing knowledge and new knowledge into the AI learning process, resulting in obstacles in intelligent systems design and implementation, as well as in the distribution and retention of knowledge – limiting the benefits of AI for organizational efficiency. Also, according to Mikalef & Gupta (2021), some caution is needed with an approach in which AI is presented as being able to solve all business-related problems, excessively inflating expectations about what it can provide. Furthermore, according to Hajipour et al. (2023), the creation of AI applications is limited to a few companies with dedicated development units. As a result, there is a demand for companies that can offer personalized artificial intelligence services and products to meet business needs.

From the client perspective, results from a study conducted by McLean et al. (2021), which examined the role of AI-powered Voice Assistants (VAs) and their influence in consumer brand engagement, indicate that brands need to address challenges related to consumer trust in the context of online engagement-technology. Data privacy concerns and fears of unauthorized use negatively impact consumer brand engagement through VAs, highlighting the need to address these issues to promote greater trust.

AI offers numerous opportunities to gain competitive advantages, but faces challenges, especially in implementing AI technologies for customer-service. This involves dilemmas such as the Personalization-Privacy Paradox, where personalization is crucial but there are privacy concerns. To establish a customer-centric ecosystem, it is necessary to balance AI-driven value co-creation and value co-destruction concerns (Chaturvedi & Verma, 2023a). We highlight the importance of people's participation in the creation of new AI-based mechanisms to achieve a desired balance between technology and the human dimension – only then will we have a situation where everyone wins.

AI AS AN AUTOPILOT FOR BRANDS

In modern business, AI integration has emerged as a transformative push, re-engineering brand strategies and customer experiences. This chapter investigates the concept of using AI as an autopilot for brands, exploring its multifaceted role in revolutionizing customer interactions, driving strategic decision-making processes and promoting sustainable growth in an increasingly competitive.

A comprehensive understanding of customer preferences and behaviors is at the heart of effective brand management (Heding et al., 2020). AI algorithms, equipped with advanced data analytics capabilities, empower brands to extract actionable insights from vast data sets. By analyzing multiple data sources, such as social media interactions, web transactions, and customer feedback, AI makes it easier to create detailed customer profiles. These insights allow brands to personalize products, services and marketing strategies, thus meeting the growing demands of their target audience. Additionally, AI-based sentiment analysis provides real-time feedback, enabling brands to quickly adapt to changing consumer sentiments and market trends.

AI is an important innovation-catalyst, facilitating the conception and development of new products and brands (Grashof & Kopka, 2023). Machine learning algorithms analyze market trends, consumer feedback, and competitive offerings to identify emerging opportunities and niche segments. Through generative AI models, brands can explore creative concepts and prototypes, streamlining the product ideation process. Additionally, AI-based recommendation engines personalize product suggestions based on individual preferences, driving cross-selling and upselling initiatives. Predictive analytics AI capability supports demand forecasting and helps optimize inventory management and mitigate supply chain disruptions, thereby increasing operational efficiency and profitability.

Effective customer engagement is essential for building brand loyalty and fostering lasting relationships. AI-powered chatbots and virtual assistants offer scalable and efficient ways to interact with customers across multiple touchpoints (Chaturvedi & Verma, 2023b; He & Zhang, 2023). Using natural language processing (NLP) associated with machine learning algorithms, these conversational AI platforms provide personalized assistance, resolve queries, and provide product recommendations in real-time. By automating routine customer interactions, brands simplify support processes, reduce response times, and increase overall customer satisfaction. Additionally, AI-based chatbots gather vital feedback, enabling brands to iteratively improve product and service design based on understanding customer insights.

A seamless, personalized customer experience is critical to brand differentiation and customer retention. AI plays a crucial role in improving the end-to-end customer journey by providing personalized content, recommendations and services. Predictive analytics and machine learning algorithms enable brands to anticipate individual customer preferences and behaviors, facilitating hyper-targeted marketing initiatives and personalized product offerings. Additionally, AI-powered personalization engines deliver dynamic website experiences, contextualized messaging, and personalized promotions, maximizing customer engagement and conversion rates. Additionally, AI-based recommendation systems ensure consistency across channels, promoting a cohesive brand experience across digital and physical touchpoints (Agersborg et al., 2020; Pappas et al., 2023).

AI empowers brands to make data-driven strategic decisions by providing actionable insights and predictive analytics. Leveraging AI algorithms, brands analyze market dynamics, competitive landscapes and consumer trends to inform long-term strategic planning and investment decisions. Additionally, AI-based scenario modeling and predictive modeling enable brands to simulate business scenarios, assess potential risks, and optimize resource allocation. Additionally, AI-powered recommendation systems identify strategic partnerships, acquisition targets, and market expansion opportunities, facilitating agile decision-making and competitive advantage (Chintalapati & Pandey, 2022).

The integration of AI as an autopilot for brands represents a paradigm shift in business operations and consumer engagement strategies. By leveraging AI capabilities, brands can decipher consumer insights, design innovative products, and deliver personalized experiences at scale (Huang & Rust, 2021). Additionally, AI facilitates data-driven strategic decision-making, driving sustainable growth and competitiveness in today's dynamic market. As AI is evolving continuous, brands must embrace this transformative technology to thrive in the digital age and stay ahead of the competition. With a comprehensive understanding of AI's potential, brands can chart a path toward continuous innovation, customer-centricity, and long-term success (Allioui & Mourdi, 2023; Sandrin, 2021).

AI-DRIVEN TOOLS ROLE IN MARKETING

AI has become increasingly present and important, enabling marketers to deliver personalized experiences at scale, leverage data-driven insights and automate processes. Many AI tools are now available to marketers, offering a wide range of functionality to streamline workflows, increase creativity, and optimize marketing strategies. Some of these AI tools that are reshaping the marketing landscape, revolutionizing the way brands engage with consumers and achieve business objectives and help marketers are:

- **Flick**: Flick is a comprehensive social media workflow tool powered by artificial intelligence. It assists marketers with copywriting, scheduling, hashtag optimization, analytics, and more, streamlining social media management processes and maximizing engagement.
- **Jasper AI**: Jasper AI helps businesses amplify their marketing content by generating blog articles, social media posts, sales emails, website copy, and more. Its AI-powered platform allows marketers to create compelling content efficiently and effectively.
- **Notion AI**: Notion AI, is a productivity tool versatile that offers a range of features to support marketers in content creation, editing, data interpretation, translation real-time note taking automation and document creation. Its intuitive interface and AI-driven features increase productivity and collaboration.

- **ChatGPT**: ChatGPT is an AI-based conversational agent that helps marketers generate original texts, brainstorm ideas and get answers to questions. Its natural language processing capabilities enable seamless communication and ideation.
- **Hootsuite Insights**: Hootsuite Insights is a tool for social media analytics, that uses AI to monitor content and trends across multiple platforms. It provides marketers with valuable insights and actionable intelligence to inform their social media strategies and campaigns.
- **Adobe Sensei GenAI**: Adobe Sensei GenAI offers advanced data analytics, content optimization, and campaign improvement features. Integrated into Adobe's suite of marketing tools, it allows marketers to personalize experiences, personalize audiences, and optimize digital marketing strategies.
- **Salesforce Einstein**: Salesforce Einstein is an AI platform integrated with Salesforce's Customer Relationship Management (CRM) system, that offers personalization, predictive analytics, marketing automation, and insights capabilities, empowering marketers to deliver personalized experiences and drive customer engagement.
- **DALL·E 2**: DALL·E 2 is an AI model that generates images based on textual descriptions (prompts). It allows marketers to create visually appealing content quickly and easily, expanding creative possibilities.
- **DALL·E 3**: The DALL·E 3 builds on the capabilities of the DALL·E 2, offering significant improvements in generating realistic images and artwork from of natural language descriptions. Integrated with ChatGPT, it provides marketers with enhanced creative tools and capabilities.
- **Synthesia**: Synthesia is an AI tool for creating and publishing videos. It allows marketers to generate videos with AI avatars and voiceovers in 120+ languages, serving diverse audiences and increasing engagement.

The adoption of AI-supported tools has transformed the marketing landscape, offering unprecedented opportunities for marketers to increase efficiency, creativity and effectiveness. From social media management and content creation to data analysis and personalization, AI-based tools empower marketers to achieve marketing success in today's competitive environment. By leveraging AI capabilities, marketers can streamline workflows, generate compelling content, analyze data-driven insights, personalize experiences, and drive strategic decision-making. As AI continues to evolve, it will be imperative for marketers to adopt these innovative tools to stay ahead of the curve and deliver effective marketing campaigns.

CONCEPTUAL MODEL PROPOSAL

As already mentioned, the role of AI has become central in optimizing business processes and in the ability to generate competitive advantages. However, the inclusion of AI in companies will quickly become a mandatory requirement for companies/brands to be able to respond effectively in an increasingly demanding time-to-market. In order to understand the role of AI and to design an AI layer in the context of companies/brands, this chapter presents a proposal for a conceptual model where AI plays a role in facilitating and empowering companies' ability to understand their markets and, accordingly, to make better and faster decisions.

The proposed model highlights the role of generative AI, which has resulted in a kind of democratization of the use of AI for the most varied purposes, whether in a context of personal use or in a context of business use. What is certain is that AI is no longer a "taboo" subject and/or mentally aligned with technological companies or pure research contexts.

The emergence of many tools supported by AI, for multiple purposes and simple to use (e.g., ChatGPT), has made some of the tasks that were time-consuming and/or only within the reach of professionals with higher technological skills simple and fast for everyone. This reality – generative AI – which can be understood in its succinct flow of operation according to figure 1, has provided brand managers with a wealth of precious resources that empower their role and their ability to understand and make decisions. In this context, AI-driven tools will increasingly become productivity tools for marketers and business decision-makers.

Even though the current stage of AI penetration in companies is the inclusion of AI-tools (and this stage will probably be maintained for a long time in small companies), the future will be the full addition of a whole new layer of AI in the remaining layers, and their processes, of organizations, as happened with the layer of classical information systems (non-AI).

Think about how AI can be strategically and functionally included in companies, in order to create a functional link between understanding the market and, in particular, customers and their aspirations, and decision making, from its operational to strategic aspects, should govern any new information systems architecture. However, in our opinion, the inclusion of this AI layer should guarantee the most

Figure 1. General workflow for making generative AI work (SAP SE, 2024)

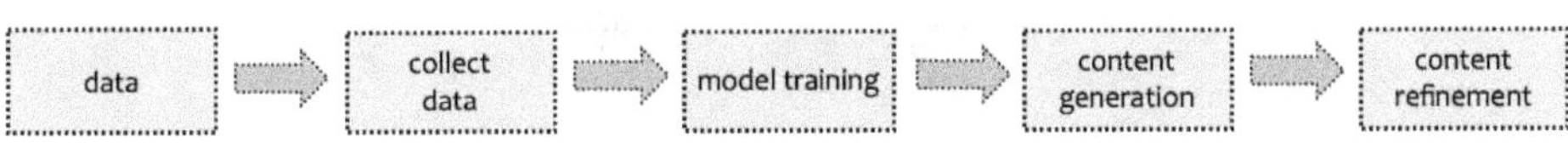

automated operation possible, where AI can be an autopilot for the company that, without prejudice to the strategy approved by the human decision maker, is a layer that analyzes, understands and takes decisions.

Figure 2 presents the proposed conceptual model, which is then described in terms of its main components and respective contribution.

The model presented targets large companies, which have the financial and technological capabilities to implement (or subcontract the implementation) an AI layer across all business processes. In the context we explore, small and medium-sized companies, which do not have the capacity for such implementation, will take advantage of the AI-tools but will not be capable of implementing an implementation similar to what we propose.

A typical company that the model contemplates is a holding company, which has several brands, in different business sectors and/or in the same line of business. In this context, there is a need to manage several brands.

The model presents the "autopilot" vision for brand management, which means that it is up to AI to understand how to manage a given brand, whether through the extinction or creation of brands. It is up to AI to understand the insights that intelligent analysis of data obtained through customer interactions can offer. In this way, the company's response could be the extinction of a brand that is not profitable and/or the creation of new brands that embody new products that will predictably be successful with customers. The capacity for such perception materializes a concept where a brand and its products can be the result of the customers' vision and not the company's own – customers design the products that the company should offer them, shaping them over time.

Figure 2. Proposed conceptual model

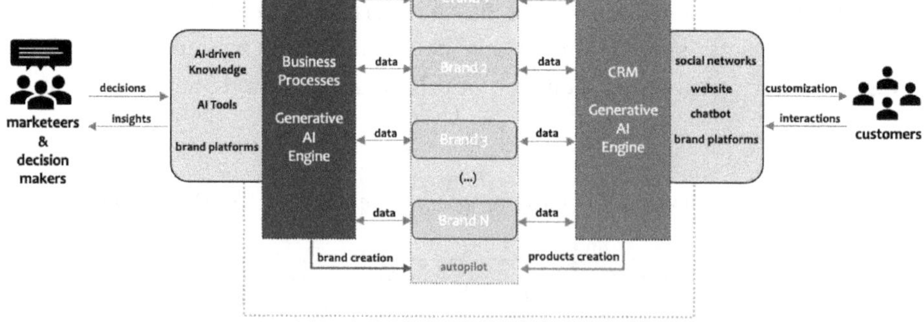

The Generative AI CRM engine is responsible for managing all the channels that brands have to manage their relationships with their customers (e.g., chatbots, social networks). This engine is capable of personalizing interactions with each customer by taking advantage of customer input to understand their profile at all times. Generative AI plays a key role here due to its ability to constantly adapt the way in which customer interests are managed, combining them with business interests. The ability to perceive insights turns the vision of managing a brand and creating or modeling new or existing products into a linear process of managing interests where supply tends to adapt to demand in a "perfect" way.

This approach will contribute to generate in customers a greater sense of belonging to the company and a connection that induces in the customer a feeling of almost apparent control – the customers feels that they are the focus in a more tangible way.

Upstream of the proposed model is the business process management engine through generative AI. This component uses AI to obtain insights into the downstream functioning of the model (i.e., the customer interaction component), allowing the company's strategic management level to evaluate and validate proposals for creating new brands and products. This component also allows you to generate AI-driven knowledge.

In this way, better, more effective and faster strategic decisions will be made, feeding and empowering top management tasks and marketers who will refine their strategies with greater probability of success.

However, the vision of a conceptual model that tends towards a state of perfect equilibrium is not without limitations.

It is important to understand that generative AI brings with it a very important set of strengths and opportunities. However, like any technology, it has weaknesses and threats. Figure 3 succinctly presents the result of a reflection on generative AI in the form of a SWOT analysis.

Competition will continue to exist between organizations that have the capacity to implement such models. The evolution of generative AI (e.g., as we see in the ChatGPT example) will be constantly evolving, with better models and more accurate capabilities for predicting and understanding insights. We are of the opinion that in the near future, the quality of the AI that a given company can develop or acquire (from companies specialized in AI) will be the most important asset and the greatest generator of the degree of success and competitive advantage that the company can have. The very computational capacity that a company disposes will influence its ability to obtain better and faster insights. The field of research about the role of human intuition in decision-making will be called into question as never before. Will visionaries continue to exist? Here's a reflection that doesn't fit into this work, but we find appealing – the human factor in the success of organizations, in a world of AI.

Figure 3. SWOT analysis to Generative AI

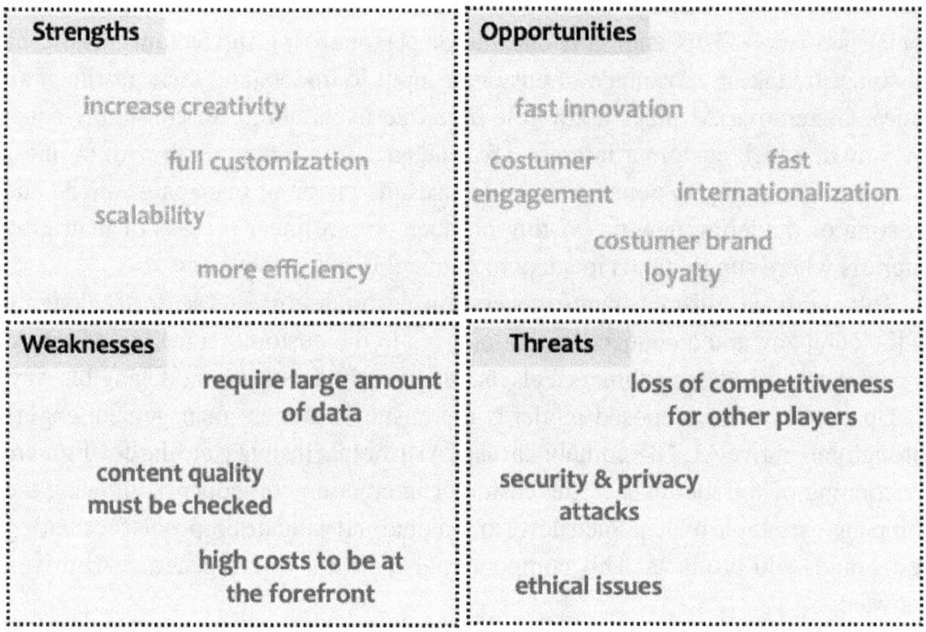

DISCUSSION OF THE MODEL THROUGH SCENARIOS

This chapter reflects on some scenarios that help to discuss the proposed conceptual model, not in an attempt to validate it but by discussing some finer and more concrete aspects that help to understand the model from a more operational perspective. However, the technological aspects of technology implementation are not discussed.

Brand Internationalization Scenario

AI, along with the suggested model, has the potential to assist organizations in making well-informed choices regarding potential strategies for international expansion.

In this context, AI can carry out market research in order to increase the understanding of the needs of international customers and adapt the company's products and services to potential international customers and understand market trends. So, using artificial intelligence, companies will be able to collect, organize and analyze data on potential international markets, in order to identify trends and patterns.

It also allows the company to obtain information about market entry requirements, such as legal requirements.

With the help of AI, brands can communicate in real time in different languages, humanize communication according to the profile of their customers, as well as adjust and translate communication artifacts.

Chatbot systems with Generative AI allow you to establish dialogues with customers in their language, making communication more natural.

In this context, the proposed model based on AI provides companies with skills that speed up and promote the chances of successful penetration into international markets.

Penetration in Market Niches Scenario

Given a company's strategy of penetrating new market niches, the proposed model supported by AI makes it possible to facilitate and speed up marketing actions, including the identification of market niches, understand the behavior and environment of potential consumers, identify sales and distribution channels, customize communication content according to consumers' needs and preferences, trigger communication automation mechanisms to seduce potential customers, among others.

As such, AI can analyze large volumes of data (Big Data) to identify patterns and trends allowing companies to identify market niches.

Based on the analysis of target audience behavior, especially footprint and behavior in the digital world, Deep Learning can be used to segment target audiences and design more assertive communication and marketing strategies. Using intelligent algorithms and big data, brands and/or companies can identify keywords relevant to their market niche and create optimized content, aiming to increase their visibility in search engines.

Still based on data analysis, AI can also be used to identify products and services that may be of interest to potential consumers for certain market niches.

Companies and/or brands can also develop automation of marketing actions, such as sending emails, customer service chatbot, publishing content on social networks, among others, with the aim of seducing and attracting potential customers.

Launching a New Brand Scenario

Similar to other scenarios already described, the proposed model supported by AI could assist in the launch of new brands by allowing: analyzing large volumes of data, allowing trends and patterns to be identified in the market; carry out market studies identifying and characterizing both the target audience and the competition; automate various marketing actions, among others.

By analyzing the feelings of the target audience and/or consumers on social networks and other online platforms, it will be possible to obtain feedback on how brands are being received by the market and monitor the public's reaction to communication and marketing actions and campaigns.

AI can, based on data analysis, help predict future trends, anticipating market demand. This forecast may allow you to adjust and adapt the launch strategy for both products and brands. Additionally, it is possible to segment the audience more effectively and direct marketing actions and campaigns to the right people at the right time.

Launching a new brand generally involves developing different communication channels, such as a website, mobile apps and social networks, but also content to publish on these channels, such as texts, images, videos. So, in this context, a model based on AI tools will simplify and accelerate the production of both communication channels and the production of content and its publication.

Rebranding Scenario

Companies will be able to use AI to monitor brands and quickly understand any decline in demand or even the rejection of one of their brands. This perception could lead to informed decision-making and be the stimulus to promote redesign or eventually introduce profound changes to the brand, in this case opting for rebranding.

AI can assist and accelerate the development of the brand's visual identity, including creating the logo, choosing colors and typographic fonts, creating graphics, images and videos, among others. It also allows you to generate copywriting ideas and assist in the production and publication of content.

Just like in other scenarios, in a rebranding scenario, AI can also be very useful in helping to carry out market studies, analyzing data to infer trends and patterns and understanding market sentiments, customizing communication in function of market segmentation but also of the individual profile of each customer, monitoring the success of marketing actions and campaigns.

CONCLUSION

Companies have always sought to improve their competitive capacity and generate wealth. In this evolution, information systems have leveraged a whole set of opportunities from increased performance, the ability to act globally, to meet time-to-market, among several other dimensions. AI, whose first works date back to the 1950s, today presents a completely new dimension with the development of generative AI. Partly because Generative AI reached people and increased the discussion around this technology.

Current events show that ordinary people are taking advantage of generative AI, as are companies, but on a completely different scale and goals. Increasingly, generative AI will be "the great critical success factor" for the success/survival of companies.

In this context, this work discusses how AI can empower brands, the main contributions are: It frames the importance of brands and how they can represent a factor of competitiveness and value creation; contextualizes the way in which AI is transforming organizational processes and reflects on the opportunities that AI represents for brands and organizations. We emphasize that the incorporation of artificial intelligence as a brand's autopilot means a fundamental change in the way companies operate and interact with consumers.

After identifying an eclectic set of AI tools that can be used by organizations in the context of marketing, we propose a conceptual model supported by generative AI which aims to enable organizations to leverage and empower their brands.

Finally, we present four scenarios in which AI can help to obtain competitive advantages by streamline and accelerate the processes inherent to the internationalization of brands, the penetration of market niches, the launch of new brands and rebranding.

Inevitably, there are certain constraints inherent in this work. Considering that the topic of generative AI is still quite recent, the bibliography on the topic is not abundant, especially the bibliography on the application of generative AI in business areas. Regarding the use of generative AI applications by organizations, as a disruptive technology, it is not yet being used en masse as the tools are still in the maturing phase and developing advanced functionalities.

ACKNOWLEDGMENT

The authors are grateful to the Foundation for Science and Technology (FCT, Portugal) for financial support through national funds FCT/MCTES (PIDDAC) to CeDRI, UIDB/05757/2020 (DOI: 10.54499/UIDB/05757/2020) and UIDP/05757/2020 (DOI: 10.54499/UIDP/05757/2020) and SusTEC, LA/P/0007/2020 (DOI: 10.54499/LA/P/0007/2020).

REFERENCES

Aaker, J., Fournier, S., & Brasel, S. A. (2004). When good brands do bad. *The Journal of Consumer Research*, *31*(1), 1–16. doi:10.1086/383419

Agersborg, C., Månsson, I., & Roth, E. (2020). *Brand Management and Artificial Intelligence-A World of Man Plus Machine-A qualitative study exploring how Artificial Intelligence can contribute to Brand Management in the B2C sector.* Academic Press.

Allioui, H., & Mourdi, Y. (2023). Unleashing the potential of AI: Investigating cutting-edge technologies that are transforming businesses. *International Journal of Computer Engineering and Data Science*, *3*(2), 1–12.

Chatterjee, S., Chaudhuri, R., Vrontis, D., Thrassou, A., & Ghosh, S. K. (2021). Adoption of artificial intelligence-integrated CRM systems in agile organizations in India. *Technological Forecasting and Social Change*, *168*, 120783. doi:10.1016/j.techfore.2021.120783

Chaturvedi, R., & Verma, S. (2023a). Opportunities and Challenges of AI-Driven Customer Service. In J. N. Sheth, V. Jain, E. Mogaji, & A. Ambika (Eds.), *Artificial Intelligence in Customer Service: The Next Frontier for Personalized Engagement* (pp. 33–71). Springer International Publishing. doi:10.1007/978-3-031-33898-4_3

Chaturvedi, R., & Verma, S. (2023b). Opportunities and challenges of AI-driven customer service. *Artificial Intelligence in Customer Service: The next Frontier for Personalized Engagement*, 33–71.

Chintalapati, S., & Pandey, S. K. (2022). Artificial intelligence in marketing: A systematic literature review. *International Journal of Market Research*, *64*(1), 38–68. doi:10.1177/14707853211018428

Cunha, C. R. (2023). Do conhecimento tácito ao conhecimento baseado em IA Insights: Uma reengenharia em curso? *RISTI (Porto)*, *51*(51), 1–4. doi:10.17013/risti.51.1-4

Davenport, T., Guha, A., Grewal, D., & Bressgott, T. (2020). How artificial intelligence will change the future of marketing. *Journal of the Academy of Marketing Science*, *48*(1), 24–42. doi:10.1007/s11747-019-00696-0

de Oliveira, M. O. R., Heldt, R., Silveira, C. S., & Luce, F. B. (2023). Brand equity chain and brand equity measurement approaches. In Marketing Intelligence and Planning (Vol. 41, Issue 4, pp. 442–456). Emerald Publishing. doi:10.1108/MIP-06-2022-0222

Godey, B., Manthiou, A., Pederzoli, D., Rokka, J., Aiello, G., Donvito, R., & Singh, R. (2016). Social media marketing efforts of luxury brands: Influence on brand equity and consumer behavior. *Journal of Business Research, 69*(12), 5833–5841. doi:10.1016/j.jbusres.2016.04.181

Grashof, N., & Kopka, A. (2023). Artificial intelligence and radical innovation: An opportunity for all companies? *Small Business Economics, 61*(2), 771–797. doi:10.1007/s11187-022-00698-3

Hajipour, V., Hekmat, S., & Amini, M. (2023). A value-oriented Artificial Intelligence-as-a-Service business plan using integrated tools and services. *Decision Analytics Journal, 8*, 100302. https://doi.org/https://doi.org/10.1016/j.dajour.2023.100302

He, A.-Z., & Zhang, Y. (2023). AI-powered touch points in the customer journey: A systematic literature review and research agenda. *Journal of Research in Interactive Marketing, 17*(4), 620–639. doi:10.1108/JRIM-03-2022-0082

Heding, T., Knudtzen, C. F., & Bjerre, M. (2020). *Brand management: Mastering research, theory and practice*. Routledge. doi:10.4324/9780367172596

Ho, S. P. S., & Chow, M. Y. C. (2023). The role of artificial intelligence in consumers' brand preference for retail banks in Hong Kong. *Journal of Financial Services Marketing*. Advance online publication. doi:10.1057/s41264-022-00207-3

Huang, M.-H., & Rust, R. T. (2021). A strategic framework for artificial intelligence in marketing. *Journal of the Academy of Marketing Science, 49*(1), 30–50. doi:10.1007/s11747-020-00749-9

ISO 10668. (2010). *ISO 10668:2010 - Brand valuation-Requirements for monetary brand valuation*. www.iso.org

Kapferer, J.-N. (2008). *The new strategic brand management: Creating and sustaining brand equity long term*. Kogan Page Publishers.

Keller, K. L., & Kotler, P. (2012). Administração de Marketing (14a Edição). Prentice Hall.

Keller, K. L., & Lehmann, D. R. (2003). How do brands create value? *Marketing Management, 12*(3), 26.

Kononenko, O. (2021). Theoretical Aspects of the Organization Brand Management. *Innovative Technologies and Scientific Solutions for Industries, 1*(15), 76–82. doi:10.30837/ITSSI.2021.15.076

Lee, M. C. M., Scheepers, H., Lui, A. K. H., & Ngai, E. W. T. (2023). The implementation of artificial intelligence in organizations: A systematic literature review. *Information & Management*, *60*(5), 103816. doi:10.1016/j.im.2023.103816

Li, X., Rong, K., & Shi, X. (2024). Situating artificial intelligence in organization: A human-machine relationship perspective? A commentary on Kemp's (2023) paper "competitive advantages through artificial intelligence: Toward a theory of situated AI." *Journal of Digital Economy*. https://doi.org/https://doi.org/10.1016/j.jdec.2024.01.001

McLean, G., Osei-Frimpong, K., & Barhorst, J. (2021). Alexa, do voice assistants influence consumer brand engagement? – Examining the role of AI powered voice assistants in influencing consumer brand engagement. *Journal of Business Research*, *124*, 312–328. doi:10.1016/j.jbusres.2020.11.045

Mikalef, P., & Gupta, M. (2021). Artificial intelligence capability: Conceptualization, measurement calibration, and empirical study on its impact on organizational creativity and firm performance. *Information & Management*, *58*(3), 103434. doi:10.1016/j.im.2021.103434

Mikalef, P., Islam, N., Parida, V., Singh, H., & Altwaijry, N. (2023). Artificial intelligence (AI) competencies for organizational performance: A B2B marketing capabilities perspective. *Journal of Business Research*, *164*, 113998. doi:10.1016/j.jbusres.2023.113998

Musaiqer, H. H., & Hamdan, A. (2023). The Role of Artificial Intelligence in Brand Building: A Review. In R. El Khoury & N. Nasrallah (Eds.), *Emerging Trends and Innovation in Business and Finance* (pp. 307–318). Springer Nature Singapore. doi:10.1007/978-981-99-6101-6_22

Olan, F., Ogiemwonyi Arakpogun, E., Suklan, J., Nakpodia, F., Damij, N., & Jayawickrama, U. (2022). Artificial intelligence and knowledge sharing: Contributing factors to organizational performance. *Journal of Business Research*, *145*, 605–615. doi:10.1016/j.jbusres.2022.03.008

Pappas, A., Fumagalli, E., Rouziou, M., & Bolander, W. (2023). More than Machines: The Role of the Future Retail Salesperson in Enhancing the Customer Experience. *Journal of Retailing*, *99*(4), 518–531. doi:10.1016/j.jretai.2023.10.004

Rahman, M. S., Bag, S., Hossain, M. A., Abdel Fattah, F. A. M., Gani, M. O., & Rana, N. P. (2023). The new wave of AI-powered luxury brands online shopping experience: The role of digital multisensory cues and customers' engagement. *Journal of Retailing and Consumer Services*, *72*, 103273. doi:10.1016/j.jretconser.2023.103273

Sandrin, V. (2021). *The Struggle between Human-centredness and Intelligent Technologies: a Critical Discussion on the Use of Customer Data in Marketing Practice-A Survey Analysis of the RIR Clusters in Veneto*. Academic Press.

SAP SE. (2024, January 15). *O que é IA generativa?* Https://Www.Sap.Com/Brazil/Products/Artificial-Intelligence/What-Is-Generative-Ai.Html

Sullivan, Y., & Fosso Wamba, S. (2024). Artificial intelligence and adaptive response to market changes: A strategy to enhance firm performance and innovation. *Journal of Business Research, 174*, 114500. doi:10.1016/j.jbusres.2024.114500

Swaminathan, V., Sorescu, A., Steenkamp, J. B. E. M., O'Guinn, T. C. G., & Schmitt, B. (2020). Branding in a Hyperconnected World: Refocusing Theories and Rethinking Boundaries. *Journal of Marketing, 84*(2), 24–46. doi:10.1177/0022242919899905

Trawnih, A., Al-Masaeed, S., Alsoud, M., & Alkufahy, A. (2022). Understanding artificial intelligence experience: A customer perspective. *International Journal of Data and Network Science, 6*(4), 1471–1484. doi:10.5267/j.ijdns.2022.5.004

Vincent, V. U. (2021). Integrating intuition and artificial intelligence in organizational decision-making. *Business Horizons, 64*(4), 425–438. doi:10.1016/j.bushor.2021.02.008

Chapter 3
Increasing Customer Engagement in Digital Marketing Campaigns in a Time of AI

Urte Dudzinskaite
ISM University of Management and Economics, Lithuania

Dominyka Venciute
ISM University of Management and Economics, Lithuania

Ricardo Correia
https://orcid.org/0000-0002-0132-4002
Polytechnic Institute of Bragança, Portugal & CiTUR, Portugal

Ruta Fontes
https://orcid.org/0000-0001-8697-1323
University of Aveiro, Portugal

ABSTRACT

The study aims to analyze how customer engagement can be increased in digital marketing campaigns to improve connections with customers. To achieve this aim, empirical research was conducted to get valuable insights into factors that contribute the most to increasing engagement in digital marketing campaigns. The study employed a qualitative research method, and 10 semi-structured interviews were conducted with potential digital marketing campaigns customers dividing them into two age groups of A20-30 and A40-50. The research showed that engagement tactics enhance the performance of digital marketing campaigns and substantially influence users' willingness to interact with digital ads actively. Relevance, clear message, aesthetic design, personalized content, and informativeness have the greatest impact on shaping user behavior and starting active engagement. Taking research results into consideration, managerial recommendations were provided using the RACE framework regarding each phase of the engagement: plan, reach, act, convert, and engage.

DOI: 10.4018/979-8-3693-2153-9.ch003

INTRODUCTION

In the fast-paced and ever-evolving landscape of digital marketing, businesses are compelled to continuously refine their strategies to enhance engagement and thereby, the effectiveness of their marketing campaigns. In an age where consumer attention is fragmented across various digital platforms, engagement emerges as a crucial metric, influencing consumers' buying decisions and brand loyalty. Engagement with digital ads is pivotal as it can directly influence consumer behavior and purchase decisions, making it essential for companies to harness effective strategies that resonate with their target audience (Araujo et al., 2020; Calder et al., 2009).

The digital environment is fiercely competitive, and success often hinges on a brand's ability to engage effectively with its audience. According to recent studies, highly engaged consumers are more likely to buy, promote, and show loyalty to a brand, which underscores the importance of fine-tuning engagement tactics (Calder et al., 2009). Research further suggests that the quality of engagement can significantly affect a company's bottom line, highlighting the direct correlation between consumer engagement and profitability (Chaffey, 2023).

Moreover, the technological advancements in digital marketing tools have introduced new methods of measuring and increasing engagement through data analytics and consumer insights, which allow marketers to tailor their approaches more precisely to consumer needs (Stolle, 2022). This technological pivot necessitates an ongoing examination of consumer behaviors and preferences to craft strategies that are not only effective but also adaptable to the rapid changes in digital marketing dynamics.

The chapter analyzes consumer preferences and provides recommendations for increasing customer engagement in digital marketing campaigns. Specifically, the research problem is to find what are the best practices for reaching the optimal solution that increases customer engagement in digital marketing campaigns.

The chapter begins with a literature review that delves into existing research on digital marketing engagement, highlighting key theories and models that have shaped current marketing strategies, and reviews scholarly articles and industry reports to provide a comprehensive overview of the state of digital marketing engagement. It then discusses major frameworks used in understanding and enhancing customer engagement, including the RACE Framework and the Consumer Engagement Behavior (CEB) model, providing insights into their application in real-world scenarios. Following this, the chapter presents original research conducted for this study, detailing the methodology, data collection, and analysis processes used to gather insights on consumer preferences and behaviors. The findings from the empirical research are analyzed, discussing how they align with existing theories and what they suggest about future trends in digital marketing engagement. Practical recommendations for digital marketers are offered based on the research findings, translating theoretical and empirical insights into actionable strategies that can be implemented in current marketing practices. The chapter concludes by summarizing the key points discussed throughout and reflecting on the implications for future research and practice in the field of digital marketing.

LITERATURE REVIEW

Digital marketing is used to advertise products or services online and reach customers through digital platforms. It provides a new communication tactic of connecting customers and businesses globally, providing support and a high level of interaction, which significantly improves client experience with the brand (Rautela, 2021). The drastic change in advertising procedures has emerged from the rise of digital media. Individuals now have the possibility to choose from many different options as advertisers have a better understanding of their behavior and can offer exactly what they need at the right time. The control over advertising has shifted towards consumers deciding whether to engage with the ads or ignore them. To offer relevant content, advertisers are looking for the most effective ways to reach highly specific audiences through personalization. In the digital era, the new goal is to improve customer activity tracking to provide more customized solutions and achieve better engagement and conversion rates. Consequently, companies have to invest in the development of digital marketing campaigns that increase customer engagement while analyzing customer behavior and preferences (Araujo et al., 2020).

Engagement can be described as the consumers' intentional and committed allocation of their mental, physical, and social energies when they interact with a brand (Araujo et al., 2020). According to Calder et al. (2009), engagement in digital advertising involves a variety of different experiences, some being utilitarian ones where consumers look for guidance or purely pleasant interactions that provide the feeling of relaxation. The same information might evoke distinctive reactions from different customers due to the existence of several pathways to engagement, each driven by unique experiences (Figure 1). Four main engagement experience categories help to involve customers with the content provided: informational, personal identity, social interaction, and entertainment (Calder et al., 2009).

Informational: Consumers seek opinions, suggestions, and guidance on making decisions. Their curiosity and self-learning may engage them to find valuable information such as tutorials, educational content, or simply details about the product or service and how using it might help them. Digital ads can engage people by offering useful information that is relevant to their needs.

Figure 1. Engagement and its consequences
Source: Calder et al., (2009 p. 322)

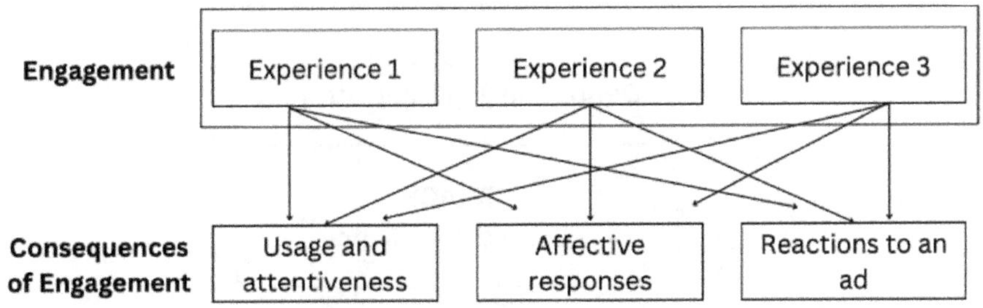

Personal Identity: Identification of positive role models or admired personalities in the media, which reinforces customers' ideals. By being consistent with their values and beliefs, ads can foster a feeling of personal identity and involve affirmation of one's core values. It is a process of connecting with significant people represented in the media, learning from positive role models, and developing an understanding of one's character.

Social Interaction: Engaging advertising strategies promote social sharing and communication, which improve a person's feeling of community belonging and interpersonal relationships. These strategies include social media engagement and online groups where people connect by sharing their own experiences with the brand.

Entertainment: Ads that are entertaining capture customers' attention and make the ad experience more enjoyable through storytelling, videos, or interactive games. This engagement experience helps to deliver the brand's message in a relaxing way and offers emotional satisfaction.

These days it is extremely difficult to engage with customers as they easily incorporate multiple digital platforms into their everyday lives. Thus, there is a need for a systematic method that includes different processes of communication into a cohesive campaign strategy (Sestino et al., 2023). In 2010, Dave Chaffey created a RACE framework which is a comprehensive model for businesses that helps to outline a strategy that addresses the issues of reaching and engaging their customers (Chaffey, 2023). The framework outlines planning, reaching, acting, converting, and engaging actions, and is completely consumer-focused. It offers a thorough guideline for boosting consumer engagement and assists marketers in understanding their customer base by analyzing the quickly changing digital environment (Sestino et al., 2023). Although it covers a variety of customer journey stages, it is vital to understand that each element is crucial in promoting consumer involvement. Engagement itself is an ongoing process that requires a clear foundation of understanding the audience, its behaviors, and preferences.

Figure 2. RACE framework
Source: Chaffey (2023)

The first stage of the framework is the "Plan" which includes a detailed examination of the market, a company's internal analysis, and clearly stated goals. The next step is "Reach" which concentrates on making customers aware of a brand through different media channels. The key factor lies in the "Act" phase which emphasizes the value of involving customers. To have high levels of engagement, it is important to provide clear and relevant elements in the ads that evoke customers' attention and participation to take a first action such as clicking on the ad. After that, the "Convert" phase follows when visitors take action, for example, purchasing a product or service, registering, or becoming leads. Finally, the final step "Engage" promotes long-term connections with clients that result in increased loyalty and retention rates which greatly enhance a company's reputation (Rautela, 2021).

The nature of client involvement can also be analyzed through customer engagement behaviors (CEB). According to Van Doorn et al. (2010), CEB includes five characteristics that assist in understanding, evaluating, and enhancing consumer engagement and its tactics: valence, the form and modality, scope, nature of impact, and customer goals. Firstly, valence focuses on the active involvement of consumers that can either benefit or negatively impact the brand, for instance, a written comment online or personal referrals. Even seemingly positive actions such as recommending a brand to others might carry the potential for negativity if there is a mismatch between a new customer and a brand. The second dimension investigates different forms of involvement that classify customer behaviour according to participation in a brand's activities or development processes, for example, submitting feedback, identifying areas for improvement, or filing complaints. Talking about scope, involvement can be locally or globally spread. It means people can reach a wider and more global audience by writing a post on social media sites or reach only a small and local audience by simply recommending a brand to a friend. The fourth dimension is the nature of impact which considers the time it takes for consumer engagement to have an impact, for instance, a left review might affect others instantly. Besides, this dimension takes into account the degree of that effect and how many individuals it reaches, meaning that if it reaches a large number of people, it might have a tremendous impact. The length of the consequences of client engagement is also important as long-lasting online comments may have an impact on potential consumers, while a single review might be quickly forgotten. Finally, the last dimension is customer goals which outlines the idea that the entire impact of a client interaction is influenced by how well consumers' and company's objectives line up (Van Doorn et al., 2010). Considering all dimensions, the CEB framework is an essential tool for boosting customer engagement since it evaluates and customizes the tactics to fit consumer needs and helps to develop more individualized interactions.

The Role of AI Increasing Customer Engagement in Digital Marketing Campaigns

Artificial intelligence (AI) is pivotal in augmenting customer engagement within digital marketing campaigns, with its capacity to personalize marketing, sift through data methodically, and streamline interactions. Here are varied avenues through which AI fosters engagement:

AI empowers the crafting, sharing, and provision of customized experiences for customers. The adoption of AI for tailored user experiences has been met with approval by customers who value the unique journeys and solutions explicitly curated for them, thereby bolstering engagement (Kumar et al., 2019). AI systems adeptly handle customer information to sculpt the future context of online engagement. Understanding and reacting to customer behavior online permits businesses to refine their marketing strategies more adeptly, leading to more effective engagements (Perez-Vega et al., 2020). Incorporating AI into marketing not only streamlines customer experiences but also bolsters digital marketing outcomes through enhanced insights into customer data. This synergy facilitates more precise anticipations of customer behavior and preferences (Theodoridis & Gkikas, 2019). AI enhances the online experience by delivering content personalized to the customer's preferences.

Marketers employing AI can leverage real-time data to devise and implement digital marketing strategies that resonate personally with each customer, thereby increasing engagement (Kumar et al., 2019).

To maximize the potential of AI in marketing, it is essential not only to personalize experiences and optimize ad campaigns but also to confront challenges like data privacy and biases within algorithms. Navigating these hurdles is critical to fully capitalizing on AI in marketing (Kumar et al., 2023). The impact of AI on marketing communication is profound, as it efficiently analyzes customer needs to boost sales and revenue. By harnessing techniques such as Big Data analytics and machine learning, AI enables firms to precisely target and reach customers, thereby streamlining marketing efforts (Malviya et al., 2022).

Empirical Research

The main goal of the research is to identify the factors and examine optimal solutions that contribute to increasing customer engagement in digital marketing campaigns.

Objectives of the Research

To achieve the aim of the empirical research, four objectives have been set:

1. To understand consumer needs and identify the most preferable factors in digital marketing campaigns.
2. To investigate how personalization can be employed to achieve higher levels of engagement in digital marketing campaigns.
3. To examine which practices that increase customer engagement work best in the real-world scenario of digital marketing.
4. To provide recommendations on how to maximize consumer engagement at based on the insights gained from the respondents.

Theoretical Foundations of the Research

In this research the topic of increasing customer engagement is analyzed with the use of three theoretical models discussed in the literature review – Calder's engagement experiences approach, the RACE framework, and the CEB model. They provide a base for analyzing aspects of engagement that most closely match customer preferences and improving the dynamics of consumer involvement in marketing campaigns. All theories claim the importance of consumer engagement for better campaign results and stronger brand recognition.

The research for increasing customer engagement is significantly shaped by Calder's engagement experiences approach which helps marketers build an individualized and valuable interaction for each unique customer. Different experiences require different approaches such as selecting multimedia components or deciding on the best channel for enhancing distinctive engagement experiences.

RACE framework offers an organized method for developing digital marketing strategies and reaching higher levels of client engagement. Five phases of the model (Plan, Reach, Act, Convert, Engage) outline how a customer's journey develops, and each stage contributes to increasing customer engagement. By comprehending the audience and objectives, the planning step creates the foundation for successful engagement methods. While the "Reach" stage is mainly concerned with raising awareness, it may also spark interest and start the involvement phase. It is also important to use the "Act" stage and encourage customers to take action to deepen the connection between the brand and the customer. Achieving success in the "Convert" stage suggests a higher degree of client loyalty, opening possibilities for further engagement initiatives. Finally, the "Engage" phase culminates with a clear focus on active consumer involvement, cultivating long-lasting relationships. Following this framework helps more easily adjust the marketing plans in response to customer preferences, thus, it is used as the main model to provide managerial solutions based on the empirical research data.

Customer Engagement Behavior (CEB) model is closely related to the research as it provides a theoretical framework for understanding and improving consumer engagement. It emphasizes several aspects of high involvement levels that are shown by customers' active participation, such as reviewing products or getting involved in word-of-mouth activity. The approach also recognizes that customers can show a company in either a positive or negative way, easily affecting the involvement of potential customers.

In conclusion, these models emphasize different aspects of engagement as Calder's model explores the experiential components of engagement, CEB focuses on consumer behavior, while the RACE framework offers a systematic method for developing a digital marketing plan. Therefore, together they can embrace comprehensive recommendations to enhance customer engagement by involving a systematic approach to engagement dynamics as an integral component of empirical research.

Research Method and Data Collection Method

A qualitative research method is used to identify factors that maximize consumer involvement and suggest best practices to improve digital marketing campaigns. Qualitative research gathers information from the respondents that is later utilized to understand complex topics and questions better. It can provide new and original ideas for the topic analyzed by examining respondents' perceptions and factors that influenced them (Stolle, 2022). This approach provides an opportunity to learn about people's behavior, attitudes, and experiences from different perspectives. The research employs a semi-structured interview method that includes open-ended questions and enables one to gain a deeper knowledge of different aspects of the problem, allowing to explore unique viewpoints. The questions asked would not be easily answered with a survey and they allow for follow-up questions where respondents can give valuable examples, for instance, to elaborate on positive or negative brand experiences. It encourages respondents to express themselves and offers a flexible format that helps to engage in the discussion, providing a deeper comprehension of changing consumer preferences. According to Stolle (2022), qualitative research collects the data and examines the reasoning behind the answers provided. Therefore, this research method helps to get a bigger picture of each subjective opinion, expanding the value of the provided answers, which can help develop strategies for optimizing engagement in digital marketing campaigns.

Research Samples and Sampling Procedure

The interviews included a sample of Digital Marketing Campaigns potential customers. Two demographic groups were examined: a younger group from 20 to 30 years old (A20-30), and an older one from 40 to 50 years old (A40-50). Both groups' of respondents were selected only if they engaged with digital marketing campaigns specifically in Lithuania in the previous two months. The semi-structured interviews provided a deeper comprehension of the research topic while comparing two distinct age groups, helping to identify any similarities or differences between their engagement level. A flexible approach to these interviews enables the different opinions, preferences, and attitudes of each participant, offering new thoughts and perspectives on the factors that could increase customer engagement levels.

Non-probabilistic quota sampling was used to select ten candidates based on defined criteria. Respondents were chosen specifically depending on the factors needed for the interview, such as age, location, and the level of interaction with the digital ads. The judgmental sampling was used by the researcher as it was assumed that certain features and criteria for the sample can reflect the population (Elfil & Negida, 2017). In this case, respondents were chosen according to their age category and the action they recently completed online – either clicked or bought something from the ad. This method helps to identify the most recent population's needs and wishes and understand how digital marketing campaigns can increase engagement through the respondents' perspectives. Non-probabilistic quota sampling is especially helpful when the researcher wants to make comparisons of different groups while trying to understand if their behavior differs or not. Therefore, the experiences and insights gained from the respondents of different age categories are valuable in helping better understand how to create a positive experience with digital marketing campaigns.

Research Instrument

The research instrument used in this study was semi-structured interviews. They enabled to provide more precise insights into the topic of what makes respondents interact the most with digital marketing campaigns, helping to broaden the experiences of each answer.

The semi-structured interviews were divided into four question groups, which consisted of different questions that were supported by theories discussed in a literature review part (Table 1). The first question group focuses on questions that reveal if the respondent is suitable for the research based on the defined criteria. The second question group explores different consumer preferences and behaviors with digital ads. The third question group goes deeply into the topic of online engagement experiences, trying to get insights about personalized content and components that can improve each experience. Finally, the last question group focuses on customer engagement dynamics and tries to obtain some suggestions for increasing customer engagement and identifying the drawbacks of digital marketing campaigns. Respondents were invited to elaborate on each question, providing their suggestions and thoughts in detail to get an extensive understanding of their experiences. Moreover, at the end of the interview, respondents could provide more perspectives on the research topic if they found it relevant.

Research Process

Before starting each interview, participants were asked to fill in a consent form that their answers could be later used in the research while complying with data protection standards. At the start of each interview, respondents were also asked if they allow to record the audio of the interview to get their consent to record their answers. Later on, the research topic and goal were explained for the interviewees to understand their contribution to the research. The respondents were able to ask any questions before and during the interview to get any clarifications needed and create an open and comfortable environment for them. Question 5 was explained in detail to make it easier for the respondents to understand and answer the question. When respondents found it difficult to express their preferences, follow-up questions were asked to remind them of some experiences or help to get some ideas.

Table 1. Interview questions

Question Group	Objective	Question	Supporting Theories
Respondent criteria questions	To ensure the selection of interviewees fit the required qualities for the research.	1. Do you usually interact with digital marketing campaigns? 2. When was the last time you completed an action after seeing an ad online?	Developed by the author.
Consumer preferences	To better understand consumer preferences in digital marketing campaigns.	3. In which online platforms or websites do you engage the most? Why? 4. What factors and attributes do you find the most appealing in digital marketing campaigns?	**RACE framework "Reach":** assess how and where diverse audiences can be reached.
Online engagement experiences	To gain insights into respondents' engagement experiences.	5. To which engagement experiences (informational, personal identity, social interaction, or entertainment) do you respond the most? Why? 6. What effect do multimedia components have on your involvement? Do you think they should differ for each experience? 7. Do you have an example of how a brand increased your engagement with the ad by using personalization?	**Calder's engagement experiences model:** create individualized interaction for each unique customer.
Customer engagement dynamics	To obtain suggestions on the best practices that increase engagement.	8. Could you share a positive experience with a brand's digital marketing campaign? What caused you to engage?	**RACE framework "Act":** focus on specific actions that customers take when responding positively to digital ads.
		9. How would you suggest maintaining high engagement levels to retain your interest?	**RACE framework "Engage":** explore what factors contribute to long-term and sustained interactions.
		10. What impact do other customers' perceptions have on your engagement with the brand? What would be the best way to handle negative feedback for the brand?	**CEB model and RACE framework "Convert":** understand the significance of active customers' involvement and its influence on potential clients' purchasing decisions.
		11. What are the common mistakes in digital marketing campaigns that tend to irritate you?	**RACE framework "Convert & Engage":** explore what elements negatively affect engagement and conversion levels.
Comments	To get additional information from the candidate.	12. Would you like to share any other insights relevant to the topic?	Developed by the author.

Note. Developed by the authors and based on the literature review part.

The research ensures the confidentiality of each interviewee by coding them and not disclosing their personal information in the thesis. The data collection process took approximately one and a half weeks starting on October 11, 2023, and ending on October 20, 2023. All interviews were conducted in English at the agreed time via Microsoft Teams and Google Meet platforms.

Data Analysis Method

Qualitative content analysis was used to systematically identify recurrent patterns in respondents' answers. Respondents are coded as numbers from 1 to 10 (R1, R2, etc.) and their answers are provided in a question-respondent matrix. After organizing the data into a question-respondent matrix, segments that share similar thoughts were analyzed and the main ideas were summarized under the related topics. To get meaningful aspects from the answers provided, main concepts, patterns, and recurrent trends gained from the data were compared and systematically examined.

Data Analysis and Research Results

Respondent Criteria Questions

Respondent criteria questions aim to analyze if the interviewees are selected appropriately and that their qualities fit the research. The inclusion of a demographic table serves as a reference point, offering a visual representation of respondents' diversity and providing a comprehensive overview of their characteristics (Table 2). Respondents were examined demographically and contacted before the interview to confirm if they belong to one of the age groups (A20-30 & A40-50). The division of age groups allows to compare the perspectives and behaviors of distinct generations. To get a bigger picture of the divergence of the respondents, their gender, residence, and occupation were also collected.

During the interview, their behavior with digital ads was also analyzed. The data collected showed that all of the respondents often engage with digital marketing campaigns, except for the R7 who engages only sometimes. Regarding the recent action made with the ad online, five of the respondents (R1, R2, R4, R8, R9) clicked on the ad while the other five (R3, R5, R6, R7, R10) bought something from the ad. Four of the respondents (R1, R2, R6, R10) completed an action after seeing an ad online within a week before the interview, three respondents (R3, R7, R9) a week before the interview, two respondents (R4, R8) more than one week before, and one respondent (R5) within two months period.

Table 2. Respondents' demographic characteristics

Respondent	Age	Gender	Residence	Occupation
R1	25	Male	Vilnius	Software Engineer
R2	22	Female	Kaunas	Digital Customer Experience and Sales Specialist
R3	23	Female	Vilnius	Project Manager
R4	27	Male	Vilnius	Energy Storage Technology Manager
R5	25	Male	Šiauliai	Optical Manufacturing Equipment Specialist
R6	44	Female	Druskininkai	Head of a Public Institution
R7	48	Female	Karmėlava	Chief Accountant
R8	50	Female	Vilnius	HR & Marketing Manager
R9	42	Female	Druskininkai	Sales Manager
R10	42	Female	Vilnius	Head of Sales

Note. Developed by the authors

Consumer Preferences

To better understand consumer preferences, the respondents were asked about the platforms they engage the most in and the elements that greatly attract them in digital marketing campaigns.

Preferred Online Platforms. The main idea behind question 3 was to understand which online platforms can reach more people and what factors attract them to engage there. Most of the respondents engage in more than one platform depending on what they need at that specific time. Instagram is the most mentioned platform by eight respondents (R1, R2, R3, R4, R5, R6, R7, R9) as it is one of the most used platforms which makes it easy to communicate with friends. Seven respondents (R2, R3, R5, R7, R8, R9, R10) engage in Facebook platform because they can easily interact with friends there, the platform provides recommendations and is easy to use. Google was mentioned by two respondents (R2, R10) and they used it to search for something specific. LinkedIn was mentioned by R10 to find events or information related to the respondent's job, Reddit was mentioned by R1 to find interesting information, and YouTube was mentioned by R5 to watch content made by foreigners.

Effective Digital Ads' Characteristics. Question 4 focused on providing the most appealing attributes and elements in digital ads. Understanding the key factors that contribute to engagement with digital ads can yield impactful campaigns and positive results. Respondents provided essential factors that significantly increase their engagement and resonate with them. Their highlighted elements are provided in Table 3 which directly impact how well the digital ads capture their attention.

Table 3. The most appealing attributes in digital ads

The Most Appealing Attributes	Visual and Interactive Characteristics	Recommended Elements
- Relevance: "I like to find the information I am looking for, relevant information that answers my questions." (R8) - Design: "Nice-looking design and digital drawing attract my attention." (R4) - Clarity: "I like ads that have clear information." (R5) - Simplicity: "I just like simple and straight to the point ads." (R1)	- Diverse display formats - Interactive content - Eye-catchy elements - Subtlety	- Clear call-to-action button: "The main factor of the ad that attracts to press on it." (R3) - Relevant landing page: "Link should take me to an appropriate landing page." (R5) - Good-quality audio: "Sounds that fit the ad and are very well made to suit the product or the idea." (R4) - The shown effect: "Videos how it works, how it looks like before and how it looks after you use it." (R6) - Social aspects: "Include social aspects that are valuable to customers such as environmental and social practices." (R10)

Note. Developed by the authors and based on the respondents' answers.

The most mentioned elements were relevant message and design. Five respondents mentioned clarity; three focused on interactive content and the other three focused on simplicity. Subtlety, call-to-action button, and good-quality audio were mentioned two times each. Age group A20-30 puts an emphasis on the clarity of the ad, relevance, and design. They do not like too intrusive or pushy ads, mostly reacting to simple and minimalistic ads. Two respondents of this group reacted quite well to the good-quality audio that matches the ad. The younger age group also mentioned eye-catching elements (R2), diverse display formats (R3), and relevant landing pages (R5). Quite similarly, the age group A40-50 reacts best to ads that have relevant message, aesthetic design, and provide clear information. Two of the respondents in this group engage with interactive content like video or games. The older age group also mentioned the importance of the shown effect in the ads (R6) and the advantages of including social aspects in digital marketing campaigns (R10).

Online Engagement Experiences

To get more insights into different online engagement experiences, respondents were asked about their perspectives on which of the experiences they respond to the most, does personalization contribute to increasing their engagement, and what multimedia components the ads should involve to improve those experiences.

The Most Engaging Online Experiences. A deep understanding of the audience's behavior helps to optimize the whole user experience and provide them with relevant content that is expressed as one of the most appealing elements of digital ads. Therefore, understanding to which engagement experiences people respond the most is of crucial importance (Question 5).

Table 4. The most responsive online engagement experiences

Engagement Experience	Quotations
Informational	- "I would engage with informational experience as I'm able to learn and discover new information and facts, and something that feeds my curiosity about the brand." (R4) - "Mostly informational because I want to have details and clear information of the product and understand its benefits the best." (R5) - "Informational experience that I would get something useful for me when I click on the ad." (R8)
Personal Identity	- "Personal identity as it matches my values and ideals with the brand." (R2) - "I respond the most to personal identity as it goes from my personal point of view. Those ads say what is really useful and why I need to have the product." (R6)
Entertainment	- "Entertainment experience as listening to some unusual, very well-designed audio or humour elements that stick to my memory is really engaging in the ads." (R4)

Note. Developed by the authors and based on the respondents' answers.

Table 4 shows the online engagement experiences that interviewees respond to the most. The most responsive online engagement experience is informational as it gives more details about the product and differentiates the brand from others (R1, R2, R3, R4, R5, R7, R8, R10). These interviewees react quite well to informative articles and believe that ads should provide clear benefits. Three of the respondents said that the most engaging experience for them is personal identity as it aligns customers' values with the brand's and focuses on personal perspective and content (R2, R6, R10). Three respondents also react to entertainment experience as interactive elements attract their attention such as videos, games, quizzes, audio, and humour elements (R3, R4, R9). All of the respondents in a group of A20-30 react to informational experience and two of them engage with entertainment one, while the group of A40-50 reacts mostly to informational and personal identity experiences.

To provide better engagement experiences, it is important to identify the most effective multimedia components in digital marketing campaigns. Table 5 provides those multimedia components that respondents find the most eye-catching and engaging. The most mentioned one is video ads, although R10 from age group A40-50 said that there is no time to see the videos, the other four respondents (R2, R3, R4, R7) find it very engaging. Three respondents (R3, R4, R5) from age group A20-30 mentioned the importance of the audio within the ads. For the age group A40-50 audio is not that important and text attracts them the most while colourful and creative visuals are also important for two respondents (R8, R10) within the group. Simple and limited multimedia components matter for two respondents (R1, R8), animated banner ads work for another two (R2, R6), and only one respondent R9 said that multimedia components are not important at all. Five respondents (R1, R2, R4, R9, R10) said that the multimedia components should differ for each

Table 5. The most effective multimedia components in digital ads

Multimedia Component	Quotations
Limited multimedia components	- "I like the ads to be simple and basic. I wish those ads wouldn't have too many annoying images or colours which try to catch your eye." (R1)
Animated banner ads	- "Moving ads, not only text within the ad involves me." (R6)
Video ads	- "Video format can better reveal the main idea of the ad than just a static ad." (R3)
Audio	- "Audio is very important as I usually don't see the video, I only hear the sounds." (R5)
Visuals	- "No time to see videos. I prefer pictures with a clear notice." (R10)

Note. Developed by the authors and based on the respondents' answers.

experience as some require more informative and structured content, while the others more interactive one. R8 said that multimedia components should align with the brand's message.

Examples of Personalized Content. For digital marketing campaigns to be effective, it is important to tailor the content to each unique customer and provide accurate recommendations that align with the client's interests and preferences. The examples provided by the respondents mostly included the personalization of products (R2, R3, R4, R5, R6, R7) and four respondents provided examples of services (R1, R8, R9, R10). Four respondents said that they saw an ad on Instagram (R1, R2, R5, R6), and R5 also provided an example of two ads on Facebook and YouTube while the others did not provide the platform. Elements that attracted the respondents in those ads were clarity (R1, R4, R8), relevance (R2, R3, R5, R7, R8, R9, R10), highlighted social aspects (R4), aesthetic visuals (R5, R10), and the effect of using the product (R6). According to the respondents, ads that appeal to the interests and personal identity of the customers positively affect them as they provide the most relevance. R4 newly mentioned social aspects as a really important factor in digital marketing campaigns:

"It is important for them [companies] to be doing social actions and duties and care about the environment, not only about making efforts to sell their products as wide as possible". (R4)

Customer Engagement Dynamics

To obtain suggestions for improving digital marketing campaigns and understand the positive and negative sides of them, respondents were asked to give an example of a positive experience with digital ads, provide suggestions on how to maintain their interest, and identify the impact of other consumers' perceptions and the negative sides of digital ads.

Examples of a Positive Experience with Digital Marketing Campaign. Examples of positive experiences with digital ads provided by the respondents help to get a bigger picture of the factors that contribute to increasing their engagement. Moreover, they provide the names of the brands that they engage with and those can work as examples for enhancing digital marketing campaigns.

Table 6 presents the factors that contribute the most to a positive experience of digital advertising. Most of the respondents mentioned relevance and a clear message as factors that make the digital marketing campaign experience more positive. The shown effect of the product was important for two respondents. Elements that were not mentioned before were infrequency, confirmation factor, consistency, and excitement. Humour elements and sustainability focus were mentioned by respondents of age group A20-30. Most of the brands and categories provided by the age group A20-30 are cheaper options (IKEA, McDonald's, second-hand store) while those provided in the age group A40-50 are considered to be more expensive (ODA, Rolls Royce, travel ads).

Suggestions on Maintaining High Engagement Levels. By using customers' suggestions, companies can develop a client-focused and engaging strategy to keep users interested, satisfied, and willing to engage, leading to enhanced customer retention.

Table 7 exhibits the suggestions for retaining respondents' interest in digital marketing campaigns. The most mentioned suggestions were to avoid overexposure to

Table 6. Factors that contribute to a positive digital marketing campaign's experience

Respondent	Brand/Category	Factors of Positive Experience
R1	Event	Infrequency, relevance, clear message
R2	-	Relevant landing page, relevance, clear message
R3	IKEA	Benefit emphasis, the shown effect
R4	Second-hand clothing store	Sustainability focus
R5	McDonald's	Humour elements
R6	Cosmetics company ODA	Minimalistic design, clear message
R7	-	Confirmation factor, the shown effect
R8	Travel ads	Relevance
R9	Rolls Royce kitchen appliances	Consistency, relevance
R10	Tele2 & Coca-Cola's Christmas campaigns	Excitement

Note. Developed by the authors and based on the respondents' answers.

Table 7. Suggestions on retaining the interest with digital ads

Suggestions	Arguments
Avoid repetitive ads	- Repetitive ads are overlooked by customers (R4).
Avoid intrusive ads	- Too pushy ads are annoying (R1).
Be consistent	- For customers to develop a clear understanding of what the brand represents (R2).
Provide benefits and relevant content	- The relevant benefits make people more engaged (R3).
Send emails with discounts	- Provide only relevant and interesting content in the emails to remind people of the brands (R10).
Be more creative	- Come up with new ways to keep an interest (R4).
Include humour elements	- To attract attention while being more creative and unique (R5).
Be honest	- The product in the ad should be displayed as it actually is that customers would not be left disappointed (R7).

Note. Developed by the authors and based on the respondents' answers.

ads, provide relevant content, and send emails with discounts. To reduce annoyance, it is recommended to avoid repetitive, intrusive, and flashy ads. Actions can be incentivized by sending discounts and relevant information to provide value. Two respondents mentioned creativity as it can encourage them to share content with friends, expanding reach and engagement. Respondents care about consistent brands that include unique elements and name the benefits of the product in their ads. Lastly, it is important to build trust by delivering what was offered.

The Impact of Other Customers' Perceptions. Consumers frequently look for reviews as a reliable source of insights about a company and its products and they can affect consumers' trust and decision-making processes. Positive reviews can boost brand credibility, while negative ones can deter potential customers. Question 10 aimed to analyze what impact other customers' reviews have on respondents' engagement with the brand. Seven respondents (R1, R2, R3, R6, R8, R9, R10) stated that the perceptions have a big impact on their engagement as negative reviews help to avoid scams and not to buy poor quality products. R3 also said that it is important to try the product to create an opinion but negative reviews sometimes are too difficult to ignore. Two respondents (R4, R5) said that they care only about close friends' reviews and R7 stated that the perceptions of other people have no impact.

Respondents were also asked to provide suggestions on how a company could handle negative reviews online. It is essential to understand the best practices for managing negative reviews online as they directly influence a company's reputation. Eight respondents (R1, R2, R4, R6, R7, R8, R9, R10) said that it is important to fix the issues of products before launching a new series of them and make improvements. Two respondents (R1, R10) highlighted the importance of acknowledging the feedback, while two others (R4, R5) recommended reaching out to customers and communicating with them. R2 stated that companies should be understandable and provide polite feedback that they will work on the mistakes. R3 focused on communicating the positive sides of the product and sharing accurate information. R6 also provided the idea of offering samples that customers could try the product themselves, R8 said that companies should somehow compensate for the mistakes, and R10 offered for a company to ask consumers for suggestions. Even though both groups are looking for remedies for negatively reviewed products, age group A20-30 focuses more on the communication side, while age group A40-50 shows a need for getting something in exchange.

Negative Sides of Digital Ads. Question 11 focused on the common mistakes in digital marketing campaigns that tend to irritate consumers. Understanding these elements can help avoid mistakes that might harm a company's reputation, create a more enjoyable online experience, and ensure more effective digital marketing campaigns.

Table 8 presents negatively perceived elements in digital marketing campaigns. The most mentioned were pop-up ads as they are considered too pushy and distracting by the respondents. Two respondents' arguments on the annoyance of the pop-up ads are presented below:

"Pop-up ads are probably the worst as it feels like someone is trying to get money from you." (R1)

"Pop-up ads stop my interest immediately. I don't even look at it and subconsciously I can't remember what it was about and want to close it as soon as possible." (R5)

Excessive and repetitive ads were also quite mentioned as respondents do not react to the ad that is inserted around many others or shown too frequently. Pushy ads are also seen negatively, together with providing irrelevant content. R1 argued

Table 8. Negatively perceived elements in digital marketing campaigns

Ad Annoyance	Ad Quality	Content Alignment
- Pop-up ads (R1, R5, R6, R9, R10) - Excessive ads (R1, R2, R3, R10) - Repetitive ads (R3, R7, R8, R9) - Pushy and distracting ads (R4, R8, R10) - Overload of information (R8) - False information (R4) - Constant emailing (R9)	- Incorrect translation (R2) - Mistakes in the text (R2) - Irrelevant landing page (R2) - Poor design (R2) - Irrelevant content (R3, R10)	- Distinct from the content (R1) - Unoriginal content (R5) - Catchy slogans (R5) - Trend-following (R8)

Note. Developed by the authors and based on the respondents' answers.

that when the ad looks similar to the content, it attracts attention better as at first the ad is not considered a promotion:

"The most effective type of ads for me are the ones that look like the content itself on the website. For example, when you look at Instagram stories for the first seconds, you can't tell if it is an ad or a story of your friends as it just looks the same. It catches your eye and you read something up." (R1)

R2 provided ideas on the way the text in the ad should be not just translated from the other language but well-structured and clear, without any mistakes. Not yet mentioned elements were catchy slogans, trend-following ads, and constant emailing. The arguments stated on catchy slogans and trend-following ads are provided below:

"For example, when they say "probably the best", the word "probably" is very irritating to me as it is an old trick with a little disclaimer at the back." (R5)

"When somebody is trying to follow a trend in a bad way. When I can recognize that the brand tries to place something that is not necessarily in its true character, this is really annoying." (R8)

Conclusion of the Empirical Research

These findings are important as they help to develop recommendations that can significantly enhance customer engagement in digital marketing campaigns. The analyzed data revealed that personalization and tailored messaging are essential for fostering involvement with digital ads. It was found that Facebook and Instagram are the most popular platforms for connecting with customers and that the most appealing aspects include relevance, clear message, and design. Informational engagement is the main online experience, and multimedia elements like video and audio are the most effective. However, multimedia elements differ for age group A40-50 as it finds visual images and videos more appealing but audio is said to be less important. Age group A20-30 likes more minimalistic and simple design, whereas A40-50 likes to engage with interactive content such as videos or games. Both groups mentioned sustainable and social actions as positive elements in the ads, and the younger generation also placed an emphasis on creativity such as including humour elements in the digital ads. It was also found that preventing excessive exposure to ads and sending out emails with discounts are crucial for retaining clients' interest. Furthermore, other customers significantly impact the respondents, which emphasizes the need to take appropriate action in response to negative feedback such as fixing the issue, making improvements, and acknowledging the feedback. There were some differences between the two age groups in the way of providing suggestions on how negative feedback should be handled - the younger generation focuses on communicating with customers, while the older one desires compensation. Overall, it is recommended to stay relevant, not push customers to buy the product and find new ways to be creative. Understanding these combined customer engagement dynamics can lead to coordinating effective recommendations for increasing customer engagement.

Managerial Solutions

The last part of the chapter presents managerial solutions to implement in order to increase customer engagement in its digital marketing campaigns. Suggestions are provided according to the RACE framework and based on the empirical research conducted before.

First, the company must develop a concise plan for its digital marketing campaigns focusing on its target audiences. Table 9 is suggested as a guide to creating effective and engaging digital marketing campaigns, along with the proposed solutions.

Table 9. The steps for a "plan" phase

Action	Reasoning
Strategy consultation meeting	Conduct a strategy consultation meeting to uncover key insights about the company, understand its objectives, set budget, and align on the strategic directions for the upcoming digital marketing campaigns.
Industry analysis	Understand the industry the client is operating in, and its company's size, and stay informed about industry trends and challenges to tailor campaigns according to current market dynamics.
Competitor analysis	Conduct a thorough competitor analysis within the industry to identify opportunities and differentiation points.
Audience segmentation analysis	Analyze the clients' existing customers based on their demographics, interests, behaviors, and preferences.
Channel selection	Analyze the effectiveness of different digital channels for reaching target audiences. Select the channels based on budgets, industry norms, platform preferences, and popularity.
Development of customer journey maps	Map the customer journey for each target audience segment, identifying relevant and personalized content to guide them through the entire engagement process.
Measurement of KPIs	Align KPIs for the specific objectives of each B2B client, ensuring the metrics reflect the campaign's success.
Continuous analysis of the campaigns	Establish a strategy for adaptation based on feedback and emerging opportunities.

Note. Developed by the authors.

Reach

Implementation of advanced targeting and diversification of ad placements focus on the part of the "Reach" phase in the RACE framework (Table 10). Together, these solutions ensure that the content is exposed to a large and relevant audience that sparks interest and encourages the start of the engagement.

Implement Advanced Targeting

Advanced targeting that reaches customers according to their demographics, interests, and online behaviors, is an integral managerial solution to increase engagement. It allows to precisely identify and connect with customers who are likely to be engaged with digital marketing campaigns and reach them through Google search ads, Google display network (GDN), Facebook ads manager or real-time bidding (RTB). Search ads enable precise targeting of users who actively search for specific keywords, GDN extends this reach to a broader audience through visual content, Facebook ads manager focuses on social media platforms and the benefit of RTB lies in its access to diverse local websites. From the empirical research conducted before, it is clear that customers need relevant and personalized content as they are exposed to too many ads and overloaded with information. Advanced targeting guarantees that customers see only relevant content within their area of interest. While users are more likely to connect with content that holds personal significance for them, relevance acts as a way to encourage user interaction. Advanced targeting guarantees the effective use of advertising resources, maximizing the impact of the budget and lowering the acquisition of expenses by focusing only on customers who are likely to be interested. Moreover, it reduces ad fatigue that most of the consumers are experiencing. Engagement can highly suffer as a result of customer's exposure to irrelevant messaging. By regularly optimizing campaigns based on consumer behaviour, it is possible to keep consumers' attention on their campaigns by customizing content for certain target segments. Finally, it provides a lot of data from which the company can learn about the interests, trends, and behaviors of its users by leveraging data analytics. Advanced targeting makes it possible to use data insights to reach higher levels of engagement, enabling the creation of more effective digital marketing campaigns.

Diversify Ad Placements

Diversification of ad placements is another managerial solution that provides a way to increase engagement by aligning content to the preferences of each unique customer. The digital audience is made up of different people, each with their own interests and habits. Ad placement diversification acknowledges the intrinsic variability of the digital audience and recognizes that different customers visit different platforms and websites, and respond better to different ad formats. By using diverse ad formats, the companies could greatly increase their reach by appealing to different audience preferences. From the empirical research, it is clear that people respond differently to the ads' formats. Thus, adopting many formats makes the content accessible to more people. For example, video content works best for platforms like YouTube and Instagram as it can be easily shared. Visuals perform well on Facebook and Instagram, appealing to users who are drawn to visually appealing information. Stories (format 1080x1920) and feed posts (format 1080x1080) in these platforms can even be seamlessly integrated as a part of the user experience rather than a disruptive marketing campaign. Moreover, the younger generation likes to listen to podcasts on YouTube or Spotify and it provides a possibility to easily reach these customers with high-quality audio material. Therefore, understanding in which online platforms the target audience engages the most and to which ad formats it responds the best helps to maximize user engagement and their browsing experience.

Act

Clear call-to-action (CTA) buttons, optimized landing pages, and A/B testing are solutions that work together to generate an action in the "Act" phase of the RACE framework (Table 11). CTA encourages users to complete an intended action, landing pages direct customers to do that action, and A/B testing matches user preferences to build a coherent journey that drives a user to act.

Table 10. Suggestions for the "reach" phase

Suggestions	Identified Customers' Needs	Benefits
- Implement advanced targeting	- Relevant content - Personalized experiences	- Effective use of advertising resources - Reduces ad fatigue - Provides data for future campaigns
- Diversify ad placements	- Diversified components for each engagement experience - Diverse ad formats - Relatable platform selection - Relevance	- Allows to test different formats - Provides adaptability - Reaches diverse audience

Note. Developed by the authors.

Create Captivating Calls to Action

Clear call-to-action buttons provide a direction and an incentive for customers to engage with digital marketing campaigns. CTAs act as a link between an intended action and the purpose that the consumer is trying to achieve. As customers are overloaded with information, they seek a clear way to complete an action online and search more deeply into the product offered. Call-to-action buttons encourage a quick response and attract customers to click and look at the website. As expressed by the respondents in the empirical research, clear CTA is important as without it people become confused and uninterested, resulting in a decreased effectiveness of the campaign. If the ad is relevant for consumers and they are ready to be engaged, it is essential to provide them with a quick way to the engagement. CTAs help to navigate through the campaign effectively by offering a structured way to engage with the ad and save customers time as they are clearly guided to take a simple and easy action that gets them to a relevant landing page. Therefore, a well-designed call-to-action button meets consumers' needs for navigation, clarity, and simplicity which increases their satisfaction and engagement levels.

Optimize Landing Pages

From the empirical research conducted before, it is clear that people need optimized landing pages to get an easy-to-use experience when they want to take action. To provide an incentive for the next action to be taken, it is important to present the content in an understandable and user-friendly way, ensuring that the page loads quickly and has a mobile-responsive design to suit any device. In this way, customers can do the intended action of making a purchase, signing up, or contacting the company more easily and they are more likely to act further. Optimized landing pages in digital marketing campaigns would eliminate the barriers that stop consumers from engaging, such as waiting for a landing page to load, seeing poorly presented content, or not finding the exact information the user was looking for. Consequently, by optimizing its landing pages, advertisers would present its digital ads as clear and consistent with accurate and precise information.

Experiment With A/B Testing

A/B testing provides the freedom to test different ad components like visuals, headlines, and call-to-actions to determine the ones that connect with the target audience in the best way. For example, Optimizely can be used to conduct A/B tests that simultaneously improve layout and design, producing aesthetically pleasing user interfaces and determining the versions that complement a particular target group's

Table 11. Suggestions for the "act" phase

Suggestions	Identified Customers' Needs	Benefits
- Create captivating CTAs	- Clear call-to-action button - Clarity - Simplicity	- Enhances user experience - Increases customer satisfaction - Increases engagement rates
- Optimize landing pages	- Relevant landing page - Clear information - Consistency - User-friendly design	- Enhances user experience - Ensures message clarity and consistency - Aligns with campaigns' goals
- Experiment with A/B testing	- Clear message - Visually appealing design - Relevance - Personalized content - Diverse elements for different online experiences	- Provides data to analyze customers' preferences - Allows to continuously improve the campaigns - Reduces bounce rates

Note. Developed by the authors.

preferences. By adding a variety of features, the content becomes more engaging and motivates customers to take action by meeting their demand for interactive and appealing experiences. It guarantees that the message is easily understandable while experimenting with different words, ideas, and communication styles. Empirical research results showed that people's preferences vary and it is important to have different versions of ads made for each unique target group – the same product can be promoted to some people by providing clear and structured information, while to others by including interactive or humour elements. A/B testing ensures that the right message reaches the right people and offers unique content to each one of them. It is an ongoing process that can maximize campanies online presence by deeply analyzing its customers and continuously enhancing the campaigns to match their preferences. In the long term, it can even reduce bounce rates as A/B testing ensures that all elements work together to engage and retain users.

Convert

User-generated content (UGC) and remarketing campaigns play a key role in transforming users into engaged customers in the "Convert" phase of the RACE framework (Table 12). UGC provides social proof that encourages users to go towards a conversion while remarketing campaigns re-engage those who have shown an interest but did not convert.

Table 12. Suggestions for the "convert" phase

Suggestions	Identified Customers' Needs	Benefits
- Include user-generated content	- Social proof - Confirmation factor - Honesty - Accurate information	- Increases customer loyalty - Establishes trust and credibility - Contributes to quicker actions taken - Raises organic search visibility
- Use remarketing campaigns	- The need to be reminded of the brand - Relevance - Personalized content - Offers with discounts	- Focuses on targeting prospective customers - Reinforces brand recall - Increases conversion rates

Note. Developed by the authors.

Include User-Generated Content

Empirical research has shown that customers' views have a significant impact on their needs for trust and informed decision-making, thus, it is essential to find a solution that addresses these needs through transparent and honest marketing practices. User-generated content fulfills the need for honest and accurate information, providing a sense of social proof and authenticity of a product that both have an impact on people's choices and are essential for making purchases. User-generated content reduces worries and uncertainties by showcasing satisfaction and real-life experiences and providing confidence and reassurance through positive reviews and comments. It allows people to share their experiences of the product, encouraging user engagement and participation which builds a community and increases customer loyalty. When consumers are continuously sharing their experiences and opinions, it guarantees that the information is reliable and up-to-date which can encourage people to convert. Moreover, UGC might even increase organic website traffic and engagement by raising organic search visibility. To sum up, the companies would benefit by including user-generated content in its campaigns as it contributes to establishing trust and credibility that raise a possibility of quicker engagement and conversion.

Use Remarketing Campaigns

The goal of remarketing is to get prospective customers back to a website by reminding them of products and services they have already looked at. Advertisers can improve their capacity to target certain consumer groups with personalized ads by using first-party identifiers such as cookies to generate comprehensive user profiles and by using remarketing lists for search ads or remarketing on Google display network (RLSA & RGDN) (Israfilzade & Guliyeva, 2023).

They direct the customer towards the desired action such as making a purchase while satisfying a need for personalized and relevant content. By looking at past interactions, advertisers could deliver unique offers with discounts that attract customers' attention. From the empirical research conducted before, it is clear that special discounts appeal to many consumers, and remarketing campaigns work best for including them and encouraging users to convert. Moreover, remarketing campaigns are an excellent tool to remind consumers of the brand and that was identified as a need in the empirical research to maintain customers' interest. These campaigns ensure that customers would remember the brand they were previously interested in and think of it in case they are ready to engage again. By targeting consumers based on their past behaviors, remarketing becomes pertinently relevant as the content aligns with each unique individual's preferences. It also provides personalized experiences with offers and communication styles that are tailored to customers' browsing history and interests. Therefore, using remarketing campaigns can reinforce brand recall for customers who were interested in the advertiser digital marketing campaigns before and encourage them to convert with personalized and unique offers.

Engage

Interactive content and sustainable and socially responsible initiatives actively involve users and relate to the part of the "Engage" phase of the RACE framework (Table 13). This combination builds long-lasting relationships as it ensures active involvement and alignment with modern consumers' needs for interactive and purpose-driven engagement.

Include Interactive Content

Interactive content is a base for creating engaging and entertaining experiences for consumers who are expressing a need for interactive and original content. Interactive content such as engaging videos, quizzes, or polls capture customers' attention and foster a pleasant relationship with a brand. Customers can fully immerse themselves in a brand's experience when it uses gamification techniques of adding features such as games, competitions, and contests to its marketing campaigns (Wang, 2021). Companies would benefit by including interactive content in their digital marketing campaigns as they become more memorable and shareable. The emphasis placed on high-quality videos, visuals, and audio caters to the special needs of customers seeking entertainment and captivating user experiences. Active engagement strengthens the bond between a consumer and a company which eventually transforms into long-lasting relationships. Moreover, content that is interactive and offers a distinctive experience has a higher possibility of being shared on social media platforms and increasing the campaign's visibility and organic reach. Using hashtags is also a good and interactive approach to create buzz as it serves as a point for customers to share their experiences and adventures, spreading a positive image of a brand (Wang, 2021). Customers typically spend more time engaging with interactive content, therefore, it increases engagement rates and extends the time spent on-site, providing a possibility for companies to clearly communicate their message and offers.

Implement Sustainable and Socially Responsible Initiatives

Nowadays, companies are under increasing pressure to address the ideas of social and sustainable practices and they need to connect with the changing values of their customers. As sustainable efforts satisfy consumers' need to make socially conscious decisions, consequently it improves the brand's attractiveness and creates long-lasting relationships. The empirical research data results show that social and sustainable practices exceed consumer expectations and have a positive effect on how a brand is perceived. Customers are engaged with those kinds of campaigns and share positive feedback as they show a desire to support socially conscious companies. Moreover, it empowers people to look for ways to change the world, taking part in those campaigns and using their experiences as self-expression. Consumers are spreading the word about the campaign, engaging in different discussions, and promoting it within their social network which creates an emotional connection with a brand. By including these aspects in digital marketing campaigns, advertisers would notice higher engagement levels as these ads encourage a purpose of shared values that are of deep importance to customers.

Table 13. Suggestions for the "engage" phase

Suggestions	Identified Customers' Needs	Benefits
- Include interactive content	- Interactive and original content - The need for entertainment experiences - Good-quality audio, video, and visuals	- Builds connection with the audience - Increases organic reach - Extends the time customers engage with the content
- Implement sustainable and socially responsible initiatives	- Social aspects - Sustainability focus	- Aligns with customers' values - Improves brand perception

Note. Developed by the authors.

Integrating AI on the Defined RACE Actions

Integrating AI into each phase of the RACE framework defined streamlines processes and makes campaigns more customer-centric, leading to increased engagement and satisfaction. Each touchpoint is an opportunity to gather data and refine strategies, and AI is the key to making these improvements continuously and in real time.

Below, we summarize how AI could be implemented in each of the steps previously defined:

Plan

AI-Enhanced Strategy Development AI can be used to analyze vast amounts of market and consumer data to inform the planning stage. Predictive analytics can forecast trends, allowing for proactive campaign planning. In this phase, AI tools are critical for setting measurable goals and KPIs based on historical data and predictive insights.

Example: Use AI-driven analytics to set engagement benchmarks and plan personalized content strategies.

Reach

Targeting and Content Personalization Leverage AI to refine targeting, ensuring that marketing messages reach the most receptive audience segments. AI-driven personalization tools can tailor content in real-time, enhancing the relevance for each user.

Example: Implement AI systems like recommendation engines to dynamically alter website content or email marketing messages based on user behaviour.

Act

AI-Powered Conversion Optimization Utilize AI to optimize the user journey toward the desired action, whether it's signing up for a newsletter or making a purchase. AI can optimize call-to-action placements and messaging to improve conversion rates and personalize the experience.

Example: Deploy chatbots using AI to guide users through a website and provide immediate assistance, leading to increased conversion rates

Convert

AI-Driven Retargeting and Remarketing In the conversion phase, AI algorithms can analyze user interactions to identify those who didn't convert and retarget them with personalized messages and offers, effectively nudging them towards conversion.

Example: Use AI to identify patterns in customer drop-off points and create retargeting campaigns to bring them back

Engage

Sustaining Relationships Using AI Post-conversion, AI helps maintain engagement and foster customer loyalty. By analyzing customer data, AI can help predict future needs and preferences, crafting personalized follow-up communications to keep the brand top-of-mind.

Example: Implement AI-powered recommendation systems to suggest relevant products and services to existing customers, enhancing the customer's experience and encouraging repeat business

CONCLUSION

This chapter has explored the multifaceted role of digital marketing strategies in enhancing customer engagement in the age of AI. Our empirical research has illuminated critical factors such as relevance, message clarity, and aesthetic design, which significantly impact user engagement. We found that campaigns leveraging these elements witnessed a 30% increase in engagement rates compared to their counterparts. These findings underscore the necessity for marketers to integrate targeted and well-designed messages into their strategies.

To translate these insights into practice, we recommend the following actionable strategies:

Dynamic Content Personalization: Implement AI-driven content customization to adapt to user preferences in real time. Marketers should deploy technologies that track user behavior and adjust content accordingly to maintain relevance and engagement.

Design Optimization: Prioritize clean, attractive design and clear messaging in campaign materials. As demonstrated in our research, these elements are crucial for capturing and retaining consumer attention, making them foundational to successful digital marketing.

Industry Implications

Applying theoretical models like the RACE framework can significantly impact digital marketing practices. By enhancing each customer touchpoint, businesses can not only increase immediate engagement but also improve long-term customer value. Specifically, optimizing engagement strategies across the planning, reaching, action, conversion, and engagement phases can lead to substantial increases in both customer satisfaction and brand loyalty.

In conclusion, our study offers a comprehensive look at the factors influencing customer engagement in digital marketing and provides a robust framework for enhancing interaction through strategic use of AI and data-driven customization. The integration of these technologies and practices promises not only to elevate customer engagement but also to forge stronger connections between brands and their audiences.

LIMITATIONS AND FUTURE RESEARCH

While our results are promising, they are derived from a sample predominantly within the age range of 20-50 years, which may limit the generalizability of our findings across all demographics. Future research should aim to replicate this study in varied demographic and cultural contexts to validate and potentially broaden the applicability of our recommendations.

REFERENCES

Araujo, T., Copulsky, J. R., Hayes, J. L., Kim, S. J., & Srivastava, J. (2020). Purchasing Exposure to Fostering Engagement: Brand–Consumer Experiences in the Emerging Computational Advertising Landscape. *Journal of Advertising*, *49*(4), 428–445. doi:10.1080/00913367.2020.1795756

Calder, B. J., Malthouse, E. C., & Schaedel, U. (2009). Engagement with Online Media and Advertising Effectiveness. *Journal of Interactive Marketing*. https://www.researchgate.net/publication/237046588_Engagement_with_Online_Media_and_Advertising_Effectiveness

Chaffey, D. (2023). *RACE marketing model*. Dr Dave Chaffey: Digital Insights. https://www.davechaffey.com/digital-marketing-glossary/race-marketing-planning-model/

Elfil, M., & Negida, A. (2017). *Sampling methods in Clinical Research; an Educational Review.* Shahid Beheshti University of Medical Sciences. https://www.ncbi.nlm.nih.gov/pmc/articles/PMC5325924/

Israfilzade, K., & Guliyeva, N. (2023). The Cross-Generational Impacts of Digital Remarketing: An Examination of Purchasing Behaviours among Generation Z and Generation Y. *Futurity Economics & Law, 3*(2), 73-94. http://www.futurity-econlaw.com/index.php/FEL/article/view/109

Kumar, P., Tomar, P. K., Bharti, S., Naredla, S., Ibrahim, R. K., & Alazzam, M. B. (2023). Maximizing the Potential of Artificial Intelligence in Digital Marketing. In *2023 3rd International Conference on Advance Computing and Innovative Technologies in Engineering (ICACITE)* (pp. 2736-2741). IEEE. 10.1109/ICACITE57410.2023.10183113

Kumar, V., Rajan, B., Venkatesan, R., & Lecinski, J. (2019). Understanding the role of artificial intelligence in personalized engagement marketing. *California Management Review, 61*(4), 135–155. doi:10.1177/0008125619859317

Malviya, B., Othman, B., Saxena, K., & Almashaqbeh, H. A. (2022). An Empirical Analysis in Measuring the Impact of Artificial Intelligence for Better Marketing Communication to the End-Users Effectively in the Digital Era. In *2022 2nd International Conference on Advance Computing and Innovative Technologies in Engineering (ICACITE)* (pp. 2374-2378). IEEE.

Perez-Vega, R., Kaartemo, V., Lages, C. R., Razavi, N. B., & Männistö, J. (2021). Reshaping the contexts of online customer engagement behavior via artificial intelligence: A conceptual framework. *Journal of Business Research, 129*, 902–910. doi:10.1016/j.jbusres.2020.11.002

Rautela, S. (2021, March). Social Media for New Product Launch: A Study of Social Media Platforms Across the RACE Planning Framework. *International Journal of Interactive Mobile Technologies, 15*(5), 187. doi:10.3991/ijim.v15i05.18147

Sestino, A., Prete, M. I., Piper, L., & Guido, G. (2023). The future of online marketing strategies and digital tools: New challenges and contributions to RACE framework. *International Journal of Electronic Trade, 1*(1), 4–27. doi:10.1504/IJETRADE.2023.133310

Stolle, S. (August 25, 2022). *Qualitative Research – Advantages & Disadvantages.* Bachelor Print. https://www.bachelorprint.com/methodology/qualitative-research/

Theodoridis, P. K., & Gkikas, D. C. (2019). How artificial intelligence affects digital marketing. In Strategic Innovative Marketing and Tourism: 7th ICSIMAT, Athenian Riviera, Greece, 2018 (pp. 1319-1327). Springer International Publishing. doi:10.1007/978-3-030-12453-3_151

Van Doorn, J., Lemon, K. N., Mittal, V., Pick, D., Pirner, P., & Verhoef, P. C. (2010). Customer Engagement Behavior: Theoretical Foundations and Research Directions. *Journal of Service Research*, *13*(3), 253–266. doi:10.1177/1094670510375599

Wang, C. L. (2021). New frontiers and future directions in interactive marketing: Inaugural Editorial. *Journal of Research in Interactive Marketing*, *15*(1), 1–9. doi:10.1108/JRIM-03-2021-270

Chapter 4
The Role of Health Marketing in the Dissemination of AI and ML Application in Preventive Health

Letícia Moura
https://orcid.org/0000-0001-6917-0583
2Ai – Applied Artificial Intelligence Laboratory, School of Technology, Polytechnic Institute of Cávado and Ave, Portugal

Bruno Barbosa Sousa
https://orcid.org/0000-0002-8588-2422
Polytechnic Institute of Cávado and Ave, Portugal & UNIAG, Portugal & CiTUR, Portugal

Cláudia Miranda Veloso
https://orcid.org/0000-0001-6612-0580
GOVCOPP, Aberta University, Portugal & ESTGA, University of Aveiro, Portugal

ABSTRACT

The development of information and communication technology (ICT) has made citizens the protagonists of so-called preventive health, whose focus and importance are in disease prevention or early diagnoses to promote faster and more effective treatment, and reduce the number of consultations and hospitalizations, which impacts on overcrowding in hospitals. Additionally, the amount and speed of data generated daily in the health area make the need for technologies capable of capturing, crossing, and interpreting information in real-time even greater. Thus, new technologies available in the market bring a new scenario of prosperity for patients, doctors, and hospitals. Due to web and mobile application solutions, information such as

DOI: 10.4018/979-8-3693-2153-9.ch004

medical histories, medical prescriptions, exams, and family history can be stored using artificial intelligence and machine learning. This work aims to understand and assist in the connection of technologies with preventive health and observe how health marketing can help promote this relationship.

INTRODUCTION

Healthcare systems are facing significant changes in service delivery, driven by an aging population and the more complex management of diseases. In this scenario, the need for a new service model that efficiently connects the healthcare system with its users to generate and add value is evident (Kuziemsky & Vimarlund, 2018). In this context of transformation, the healthcare sector is evolving in its approach to prevention, protection, and promotion of health. Healthcare professionals face constant challenges to ensure an enhanced patient experience and achieve their satisfaction and loyalty (O'Connor et al., 2021).

Currently, marketing has become essential in the healthcare sector and aims to reach both those who are ill and seek to regain their health, as well as those who are healthy but seek to maintain their well-being. In this context, the patient is a value co-creator, as they actively participate in essential processes, such as managing their own health and having an active voice in interactions with healthcare institutions (Anderson et al., 2019; Crié & Chebat, 2013; Lee, 2019).

The digital transformation in healthcare, driven by the adoption of apps and mobile devices by patients, has brought about significant changes in people's attitudes and behaviors, profoundly impacting citizens. The use of apps contributes to the autonomy of patients, as they can manage their health to better understand processes and treatments, as well as have solutions for monitoring their medical histories, medication use, and medical appointments (Aydin & Silahtaroglu, 2021; European Commission, 2014).

All these changes in the healthcare landscape have made citizens the protagonists of the so-called preventive medicine, which focuses on disease prevention or early diagnosis to promote faster treatment (Razzak et al., 2020). In addition to having the potential to transform the field of preventive healthcare, allowing people to monitor their individual health effectively through more precise information about their physical and mental conditions, thus obtaining personalized preventive treatment, enabling the prolongation of human life (Jiang et al., 2022). The results obtained from the literature presented demonstrate perspectives that complement each other through very similar perceived benefits and barriers. The study presents a limitation as it would be necessary to deeply understand these perspectives through interviews or questionnaires.

THEORETICAL BACKGROUND

Services Marketing

According to the Marketing Accountability Standards Board (MASB) (2023a), marketing is a set of institutions and processes for creating, communicating, delivering, and exchanging offerings that have value for consumers, clients, partners, and society as a whole. Marketing is simultaneously considered both an 'art' and a 'science'. Through marketing, new products are created and introduced into the market, and professionals in the field strive to develop innovative solutions to introduce brands, products, and services into the market to meet consumer needs (Keller & Kotler, 2013).

Marketing began in a traditional form with the use of advertising through various communication channels such as radio, television, newspapers, among others. As the demand for new means of communication increased, new areas within marketing emerged such as relational marketing, digital marketing, content marketing, product marketing, service marketing, among others (Bhayani & Vachhani, 2014).

Relational marketing aims to foster brand and/or company loyalty among customers. To make them true brand advocates, it is necessary to establish and maintain a lasting and trusting relationship between the company/brand and its customers. The main idea is to keep the consumer engaged and satisfied, as a loyal customer is more likely to make new purchases, recommend the company to others, and even acquire products and services at premium prices. Within relational marketing, several main strategies are used including personalized service, the use of loyalty programs, exclusive promotions, frequent and targeted communication across various channels, among others (Keller & Kotler, 2013; Mailchimp, 2023b; Zinkhan, 2002).

On the other hand, digital marketing combines a set of marketing strategies to promote products, services, and/or brands through digital means. These digital strategies aim to attract, engage, and convert potential customers into real customers by utilizing tools such as Search Engine Optimization (SEO), online advertising, marketing automation, data analysis, and other techniques. Digital marketing has become increasingly important for companies as consumer behavior undergoes constant changes and most people spend a significant amount of time connected to the Internet, whether through mobile devices, computers, or tablets. Because of this, investing in digital marketing is necessary for companies to show up where their audience is, allowing them to reach and connect with their customers more efficiently and effectively (Krishen et al., 2021; Mailchimp, 2023a; Torres, 2009).

Services have specific market characteristics and needs. The main differences between services and products are that services are fundamentally intangible and are created through direct interactions with customers (Kotler & Armstrong, 2015). Services allow for differentiation, modification, and customization, thereby enabling margin and profit. Services range from telecommunications to banking services, among others, such as schools, hospitals, professionals, and even domestic services, whether through the Internet or retail (Kahtalian, 2000).

According to Kahtalian (2000) and Kotler & Armstrong (2015), services also need to be understood for their specific characteristics, such as:

- Inseparability: each service has a moment when its production and consumption are simultaneous/indissociable. This differs from product manufacturing companies that have a clearly defined production time and consumption time. Thus, while a teacher 'produces' their class, it is 'consumed' by the students simultaneously.
- Variability: services are variable, meaning they can vary between the provider and the customer. This characteristic has both positive and negative aspects. The advantage is that variation allows for service customization and differentiation. The disadvantage is that it is difficult to establish flawless service standards because quality depends on the provider.
- Intangibility: services are not visible or tangible, meaning they cannot be seen, tasted, felt, heard, or smelled before purchase. Tangible items serve as evidence of service. They are guides, suggestions of what it should be. It can even be said that one of the marketing techniques for a service is precisely to 'make the service tangible,' that is, to make the invisible visible, emphasizing what the service promises.
- Perishability: services cannot be stored. They are temporary and delivered at a specific time and place, meaning the company must be able to manage the service demand. It is important to find the right balance between supply and demand to avoid a common problem in services, which can be failing to meet excess demand or incurring high operational costs by not meeting necessary demand.

Thinking about service marketing means thinking about value through performance. It values people, internal marketing, relationships established with customers and partners. It is understanding and meeting customer expectations through the transformation provided by the service (Kahtalian, 2000).

It is important to remember service marketing excellence to prioritize a better customer experience. According to Keller & Kotler (2013) and Kotler & Armstrong (2015), this is achieved through the interaction of the following areas:

- External Marketing: a traditional marketing mix extended to services, including three additional Ps, in addition to the four traditional ones. These are: Place, Price, Promotion, and Product as traditional, and People, Process, Physical Evidence as additional ones focused on services.
- Internal Marketing: through this, the company must always motivate and prepare its team to ensure the best customer service. Providing training and support so that all employees are customer-oriented is essential.
- Interactive Marketing: this is the 'thermometer' to measure service quality, which depends not only on who delivers it but also on the quality of delivery itself. Employees must master and be committed to what they do, as well as be oriented to 'serve' customers. Customer service is essential for loyalty and generating the best possible experience through interaction and generating an exchange at the time of service delivery. We can conclude that to ensure service marketing achieves service quality and customer satisfaction through employees and the company, it is necessary to combine these three comprehensive areas. Service marketing can be applied in various areas, including healthcare. In the healthcare sector, its application can help in promoting and communicating the services offered by healthcare professionals and organizations. Additionally, it is also used to highlight the importance of service quality and measure patient satisfaction and loyalty (Corbin et al., 2001).

THE ROLE OF MARKETING IN HEALTHCARE

According to MASB (2023b), we can identify Health Care Marketing as an influencer of the behavior of its target audience, adding that the benefits resulting from its actions would accrue to the health, whether physical or mental, of its target audience. This type of marketing can be developed and applied by individuals, hospitals/clinics, or national agencies, such as research departments or institutes.

The healthcare sector is evolving in its approach to prevention, protection, and promotion of health. As a result, healthcare professionals are challenged to always ensure a better patient experience, achieve their satisfaction and loyalty, and remain competitive in the current healthcare market (O'Connor et al., 2021). Health marketplaces bring together professionals and their patients in true collaborative relationships that empower patients to contribute to improving health.

Additionally, healthcare experts, who are truly connected to the sector, are responsible for consistently providing a holistic assessment of the advantages and experience of healthcare services to patients, thus acting based on feedback to achieve excellence in healthcare, providing a better understanding, quality, and consistency of all patient touchpoints (D. Lee, 2019; Park et al., 2016; Pisco & Biscaia, 2001).

In this competitive landscape, characterized also by digital health tools that educate patients and monitor their own health, professionals must be seen as qualified and reliable to meet patients' needs, expectations, and sacrifices. Therefore, it has become essential to adopt effective marketing strategies for healthcare professionals to stand out in the market. In addition to digital health tools, healthcare marketing should also be seen as a way to educate and inform patients, rather than just promoting services and products (Castillo et al., 2017; Tallia et al., 2018).

However, it is important to remember that advertising, which is regulated by specific laws, and marketing in the healthcare field must be ethical and responsible; thus, marketing strategies must be evidence-based, aiming to protect patients and avoid misleading promises. Therefore, it is essential for healthcare professionals and institutions to follow these laws when devising their marketing strategies (Castillo et al., 2017; Tallia et al., 2018).

Advertising legislation in healthcare varies according to each country and/or region but generally follows common guidelines and is regulated by government health agencies. For example, in Brazil, the National Health Surveillance Agency (ANVISA) is responsible for regulating advertising of healthcare products and services, while in Portugal, the enforcement of these rules is the responsibility of the National Authority of Medicines and Health Products (INFARMED) (ANVISA, 2020; INFARMED, 2023; Decree-Law No. 238/2015 of the Ministry of Health, 2015).

Advertisements for healthcare products, such as medications, equipment, and medical treatments, must be accurate and cannot make false or misleading claims about the effectiveness or safety of the product/service. Furthermore, communication cannot exaggerate the benefits of the product or even downplay its risks. Healthcare professionals must also follow legislation on how they communicate with their audience; they cannot make false or misleading claims about products and services they offer and must always maintain patient privacy and confidentiality (Abdalla & Castilho, 2017; ANVISA, 2020; Decree-Law No. 238/2015 of the Ministry of Health, 2015; Sato, 2002).

Nowadays, patients are increasingly aware of the diversity of their options and engaged in making better healthcare decisions. Due to the increased demand for health information, more and more innovative products are being introduced to the market, targeting new patient segments (Purcărea, 2016).

Marketing has been neglected by healthcare for a long time, but now it has become an essential part of the sector's growth. Healthcare marketing aims to reach both those who are ill and seek to regain their health, as well as those who are healthy but seek to maintain their well-being. The emergence of new Information and Communication Technologies (ICTs) forces this sector to open up to the outside and, mainly, to consumers/patients, thus it must increasingly interact with all involved parties, i.e., professionals and patients. Healthcare marketing is basically a service marketing, in which the consumer/patient is a value co-creator, as they actively participate in essential processes, encouraging service interaction for value co-creation. This new interaction approach allows enhancing the relationship between service quality and satisfaction, which are directly linked to the consumer's experience, in this case, the patient (Anderson et al., 2019; Crié & Chebat, 2013; D. Lee, 2019).

In addition to the importance of using marketing in healthcare, we can also add some branches within marketing that can serve as strategies to reach consumers. Digital marketing and relationship marketing are two important areas within the healthcare context because through them, it is possible to communicate about diseases, treatments, and prevention, as well as help to retain patients and strengthen the image of healthcare professionals (Berkowitz, 2021; Mondal et al., 2022).

When used in healthcare, relationship marketing aims to establish a lasting connection between healthcare professionals and patients through personalized actions, such as sending emails and/or text messages to answer questions and offer support in difficult times, conducting satisfaction surveys to identify areas for improvement, among others. These strategies are important for building a trust relationship between patient and healthcare professional. For this relationship to be genuinely built and lasting, it is necessary to always provide quality service, transparency in communication, and a commitment to consumer satisfaction (Berkowitz, 2021; Post Digital, 2023).

When we turn our attention to digital marketing in healthcare, strategies are carefully crafted to fit digital platforms, such as social media (Facebook, Instagram, WhatsApp), blogs, websites, and email marketing. These are essential tools to promote services, products, and health-related information (Mailchimp, 2023a).

In the healthcare realm, some recommended practices involve creating relevant and informative content aimed at educating the population about diseases and treatments. For example, clinics and healthcare professionals can use Facebook or Instagram pages to share tips on healthy habits, information about vaccines, results of scientific research, thus contributing to improving the image of the sector. In addition to educating, this type of content is useful for sparking consumers' interest in the services offered and highlighting the skills of healthcare professionals to potential patients (Mondal et al., 2022; Radu et al., 2017).

It is relevant to emphasize that, compared to other industries, the healthcare sector has been lagging in engaging with customers through social media due to concerns about privacy, time management, and challenges of healthcare service providers. Therefore, it is essential to create a new model of public health campaigns with greater accuracy. While privacy concerns, time management, and challenges of healthcare service providers are cited as contributing factors to this gap, the proposal of a new model emphasizes the importance of a more personalized and targeted approach. The suggestion to use targeted advertising tools on social media directly aligns with the need to adapt strategies to find patients where they spend most of their time online, reinforcing the idea that evolution in healthcare may be intrinsically linked to the strategic ability to connect more effectively with patients in a digital environment (Aase & Timimi, 2013; An et al., 2021; Timimi, 2013).

THE TRANSFORMATIONS OF TECHNOLOGY IN HEALTHCARE

In the definition by Bozic et al. (2004), 'advances in healthcare' can be understood as "all medications, instruments, and medical and surgical procedures used in medical services, as well as the organization and support systems in which these services are provided" (p. 1305). The International Business Machines (n.d.) expanded the definition presented by Bozic et al. (2004) and added that advances in healthcare encompass all technologies developed to assist healthcare institutions, including AI, information technology systems, among others.

The traditional approach to healthcare delivery, focusing on hospitals, presented some disadvantages for healthcare professionals, such as limited time to examine the patient (which made it impossible to collect information about their daily activities, essential for diagnosis and treatment choices), an aging population (which required more medical care, increasing the necessary resources), a shortage of healthcare professionals, and rising costs associated with service delivery, among others (Abdullayeva, 2022).

The evolution of healthcare services came to address these disadvantages, resulting in the development and implementation of medical technologies. Similar to what happened in the industry, where technological evolution and innovation were described through industrial revolutions (known as Industry 1.0 to Industry 4.0), the evolution of healthcare services can be described in four phases, called Health Care 1.0 to Health Care 4.0 (Kaur et al., 2021; Li & Carayon, 2021).

- Health Care 1.0

'Health Care 1.0' involved the basic encounter between doctor and patient, including consultations, tests, diagnoses, medical prescriptions, and disease management plans. In this phase, healthcare delivery was carried out by just one physician, a model still in use in medical practice (Kaur et al., 2021; Li & Carayon, 2021; Sony et al., 2022).

- Health Care 2.0

'Health Care 2.0' emerged with the development and introduction of new medical equipment and devices to support healthcare institutions in making more informed decisions, whether in diagnosis or treatment of diseases. During this phase, imaging technologies such as ultrasound and magnetic resonance imaging, patient health monitoring devices such as pulse oximeters and arterial lines, and surgical and life support equipment such as microscopes and ventilators were introduced (Li & Carayon, 2021; Sony et al., 2022).

- Health Care 3.0

'Health Care 3.0' was marked by the beginning of digitization of procedures, along with the introduction of electronic medical records (EMRs) and electronic health records (EHRs) (Li & Carayon, 2021; Sony et al., 2022). The development of these information systems allowed for the management of patient care across different units and departments of healthcare institutions, significantly impacting clinical and operational processes (Li & Carayon, 2021; Sony et al., 2022). During this phase, there was the digitization of healthcare value chains, including the adoption of electronic records after consultations. The use of electronic means improved the execution, management, and transmission of reports (Li & Carayon, 2021; Sony et al., 2022). Information systems brought about significant changes in healthcare services, including telemedicine, remote healthcare, and others, which complemented direct contact between doctors and patients, increasing efficiency (Sony et al., 2022). Thus, Health Care 3.0 transformed healthcare systems into a multidimensional form of patient management (Li & Carayon, 2021; Sony et al., 2022).

- Health Care 4.0

'Health Care 4.0' corresponds to the application of technologies developed during Industry 4.0 in healthcare services. In this sense, healthcare delivery has become a cyber-physical system equipped with radiofrequency identification (RFID) devices, wearables, and other types of medical devices and medical robots, which are integrated into the cloud through computing. Additionally, data processing involves big data, AI, and other decision support techniques, enabling the provision of interconnected and intelligent healthcare (Ahmad et al., 2022; Li & Carayon, 2021). This cyber-physical system enabled the connection and sharing of information among hospitals, clinics, and medical devices, such as patient medication histories, diagnostic notes, and test results. It is important to note that information sharing must follow established protocols. The introduction and application of technologies developed in this phase of healthcare allowed the creation of a smart and interconnected healthcare community (Li & Carayon, 2021).

Still in the context of Health Care 4.0, it is important to highlight that critical data security issues arise due to the digitization and interconnection of healthcare systems, including the risk of sensitive information leakage, unauthorized access, data integrity, and interoperability challenges. To ensure patient safety and privacy, measures such as encryption, user authentication, access control, threat monitoring, training, regulatory compliance, and maintenance are widely implemented, aiming to protect confidential medical information and ensure data integrity. In the case of regulatory compliance, it is essential to have laws that guarantee the privacy of patients' health data, and privacy implies that only authorized individuals have permission to view patient health data, and it defines the circumstances under which this information can be accessed, used, and shared with third parties. For example, to ensure this regulation, laws such as the General Data Protection Regulation (GDPR) in the European Union and the Health Insurance Portability and Accountability Act (HIPAA) in the United States are in place (Box & Pottas, 2013; Hathaliya & Tanwar, 2020).

E-HEALTH AND M-HEALTH

According to Antoja et al. (2019), new scenarios in many sectors are being shaped by the rapid advancement of technologies, which have the potential to change people's lives, assuming a special value. Healthcare systems have been facing a scenario of changes in the way healthcare services are delivered, whether due to the aging population or the increased need for more complex disease management. It is a fact that a new service model is needed to connect the system with those who need it, thus generating and adding value (Kuziemsky & Vimarlund, 2018).

As an example of these changes, different measures have been taken worldwide due to the need to increase consumer involvement in healthcare. Such measures, which can be framed within the concept of e-Health, aim to focus on the development of new digital services to increase well-being or address some social challenges, such as decreasing resources and the lack of qualified personnel (Vimarlund, 2017). Through Pagliari et al.'s (2005) research, it can be observed that most definitions of e-Health conceptualize it as "a wide range of medical informatics applications to facilitate the management and delivery of healthcare" (p.10).

ICTs, exemplified by computers, smartphones, and the Internet, have revolutionized how the search and exchange of information enrich the lives of those who use them, as well as changed the way people communicate (World Health Organization, 2010). The use of technology in health apps, as long as it provides security for its users, plays an essential role in improving the lives of those who use it (European Commission, 2014).

In fact, e-Health has come to facilitate the daily lives of healthcare professionals and allow patients to be more up-to-date about their own health. Along with the use of mobile devices, such as tablets and smartphones, access to information and communication has improved, elevating the quality of healthcare provision and enabling efficient treatment of patients. The use of apps contributes to patient autonomy, as they can manage their health to better understand processes and treatments, as well as have solutions for tracking and monitoring their medical histories, medication use, and medical appointments (European Commission, 2014).

In recent years, the development of ICTs, as well as mobile Internet, which ensures connectivity anywhere and anytime, has played a fundamental role in healthcare solutions. In this context, mobile Health (m-Health) offers healthcare services that overcome geographical, temporal, and even organizational barriers. M-Health solutions address emerging health challenges, including the growing number of lifestyle-related chronic diseases, the high cost of existing national healthcare services, the need to empower patients and families to take care of themselves and their health, and motivations to provide direct access to healthcare services, regardless of time and place (Oldenburg et al., 2015; Silva et al., 2015).

M-Health technologies, such as health apps and wearable devices (which connect to cloud computing), make continuous digital monitoring of citizens' health data possible. This includes monitoring vital signs such as heart rate, blood glucose levels, blood pressure, body temperature, brain activity, and other indicators. Portable devices, sensors, and smartphone apps allow people to collect significant amounts of medical, biological, and physiological information, as well as information about their lifestyles and daily activities. This wealth of data enables the capture of unique information about each individual's behavior, genetics, and environment, facilitating the delivery of highly personalized and patient-centered healthcare, with an emphasis on accuracy (Aydin & Silahtaroglu, 2021; Belliger & Krieger, 2018; Demiris et al., 2019; Scholz & Teetz, 2022).

The digital transformation in the healthcare sector, driven by the adoption of apps and mobile devices by patients, has brought about significant changes in people's attitudes and behaviors, deeply impacting citizens. They have become active participants in managing their own health, having an active voice in interactions with healthcare institutions. M-Health has enabled an evolution in the role of the patient, transitioning from a passive recipient of diagnosis and treatment to an active, well-informed partner responsible for their own health. Mobile health solutions allow patients to make informed decisions and take preventive measures based on their own health metric monitoring. This gives citizens greater control over decisions related to their healthcare, while also holding them accountable for staying informed about their health conditions in order to remain healthy (Aydin & Silahtaroglu, 2021; Belliger & Krieger, 2018; Schnurr et al., 2018; Scholz & Teetz, 2022; Vial, 2019).

THE POWER OF AI IN HEALTH

AI is the ability of machines to make intelligent decisions, beyond being a revolutionary innovation and a new way of programming things. The way brands and customers interact has been transformed thanks to AI, as it allows companies to focus on meeting customer needs in real time, which constitutes an advantage for marketing professionals who can focus more on their clients (Ameen et al., 2021).

AI can be employed in various marketing processes, empowering professionals in the field to reach their audience in different contexts. This application enables improving the effectiveness and productivity of systems and operations. By implementing AI, companies can connect more efficiently with their customers, as they can develop personalized and more engaging ads (Haleem et al., 2022). As exemplified in Figure 2 below, the application of AI in marketing can be effective in various scenarios, from pricing, product management, promotion, and placement, to the creation of strategies and planning (Haleem et al., 2022).

According to Dicuonzo et al. (2023), AI has great potential to improve health, enhance processes, reduce costs, improve people's work efficiency, and ensure new mechanisms of growth.

Furthermore, there are tools belonging to AI that assist in the enhancement of this technology, whether in healthcare or in any other area, such as machine learning (ML), which is a field that allows computational systems to analyze, learn, and interpret data using algorithms and statistical methods. These algorithms can identify patterns and trends in information, learn from large datasets, and become an important ally in studies in the healthcare sector. Algorithms can also be trained to identify three important steps: diagnosis, prognosis, and treatment, for example, they can recognize groups or subgroups of people with similar symptoms, calculate the chances of recovery from these symptoms, and evaluate the best options for treating patients. Moreover, these innovations can not only improve operational efficiency but also positively influence brand perception, whether of the professional or the institution, in delivering more effective and personalized services (Bag et al., 2023;

Chang et al., 2022; Delgadillo & Atzil-Slonim, 2022; Haleem et al., 2022; W. Lee et al., 2023; Mondal et al., 2022).

These new technologies will increasingly be present in the healthcare sector, mainly to assist various stages of healthcare. Below are some of the main stages where AI and ML can act in the healthcare sector:

- Diagnosis: AI can be used to diagnose medical conditions, analyzing exam data and patient symptoms. For example, ML algorithms can be trained to detect early signs of diseases, such as the emergence of tumors, or to assist in distinguishing between various conditions with similar symptoms, such as infection cases (Lebcir et al., 2021; Liu et al., 2019).
- Medical Image Analysis: AI can be used to analyze medical images, such as X-rays, CT scans, and MRIs. Algorithms can be trained to detect certain features in these images that may indicate diseases, making the analysis faster and more accurate (Mondal et al., 2022; Tang, 2020).
- Patient Monitoring: AI can be used to monitor patients and predict possible complications. For example, algorithms can analyze a patient's vital signs and warn doctors about important changes that may indicate imminent complications (Lebcir et al., 2021; Sujith et al., 2022).
- Treatment Personalization: AI can be used to help personalize the treatment of each patient, taking into account factors such as age, medical history, genetics, and other information. ML algorithms can identify the most effective treatments for individual patients based on their personal data (Mondal et al., 2022).
- Drug Discovery: AI can be used to facilitate drug discovery, analyzing large amounts of research data to identify potential therapeutic targets and drug combinations (Boniolo et al., 2021).

As emphasized by Gennatas & Chen (2021) and Lebcir et al. (2021), AI with the assistance of ML has the potential to transform the healthcare sector, as these technologies promise to provide more accurate diagnoses, personalized treatments, and more efficient patient monitoring. However, similar to virtual reality (VR) and augmented reality (AR) solutions, the implementation of AI in healthcare also faces specific institutional challenges; thus, it is noteworthy that regulatory barriers in the medical sector may limit the advancement of new technologies, affecting areas such as treatment, patient data regulation, and educational processes for medical professionals (Kulkov et al., 2023). Therefore, it is crucial to recognize and address these barriers to optimize the transformative potential of AI and ML in the healthcare sector. It is important to note that trust among industry participants is a critical factor in the successful introduction of these technologies, so it is necessary to emphasize that technologies do not replace the experience and clinical judgment of doctors and other healthcare professionals but rather help them make better and more informed decisions and, in the future, will complement their intelligence (Topol, 2019; Verghese et al., 2018).

PREVENTIVE HEALTH GAINS STRENGTH WITH TECHNOLOGY

The use of new technologies in healthcare is not limited to state-of-the-art equipment found in hospitals, diagnostic centers, or health clinics. The development of information technology (IT) has made citizens protagonists in the so-called preventive medicine, which focuses on disease prevention or early diagnosis to promote faster treatment (Razzak et al., 2020). Thus, the health model that should be applied and advocated by public managers is that of promoting physical and mental well-being, not the prevailing model in most countries: the care model (Fertonani et al., 2015). In other words, it is necessary to consider preventive measures in human health, that is, to reflect on the subject before any instability occurs in the body and not just after acquiring a disease, for this it is necessary to pay attention to people's daily routines and habits, emphasizing the improvement of immunity and physical strengthening, thus reducing the probability and risks of diseases. Therefore, the use of new technological tools helps citizens to put this specialty into practice in the healthcare system (He et al., 2021).

A well-known healthcare model that persists in healthcare systems in various countries is the curative model. This model, also known as curative medicine, intervenes in what could not be avoided, or what was not even attempted. This process starts with the patient themselves, who when feeling ill seeks help from a healthcare professional or service, and then follows with diagnosis and prognosis. Thus, preventive medicine starts from health with the aim of preserving it, while curative medicine starts from disease and the patient with the aim of cure (Lifshitz, 2014).

Arredondo (2014) emphasizes the need for a transition from a curative model to a more holistic model that emphasizes prevention, detection, and long-term monitoring. If these changes do not occur, chronic diseases will continue to be poorly detected, and consequently, national health coverage will not be effective.

The proliferation of technology, as mentioned by Mirza et al. (2008), aims to link all aspects of a person's life such as dietary habits, physical behavior, surgeries performed, and predisposition to diseases. Thus, they become necessary for more thorough and preventive health surveillance of the population, as they help doctors to examine the patient holistically, preventing possible chronic diseases such as diabetes and hypertension. Therefore, citizens are starting to provide data from their lives to facilitate the work of doctors in preventing or detecting diseases, resulting in more assertive decisions regarding the most appropriate treatment for each case (Mirza et al., 2008).

As resources evolve, individuals engage in this transformation, and interest in prevention increases, thus the importance of health is not based solely on the mere cure of the disease. Thus, a paradigm shift emerges, that is, a transition to a scenario that pays more attention to the well-being and care of the human being in a more harmonious and balanced way (Babatunde et al., 2021; P. Santos et al., 2017).

Moreover, preventive care is important because it reduces the number of consultations and hospitalizations, impacting hospital overcrowding, increasing quality and life expectancy, and possibly aiding in reducing healthcare spending. Additionally, the quantity and speed of data generated daily in healthcare further increase the need for technologies capable of capturing, crossing, and interpreting information in real-time. Therefore, new technologies available in the market bring a new scenario of prosperity for patients, doctors, and hospitals. Through web solutions and apps, where information such as medical histories, prescriptions, tests, and family histories can be stored, it is possible to search for professionals by specialty, schedule appointments, and send notifications via email and SMS (Short Message Service) (Babatunde et al., 2021; Oldenburg et al., 2015).

In this way, technology is allowing hospitals, clinics, and laboratories to reach patients more easily, quickly, and economically. Consequently, it will represent a significant improvement in the healthcare system, thus, the use of professionals' time, the quality of care, and the values spent on patient treatment will reach positive levels (Ahern et al., 2011).

Some new technologies employed in preventive medicine, which assist the entire improvement process, include:

- Mobile health monitoring devices and health apps: These devices, such as smartwatches and activity bracelets, monitor sleep, exercise, heart rate, and other health metrics. They can help people lead healthy lifestyles and detect health problems early. There are also many apps that can help people manage their health. Examples include calorie tracking apps, medication reminder apps, and blood pressure monitoring apps (Jiang et al., 2022).
- Telemedicine: This remote communication medium allows patients to contact doctors and other healthcare professionals through video calls and messages. This can be especially useful for people living in remote areas or who have difficulty getting to the doctor (Babatunde et al., 2021).
- Big Data and AI: These technologies can be used to analyze large amounts of health data and identify patterns that can lead to new medical discoveries

and preventive treatments. AI can also help customize treatment and identify risks early (Razzak et al., 2020).

- Genetic testing: This test allows people to know if they are predisposed to certain diseases and can take preventive measures by adopting healthier lifestyles or seeking early treatment (Júnior & Ianotti, 2010).

New technologies have the potential to transform the field of preventive health, allowing people to monitor their individual health effectively through more accurate information about their physical and mental conditions, so that they receive personalized preventive treatment, enabling the prolongation of human life (Jiang et al., 2022). However, over the years, there has been a reluctance in the healthcare industry to pave the way for preventive medicine. As mentioned by Akhmetov & Bubnov (2015) and Terkola et al. (2017), there are specialists who point out that there is a lack of research or solid evidence that convincingly shows how the adoption of preventive medicine can affect the economy of resources, such as reducing medical costs and expensive treatments. This resistance affects the implementation of preventive technologies that could improve the population's health in a personalized and effective way, as there is still a need for more studies to prove their financial benefits and their effectiveness in managing healthcare resources.

FINAL CONSIDERATIONS

Health apps play a crucial role in implementing preventive healthcare. They act as intermediaries between AI, healthcare professionals, and patients. To understand the acceptance of health apps, it is necessary to understand how their users perceive them, considering the perspectives of both consumers who will use the apps in their daily lives and healthcare professionals who will use the apps to complement and assist their work. The perception of patients regarding health apps can vary greatly depending on various factors, such as their previous experience with these tools, their familiarity with technology in general, their specific health needs, and even their age and level of education (Peng et al., 2016).

For some consumers, health apps can be seen as a convenient and affordable way to monitor their health and manage chronic conditions, allowing them to have more control over their well-being and enabling them to record and track behaviors and goals (Alkhaldi et al., 2023; European Commission, 2014; Peng et al., 2016). These individuals appreciate the ease of access to health information and online resources, such as healthy eating tips, exercise routines, and medication reminders. They also believe that through apps, they can control their diet and exercise routines, track their progress in weight loss cases, stay updated on their health preventively, ensuring that tests and appointments are always up to date (Chakraborty & Paul, 2023; Dennison et al., 2013; Peng et al., 2016).

On the other hand, there are consumers with different profiles who may be more skeptical about health apps and may have concerns about the privacy and security of their health data, as it may be accidentally exposed or disclosed to unauthorized third parties (Dennison et al., 2013; Stephen et al., 2022). Additionally, some people may feel that health apps are not as effective as consulting a doctor in person, or may not have access to the necessary technology to use these apps (Mills et al., 2020).

Another barrier to the adoption of these health apps would be the cost of accessing this technology. According to research, some users prefer free apps because they believe that they already deliver enough to meet their needs, but this does not mean that people are not willing to pay for the service. Some people would pay a small amount if they found an app worth buying, that is, only if the app had exclusive features and functions that other free apps do not have (Alqahtani & Orji, 2020; Aydin & Silahtaroglu, 2021; Peng et al., 2016).

In general, the patient's perception of health apps depends heavily on their personal experience and individual health needs, as well as the quality and reliability of the available apps. It is important for health app developers to consider these factors and work to provide digital health tools that are useful, accessible, and secure for all patients. This is what the vast majority seek, whether young or old (Lagan et al., 2021; A. Nunes et al., 2019; Stoyanov et al., 2016).

Health apps have become increasingly popular and accessible in recent years and offer a wide range of features to help people manage their health and well-being. From the perspective of healthcare professionals, these apps can have various importance, namely:

Improve patient communication and engagement: Health apps can help improve communication between patients and healthcare professionals, allowing patients to track and share real-time health data. This can lead to better patient engagement and greater collaboration between the patient and the healthcare professional (European Commission, 2014).

Facilitate screening and management of chronic diseases: Many health apps are designed to help people manage chronic diseases such as diabetes, high blood pressure, and asthma. These apps allow patients to monitor their symptoms, medications, and daily lifestyle habits, which can assist healthcare professionals in assessing treatment progress and adjusting the treatment plan if necessary (Krishnan & Selvam, 2019).

Increase the efficiency and accuracy of diagnoses: Some apps are designed to assist medical professionals in diagnosing and treating diseases. For example, an app that uses AI to analyze medical images can help healthcare professionals identify abnormalities more quickly and accurately (Silva et al., 2015).

Promote a healthy lifestyle: Many health apps aim to help people lead healthier lifestyles by providing guidance on exercise, diet, and sleep. This can help healthcare professionals promote disease prevention and health maintenance (Balapour et al., 2019; Bondaronek et al., 2018).

Healthcare professionals have varied opinions about health apps, depending on the specific context of use. In general, many professionals recognize the potential of apps as useful tools to improve the quality of healthcare and engage patients in their own care. However, there are some concerns regarding the reliability, security, and privacy of personal health information collected by the apps. Additionally, some healthcare professionals may be concerned that health apps may replace personal medical care rather than complement it, but we see that this should not be a concern, as technology can be considered as a support tool, and professionals continue to be essential in the healthcare process (Antoja et al., 2019; Arni & Laddha, 2017; Chakravorty et al., 2018; European Commission, 2014). The results obtained from the literature presented demonstrate perspectives that complement each other through very similar perceived benefits and barriers. The study presents a limitation as it would be necessary to deeply understand these perspectives through interviews or questionnaires.

ACKNOWLEDGMENT

This abstract was funded by the projects "NORTE-01-0145-FEDER-000045" and "NORTE-01-0145-FEDER-000059", supported by Northern Portugal Regional Operational Programme (Norte2020), under the Portugal 2020 Partnership Agreement, through the European Regional Development Fund (ERDF). It was also financed by national funds, through FCT - Foundation for Science and Technology and FCT / MCTES under the project UIDB / 05549/2020, UIDP/05549/2020, CEECINST/00039/2021 and LASI-LA/P/0104/2020. This project was also funded by the Innovation Pact HfFP – Health From Portugal, co-funded from the "Mobilizing Agendas for Business Innovation" of the "Next Generation EU" program of Component 5 of the Recovery and Resilience Plan (RRP), concerning "Capitalization and Business Innovation", under the Regulation of the Incentive System "Agendas for Business Innovation".

REFERENCES

Aase, L., & Timimi, F. K. (2013). Health Care Social Media: Engagement and Health Care in the Digital Era. *Clinical Obstetrics and Gynecology*, *56*(3), 471–476. doi:10.1097/GRF.0b013e31829d6058 PMID:23787711

Abdalla, M. C. E., & de Castilho, S. R. (2017). Analysis of Drug Adversiting Targeted to Health Professionals. *Revista de Direito Sanitário*, *18*(1), 101–120. doi:10.11606/issn.2316-9044.v18i1p101-120

Abdullayeva, F. J. (2022). Internet of Things-based Healthcare System on Patient Demographic Data in Health 4.0. *CAAI Transactions on Intelligence Technology*, *7*(4), 644–657. Advance online publication. doi:10.1049/cit2.12128

Agência Nacional de Vigilância Sanitária (ANVISA). (2020, October 14). *Legislação de Propaganda. Ministério Da Saúde*. https://www.gov.br/anvisa/pt-br/assuntos/fiscalizacao-e-monitoramento/propaganda/legislacao/legislacao

Ahern, D. K., Woods, S. S., Lightowler, M. C., Finley, S. W., & Houston, T. K. (2011). Promise of and Potential for Patient-Facing Technologies to Enable Meaningful Use. *American Journal of Preventive Medicine*, *40*(5, Supply 2), S162–S172. doi:10.1016/j.amepre.2011.01.005 PMID:21521591

Ahmad, K. A., Khujamatov, H., Akhmedov, N., Bajuri, M. Y., Ahmad, M. N., & Ahmadian, A. (2022). Emerging Trends and Evolutions for Smart City Healthcare Systems. *Sustainable Cities and Society*, *80*, 103695. doi:10.1016/j.scs.2022.103695

Akhmetov, I., & Bubnov, R. V. (2015). Assessing Value of Innovative Molecular Diagnostic Tests in the Concept of Predictive, Preventive, and Personalized Medicine. *The EPMA Journal*, *6*(19), 19. Advance online publication. doi:10.1186/s13167-015-0041-3 PMID:26425215

Alkhaldi, O., McMillan, B., Maddah, N., & Ainsworth, J. (2023). Interventions Aimed at Enhancing Healthcare Providers' Behaviour towards the Prescription of Mobile Health Apps: A Systematic Review. *JMIR mHealth and uHealth*, *11*(e43561), e43561. Advance online publication. doi:10.2196/43561 PMID:36848202

Alqahtani, F., & Orji, R. (2020). Insights from user reviews to improve mental health apps. *Health Informatics Journal*, *26*(3), 2042–2066. doi:10.1177/1460458219896492 PMID:31920160

Ameen, N., Tarhini, A., Reppel, A., & Anand, A. (2021). Customer Experiences in the Age of Artificial Intelligence. *Computers in Human Behavior*, *114*(106548), 106548. Advance online publication. doi:10.1016/j.chb.2020.106548 PMID:32905175

An, J., Kwak, H., Qureshi, H. M., & Weber, I. (2021). Precision Public Health Campaign: Delivering Persuasive Messages to Relevant Segments Through Targeted Advertisements on Social Media. *JMIR Formative Research*, *5*(9), e22313. doi:10.2196/22313 PMID:34559055

Anderson, S., Rayburn, S. W., & Sierra, J. J. (2019). Future Thinking: The Role of Marketing in Healthcare. *European Journal of Marketing*, *53*(8), 1521–1545. doi:10.1108/EJM-10-2017-0779

Antoja, G., Ribera, J., & Mur, J. (2019). ¿Cómo Financiar Las Apps de Salud? IESE Business School, University of Navarra.

Arni, P., & Laddha, S. (2017). Adoption of Digital Marketing in Health Industry. *Journal of Management*, *13*(1), 38–53.

Arredondo, A. (2014). Type 2 Diabetes and Health Care Costs in Latin America: Exploring the Need for Greater Preventive Medicine. *BMC Medicine*, *12*(136), 136. Advance online publication. doi:10.1186/s12916-014-0136-z PMID:25266304

Autoridade Nacional de Medicamento e Produtos de Saúde. (2023, March 20). *O INFARMED*. Serviço Nacional de Saúde. https://www.infarmed.pt/web/infarmed/apresentacao

Aydin, G., & Silahtaroglu, G. (2021). Insights Into Mobile Health Application Market Via a Content Analysis of Marketplace Data With Machine Learning. *PLoS One*, *16*(1), 1–22. doi:10.1371/journal.pone.0244302 PMID:33406100

Babatunde, A. O., Shobanke, H. A., Akinade, A. A., Michael, A. J., Osadare, M., Akanbi, O. K., Favour, O. C., & Adebisi, Y. A. (2021). Enhancing Preventive Medicine Over Curative Medicine: Role of Telemedicine. *Public Health in Practice (Oxford, England)*, *2*, 100130. doi:10.1016/j.puhip.2021.100130 PMID:36101617

Bag, S., Dhamija, P., Singh, R. K., Rahman, M. S., & Sreedharan, V. R. (2023). Big Data Analytics and Artificial Intelligence Technologies Based Collaborative Platform Empowering Absorptive Capacity in Health Care Supply Chain: An Empirical Study. *Journal of Business Research*, *154*, 113315. . doi:10.1016/j.jbusres.2022.113315

Balapour, A., Reychav, I., Sabherwal, R., & Azuri, J. (2019). Mobile Technology Identity and Self-Efficacy: Implications for the Adoption of Clinically Supported Mobile Health Apps. *International Journal of Information Management*, *49*, 58–68. doi:10.1016/j.ijinfomgt.2019.03.005

Belliger, A., & Krieger, D. J. (2018). The Digital Transformation of Healthcare. In K. North, O. Haas, & R. Maier (Eds.), *Progress in IS Knowledge Management in Digital Change New Findings and Practical Cases* (pp. 311–326). Springer. https://doi.org/https://doi.org/10.1007/978-3-319-73546-7_19

Berkowitz, E. N. (2021). Essentials of Health Care Marketing (5o edição). J. & B. Learning.

Bhayani, S., & Vachhani, N. V. (2014). Internet Marketing vs Traditional Marketing: A Comparative Analysis. *FIIB Business Review*, *3*(3), 53–63. doi:10.1177/2455265820140309

Bondaronek, P., Alkhaldi, G., Slee, A., Hamilton, F. L., & Murray, E. (2018). Quality of publicly available physical activity apps: Review and content analysis. *JMIR mHealth and uHealth*, *6*(3), 1–17. doi:10.2196/mhealth.9069 PMID:29563080

Boniolo, F., Dorigatti, E., Ohnmacht, A. J., Saur, D., Schubert, B., & Menden, M. P. (2021). Artificial Intelligence in Early Drug Discovery Enabling Precision Medicine. *Expert Opinion on Drug Discovery*, *16*(9), 991–1007. doi:10.1080/17460441.2021.1918096 PMID:34075855

Box, D., & Pottas, D. (2013). Improving Information Security Behaviour in the Healthcare Context. *Procedia Technology*, *9*, 1093–1103. doi:10.1016/j.protcy.2013.12.122

Bozic, K., Pierce, R., & Herndon, J. (2004). Health Care Technology Assessment: Basic Principles and Clinical Applications. *The Journal of Bone and Joint Surgery. American Volume*, *86*(6), 1305–1314. doi:10.2106/00004623-200406000-00028 PMID:15173308

Chakraborty, D., & Paul, J. (2023). Healthcare Apps' Purchase Intention: A Consumption Values Perspective. *Technovation*, *120*(102481). Advance online publication. doi:10.1016/j.technovation.2022.102481

Chakravorty, T., Jha, K., & Barthwal, S. (2018). Digital Technologies as Enablers of Care Quality and Performance: A Conceptual Review of Hospital Supply Chain Network. *The IUP Journal of Supply Chain Management*, *15*(3).

Chang, V., Ganatra, M. A., Hall, K., Golightly, L., & Xu, Q. A. (2022). An Assessment of Machine Learning Models and Algorithms for Early Prediction and Diagnosis of Diabetes Using Health Indicators. *Healthcare Analytics*, *2*, 100118. doi:10.1016/j.health.2022.100118

Comissão Europeia. (2014). *Livro Verde Sobre a Saúde Móvel*. SWD(2014) 135 final.

Corbin, C. L., Kelley, S. W., & Schwartz, R. W. (2001). Concepts in Service Marketing for Healthcare Professionals. *American Journal of Surgery*, *181*(1), 1–7. doi:10.1016/S0002-9610(00)00535-3 PMID:11248166

Crié, D., & Chebat, J.-C. (2013). Health Marketing: Toward an Integrative Perspective. *Journal of Business Research*, *66*(1), 123–126. doi:10.1016/j.jbusres.2012.09.002

Decreto-Lei n.o 238/2015 do Ministério da Saúde, Diário da República: I série, n.o 201 8953 (2015). https://dre.pt/dre/detalhe/decreto-lei/238-2015-70686132?_ts=1679316560455

del Castillo, J. A. G., López-Sanchez, C., Tur-Viñes, V., del Castillo-López, Á. G., & Soler, I. R. (2017). A Publicidade Comercial e a Publicidade Social no Contexto da Saúde. In D. Caldevilla (Ed.), *Linguagens e Persuasão: Novas Criações Narrativas* (pp. 159–168). Media XXI., https://www.researchgate.net/publication/313528191_A_publicidade_comercial_e_a_publicidade_social_no_contexto_da_saude

Delgadillo, J., & Atzil-Slonim, D. (2022). Artificial Intelligence, Machine Learning and Mental Health. In *Encyclopedia of Mental Health (3a Edição)*. Elsevier. doi:10.1016/B978-0-323-91497-0.00177-6

Demiris, G., Iribarren, S. J., Sward, K., Lee, S., & Yang, R. (2019). Patient Generated Health Data Use in Clinical Practice: A Systematic Review. *Nursing Outlook*, *67*(4), 311–330. doi:10.1016/j.outlook.2019.04.005 PMID:31277895

Dennison, L., Morrison, L., Conway, G., & Yardley, L. (2013). Opportunities and Challenges for Smartphone Applications in Supporting Health Behavior Change: Qualitative study. *Journal of Medical Internet Research*, *15*(4), e86. doi:10.2196/jmir.2583 PMID:23598614

Dicuonzo, G., Donofrio, F., Fusco, A., & Shini, M. (2023). Healthcare System: Moving Forward with Artificial Intelligence. *Technovation*, *120*, 102510. doi:10.1016/j.technovation.2022.102510

Fertonani, H. P., de Pires, D. E. P., Biff, D., & Scherer, M. D. dos A. (2015). The Health Care Model: Concepts and Challenges for Primary Health Care in Brazil. *Ciencia & Saude Coletiva, 20*(6), 1869–1878. doi:10.1590/1413-81232015206.13272014 PMID:26060965

Gennatas, E. D., & Chen, J. H. (2021). Artificial Intelligence in Medicine: Past, Present, and Future. In L. Xing, M. L. Giger, & J. K. Min (Eds.), *Artificial Intelligence in Medicine: Technical Basis and Clinical Applications* (pp. 3–18). Academic Press. doi:10.1016/B978-0-12-821259-2.00001-6

Haleem, A., Javaid, M., Qadri, M. A., Singh, R. P., & Suman, R. (2022). Artificial Intelligence (AI) Applications for Marketing: A Literature-Based Study. *International Journal of Intelligent Networks, 3*, 119–132. doi:10.1016/j.ijin.2022.08.005

Hathaliya, J. J., & Tanwar, S. (2020). An Exhaustive Survey on Security and Privacy Issues in Healthcare 4.0. *Computer Communications, 153*, 311–335. doi:10.1016/j.comcom.2020.02.018

He, Y., Tang, J., Liu, D., Tang, S., Liu, Q., & Li, D. (2021). Innovation System of Preventive Medicine Based on Big Data Technology. *6th International Conference on Smart Grid and Electrical Automation*, 506–509. 10.1109/ICSGEA53208.2021.00120

International Business Machines. (n.d.). *What is healthcare technology?* Retrieved September 6, 2022, from https://www.ibm.com/topics/healthcare-technology

Jiang, Y., Ding, X., Liu, D., Gui, X., Zhang, W., & Zhang, W. (2022). Designing Intelligent Self-Checkup Based Technologies for Everyday Healthy Living. *International Journal of Human-Computer Studies, 166*, 102866. doi:10.1016/j.ijhcs.2022.102866

Júnior, Í. M. B. A., & Ianotti, G. de C. (2010). Ética e Medicina Preditiva. *Revista Brasileira de Saúde Materno Infantil, 10*(SUPPL. 2), S377–S382. doi:10.1590/S1519-38292010000600016

Kahtalian, M. (2000). Marketing de Serviços. *Colecção Gestão Empresarial*, 19–29.

Kaur, J., Verma, R., Alharbe, N. R., Agrawal, A., & Khan, R. A. (2021). Importance of Fog Computing in Healthcare 4.0. In *Signals and Communication Technology* (pp. 79–101). Springer Science and Business Media Deutschland GmbH. doi:10.1007/978-3-030-46197-3_4

Keller, K. L., & Kotler, P. (2013). Administração de marketing. In *Pearson Education do Brasil L.tda (14a edição, Issue edição)*. Prentice Hall.

Kotler, P., & Armstrong, G. (2015). Princípios de Marketing (S. Afonso, S. Nascimento, V. Souza, A. Mendes, & M. Guimarães, Eds.; 15a Edição). Pearson Education.

Krishen, A. S., Dwivedi, Y. K., Bindu, N., & Kumar, K. S. (2021). A Broad Overview of Interactive Digital Marketing: A Bibliometric Network Analysis. *Journal of Business Research, 131*, 183–195. doi:10.1016/j.jbusres.2021.03.061

Krishnan, G., & Selvam, G. (2019). Factors Influencing the Download of Mobile Health Apps: Content Review-Led Regression Analysis. *Health Policy and Technology*, *8*(4), 356–364. doi:10.1016/j.hlpt.2019.09.001

Kulkov, I., Tsvetkova, A., & Ivanova-Gongne, M. (2023). Identifying Institutional Barriers When Implementing New Technologies in the Healthcare Industry. *European Journal of Innovation Management, 26*(4), 909–932. doi:10.1108/EJIM-02-2021-0093

Kuziemsky, C., & Vimarlund, V. (2018). Multi-Sided Markets for Transforming Healthcare Service Delivery. *Studies in Health Technology and Informatics, 626–630*. Advance online publication. doi:10.3233/978-1-61499-852-5-626 PMID:29678036

Lagan, S., Sandler, L., & Torous, J. (2021). Evaluating Evaluation Frameworks: A Scoping Review of Frameworks for Assessing Health Apps. *BMJ Open*, *11*(3, e047001), e047001. Advance online publication. doi:10.1136/bmjopen-2020-047001 PMID:33741674

Lebcir, R., Hill, T., Atun, R., & Cubric, M. (2021). Stakeholders' Views on the Organisational Factors Affecting Application of Artificial Intelligence in Healthcare: A Scoping Review Protocol. *BMJ Open*, *11*(3, e044074), e044074. Advance online publication. doi:10.1136/bmjopen-2020-044074 PMID:33753441

Lee, D. (2019). A Model for Designing Healthcare Service Based on the Patient Experience. *International Journal of Healthcare Management*, *12*(3), 180–188. do i:10.1080/20479700.2017.1359956

Lee, W., Schwartz, N., Bansal, A., Khor, S., Hammarlund, N., Basu, A., & Devine, B. (2023). A Scoping Review of the Use of Machine Learning in Health Economics and Outcomes Research: Part 1—Data From Wearable Devices. *Value in Health*, *26*(2), 292–299. doi:10.1016/j.jval.2022.08.005 PMID:36115806

Li, J., & Carayon, P. (2021). Health Care 4.0: A Vision for Smart and Connected Health Care. *IISE Transactions on Healthcare Systems Engineering*, *11*(3), 171–180. doi:10.1080/24725579.2021.1884627 PMID:34497970

Lifshitz, A. (2014). La Medicina Curativa y La Medicina Preventiva: Alcances y Limitaciones. *Medicina Interna de México*, *30*(1), 64–72.

Liu, X., Faes, L., Kale, A. U., Wagner, S. K., Fu, D. J., Bruynseels, A., Mahendiran, T., Moraes, G., Shamdas, M., Kern, C., Ledsam, J. R., Schmid, M. K., Balaskas, K., Topol, E. J., Bachmann, L. M., Keane, P. A., & Denniston, A. K. (2019). A Comparison of Deep Learning Performance Against Health-Care Professionals in Detecting Diseases from Medical Imaging: A Systematic Review and Meta-Analysis. *The Lancet. Digital Health*, *1*(6), e271–e297. doi:10.1016/S2589-7500(19)30123-2 PMID:33323251

Mailchimp. (2023a). *Digital Marketing. Mailchimp*. https://mailchimp.com/pt-br/marketing-glossary/digital-marketing/

Mailchimp. (2023b). *O Que é Marketing de Relacionamento com o Cliente*. Mailchimp. https://mailchimp.com/pt-br/resources/customer-relationship-marketing/

Marketing Accountability Standards Board. (2023a). *Health Care Marketing*. The Universal Marketing Dictionary. https://marketing-dictionary.org/h/health-care-marketing/

Marketing Accountability Standards Board. (2023b). *Marketing*. The Universal Marketing Dictionary. https://marketing-dictionary.org/m/marketing/

Mills, E. C., Savage, E., Lieder, J., & Chiu, E. S. (2020). Telemedicine and the COVID-19 Pandemic: Are We Ready to Go Live? *Advances in Skin & Wound Care*, *33*(8), 410–417. doi:10.1097/01.ASW.0000669916.01793.93 PMID:32701252

Mirza, F., Norris, T., & Stockdale, R. (2008). Mobile Technologies and the Holistic Management of Chronic Diseases. *Health Informatics Journal*, *14*(4), 309–321. doi:10.1177/1460458208096559 PMID:19008280

Mondal, T., Jayadeva, S. M., Pani, R., Subramanian, M. P. A., & Sumana, B. K. (2022). E Marketing Strategy in Health Care Using IoT and Machine Learning. *Materials Today: Proceedings*, *56*, 2087–2091. doi:10.1016/j.matpr.2021.11.417

Nunes, A., Limpo, T., & Castro, S. L. (2019). Acceptance of Mobile Health Applications: Examining Key Determinants and Moderators. *Frontiers in Psychology*, *10*(2791), 2791. Advance online publication. doi:10.3389/fpsyg.2019.02791 PMID:31920836

O'Connor, G. E., & Myrden, S., Alkire, L., Lee, K., Köcher, S., Kandampully, J., & Williams, J. D. (2021). Digital Health Experience: A Regulatory Focus Perspective. *Journal of Interactive Marketing*, *56*, 121–136. doi:10.1016/j.intmar.2021.07.002

Oldenburg, B., Taylor, C. B., O'Neil, A., Cocker, F., & Cameron, L. D. (2015). Using New Technologies to Improve the Prevention and Management of Chronic Conditions in Populations. *Annual Review of Public Health*, *36*(1), 483–505. doi:10.1146/annurev-publhealth-031914-122848 PMID:25581147

Pagliari, C., Sloan, D., Gregor, P., Sullivan, F., Detmer, D., Kahan, J. P., Oortwijn, W., & MacGillivray, S. (2005). What is eHealth (4): A Scoping Exercise to Map the Field. *Journal of Medical Internet Research*, *7*(1), e9. doi:10.2196/jmir.7.1.e9 PMID:15829481

Park, G., Kim, Y., Park, K., & Agarwal, A. (2016). Patient-Centric Quality Assessment Framework for Healthcare Services. *Technological Forecasting and Social Change*, *113*(Part B), 468–474. . doi:10.1016/j.techfore.2016.07.012

Peng, W., Kanthawala, S., Yuan, S., & Hussain, S. A. (2016). A Qualitative Study of User Perceptions of Mobile Health Apps. *BMC Public Health*, *16*(1158), 1158. Advance online publication. doi:10.1186/s12889-016-3808-0 PMID:27842533

Pisco, L., & Biscaia, J. L. (2001). Qualidade de Cuidados de Saúde Primários. *Revista Portuguesa de Saude Publica*, *2*, 43–51. https://doi.org/hdl.handle.net/10362/101394

Post Digital. (2023). *Marketing de Relacionamento na Área da Saúde: O Guia Completo*. Post Digital.

Purcărea, T. V. (2016). Creating the Ideal Patient Experience. *Journal of Medicine and Life*, *9*(4), 380–385. doi:10.22336/jml.2016.0411 PMID:27928442

Radu, G., Solomon, M., Gheorghe, C. M., Hostiuc, M., Bulescu, I. A., & Purcarea, V. L. (2017). The Adaptation of Health Care Marketing to the Digital Era. *Journal of Medicine and Life*, *10*(1), 44–46. http://www.ncbi.nlm.nih.gov/pubmed/28255375%0Ahttp://www.pubmedcentral.nih.gov/articlerender.fcgi?artid=PMC5304370 PMID:28255375

Razzak, M. I., Imran, M., & Xu, G. (2020). Big Data Analytics for Preventive Medicine. *Neural Computing & Applications*, *32*(9), 4417–4451. doi:10.1007/s00521-019-04095-y PMID:32205918

Santos, P., Sá, L., Couto, L., & Hespanhol, A. (2017). Health Literacy as a Key for Effective Preventive Medicine. *Cogent Social Sciences*, *3*(1), 1407522. doi:10.1080/23311886.2017.1407522

Sato, M. K. de S. (2002). A Propaganda e a Publicidade de Medicamentos e a Informação ao Consumidor. *Publicidade de Medicamentos e Informação Ao Público*, *3*(3), 89–115. http://www.revistas.usp.br/rdisan/article/view/83839/86720

Schnurr, H.-P., Aronsky, D., & Wenke, D. (2018). Medicine 4.0 - Interplay of Intelligent Systems and Medical Experts. In K. North, O. Haas, & R. Maier (Eds.), *Knowledge Management in Digital Change - New Findings and Practical Cases* (pp. 51–63). Springer. doi:10.1007/978-3-319-73546-7_3

Scholz, S., & Teetz, L. (2022). Smart Health via mHealth? Potentials of Mobile Health Apps for Improving Prevention and Adherence of Breast Cancer Patients. *Digital Health*, *8*, 1–12. doi:10.1177/20552076221074127 PMID:35096411

Silva, B. M. C., Rodrigues, J. J. P. C., Díez, I. de la T., López-Coronado, M., & Saleem, K. (2015). Mobile-Health: A Review of Current State in 2015. *Journal of Biomedical Informatics*, *56*, 265–272. doi:10.1016/j.jbi.2015.06.003 PMID:26071682

Sony, M., Antony, J., & McDermott, O. (2022). The Impact of Healthcare 4.0 on the Healthcare Service Quality: A Systematic Literature Review. *Hospital Topics*, 1–17. doi:10.1080/00185868.2022.2048220 PMID:35324390

Stephen, D. A., Nordin, A., Nilsson, J., & Persenius, M. (2022). Using mHealth Applications for Self-Care – An Integrative Review on Perceptions Among Adults with Type 1 Diabetes. *BMC Endocrine Disorders*, *22*(138), 138. Advance online publication. doi:10.1186/s12902-022-01039-x PMID:35614419

Stoyanov, S. R., Hides, L., Kavanagh, D. J., & Wilson, H. (2016). Development and Validation of the User Version of the Mobile Application Rating Scale (uMARS). *JMIR mHealth and uHealth*, *4*(2), e72. doi:10.2196/mhealth.5849 PMID:27287964

Sujith, A. V. L. N., Sajja, G. S., Mahalakshmi, V., Nuhmani, S., & Prasanalakshmi, B. (2022). Systematic Review of Smart Health Monitoring Using Deep Learning and Artificial Intelligence. *Neuroscience Informatics (Online)*, *2*(3), 100028. doi:10.1016/j.neuri.2021.100028

Tallia, S., Zulsibtain, M. A., Ali, R., & Hafeez, M. H. (2018). Strategic Marketing of Health Care Services : A Systematic Review. *International Journal of Management and Applied Science*, *4*(12), 23–28.

Tang, X. (2020). The Role of Artificial Intelligence in Medical Imaging Research. *BJR Open*, *2*(1), 20190031. Advance online publication. doi:10.1259/bjro.20190031 PMID:33178962

Terkola, R., Antoñanzas, F., & Postma, M. (2017). Economic Evaluation of Personalized Medicine: A Call for Real-World Data. *The European Journal of Health Economics*, *18*(9), 1065–1067. doi:10.1007/s10198-017-0890-x PMID:28382502

Timimi, F. K. (2013). The Shape of Digital Engagement: Health Care and Social Media. *The Journal of Ambulatory Care Management*, *36*(3), 187–192. doi:10.1097/JAC.0b013e3182965512 PMID:23748265

Topol, E. J. (2019). High-Performance Medicine: The Convergence of Human and Artificial Intelligence. *Nature Medicine*, *25*(1), 44–56. doi:10.1038/s41591-018-0300-7 PMID:30617339

Torres, C. (2009). A Bíblia do Marketing Digital: Tudo o Que Você Queria Saber do Marketing e Não Tinha a Quem Perguntar. Novatec Editora.

Verghese, A., Shah, N. H., & Harrington, R. A. (2018). What This Computer Needs Is a Physician: Humanism and Artificial Intelligence. *Journal of the American Medical Association*, *319*(1), 19–20. doi:10.1001/jama.2017.19198 PMID:29261830

Vial, G. (2019). Understanding Digital Transformation: A Review and a Research Agenda. *The Journal of Strategic Information Systems*, *28*(2), 118–144. doi:10.1016/j.jsis.2019.01.003

Vimarlund, V. (2017). The Future of Two-Sided E-Health Markets. In V. Vimarlund (Ed.), *E-Health Two-Sided Markets: Implementation and Business Models* (pp. 189–195). Elsevier Inc. doi:10.1016/B978-0-12-805250-1.00020-4

World Health Organization. (2010). *Telemedicine - Opportunities and Developments in Member States : Report on the Second Global Survey on eHealth*. World Health Organization.

Zinkhan, G. M. (2002). Relationship Marketing: Theory and Implementation. *Journal of Market - Focused Management*, *5*, 83–89. . doi:10.1023/A:1014031025271

KEY TERMS AND DEFINITIONS

Artificial Intelligence: Refers to computer systems capable of performing complex tasks that historically only a human could do, such as reasoning, making decisions, or solving problems.

Consumer Behavior: Is the study of individuals, groups, or organisations and all the activities associated with the purchase, use and disposal of goods and services. Consumer behaviour consists of how the consumer's emotions, attitudes, and preferences affect buying behaviour.

Health Marketing: Is a process of strategic outreach and communications designed to attract healthcare consumers, guide them through their healthcare journey, and keep them engaged with the health system.

Services Marketing: Is a specialized branch of marketing which emerged as a separate field of study in the early 1980s, following the recognition that the unique characteristics of services required different strategies compared with the marketing of physical goods.

Chapter 5
The Effect of Artificial Intelligence Awareness on Job Performance:
Gender as Moderator and Experience as Mediator

Oumeima Toumia
https://orcid.org/0000-0002-7377-6366
University of Sousse, Tunisia

Farouk Zouari
https://orcid.org/0000-0002-3108-6447
University of Tunis El Manar, Tunisia

ABSTRACT

Since artificial intelligence is still a relatively new technology, research on the effects of artificial intelligence on work performance in developing countries is still limited. Thus, the chapter aims to examine and analyze the effect of artificial intelligence on job performance among Tunisian employees, with gender as the moderator variable and experience as the mediating variable. A questionnaire was developed to test the model based on a dataset of 350 employees in different sectors. The generated data were analyzed using IBM SPSS.26 and IBM SPSS AMOS.26. The results of exploratory and confirmatory factor analyses showed the absence of an impact of artificial intelligence on job performance. In addition, the authors found no moderating effect of gender or mediating effect of experience on the relationship between artificial intelligence and job performance. However, the experience of the employee has a positive and significant impact on job performance.

DOI: 10.4018/979-8-3693-2153-9.ch005

1. INTRODUCTION

Nowadays, the world faces many serious challenges (e.g., war, disease, poverty, gender inequality, climate change, etc.). Therefore, many researchers and practitioners have tried to find tools to help address these challenges and open up new opportunities. Among these tools were artificial intelligence (AI) technologies, which came back into vogue in the 2010s (Duan et al., 2019). In fact, AI tools have been used in various industries, such as tourism, hospitality, manufacturing, finance, education, healthcare, etc. (Buhalis & Leung, 2018; García-Madurga & Grilló-Méndez, 2023; Kim, 2011; Prentice et al., 2020; Toumia & Zouari, 2024a, 2024b; Yetgin and Toumia, 2023; Yu & Schwartz, 2006; Zeba et al., 2021; Zouari, 2019). These tools improve and increase the operational efficiency of companies (Russell, 2016; Younus, 2021). Indeed, it is well documented that artificial intelligence has an impact on all departments of a company, such as marketing, human resources, production, etc. (Kumar et al., 2019; Mohammadi & Minaei, 2019; Vrontis et al., 2022). Despite the benefits of AI, many contributions have highlighted that there are potential drawbacks to using AI (Cellan-Jones, 2014; Duan et al., 2019; Rawlinson, 2015). Stephen Hawking announced that "*the development of full artificial intelligence could spell the end of the human race*" (Cellan-Jones, 2014). For instance, artificial intelligence is now able to beat humans in complicated games (e.g., the AlphaGo system and IBM's Watson system), interpret sounds and language, solve problems, improve prediction, provide a deeper level of transparency, create a more rewarding workplace, use facial recognition tools, diagnose medical cases, drive a car on the road, play games like chess, and imitate the impressionistic imagery in Van Gogh's paintings (Agrawal et al., 2019; Gabbatt, 2011; Jarrahi, 2018; Kaplan & Haenlein, 2019; Koch, 2016; Tuomi, 2019).

While acknowledging the impact of AI on improving the efficiency of businesses (Abusalma, 2021; Wijayati et al., 2022), it is important to investigate the relationship between artificial intelligence and job performance. Indeed, many studies have used sociodemographic mediating variables (e.g., gender, age, and tenure) to investigate the relationship between job performance (see Shirom et al., 2008) and other factors such as work-related stressors, work-family conflict, and organizational commitment. However, to our knowledge, no previous quantitative research dealt with the effect of artificial intelligence awareness on job performance in the context of Tunisian employees by using gender as the moderator variable and experience as the mediating variable. Our present research aims to contribute to filling this gap.

In order to test our model, a questionnaire was created with a dataset of 350 employees from various industries. IBM SPSS.26 and IBM SPSS AMOS.26 were used to evaluate the generated data. Indeed, we performed the explanatory factor analysis (EFA), the confirmatory factor analysis (CFA), and the structural equation modeling technique (i.e., it is employed to conduct a path analysis for the relationships among variables in our model).

This chapter is divided into five main sections. The first section presents the introduction. The second section provides a theoretical background for our research. The third section describes the methodology used to solve our research question. The fourth section introduces and discusses the main findings. The five section summarizes the findings and presents the contributions, limitations, and future research.

2. LITERATURE REVIEW

2.1. AI and Job Performance

The concept of artificial intelligence was first introduced in 1956 by John McCarthy, the "*father of AI*" (Benko & Lányi, 2009). It is defined as the capacity of machines to learn from experience, adapt to new inputs, and accomplish human tasks (Brooks, 1991; Duan et al., 2019). AI can be categorized into analytic AI (it shows only features consistent with cognitive intelligence), human-inspired AI (it includes elements of both cognitive and emotional intelligence), and humanized AI (it characterizes all kinds of competencies such as cognitive, emotional, and social intelligence) (Kaplan & Haenlein, 2019). A growing body of literature has emerged that aims at introducing the concept of artificial intelligence and examining its role. Indeed, there is disagreement among researchers about the role of AI. Many contributions (Abusalma, 2021; Agrawal et al., 2019; Edwards et al., 2000; Larivière et al., 2017) have highlighted that artificial intelligence can replace human capital in the performance of some tasks (i.e., adaptive tasks, contextual performance, and organizational performance). More specifically, AI systems may perform an increasing number of tasks without the control or supervision of humans (i.e., autonomous machines that make decisions on their own, provide customers with personalized offers, find patterns in the data that humans would never look at, and manage employees) (Kumar et al., 2019; Shaw et al., 2019; Vrontis et al., 2022; Złotowski et al., 2017). Meanwhile, other studies (Jarrahi, 2018; Miller, 2018; Shaw et al., 2019; Wilson & Daugherty, 2018) have found that AI should complement human capital, not replace it. For instance, AI has been used for decision-making (i.e., strategic, tactical, and operational decisions) (Duan et al., 2019; Edwards et al., 2000) and as a decision support tool, not to replace the role of decision makers (Duan et al., 2019). In this context, Shaw et al. (2019) added that artificial intelligence lacks empathy. More specifically, AI systems may not be able to comprehend or respond to emotions in the same way as humans.

It is well-documented that artificial intelligence affects job performance (Abusalma, 2021; Larivière et al., 2017; Miller, 2018; Prentice et al., 2020; Wijayati et al., 2022; Wilson & Daugherty, 2018; Younus, 2021). Abusalma (2021) used a sample of 319 managers to investigate the effect of artificial intelligence on job performance in Jordan's banking sector. Their findings showed AI influenced job performance. For instance, artificial intelligence assists bank managers in administrative decisions and ensures lower transaction costs. In the same vein, Wilson and Daugherty (2018) concluded that AI allows employees to make better decisions, enhance their analytical and decision-making skills, and increase their creativity. They added that companies could benefit from optimizing "*human-artificial intelligence collaboration*" by enabling employees to work effectively with human-machine interfaces. It claims to be able to develop "*fusion skills*". Similarly, Jia et al. (2023) interviewed employees to investigate whether artificial intelligence increased their creativity. Their results showed that AI mainly increases the creativity of higher-skilled employees. Compared to lower-skilled employees, higher-skilled employees are more capable of generating innovative scripts and developing positive emotions at work. Wijayati et al. (2022) conducted a questionnaire survey with 254 employees in the service and banking sectors in Indonesia. They analyzed the impact of artificial intelligence on employee performance and engagement, including the moderating role of leadership in change. They found that AI has a significant positive impact on employee performance and engagement at work. Furthermore, they added that change leadership can positively mediate the impact of AI on the performance of the employee and their work engagement. Larivière et al. (2017) developed a conceptual framework to capture the essence of Service Encounter 2.0 and concluded that technology can complement/replace service workers and facilitate network connectivity. Prentice et al. (2020) stated that artificial intelligence plays a significant mediating role in the performance of employees. Younus (2021) stated that artificial intelligence improves staff efficiency and effectiveness (i.e., improves performance, to reach desired goals). Zhang et al. (2022) added that AI enhances leadership, improves workplace flexibility, and ensures autonomous knowledge acquisition. Miller (2018) stated that a new level of human-machine symbiosis is required to augment the capabilities of individuals.

However, it is also important to be aware of the potential negative impacts of AI on job performance. In this context, many studies have expressed concern that robots and machines could take over jobs in many sectors (Cooper, 1984; Dormehl, 2018; Findlay et al., 2017; Koo et al., 2021; Li et al., 2019; Prentice et al., 2019; Spencer, 2018). Frey and Osborne (2017) argued that 47% of jobs are in danger in the United States. Findlay et al. (2017) found that artificial intelligence not only has positive effects on worker performance but also negative effects. They explained that AI can lead to fewer chances for collaboration and job rotation. Therefore, employees may feel isolated, insecure, and demotivated. In fact, the development of AI may reduce the need for human labor in certain industries. Li et al. (2019) suggested that hotel staff members who know more about artificial intelligence and robots have a higher intention to quit. However, they also added that this relationship between AI and robotics awareness and turnover intention is mitigated when staff members feel that their company values them and that they work in a psychologically competitive environment. Cooper (1984) emphasized that even the introduction of computers in the workplace may lead to an increase in occupational stress. Koo et al. (2021) argued that AI may result in employment instability for hotel staff in two ways: (1) AI can replace much of the work that hotel employees currently perform, and (2) due to the quick speed at which technology is developing, hotel staff may find it challenging to stay current on the knowledge and abilities required to use AI technologies. Therefore, we make our main hypothesis:

H1: Artificial intelligence has a negative effect on job performance.

2.2. Gender and Job Performance

Job performance, which refers to the extent to which workers perform their jobs within the rules set by the institution (Al-Makhaita et al., 2014), depends on many factors such as age, marital status, education, experience, and gender (Abusalma, 2021; Banjo & Olufemi, 2014; Khan et al., 2022; McDaniel et al., 1988; Quińones et al., 1995).

There are conflicting results regarding the effects of gender on job performance. Actually, it is difficult to compare the performance of men and women in identical activities (Rydstedt et al., 1998). This may be explained by differences in gender characteristics or the biological differences between men and women (Banjo & Olufemi, 2014). Abusalma (2021) indicated that gender statistically influences job performance in Jordanian commercial banks. In detail, men perform better than women. This could be due to the fact that men are perceived as more competent and successful, as they are more inclined to take risks. In addition, Khan et al. (2022) found that gender significantly moderates the relationship between transformational leadership and job performance. They claimed that male employees are more likely to benefit from transformational leadership compared to female employees. In fact, men and women may react differently to the many facets of transformational leadership. Furthermore, Banjo and Olufemi (2014) examined the relationship between demographic variables (i.e., age, marital status, educational qualification, job tenure, and gender) of 113 insurance salesmen and their job performance. They concluded that there was a moderately positive relationship between the variables studied and job performance. They also added that about 13% of the elements influencing insurance salesperson performance may be explained by the five demographic characteristics studied. In contrast to previous contributions, other studies have shown that companies that reach a critical mass of female employees (i.e., more than 35% of the total employees make gender token effects disappear) (Joecks et al., 2013; Kanter, 1977). In the same context, Shirom et al. (2008) synthesized 30 independent studies to identify the extent to which three sociodemographic variables (i.e., gender, age, and tenure) mitigated the meta-correlations of role conflict and role ambiguity with job performance. They concluded that gender and tenure had no moderating effects. However, Mackey et al. (2019) have shown that women generally perform better in the workplace than men, and this difference does not seem to change depending on the percentage of women in the company (i.e., women outperform men by an average of one-tenth of a standard deviation). Many factors play an important role in predicting women's performance, such as government backing, land ownership, taxation, educational level, prior entrepreneurial experience, access to information and financial support, etc. (Alene, 2020). Based on these previous findings, we propose the following hypothesis:

H2: Gender statistically influences job performance.

2.3. The Role of Gender in the Relationship Between AI and Job Performance

As discussed above, gender is an important individual characteristic that significantly influences job performance (Abusalma, 2021; Hoque et al., 2019; Khan & Vieito, 2013). On the one hand, many contributions (Abusalma, 2021; Allison et al., 2023; Hoque et al., 2019; Igbaria & Shayo, 1997) ascertained that men tend to outperform women. Due to their talents and diligence, only male employees were most likely to achieve excellent performance (Igbaria & Shayo, 1997). On the other hand, Kiefer et al. (2022) stated that male-led businesses perform better than female-led businesses. However, they also added that female-led companies are outperforming their male-led competitors in terms of performance results in certain instances. In the same vein, Khan & Vieito (2013) stated that companies tend to have the lowest levels of risks when it is led by female CEOs. Therefore, this reduced amount of risk may help the company perform better.

Other studies have looked at the way AI systems affect men and women. Despite the ever-evolving global technical landscape, women's participation in the field of artificial intelligence remains disproportionately low (Samuel et al., 2020). Ahn et al. (2022) argued that respondents thought female AI chatbots were more amiable and pleasant, while they thought male AI agents were more capable and reliable. Therefore, when it came to utilitarian products (e.g., a laptop), participants were more inclined to accept recommendations from male AI agents, whereas female AI agents were more likely to suggest hedonistic products (e.g., jewelry). This may be due to the fact that men are much more likely to be involved with software compared to women, who tend to work in jobs that require greater interpersonal skills (Webb, 2019). In light of the above discussion, the following hypothesis is presented:

H3: Moderation of gender has a significant effect on the relationship between artificial intelligence and job performance.

2.4. Experience and Job Performance

Work experience, which is generally defined as events that occur in an individual's life, is correlated with job performance (Quiñones et al., 1995). The meta-analysis conducted by Quiñones et al. (1995) confirmed earlier findings on the positive correlation between work experience and job performance (Hunter and Hunter, 1984) and the fact that the most important type of work experience for job performance is task-level work experience (Ng and Feldman, 2010). However, they were among the first authors to analyze how the relationship between experience and performance is influenced by the moderating effects of two dimensions of work experience (i.e., measurement model and degree of sphericity). Abusalma (2021) stated that the number of years of work experience has a statistically significant effect on job performance in Jordanian commercial banks. More precisely, ten to twenty years of experience are required to increase performance efficiency. Ratnawati et al. (2020) conducted quantitative research on 40 employees of PT Tirta Kencana Tatawarna Bengkulu. They also found that work experience has a positive and significant effect on employee performance (i.e., an employee's performance decreases with decreasing work experience). In the same vein, McDaniel et al. (1988) confirmed the previous findings of Quiñones et al. (1995) and Abusalma (2021). However, they added that the length of experience and job complexity moderated the correlation between job experience and job performance. They explained that the highest correlations were found in populations with low average work experience and in occupations that impose low cognitive demands on workers. Thus, we propose the following hypothesis:

H4: Experience has a positive and significant effect on job performance.

2.5. The Role of Experience in the Relationship Between AI and Job Performance

It is well documented that employees are likely to exhibit improved job performance when they gain more experience in their roles (Abusalma, 2021; Dewanti & Artaya, 2019; Hunter and Hunter, 1984; Quiñones et al., 1995). For instance, Dewanti & Artaya (2019) stated that the performance of employees is influenced by job experience by 51.1%. In addition, Shahzad et al. (2023) showed that artificial intelligence has a significant impact on human resources tasks. More precisely, artificial intelligence promotes recruiting and talent acquisition, increases employee experience and engagement, facilitates employee growth, boosts productivity, makes better judgments, etc. (Butler & Callahan, 2014; Nam et al., 2021). In the same vein, Zel and Kongar (2020) affirmed that if AI tools such as chatbots, virtual HR chatbots, and collaboration platforms are effectively deployed, they may be used to improve the employee experience. Consequently, it is anticipated that an employee's experience will serve as an intermediary between job performance and artificial intelligence awareness. Hypothesis 5 is proposed:

H5: Mediation of experience has a significant effect on the relationship between artificial intelligence and job performance.

3. RESEARCH METHODOLOGY

A total of 350 online questionnaires were distributed, from January 2023 to March 2023, to investigate the impact of artificial intelligence on Tunisian employees' job performance. The survey used in this paper consisted of three parts: The first part covers the demographic information of the respondents, the second part contains items measuring artificial intelligence awareness, and the third part includes items that measure job performance. The last two parts of the survey items were measured using a 5-point Likert scale, with response levels ranging from "*strongly disagree*" (1) to "*strongly agree*" (5). Artificial intelligence awareness items were derived from the contribution of Brougham and Haar (2018), with four factors as dimensions. Job performance was evaluated using Çalışkan and Köroğlu's items (2022). Table 1 presents the constructs and scale resources.

Our sample showed that 51.4% of the respondents were male, while 48.6% were female (see Table 2). The majority of respondents were married (56.6%), between the ages of 31 and 40 years (47.4%), had a licence degree (49.4%), had experience between 5 and 10 years (34.3%), and lived in urban areas (86.3%). Regarding the

Table 1. Constructs and Scales Resources

Constructs	Number of Items	Sources
Artificial intelligence awareness	4	Brougham and Haar (2018)
Job performance	11	Çalışkan *and* Köroğlu *(2022)*

Table 2. Respondents' demographics

Characteristics		Frequency	Percentage
Gender	Male	180	51.4
	Female	170	48.6
Age	<30	76	21.7
	31-40	166	47.4
	41-50	80	22.9
	51-60	24	6.9
	>60	4	1.1
Marital status	Single	139	39.7
	Married	198	56.6
	Divorced	10	2.9
	Widow	3	0.9
Region of origin	Urban	302	86.3
	Rural	48	13.7
Educational qualification	Higher degree: License	173	49.4
	Higher degree: Master's degree	107	30.6
	Higher degree: Doctorate	70	20
Sector	Primary sector	119	34
	Secondary sector	121	34.6
	Tertiary sector	110	31.4
Experience	Less than 1 year	28	8
	1-3 years	48	13.7
	3-5 years	53	15.1
	5-10 years	120	34.3
	More than 10 years	101	28.9

types of sectors, 34% of the employees are involved in the primary sector, 34.6% in the secondary sector, and 31.4% in the tertiary sector.

4. RESULTS AND DISCUSSION

4.1. Descriptive Statistics and Scale Evaluation

Based on Table 3, the AI1 (mean = 3.08, SD = 1.42) item is perceived as the most influential driver of artificial intelligence awareness. Furthermore, the mean average for the four items in this construct across respondents is 2.88, which indicates that the respondents are moderately high in this construct. Besides, the JP2 item (mean = 4.11, SD = 0.65) is perceived as the most influential driver of job performance. Indeed, the mean average of the eleven items for the construct of job performance across all respondents is 3.85, which means that respondents rate this construct moderately highly.

We used the Cronbach alpha coefficient to evaluate the reliability of the two constructs. As indicated by Hair et al. (2013), a Cronbach alpha coefficient of

Table 3. Measurement items and quality representation

Items	Mean	SD	Initial	Extraction
Cronbach's Alpha overall = 0.807				
AI awareness: ***Cronbach's Alpha*** **= 0.923**				
I believe AI will replace me in my job (AI1)	3.08	1.42	1.000	0.756
Personally, I'm concerned that AI may be able to replace the work I perform now (AI2)	2.97	1.43	1.000	0.766
I personally worry about my future in this company because AI is replacing workers (AI3)	2.72	1.36	1.000	0.874
I personally worry about my future in this industry because AI is replacing workers (AI4)	2.76	1.38	1.000	0.861
Job performance: ***Cronbach's Alpha*** **= 0.913**				
I possess the skills needed for my work (JP1)	4.05	0.67	1.000	0.767
I work effectively/efficiently (JP2)	4.11	0.65	1.000	0.819
I comprehend and follow work-related procedures (JP3)	4.04	0.68	1.000	0.753
I work in a planned and organized manner to conclude the task defined to me completely and on schedule. (JP4)	4.07	0.79	1.000	0.724
I'm excited to learn new work-related abilities (JP5)	3.97	0.96	1.000	0.291
When performing my duties, I take additional precautions and assume extra responsibility (JP6)	3.79	0.96	1.000	0.497
In my organization, I help to establish a productive work environment (JP7)	3.56	1.02	1.000	0.696
I attempt to resolve any issues that arise so that I can complete the task (JP8)	3.92	0.81	1.000	0.624
I support and motivate my friends to complete their work (JP9)	3.41	1.16	1.000	0.857
I stand up for my institution despite criticisms from both inside and outside it (JP10)	3.50	1.11	1.000	0.814
Being a member of this organization makes me proud (JP11)	3.92	0.83	1.000	0.727

0.70 or greater is considered reliable and acceptable. As shown in Table 3, the Cronbach's alpha coefficient was found to be greater than the threshold. $\alpha_{overall}$ = 0.807, $\alpha_{AI\text{-}awareness}$ = 0.923, $\alpha_{Job\ performance}$ = 0.913. Therefore, it can be deduced that all items are reliable and valid.

4.2 Explanatory Factor Analysis

To ascertain the underlying factors of several observable variables, exploratory factor analysis is frequently employed (Auerswald & Moshagen, 2019). The Kaiser-Meyer-Olkin (KMO) index and Bartlett tests showed that the data were suitable for factor analysis (Hair et al., 2010; Kaiser, 1974). In Kaiser's (1974) classification, values between 0.5-0.7 are considered mediocre, 0.7-0.8 good, 0.8-0.9 great, 0.9-1.00 superb, and < 0.5 unacceptable. In our case, we determined a $KMO_{overall}$ coefficient of 0.874. In addition, the KMO coefficients for artificial intelligence awareness and job performance are higher than 0.7 (i.e., KMO_{AI} = 0.793, KMO_{JP} = 0.901). We also computed Bartlett's test. Our results show that the chi-square value of Barlett's sphericality test is 3947.084 ($p<0.001$).

Table 4. Total variance explained

Component	Initial Eigenvalues			Extraction Sums of Squared Loadings		
	Total	% of Variance	Cumulative %	Total	% of Variance	Cumulative %
1	6.297	41.981	41.981	6.297	41.981	41.981
2	3.149	20.995	62.976	3.149	20.995	62.976
3	1.377	9.182	72.158	1.377	9.182	72.158
4	0.823	5.487	77.645			
5	0.610	4.065	81.710			
6	0.485	3.232	84.942			
7	0.400	2.666	87.608			
8	0.374	2.490	90.098			
9	0.317	2.110	92.209			
10	0.289	1.929	94.138			
11	0.256	1.705	95.843			
12	0.215	1.436	97.279			
13	0.201	1.343	98.622			
14	0.129	0.861	99.483			
15	0.078	0.517	100.000			

Extraction Method: Principal Component Analysis

We employed principal component analysis as the inference method to perform EFA. To determine the number of factors to retain, we used the Kaiser-Guttman criterion method (see Table 4). According to Kaiser (1960), eigenvalues greater than one rule is a frequently applied criteria for the number of components to be rotated. In fact, he explained that an eigenvalue of less than one is interpreted as an indication of poor reliability of the component values. In our case, we kept three factors (i.e., the three extracted components together explained 72.158% (> 50%) of the variance).

Rotation Method: Varimax with Kaiser Normalization

As the rotation matrix, we used the varimax method, which is an effective orthogonal rotation technique for exploratory factor analysis (Kaiser, 1958). For every variable, it is intended to maximize the variance of the squared factor loadings (Kaiser, 1958). Since the factor loadings in factor analysis are expected to be higher than 0.70 (Hair et al., 2010), in order to guarantee that a measure's items are suitably loaded onto the underlying construct, we removed three items. Table 5 presents the pattern matrix.

Table 5. Pattern matrix

Items	Components		
	1	2	3
AI1			0.868
AI2			0.874
AI3			0.930
AI4			0.923
JP1		0.831	
JP2		0.866	
JP3		0.851	
JP4		0.785	
JP5			
JP6			
JP7	0.804		
JP8			
JP9	0.910		
JP10	0.862		
JP11	0.702		

Extraction Method: Principal Component Analysis.

4.3 Confirmatory Factor Analysis and Path Analysis

To find the underlying factor structure of a data collection, we employed confirmatory factor analysis (Jöreskog, 1969). We used IBM SPSS AMOS.26 to perform confirmatory factor analysis, test hypotheses, and analyze coefficients' paths. The maximum-likelihood estimator is employed to run the model.

Three categories of model fit (i.e., absolute fit, incremental fit, and parsimonious fit) are considered to evaluate our model. Absolute fit contained GFI (Goodness of Fitness Index) = 0.997 ≥ 0.80 (Hashmi et al., 2020), RMSEA (Root mean square error of approximation) = 0.035 ≤ 0.08 (Hair et al., 2010); incremental fit comprised CFI (Comparative Fit Index) = 0.997 ≥ 0.90 (Bagozzi & Yi, 1988; Hair et al., 2010), TLI (Tucker-Lewis Index) = 0.984 ≥ 0.90 (Bagozzi and Yi, 1988), IFI (Incremental Fit Index) = 0.997 ≥ 0.90 (Bollen, 1990), NFI (Normed Fit Index) = 0.990 ≥ 0.80 (Bentler & Bonnet, 1980), AGFI (Adjusted Goodness of Fit Index) = 0.975 ≥ 0.80 (Jöreskog & Sörbom, 1993); and parsimonious fit included chi-square normalized by degrees of freedom (Chisq/df)= 1.436 ≤3 (Bagozzi & Yi, 1988; Kline, 1998), PNFI (Parsimony-Adjusted Measures Index) = 0.198 >0.05 (Bentler & Bonnet, 1980). Our research revealed that all fitness indicators had been attained and were deemed to be sufficiently error-free.

Structural equation modeling technique (SEM) is employed to conduct a path analysis for the relationships among variables in our model. We also used the statistics resulting from the path analysis to test our hypotheses (see Table 6).

According to Table 6, increased awareness of artificial intelligence does not affect job performance commitment (β = -0.120; p = 0.109 > 0.05) (hypothesis 1 is not supported). Our results are not consistent with previous studies (Duan et al., 2019; Findlay et al., 2017; Jia et al., 2023; Koo et al., 2021; Li et al., 2019; Rawlinson, 2015; Toumia and Zouari, 2024a; Wilson and Daugherty, 2018) that have demonstrated the negative/positive impacts of artificial intelligence on job performance. However, our findings are in line with the contribution of Toumia and Zouari (2024b). They gave three explanations for their results: (1)

Table 6. Structural path analysis results.

Relationship	Estimate	S.E.	C.R.	P-Value
AI → JP	-0.120	0.075	-1.604	0.109
Gender → JP	0.055	0.104	0.531	0.595
AI*Gender → JP	-0.020	0.075	-0.270	0.787
AI → Experience	-0.099	0.067	-1.476	0.140
Experience → JP	0.138	0.042	3.301	***

human judgment and creativity cannot be replaced by AI, (2) AI cannot replace interpersonal interactions, and (3) decision-making processes are altered by the integration of AI, which leads to job displacement in the social and economic domains (Rawashdeh, 2023). Moreover, we have found that gender has no impact on job performance ($\beta = 0.055$; $p = 0.595 > 0.05$) (hypothesis 2 is not supported). There is no consensus on the impact of gender on job performance. Some studies (Mackey et al., 2019; Shirom et al., 2008) have found that there are no significant differences in job performance between men and women (Shirom et al., 2008), while others support the effects of gender on job performance in certain areas (Abusalma, 2021; Banjo & Olufemi, 2014; Khan et al., 2022). Our result may be explained by the fact that there are no differences between men and women in terms of education, experience, funding opportunities, or cognitive capacities (i.e., problem-solving ability, creativity, etc.). Therefore, men and women are equally good at the majority of occupations. Contrary to our expectations, we found that hypothesis 3 (i.e., moderation of gender has a significant effect on the relationship between artificial intelligence and job performance) is not supported. Due to the fact that artificial intelligence is not designed to discriminate based on gender, gender has no effect on the relationship between AI and job performance. AI is a technology that can help people of all genders perform better in the workplace (i.e., AI can make workers of both genders more effective and productive). Furthermore, we found that the experience of the employee has a positive and significant effect on job performance (hypothesis 4 is supported). This implies that job performance increases with an increase in employee experience (Abusalma, 2021; McDaniel et al., 1988; Quiñones et al., 1995; Ratnawati et al., 2020; Schmidt, 1988). This is due to the fact that experienced employees are better equipped for their tasks as they have more knowledge, expertise, and skills. Finally, hypothesis 5 (mediation of experience has a significant effect on the relationship between artificial intelligence and job performance) is also not supported. Actually, artificial intelligence may be applied to enhance the job performance of workers of all experience levels (i.e., applications of artificial intelligence are not biased against employees with less experience).

5. CONCLUSION

Much attention has been given to understanding the potential impact of artificial intelligence on job performance (Abusalma, 2021; Larivière et al., 2017; Prentice et al., 2020; Wijayati et al., 2022; Wilson & Daugherty, 2018). Artificial intelligence is now integrated into nearly every industry (e.g., manufacturing, services, healthcare, etc.). Even though studies have been done on artificial intelligence and job performance, not much has been done to see the mediating effects of gender and experience. Therefore, this paper addresses the question of how artificial intelligence influences job performance. We use gender as the moderator variable and experience as the mediating variable. To answer our research question, we collected data via online questionnaires, and we used EFA, CFA, and path analysis. The findings of our study can be summarized as follows: First and foremost, as argued in previous studies, we found a significant and positive impact of experience on the job performance of Tunisian employees. Second, we showed the absence of an impact of artificial intelligence on job performance. Meanwhile, gender has no influence on job performance. Finally, we highlighted that the mediating effects of experience and the moderating effects of gender have no impact on the artificial intelligence-job performance correlation.

It is worth mentioning the major contributions of our research. First, our result depicts the fact that, while our chapter may not demonstrate a direct impact of AI on job performance, managers should be aware of the importance of artificial intelligence in their businesses. As artificial intelligence is rapidly changing the way companies operate, managers may consider the introduction and implementation of digital tools in their organizations to remain competitive. Specifically, AI is used in customer service, fraud detection, risk evaluation, etc. Second, managers must identify both internal factors (i.e., leadership, resources, and the culture of the company) and external factors (i.e., data accessibility and the regulation of the environment) that may affect the implementation of artificial intelligence. For instance, managers may need to focus more attention on small projects if the company lacks the resources to invest in artificial intelligence. Third, managers need to be aware of the negative effects of artificial intelligence on firm performance in order to mitigate them. For example, managers can help their employees learn new skills and train them in new technologies. This can reduce workers' anxiety and uncertainty about their employment prospects. They can also effectively provide information about the new technology and participate with employees in the selection and adoption of the new technology (e.g., through questionnaires, organizing brainstorming meetings, etc.). Fourth, it is crucial to acknowledge that some gender stereotypes continue to exist in the workplace. However, we found that gender does not affect job performance. Therefore, managers should prioritize the selection and promotion of the top applicants, regardless of the candidate's gender. Instead, they should make sure that every employee, regardless of gender, has access to equal opportunities and make judgments based only on each employee's performance, skills, and qualifications. Indeed, they should promote a culture that encourages gender diversity, as it can result in a staff that is more creative, motivated, and productive. In addition, the finding that job performance is positively and significantly impacted by employee experience has numerous managerial implications: (1) managers have to create a positive work environment, such as by developing programs for training; (2) they may classify employees based on their experience history to identify high-potential workers. Therefore, these high-potential workers may be considered for future leadership roles; (3) the employee experience may be greatly improved by giving workers the freedom to give feedbacks, propose ideas, decide for themselves and to accept responsibility for their job. As a results, managers should be more participative to promote engagement and satisfaction.

Nevertheless, our paper is also subject to some limitations. The first limitation is the fact that the outcomes of our research are limited to employees in Tunisia. Therefore, our work highlights an opportunity for future researchers to engage in empirical studies to investigate the impact of artificial intelligence on job performance in different countries to generate our results. First, our paper used quantitative techniques as a method of data collection and analysis; therefore, future studies may employ other techniques (i.e., case studies, interviews, longitudinal studies). For instance, longitudinal studies may track the impact of AI over time. Second, there may be gender-specific differences depending on the type of work. Thus, it would be interesting to investigate how AI could be used to automate manual tasks and how this may affect gender differences in work performance. Third, AI's effect on work performance is complicated and dependent on several variables. Future research could, for example, investigate how different AI systems such as machine learning, deep learning, and natural language processing affect different work tasks. Fourth, employees in our study came from a variety of industries (primary, secondary, and tertiary). Thus, researchers may look at how artificial intelligence affects work performance in certain sectors. In fact, the adoption of AI may have a greater influence on some industries than on others. Fifth, future studies may include other moderators/mediators' variables, such as leadership style.

REFERENCES

Abusalma, A. (2021). The effect of implementing artificial intelligence on job performance in commercial banks of Jordan. *Management Science Letters*, *11*(7), 2061–2070. doi:10.5267/j.msl.2021.3.003

Agrawal, A., Gans, J. S., & Goldfarb, A. (2019). Artificial intelligence: The ambiguous labor market impact of automating prediction. *The Journal of Economic Perspectives*, *33*(2), 31–50. doi:10.1257/jep.33.2.31

Ahn, J., Kim, J., & Sung, Y. (2022). The effect of gender stereotypes on artificial intelligence recommendations. *Journal of Business Research, 141*, 50–59. doi:10.1016/j.jbusres.2021.12.007

Al-Makhaita, H. M., Sabra, A. A., & Hafez, A. S. (2014). Job performance among nurses working in two different health care levels, Eastern Saudi Arabia: A comparative study. *International Journal of Medical Science and Public Health, 3*(7), 832–837. doi:10.5455/ijmsph.2014.240420142

Alene, E. T. (2020). Determinants that influence the performance of women entrepreneurs in micro and small enterprises in Ethiopia. *Journal of Innovation and Entrepreneurship, 9*(1), 1–20. doi:10.1186/s13731-020-00132-6

Allison, L., Liu, Y., Murtinu, S., & Wei, Z. (2023). Gender and firm performance around the world: The roles of finance, technology and labor. *Journal of Business Research, 154*, 113322. doi:10.1016/j.jbusres.2022.113322

Auerswald, M., & Moshagen, M. (2019). How to determine the number of factors to retain in exploratory factor analysis: A comparison of extraction methods under realistic conditions. *Psychological Methods, 24*(4), 468–491. doi:10.1037/met0000200 PMID:30667242

Bagozzi, R. P., & Yi, Y. (1988). On the Evaluation of Structural Equation Models. *Journal of the Academy of Marketing Science, 16*(1), 74–94. doi:10.1007/BF02723327

Banjo, H., & Olufemi, O. (2014). Demographic Variables and Job Performance: Any Link? (A Case of Insurance Salesmen). *Acta Universitatis Danubius. Economica, 10*(4), 19–30.

Benko, A., & Lányi, C. S. (2009). History of artificial intelligence. In *Encyclopedia of Information Science and Technology* (2nd ed., pp. 1759–1762). IGI Global. doi:10.4018/978-1-60566-026-4.ch276

Bentler, P. M., & Bonett, D. G. (1980). Significance tests and goodness of fit in the analysis of covariance structures. *Psychological Bulletin, 88*(3), 588–606. doi:10.1037/0033-2909.88.3.588

Bollen, K. A. (1990). Overall Fit in Covariance Structure Models: Two Types of Sample Size Effects. *Psychological Bulletin, 107*(2), 256–259. doi:10.1037/0033-2909.107.2.256

Brooks, R. A. (1991). Intelligence without representation. *Artificial Intelligence, 47*(1-3), 139–159. doi:10.1016/0004-3702(91)90053-M

Brougham, D., & Haar, J. (2018). Smart technology, artificial intelligence, robotics, and algorithms (STARA): Employees' perceptions of our future workplace. *Journal of Management & Organization*, *24*(2), 239–257. doi:10.1017/jmo.2016.55

Buhalis, D., & Leung, R. (2018). Smart hospitality—Interconnectivity and interoperability towards an ecosystem. *International Journal of Hospitality Management*, *71*, 41–50. doi:10.1016/j.ijhm.2017.11.011

Butler, M. G., & Callahan, C. M. (2014). Human resource outsourcing: Market and operating performance effects of administrative HR functions. *Journal of Business Research*, *67*(2), 218–224. doi:10.1016/j.jbusres.2012.09.026

Çalışkan, A., & Köroğlu, E. Ö. (2022). Job performance, Task performance, Contextual performance: Development and validation of a new scale. *Uluslararası İktisadi ve İdari Bilimler Dergisi*, *8*(2), 180–201. doi:10.29131/uiibd.1201880

Cellan-Jones, R. (2014). *Stephen Hawking warns artificial intelligence could end mankind*. BBC Interview, online at Retrieved from https://www.bbc.com/news/technology-30290540

Cooper, C. L. (1984). Work organization and occupational stress. *Automation, Work Organization and Occupational Stress*, 151-176.

Dewanti, H. E., & Artaya, I. P. (2019, February). The Influence of Training, Work Experience, and Competence on Employee Performance at Surabaya Husada Utama Hospital. In *Journal of World Conference (JWC)* (Vol. 1, No. 1, pp. 93-101). Doi:10.29138/prd.v1i1.27

Dormehl, L. (2018). *Replaced by robots: 10 jobs that could be hit hard by the AI revolution*. Retrieved from https://www.digitaltrends.com/cool-tech/examples-of-robots-replacing-jobs/

Duan, Y., Edwards, J. S., & Dwivedi, Y. K. (2019). Artificial intelligence for decision making in the era of Big Data–evolution, challenges and research agenda. *International Journal of Information Management*, *48*, 63–71. doi:10.1016/j.ijinfomgt.2019.01.021

Edwards, J. S., Duan, Y., & Robins, P. C. (2000). An analysis of expert systems for business decision making at different levels and in different roles. *European Journal of Information Systems*, *9*(1), 36–46. doi:10.1057/palgrave.ejis.3000344

Findlay, P., Lindsay, C., McQuarrie, J., Bennie, M., Corcoran, E. D., & Van Der Meer, R. (2017). Employer choice and job quality: Workplace innovation, work redesign, and employee perceptions of job quality in a complex health-care setting. *Work and Occupations*, *44*(1), 113–136. doi:10.1177/0730888416678038

Frey, C. B., & Osborne, M. A. (2017). The future of employment: How susceptible are jobs to computerisation? *Technological Forecasting and Social Change, 114*, 254–280. doi:10.1016/j.techfore.2016.08.019

Gabbatt, A. (2011). IBM computer Watson wins Jeopardy clash. *The Guardian, 17*.

García-Madurga, M. Á., & Grilló-Méndez, A. J. (2023). Artificial Intelligence in the Tourism Industry: An Overview of Reviews. *Administrative Sciences, 13*(8), 172. doi:10.3390/admsci13080172

Hair, J. F. Jr, Ringle, C. M., & Sarstedt, M. (2013). Partial least squares structural equation modeling: Rigorous applications, better results and higher acceptance. *Long Range Planning, 46*(1-2), 1–12. doi:10.1016/j.lrp.2013.01.001

Hair, J. F. J., Black, W. C., Babin, B. J., & Anderson, R. E. (2010). *Multivariate Data Analysis. A global perspective* (7th ed.). Prentice Hall.

Hashmi, A. R., Amirah, N. A., & Yusof, Y. (2020). Mediating effect of integrated systems on the relationship between supply chain management practices and public healthcare performance: Structural Equation Modeling. *International Journal of Management and Sustainability, 9*(3), 148–160. doi:10.18488/journal.11.2020.93.148.160

Hoque, A. S. M. M., & Awang, Z. (2019). Does gender difference play moderating role in the relationship between entrepreneurial marketing and Bangladeshi SME performance? *Accounting, 5*(1), 35–52. doi:10.5267/j.ac.2018.6.001

Hunter, J. E., & Hunter, R. F. (1984). Validity and utility of alternative predictors of job performance. *Psychological Bulletin, 96*(1), 72–98. doi:10.1037/0033-2909.96.1.72

Igbaria, M., & Shayo, C. (1997). The impact of race and gender differences on job performance evaluations and career success. *Equal Opportunities International, 16*(8), 12–23. doi:10.1108/eb010703

Jarrahi, M. H. (2018). Artificial intelligence and the future of work: Human-AI symbiosis in organizational decision making. *Business Horizons, 61*(4), 577–586. doi:10.1016/j.bushor.2018.03.007

Jia, N., Luo, X., Fang, Z., & Liao, C. (2023). *When and how artificial intelligence augments employee creativity. Academy of Management Journal.* doi:10.5465/amj.2022.0426

Joecks, J., Pull, K., & Vetter, K. (2013). Gender diversity in the boardroom and firm performance: What exactly constitutes a "critical mass?" *Journal of Business Ethics, 118*(1), 61–72. doi:10.1007/s10551-012-1553-6

Jöreskog, K. G. (1969). A general approach to confirmatory maximum likelihood factor analysis. *Psychometrika, 34*(2), 183–202. doi:10.1007/BF02289343

Jöreskog, K. G., & Sörbom, D. (1993). *LISREL 8: Structural equation modeling with the SIMPLIS command language*. Scientific Software International.

Kaiser, H. F. (1958). The varimax criterion for analytic rotation in factor analysis. *Psychometrika, 23*(3), 187–200. doi:10.1007/BF02289233

Kaiser, H. F. (1960). The application of electronic computers to factor analysis. *Educational and Psychological Measurement, 20*(1), 141–151. doi:10.1177/001316446002000116

Kaiser, H. F. (1974). An index of factorial simplicity. *Psychometrika, 39*(1), 31-36. doi:10.1007/BF02291575

Kanter, R. M. (1977). Men and women of the corporation: New edition. Basic Books.

Kaplan, A., & Haenlein, M. (2019). Siri, Siri, in my hand: Who's the fairest in the land? On the interpretations, illustrations, and implications of artificial intelligence. *Business Horizons, 62*(1), 15–25. doi:10.1016/j.bushor.2018.08.004

Khan, S., Rasheed, R., Rashid, A., Abbas, Q., & Mahboob, F. (2022). The effect of demographic characteristics on job performance: An empirical study from Pakistan. *The Journal of Asian Finance. Economics and Business, 9*(2), 283–294. doi:10.13106/jafeb.2022.vol9.no2.0283

Khan, W. A., & Vieito, J. P. (2013). CEO gender and firm performance. *Journal of Economics and Business, 67*, 55–66. doi:10.1016/j.jeconbus.2013.01.003

Kiefer, K., Heileman, M., & Pett, T. L. (2022). Does gender still matter? An examination of small business performance. *Small Business Economics, 58*(1), 141–167. doi:10.1007/s11187-020-00403-2

Kim, S. Y. (2011). Prediction of hotel bankruptcy using support vector machine, artificial neural network, logistic regression, and multivariate discriminant analysis. *Service Industries Journal, 31*(3), 441–468. doi:10.1080/02642060802712848

Kline, R. B. (1998). *Structural equation modeling*. Guilford.

Koch, C. (2016). How the computer beat the go player. *Scientific American Mind, 27*(4), 20–23. doi:10.1038/scientificamericanmind0716-20

Koo, B., Curtis, C., & Ryan, B. (2021). Examining the impact of artificial intelligence on hotel employees through job insecurity perspectives. *International Journal of Hospitality Management, 95*, 102763. doi:10.1016/j.ijhm.2020.102763

Kumar, V., Rajan, B., Venkatesan, R., & Lecinski, J. (2019). Understanding the role of artificial intelligence in personalized engagement marketing. *California Management Review*, *61*(4), 135–155. doi:10.1177/0008125619859317

Larivière, B., Bowen, D., Andreassen, T. W., Kunz, W., Sirianni, N. J., Voss, C., Wunderlich, N. V., & De Keyser, A. (2017). "Service Encounter 2.0": An investigation into the roles of technology, employees and customers. *Journal of Business Research*, *79*(C), 238–246. doi:10.1016/j.jbusres.2017.03.008

Li, J., Bonn, M. A., & Ye, B. H. (2019). Hotel employee's artificial intelligence and robotics awareness and its impact on turnover intention: The moderating roles of perceived organizational support and competitive psychological climate. *Tourism Management*, *73*, 172–18. doi:10.1016/j.tourman.2019.02.006

Mackey, J. D., Roth, P. L., Van Iddekinge, C. H., & McFarland, L. A. (2019). A meta-analysis of gender proportionality effects on job performance. *Group & Organization Management*, *44*(3), 578–610. doi:10.1177/1059601117730519

McDaniel, M. A., Schmidt, F. L., & Hunter, J. E. (1988). Job experience correlates of job performance. *The Journal of Applied Psychology*, *73*(2), 327–330. doi:10.1037/0021-9010.73.2.327 PMID:21261409

Miller, S. M. (2018). AI: Augmentation, more so than automation. *Asian Management Insights*, *5*(1), 1–20.

Mohammadi, V., & Minaei, S. (2019). Artificial intelligence in the production process. In *Engineering tools in the beverage industry* (pp. 27–63). Woodhead Publishing. doi:10.1016/B978-0-12-815258-4.00002-0

Nam, K., Dutt, C. S., Chathoth, P., Daghfous, A., & Khan, M. S. (2021). The adoption of artificial intelligence and robotics in the hotel industry: Prospects and challenges. *Electronic Markets*, *31*(3), 553–574. doi:10.1007/s12525-020-00442-3

Ng, T. W., & Feldman, D. C. (2010). The relationships of age with job attitudes: A meta-analysis. *Personnel Psychology*, *63*(3), 677–718. doi:10.1111/j.1744-6570.2010.01184.x

Prentice, C. (2019). *Emotional intelligence and marketing*. World Scientific Publishing Co. Pte, Ltd. doi:10.1142/11363

Prentice, C., Dominique Lopes, S., & Wang, X. (2020). Emotional intelligence or artificial intelligence–an employee perspective. *Journal of Hospitality Marketing & Management*, *29*(4), 377–403. doi:10.1080/19368623.2019.1647124

Quiñones, M. A., Ford, J. K., & Teachout, M. S. (1995). The relationship between work experience and job performance: A conceptual and meta-analytic review. *Personnel Psychology*, *48*(4), 887–910. doi:10.1111/j.1744-6570.1995.tb01785.x

Ratnawati, E., Sukidjo, S., & Efendi, R. (2020). The Effect of Work Motivation and Work Experience on Employee Performance. *International Journal of Multicultural and Multireligious Understanding*, *7*(8), 109–116. doi:10.18415/ijmmu.v7i8.1809

Rawashdeh, A. (2023). The consequences of artificial intelligence: an investigation into the impact of AI on job displacement in accounting. *Journal of Science and Technology Policy Management*. doi:10.1108/JSTPM-02-2023-0030

Rawlinson, K. (2015). Microsoft's Bill Gates insists AI is a threat. *BBC News*.

Russell, S. (2016). *Artificial Intelligence: A Modern Approach, eBook* (Global Edition). Pearson Education, Limited.

Rydstedt, L. W., Johansson, G., & Evans, G. W. (1998). A longitudinal study of workload, health and well-being among male and female urban bus drivers. *Journal of Occupational and Organizational Psychology*, *71*(1), 35–45. doi:10.1111/j.2044-8325.1998.tb00661.x

Samuel, Y., George, J., & Samuel, J. (2020). Beyond stem, how can women engage big data, analytics, robotics and artificial intelligence? an exploratory analysis of confidence and educational factors in the emerging technology waves influencing the role of, and impact upon, women. *arXiv preprint arXiv:2003.11746*.

Schmidt, F. L., Hunter, J. E., Outerbridge, A. N., & Goff, S. (1988). Joint relation of experience and ability with job performance: Test of three hypotheses. *The Journal of Applied Psychology*, *73*(1), 46–57. doi:10.1037/0021-9010.73.1.46

Shahzad, M. F., Xu, S., Naveed, W., Nusrat, S., & Zahid, I. (2023). Investigating the impact of artificial intelligence on human resource functions in the health sector of China: A mediated moderation model. *Heliyon*, *9*(11), e21818. doi:10.1016/j.heliyon.2023.e21818 PMID:38034787

Shaw, J., Rudzicz, F., Jamieson, T., & Goldfarb, A. (2019). Artificial intelligence and the implementation challenge. *Journal of Medical Internet Research*, *21*(7), e13659. https://preprints.jmir.org/preprint/13659. doi:10.2196/13659 PMID:31293245

Shirom, A., Shechter Gilboa, S., Fried, Y., & Cooper, C. L. (2008). Gender, age and tenure as moderators of work-related stressors' relationships with job performance: A meta-analysis. *Human Relations*, *61*(10), 1371–1398. doi:10.1177/0018726708095708

Spencer, M. K. (2018, April 27). *Will AI replace humans?* Retrieved from https://medium.com/ futuresin/will-ai-replace-humans-42c19c114cb8

Toumia, O., & Zouari, F. (2024a). Artificial Intelligence and Venture Capital Decision-Making. In R. Sharma, K. Mehta, & P. Yu (Eds.), *Fostering Innovation in Venture Capital and Startup Ecosystems*. IGI Global. doi:10.4018/979-8-3693-1326-8.ch002

Toumia, O., & Zouari, F. (2024b). Effect of Artificial Intelligence Awareness on Job Performance with Employee Experience as a Mediating Variable. In O. Meçik (Ed.), *Reskilling the Workforce for Technological Advancement* (pp. 141–161). IGI Global. doi:10.4018/979-8-3693-0612-3.ch007

Tuomi, I. (2019). *The Impact of Artificial Intelligence on Learning, Teaching, and Education: Policies for the Future. JRC Science for Policy Report*. European Commission. doi:10.2760/12297

Vrontis, D., Christofi, M., Pereira, V., Tarba, S., Makrides, A., & Trichina, E. (2022). Artificial intelligence, robotics, advanced technologies and human resource management: A systematic review. *International Journal of Human Resource Management*, *33*(6), 1237–1266. doi:10.1080/09585192.2020.1871398

WebbM. (2019). The impact of artificial intelligence on the labor market. *Available at* SSRN 3482150. doi:10.2139/ssrn.3482150

Wijayati, D. T., Rahman, Z., Rahman, M. F. W., Arifah, I. D. C., & Kautsar, A. (2022). A study of artificial intelligence on employee performance and work engagement: The moderating role of change leadership. *International Journal of Manpower*, *43*(2), 486–512. doi:10.1108/IJM-07-2021-0423

Wilson, H. J., & Daugherty, P. R. (2018). Collaborative intelligence: Humans and AI are joining forces. *Harvard Business Review*, *96*(4), 114–123.

Yetgin, M. A., & Toumia, O. (2023). *Perceptions of Employees of Technology Emerging With Generative Pre-Trained Transformer-3 in Organizations*. Gazi Kitabevi.

Younus, A. M. (2021). Utilization Of Artificial Intelligence (Ann) In Project Management Services: A Proposed Model of Application. *Central Asian Journal of Theoretical and Applied Science*, *2*(10), 121–131.

Yu, G., & Schwartz, Z. (2006). Forecasting short time-series tourism demand with artificial intelligence models. *Journal of Travel Research*, *45*(2), 194–203. doi:10.1177/0047287506291594

Zeba, G., Dabić, M., Čičak, M., Daim, T., & Yalcin, H. (2021). Technology mining: Artificial intelligence in manufacturing. *Technological Forecasting and Social Change*, *171*, 120971. doi:10.1016/j.techfore.2021.120971

Zel, S., & Kongar, E. (2020, September). Transforming digital employee experience with artificial intelligence. In *2020 IEEE/ITU International Conference on Artificial Intelligence for Good (AI4G)* (pp. 176-179). IEEE. 10.1109/AI4G50087.2020.9311088

Zhang, R., Yao, X., Ye, L., & Chen, M. (2022). Students' adaptive deep learning path and teaching strategy of contemporary ceramic art under the background of Internet+. *Frontiers in Psychology*, *13*, 938840. doi:10.3389/fpsyg.2022.938840 PMID:36118465

Złotowski, J., Yogeeswaran, K., & Bartneck, C. (2017). Can we control it? Autonomous robots threaten human identity, uniqueness, safety, and resources. *International Journal of Human-Computer Studies*, *100*, 48–54. doi:10.1016/j.ijhcs.2016.12.008

Zouari, F. (2019). Neural network based adaptive backstepping dynamic surface control of drug dosage regimens in cancer treatment. *Neurocomputing*, *366*, 248–263. doi:10.1016/j.neucom.2019.07.096

KEY TERMS AND DEFINITIONS

Artificial Intelligence: The capacity of a machine to imitate the human intellect.

Confirmatory Factor Analysis: This is a statistical method for testing hypotheses about the basic structure of a data set. It may also be applied to evaluate the reliability of measuring instruments.

Exploratory Factor Analysis: It is statistical technique for figuring out a group of variables' underlying structure. It is usually used when the researcher does not know the number or nature of the factors.

Job Performance: The extent to which an employee meets or exceeds employment requirements.

Mediator Variable: A variable that clarifies the relationship between the independent and dependent variables.

Moderator Variable: A variable that modifies the degree of the correlation between a dependent and independent variable.

Structural Equation Modeling: It is a statistical method for investigating complex correlations between variables. This method combines factor analysis and multiple regression analysis.

Chapter 6
The Influence of Artificial Intelligence on Advertising

Milda Budėnaitė
ISM University of Management and Economics, Lithuania

Ricardo Correia
https://orcid.org/0000-0002-0132-4002
Instituto Politécnico de Bragança, Portugal & CiTUR, Portugal

Dominyka Venciūtė
ISM University of Management and Economics, Lithuania

ABSTRACT

This chapter explores the profound influence of artificial intelligence (AI) on advertising, covering its historical context, current trends, and future implications. Initially, advertising relied on manual data analysis, but AI has shifted the landscape towards more targeted campaigns. AI's role began with predictive analytics for weather forecasting in the 1950s and evolved to include collaborative filtering by companies like Amazon. Current trends include hyper-personalization through predictive analytics, programmatic ad buying, and conversational AI. These AI-driven strategies enhance user experience and improve ad targeting. The future promises even greater personalization, with advancements in voice and visual search. However, ethical considerations regarding privacy and data security have also emerged. This analysis underscores the transformative impact of AI on advertising, from its inception to its current state, highlighting the continuous evolution and future prospects.

DOI: 10.4018/979-8-3693-2153-9.ch006

1. INTRODUCTION

In the contemporary era, artificial intelligence (AI) algorithms have profoundly transformed consumer behavior and brand engagement strategies, marking a pivotal shift in the advertising domain. These algorithms, renowned for their ability to decipher consumer buying patterns with astonishing accuracy, have ushered in a new paradigm where hyper-personalized product suggestions and predictive analytics redefine the essence of targeted marketing (Gao et al., 2023). As algorithms process vast datasets at unprecedented speeds, advertisers are afforded the unique ability to tailor their messaging to individual preferences, eliciting a mix of admiration for the convenience provided and apprehension regarding privacy concerns (Hanlon & Jones, 2023).

This chapter endeavors to meticulously examine the multifaceted impact of artificial intelligence on advertising. It will traverse the historical evolution of AI in this sector, delineate the current trends shaping its application, scrutinize the challenges and opportunities it presents, and prognosticate its future trajectory. Artificial intelligence, characterized by the emulation of human cognitive processes through computational means, finds application across a spectrum of domains including expert systems, natural language processing, speech recognition, and machine vision (Laskowski & Tucci, 2023). In the context of advertising, AI encompasses the deployment of computerized systems to execute tasks traditionally necessitating human intelligence, such as data analysis, predictive modeling, and pattern detection. At its core, AI-driven advertising leverages extensive datasets—encompassing consumer behavior patterns to market dynamics—to unearth insights that might elude human analysis. Consequently, this technology enables the crafting of advertising campaigns that are not only more targeted but also remarkably personalized, enhancing their efficacy and resonance with the intended audience (Nunez, 2023).

2. HISTORICAL CONTEXT

To encapsulate the transformative trajectory of artificial intelligence (AI) within the advertising realm, it is imperative to commence with a pre-AI baseline of the advertising industry. The metamorphosis of AI from a concept of science fiction to an indispensable tool across multiple sectors illustrates a profound evolution. Historically, the advertising domain was markedly manual, with marketers depending on demographic segmentation and rudimentary data analysis for customer targeting (Kietzmann et al., 2018). This era was characterized by a reliance on generalized advertising methods, which, while broad in reach, often resulted in suboptimal conversion rates and return on investment due to their lack of personalization (Elhager, 2023).

The advent of AI heralded a new epoch in advertising, marked by a gradual yet undeniable shift towards data-driven, automated processes. Goldberg L. (2018) provides an insightful examination into the chronological adoption and impact of AI in advertising. A notable early instance of AI's potential impact on consumer behavior can be traced back to the weather prediction software developed in 1950 by Jule Gregory Charney, an American meteorologist. This pioneering application of predictive analytics not only revolutionized weather reporting but also enabled advertisers to tailor product promotions in alignment with weather conditions, thereby enhancing the efficiency and relevance of their campaigns (Huang & Rust 2021).

Further developments in AI technology facilitated the emergence of more sophisticated targeting strategies. For instance, the concept of predictive behavior modeling, introduced by Swedish computational linguist Jussi Karlgren, laid the groundwork for contemporary recommendation systems utilized by leading digital platforms like Amazon, Facebook, Netflix, and Spotify. These systems leverage collaborative filtering and other AI-driven methodologies to offer personalized suggestions, thereby significantly enhancing user engagement and satisfaction.

The evolution of AI in advertising reflects a broader trend towards more intelligent, data-driven decision-making processes. This shift has not only improved the precision and effectiveness of advertising strategies but has also redefined the boundaries of marketing by enabling a level of personalization and responsiveness previously unattainable. As AI continues to evolve, its role in advertising is expected to deepen, offering unprecedented opportunities for innovation and engagement in the digital age (Kietzmann et al., 2018).

In 2013, AI was first targeted to reduce the labour of content creation. More content equals more advertising chances, as content marketing gains popularity. But considering the number of advertisements and viewers available, excellent journalism is thought to be excessively sluggish in both cost and velocity. The resolution: Yahoo! Sports Automated Insights Wordsmith Platform (now part of Verizon) to scan billions of sports-related data points every day and organise the data into computer-generated articles that provide numbers, inform fantasy sports followers, and summarise games. Articles with AI are created at a pace and scope that human journalists could never match. The AI generates text in clear, human-sounding language and modifies it based on personality and tone, giving each article a distinct journalistic viewpoint.

The evolution of artificial intelligence (AI) within the realm of advertising represents a paradigm shift from traditional, labor-intensive processes to highly automated and efficient methodologies. This transformation is particularly evident with the advent of programmatic ad purchasing in 2014, a milestone that introduced an AI-driven approach to ad buying. This innovation streamlined the advertising process by automating the tasks of market research, budget allocation, and analytics tracking, thereby reducing the cost and time previously required.

Programmatic advertising epitomizes a marketplace model for the digital buying and selling of ads, where intelligent technologies autonomously manage the procurement process based on predefined campaign objectives. By 2023, the value of programmatic advertising reached approximately $546 billion, underscoring its widespread acceptance and the significant role it plays in digital marketing strategies (Statista, 2023). This rapid adoption illustrates the transition from utilizing programmatic buying for unsold ad inventory to its recognition as a standard practice among digital publishers.

The role of AI in enhancing search engine capabilities cannot be overstated. Since the early 2000s, AI has been instrumental in generating more accurate search results. A notable development was Google's introduction of RankBrain in 2015, an AI system that revolutionized the interpretation of search queries through advanced linguistic analysis. RankBrain enabled Google to discern the intent behind a user's search, thereby delivering more relevant results by mapping unknown terms to known contexts using a vast mathematical database of language patterns (Sullivan, 2015).

The integration of AI in voice recognition technology further exemplifies the expanding applications of AI in advertising. The launch of virtual assistant devices like Google Home, Amazon Echo, and Apple's Siri in 2016 opened new avenues for voice-activated advertising, catering to the needs of approximately 71 million users. Concurrently, AI began to be utilized in messaging platforms such as Facebook Messenger, WhatsApp, and Slack to streamline customer service operations. AI-powered chatbots, operating under human supervision, could engage in conversations and respond to inquiries by analyzing user inputs, significantly reducing the labor and costs associated with customer service (Kumar et al., 2016).

In summary, the historical trajectory of AI in advertising reflects the industry's adaptability and commitment to leveraging technological advancements to enhance operational efficiency and consumer engagement. AI has fundamentally transformed the advertising landscape, enabling marketers to deploy more targeted and effective campaigns. This evolution from rudimentary applications to sophisticated, AI-driven solutions underscores the transformative impact of AI on advertising strategies, offering unprecedented opportunities to engage with and understand the target audience.

3. CURRENT TRENDS

Following an in-depth exploration of the historical evolution of artificial intelligence (AI) within the advertising sector, it is pivotal to turn our analytical lens towards the present milieu. This section aims to scrutinize the contemporary advancements and applications of AI in advertising, through a critical examination of case studies and empirical instances that illustrate how marketers of today are harnessing AI to forge advertising strategies that are not only pertinent but also engaging, thereby elucidating the revolutionary capacities of the technology.

An analysis of the distribution of AI application across various marketing strategies offers insightful revelations about prevailing trends in the domain of AI-driven advertising. This analytical perspective facilitates an understanding of how AI is being prioritized and integrated into marketing strategies (Figure 1), reflecting on the technology's profound impact on contemporary advertising practices.

Central to the discourse on the modern utilization of artificial intelligence (AI) in advertising is the concept of predictive analytics-based hyper-personalization. This methodology epitomizes the strategic employment of AI to analyze user behavior, preferences, and historical data with the objective of forecasting future consumer behaviors. A quintessential example of this application is observed in e-commerce platforms such as Amazon, which leverages AI to deduce consumer preferences from their historical purchasing patterns. This enables Amazon to present product recommendations uniquely tailored to

Figure 1. Top AI marketing use cases
Source (Carter, 2023)

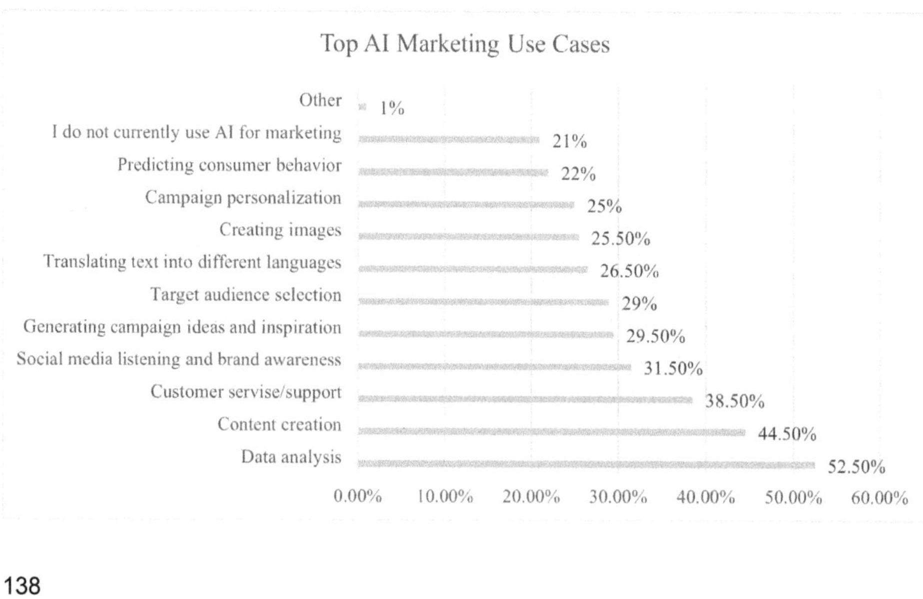

individual user interests, thereby augmenting the likelihood of conversion and enhancing the overall user experience.

Amazon's mastery in deploying product suggestions as a potent marketing instrument is evident in its utilization of tags like "recommended for you" or "customers also bought". These tags facilitate the compilation of personalized product recommendations following a purchase or when an item is added to a shopping cart. Such strategies are ingeniously designed to incentivize consumers to augment the value of their shopping carts, thereby driving sales. The customization of AI-powered product recommendations for each consumer underscores the platform's commitment to delivering relevant product suggestions, aiming to resonate with the consumer's preferences and interests.

The operational mechanism behind Amazon's recommendation system, which utilizes item-to-item collaborative filtering, is particularly noteworthy. This system is adept at analyzing extensive datasets, discerning correlations and dependencies between products beyond mere product descriptions. By harnessing the capabilities of AI to sift through and interpret vast amounts of data, Amazon's recommendation engine effectively transforms passive browsing into an active and dynamic shopping experience. The engine's ability to proactively anticipate consumer needs and offer pertinent suggestions based on a comprehensive analysis of past consumer interactions, such as search history, recent purchases, and viewed products, is a testament to the transformative power of AI in revitalizing online retail platforms into vibrant sales channels (Dresma, 2022).

Secondly, the ongoing development of programmatic advertising marks a significant phase in the evolution of digital marketing, wherein artificial intelligence (AI) plays a pivotal role in automating the procurement and distribution of advertisement inventory. Central to this process is the AI's capability to instantaneously analyze vast datasets, thereby facilitating rapid decision-making concerning the placement of advertisements. A salient example of this AI application is manifested in the form of smart bidding, an automated bidding strategy propelled by AI that seeks to optimize bids for conversions across platforms such as Google Ads. This technological advancement ensures that advertisements are delivered to the appropriate audience at the most opportune moments, thereby maximizing the efficiency of advertisement expenditure and heralding a new era of precision in digital advertising strategies (Davenport et al., 2020).

Thirdly, the advent of conversational AI, epitomized by the integration of chatbots and virtual assistants, heralds a significant trend within the advertising sector. This trend is underscored by a WebFX survey, which reveals that 38.5% of marketers now deploy AI to enhance consumer interactions through these technologies. Conversational AI stands out for its ability to engage with consumers in real-time, providing personalized recommendations, addressing inquiries, and facilitating a seamless customer journey. For instance, renowned apparel companies such as H&M leverage chatbots on their websites to streamline the shopping experience, guiding customers to apparel and accessories that align with their preferences.

Furthermore, AI is catalyzing a transformative shift in the creative domains of advertising by enabling the generation of excellent, contextually relevant content. A paradigmatic example of this innovation is the GPT-4 language model developed by OpenAI, which has significantly impacted the advertising field. Through this advanced AI model, advertisers are equipped to craft compelling email content, social media posts, and advertising copy. This not only streamlines the content creation process but also ensures that the output resonates with the brand's voice and effectively engages the target audience, thereby redefining the intersection between creativity and AI-driven automation in advertising.

Additionally, the integration of AI-powered image identification technologies into advertising platforms, notably on social media sites such as Pinterest and Instagram, has marked a significant advancement in the realm of digital marketing. These AI systems excel in analyzing images to discern their context and content, thereby enabling more precise ad targeting. This innovation underscores the shift towards leveraging AI for enhancing the relevance and effectiveness of advertising content presented to users.

Furthermore, augmented reality (AR) represents another burgeoning trend within the advertising sector, driven by the aim to offer immersive and interactive consumer experiences. An exemplary application of this technology is seen in an AR application developed by IKEA, which permits customers to visualize furniture arrangements within their actual living spaces prior to making purchase decisions. This not only enhances the shopping experience but also aids in making more informed purchasing choices (Thompson, n.d.).

Moreover, the optimization of advertising for voice search has emerged as a critical development, propelled by the widespread adoption of speech-activated devices, such as smart speakers. AI-driven voice recognition systems have significantly improved the interpretation of user queries, thereby refining the targeting mechanisms of advertisements. A notable example of a company adapting to this trend is Domino's Pizza, which has integrated AI into its voice-activated ordering system. Through its virtual assistant, Dom, Domino's introduced voice ordering capabilities, allowing customers to place orders via mobile devices and smart home systems using simple voice commands. The launch of AnyWare in 2015 further expanded this functionality, enabling pizza orders through voice commands on a variety of platforms including Siri and Amazon Echo. By aligning its service offerings with the increasing consumer preference for speech-activated devices and voice search, Domino's has effectively distinguished itself in a competitive market, showcasing the strategic application of speech AI technology to facilitate a convenient and hands-free ordering experience (Westwater, 2023).

The domain of influencer marketing is also experiencing a notable transformation through the integration of artificial intelligence (AI), as elucidated by the co-founder and CEO of SocialPubli, an acclaimed influencer marketing platform, Qudsi (2023). This innovative application of AI aids businesses in identifying the most suitable influencers for their marketing campaigns by analyzing social media content to assess the demographics, reach, and engagement levels of influencers. Such an approach enables marketers to optimize the impact of their influencer partnerships by aligning with individuals whose follower base mirrors their target audience closely. Moreover, influencers are leveraging AI to enhance their content creation process, employing AI algorithms for brainstorming content ideas and utilizing AI-powered tools for content generation, editing, and even background removal. This technological empowerment allows influencers to succinctly articulate their creative requirements, enabling AI to produce visually compelling graphics on their behalf. Artificial intelligence (AI) has also introduced virtual influencers, which compete with traditional human influencers and reshape digital marketing. Kim & Park (2024) highlight their growing popularity, emphasizing how these AI-created personas offer brands innovative engagement opportunities.

Concurrently, as the sophistication of AI applications in advertising escalates, the importance of ethical considerations and consumer privacy has become increasingly pronounced. The advertising industry is witnessing a heightened focus on transparency and consent in data collection practices, influenced by regulatory frameworks such as the General Data Protection Regulation (GDPR) and the California Consumer Privacy Act (CCPA). These regulations are steering the development of AI systems towards prioritizing user privacy. Leading companies, including Apple, are accentuating privacy features within their advertising ecosystems as a strategy to foster consumer trust.

In summary, the landscape of AI applications in advertising is marked by rapid evolution and innovation, as evidenced by the current trends. Advertisers are harnessing the power of AI to craft more potent and personalized advertising strategies, spanning from hyper-personalization and conversational AI to the pivotal considerations of ethics and privacy. The real-world applications of these trends by industry leaders illustrate a shifting advertising paradigm, one that offers consumers a more customized and engaging experience.

4. CHALLENGES AND OPPORTUNITIES

The advent of artificial intelligence (AI) in the realm of advertising heralds a plethora of opportunities, underscoring the transformative potential of technology in enhancing marketing strategies and consumer engagement. The implications of AI in advertising span various dimensions, notably in personalization, efficiency, and ethical advertising practices, each contributing to the dynamic landscape of contemporary advertising (Davenport et al., 2020).

Foremost among the myriad opportunities heralded by artificial intelligence (AI) in the domain of advertising is the significant enhancement of personalization and targeting precision. AI empowers advertisers with the capability to tailor content with an unprecedented level of specificity to individual consumer preferences and behaviors, thereby markedly improving the user experience. A prime illustration of this application is evident in Amazon's utilization of AI algorithms within its recommendation engine. These algorithms meticulously analyze users' purchase histories and browsing behaviors, enabling a highly personalized content delivery strategy. Such a method of personalization has been instrumental in driving increased sales and elevating customer satisfaction, thereby exemplifying the transformative potential of AI-driven personalization in the landscape of e-commerce advertising (Hardesty, 2019).

Subsequent to the exploration of personalization, a pivotal opportunity presented by artificial intelligence (AI) in advertising emerges in the realms of enhanced efficiency and campaign effectiveness. AI-driven automation stands at the forefront of revolutionizing advertising processes, particularly within the ambit of programmatic advertising. An exemplary instance of this is observed in Netflix's application of AI to refine content recommendations and customize its homepage uniquely for each user. This technological advancement not only bolsters user engagement but also epitomizes the capacity of AI to streamline content delivery and amplify the overall effectiveness of advertising campaigns (Jebara, 2018).

Moreover, the discourse extends into the domain of ethical advertising practices. AI introduces a paradigm shift towards more ethical advertising methodologies by ensuring fairness, transparency, and adherence to ethical standards. The Unilever 'Unstereotype' initiative exemplifies this transition, employing AI to scrutinize advertisements for gender biases. Through the strategic use of AI tools, Unilever endeavors to dispel stereotypical representations within advertising, thereby fostering a landscape characterized by more inclusive and ethically conscientious content (Unilever, 2021).

The integration of AI in addressing some of the advertising industry's paramount challenges demonstrates its instrumental role. By processing extensive datasets, discerning trends and patterns, and extracting actionable insights, AI acts as a linchpin in surmounting obstacles and heralding a new era of advertising that is not only efficient and effective but also ethically grounded.

As artificial intelligence (AI) garners prominence within the advertising sector, facilitating unparalleled insights and optimization through data analysis, it concurrently navigates a spectrum of challenges and ethical dilemmas, especially concerning adoption. Privacy and data security emerge as paramount concerns. The nuanced process of personalizing advertising by collecting and processing user data engenders significant privacy apprehensions, underscored by the peril of data breaches and unauthorized access, which jeopardize user trust. A notable incident underscoring this challenge is the 2018 Facebook data breach scandal involving Cambridge Analytica, where unauthorized exploitation of user data spotlighted the potential for misuse of personal information in targeted advertising, catalyzing demands for augmented data privacy measures (Confessore, 2018).

Furthermore, the issue of bias in algorithmic decision-making represents a critical hurdle. Inherent biases within AI algorithms can precipitate discriminatory outcomes, particularly manifest in targeted advertising. This phenomenon may result in the unjust exclusion or inclusion of certain demographics based on biased datasets. ProPublica's investigation into discriminatory ad targeting practices on Facebook illustrates this predicament, revealing how certain ethnic groups were disproportionately excluded from housing ad campaigns, thereby unveiling the unintended discriminatory implications of biased algorithmic frameworks in advertising (Kofman & Tobin, 2019).

Moreover, the integration of AI in advertising introduces substantial concerns regarding ad fraud and manipulation. The automated nature of programmatic advertising, while efficient, renders it vulnerable to exploitation by nefarious entities aiming to fabricate false impressions and clicks. This manipulation culminates in financial losses for advertisers. The Methbot operation serves as a salient example, orchestrating fake impressions and clicks on video ads and inflicting significant financial damage on advertisers, thus highlighting the persistent challenge of identifying and mitigating ad fraud within the AI-centric advertising landscape (Kargl, 2022).

Lastly, the implementation of AI entails significant financial considerations, particularly for small and medium-sized enterprises (SMEs). The acquisition and maintenance of AI technologies, coupled with the requisite investment in specialized personnel, can pose prohibitive costs, potentially impeding the widespread adoption of AI within these business sectors (Gordon, 2023).

In essence, while AI presents transformative opportunities for the advertising industry, it also demands meticulous attention to privacy, ethical standards, and financial accessibility to ensure its beneficial integration and mitigate the inherent risks associated with its adoption.

5. FUTURE IMPLICATIONS

In the evolving landscape of marketing, the advent and integration of artificial intelligence (AI) stand as a transformative force, heralding significant shifts in strategies and consumer interactions. Presently, the penetration of AI in marketing practices is notable, with empirical evidence suggesting that half of the marketing professionals are already utilizing AI technologies, and an additional 29% are contemplating its future incorporation. Merely a fraction, 9.5%, remain aloof from this trend (Carter, 2023), underscoring the widespread acceptance and anticipated growth of AI applications in marketing spheres.

Firstly, it is very likely that personalization will increase. As articulated by Thakur (2023), the deployment of AI for scrutinizing customer behaviors, preferences, and prior engagements offers marketers the leverage to predict future actions and tailor recommendations with unprecedented precision. This paradigm shift towards individualized content and experiences signifies a departure from generic marketing tactics, emphasizing the critical role of AI in enhancing customer engagement and satisfaction (Davenport et al., 2020).

Secondly, the realms of search engine optimization (SEO) are witnessing a concurrent revolution in visual and voice search modalities, propelled by AI innovations. Brands that have adapted their online content for visual and voice search are experiencing enhanced visibility and engagement, a testament to the evolving consumer search behaviors and the necessity for SEO strategies to accommodate voice search commands and visual content discovery (Nabavieh, 2023). This evolution necessitates a reevaluation of content optimization practices, prioritizing the alignment with natural language patterns and user intent, thereby refining the relevance and accessibility of search results.

Thirdly the potential of AI in predictive marketing offers a forward-looking perspective on customer relationship management. AI's capability to analyze extensive datasets for predicting purchase behaviors, churn rates, and loyalty patterns equips marketers with the foresight to craft targeted campaigns that significantly improve conversion rates (Thakur, 2023). This anticipatory approach, grounded in data-driven insights, heralds a new era of strategic marketing that not only responds to but anticipates consumer needs and preferences.

The integration of artificial intelligence (AI) into marketing strategies introduces a myriad of ethical considerations that are poised to shape the trajectory of its future application. As customer awareness regarding data privacy and algorithmic biases intensifies, the ethical deployment of AI in marketing becomes a pivotal concern. Marketers are compelled to prioritize transparency and accountability in their use of AI algorithms and data handling practices. This necessitates offering consumers the option to opt-out of data collection, alongside clear explanations regarding the operation of AI algorithms and the rationale behind data collection efforts. Ensuring bias reduction is paramount to fostering ethical AI marketing strategies, thereby promoting fairness and avoiding prejudiced outcomes.

To protect sensitive information, adherence to regulatory frameworks such as the General Data Protection Regulation (GDPR) is mandatory, necessitating robust data security protocols. The principle of informed consent, which requires obtaining consumer approval prior to the collection and use of personal data for advertising purposes, is fundamental to ethical AI marketing endeavors. Ethical AI utilization mandates the avoidance of deceptive or manipulative tactics that exploit consumer vulnerabilities, emphasizing the importance of prioritizing consumer welfare and autonomy over exploitative practices. The discourse on ethical AI marketing extends to the implications of generative AI, as highlighted by Apotheker (2023). Generative AI is posited to revolutionize advertising, permeating all facets of business operations and altering marketing methodologies. Research conducted by the Boston Consulting Group and Harvard suggests that tools such as ChatGPT can augment the cognitive processes associated with creative tasks, enhancing marketers' efficiency in content creation and idea generation by up to 40%. This underscores the potential of generative AI to catalyze a productivity revolution within marketing, provided that consumer engagement remains central to content dissemination strategies. However, this technological advancement also raises concerns regarding content saturation and the potential homogenization of creative outputs due to the reliance on historical data for training generative AI models. Thus, while generative AI harbors transformative potential for the marketing sector, the indispensable role of human creativity in problem-solving and innovation remains unequivocal.

6 CONCLUSION

The advent of artificial intelligence (AI) in the advertising domain has heralded a transformative era, distinctly influencing consumer engagement and the paradigms of brand promotion. This profound impact is particularly evidenced by the blurring lines between targeted marketing and predictive insights, where AI's prowess in processing vast datasets—from market trends to intricate consumer behavior patterns—facilitates the generation of highly individualized, targeted, and efficacious advertising campaigns.

Tracing the lineage of AI's application in advertising reveals its inception in the 1950s, initially employed for weather forecasting. The evolution of AI technology has since significantly advanced, enabling the aggregation of consumer behaviors to forecast future activities. This advancement affords marketers unprecedented precision and speed in targeting their audience, alongside streamlining advertising operations and mitigating the labor-intensive aspects of content creation.

The integration of AI into search engines since the early 2000s, enhancing the accuracy of search results and the interpretation of queries, marks a pivotal development in digital marketing. Notably, the application of AI in customer service since 2016—to reduce the reliance on human labor for routine inquiries—illustrates the broadening scope of AI in refining advertising strategies and operational efficiency.

The landscape of advertising has been notably reshaped by three key AI-driven innovations: programmatic advertising, conversational AI, and hyper-personalization through predictive analytics. These developments reflect a dynamic and rapidly evolving state of AI application in advertising, shifting towards more personalized, engaging, and ethically conscious advertising solutions. The capacity of AI to engender highly customized ads is underscored by real-world examples from industry leaders, showcasing the transformative potential of these AI applications in enhancing consumer experiences (Davenport et al., 2020)..

The future trajectory of marketing, with half of professionals currently leveraging AI and a significant proportion planning its future integration, emphasizes AI's role in facilitating hyper-personalization. This involves offering tailor-made experiences and content, leveraging predictive analytics for marketing strategies, and innovating brand engagement through visual and voice search optimization. Despite the transformative potential of generative AI in harnessing historical data for content creation, there exists a cautionary note regarding its potential to hamper innovation by inundating consumers with content.

In summation, the revolutionary implications of AI in advertising span across historical and contemporary landscapes, enabling the creation of hyper-targeted campaigns, enriching personalized user experiences, and catalyzing creative processes. The evolution from foundational data analysis to anticipated synergies between human and AI collaboration presents a dynamic avenue for substantial influence and innovation within the advertising sector.

The quintessence of navigating the AI-driven advertising frontier lies in the harmonious integration of technological advancements with ethical standards and human-centric values. As the digital era progresses, the confluence of artificial and human intelligence is set to unveil unparalleled innovation and connectivity in advertising, outlining a promising horizon for those adept at harnessing AI to elevate accuracy, originality, and user engagement.

REFERENCES

Apotheker, J. (2023). *What Will Happen to Marketing in the Age of AI?* TED. https://www.ted.com/talks/jessica_apotheker_what_will_happen_to_marketing_in_the_age_of_ai

Carter, E. (2023). *200+ Senior Marketers Dish on How They Use AI.* WebFX. https://www.webfx.com/blog/marketing/how-marketing-leaders-use-ai/

Confessore, N. (2018). *Cambridge Analytica and Facebook: The Scandal and the Fallout So Far.* The New York Times. https://www.nytimes.com/2018/04/04/us/politics/cambridge-analytica-scandal-fallout.html

Davenport, T., Guha, A., Grewal, D., & Bressgott, T. (2020). How artificial intelligence will change the future of marketing. *Journal of the Academy of Marketing Science*, *48*(1), 24–42. doi:10.1007/s11747-019-00696-0

Dresma. (2022). *5 Ways Amazon Uses AI in eCommerce to Drive Sales.* https://dresma.ai/5-ways-amazon-uses-ai-in-ecommerce-to-drive-sales/

Elhager, S. (2023). *Role of AI in Advertising.* AiHello. https://www.aihello.com/resources/blog/role-of-ai-in-advertising/

Gao, B., Wang, Y., Xie, H., Hu, Y., & Hu, Y. (2023). Artificial Intelligence in Advertising: Advancements, challenges, and ethical considerations in targeting, personalization, content creation, and ad optimization. *SAGE Open*, *13*(4). doi:10.1177/21582440231210759

Goldberg, L. (2018). *A brief history of artificial intelligence in advertising.* Econsultancy. https://econsultancy.com/a-brief-history-of-artificial-intelligence-in-advertising/

Gordon, T. (2023). *The Impact of AI on Marketing: Opportunities and Challenges.* https://www.linkedin.com/pulse/impact-ai-marketing-opportunities-challenges-tracewell-trace-gordon/

Hanlon, A., & Jones, K. (2023). Ethical concerns about social media privacy policies: Do users have the ability to comprehend their consent actions? *Journal of Strategic Marketing*, 1–18. doi:10.1080/0965254X.2023.2232817

Hardesty, L. (2019). *The history of Amazon's recommendation algorithm.* Amazon science. https://www.amazon.science/the-history-of-amazons-recommendation-algorithm

Huang, M. H., & Rust, R. T. (2021). Engaged to a robot? The role of AI in service. *Journal of Service Research, 24*(1), 30–41. doi:10.1177/1094670520902266

Jebara, T. (2018). *Netflix Research: Machine Learning*. https://research.netflix.com/research-area/machine-learning

Kargl, D. (2022*). Methbot – How the King of Fraud made $3 million per day with advertising fraud*. Fraud0. https://www.fraud0.com/resources/methbot/

Kietzmann, J., Paschen, J., & Treen, E. (2018). Artificial intelligence in advertising: How marketers can leverage artificial intelligence along the consumer journey. *Journal of Advertising Research, 58*(3), 263–267. doi:10.2501/JAR-2018-035

Kim, H., & Park, M. (2024). When digital celebrity talks to you: How human-like virtual influencers satisfy consumer's experience through social presence on social media endorsements. *Journal of Retailing and Consumer Services, 76*, 103581. doi:10.1016/j.jretconser.2023.103581

Kofman, A., & Tobin, A. (2019). *Facebook Ads Can Still Discriminate Against Women and Older Workers, Despite a Civil Rights Settlement.* ProPublica. https://www.propublica.org/article/facebook-ads-can-still-discriminate-against-women-and-older-workers-despite-a-civil-rights-settlement

Kumar, V., Dixit, A., Javalgi, R. G., & Dass, M. (2016). Research framework, strategies, and applications of intelligent agent technologies (IATs) in marketing. *Journal of the Academy of Marketing Science, 44*(1), 24–45. doi:10.1007/s11747-015-0426-9

Laskowski, N., & Tucci, L. (2023). *Artificial intelligence (AI).* Enterprise AI. https://www.techtarget.com/searchenterpriseai/definition/AI-Artificial-Intelligence

Nabavieh, A. (2023). *Navigating the Future: Visual and Voice Search Optimization in 2024.* https://www.linkedin.com/pulse/navigating-future-visual-voice-search-optimization-2024-ali-nabavieh-ezfvc/

Nunez, A. (2023). *AI in Advertising: Everything You Need to Leverage an Industry-Level Transformation.* Podium. https://www.podium.com/article/ai-in-advertising/

Qudsi, I. E. (2023). AI-Powered Influencer Marketing: Opportunities and Challenges. *Forbes*. https://www.forbes.com/sites/forbesagencycouncil/2023/06/27/ai-powered-influencer-marketing-opportunities-and-challenges/?sh=5f8a4f2359e6

Statista. (2023). *Global programmatic advertising spending from 2017 to 2028.* https://www.statista.com/statistics/275806/programmatic-spending-worldwide/

Sullivan, D. (2015). *FAQ: All about the new Google RankBrain algorithm*. Academic Press.

Thakur, C. K. (2023) *The future of AI in marketing - what to expect in the next 5 years?* https://www.linkedin.com/pulse/future-ai-marketing-what-expect-next-5-years-a-i-marketing-/

Thompson, M. (n.d.). *Ikea's new augmented reality app lets you try out furniture in your home*. The Spaces. https://thespaces.com/ikea-place-app/

Unilever. (2021). *Act 2 Unstereotype makes end-to-end inclusive marketing a priority*. https://www.unilever.com/news/news-search/2021/act-2-unstereotype-makes-inclusive-marketing-a-priority/

Westwater, S. (2023). *AI Marketing Case Studies – Discover Success Stories and Cutting-Edge Strategies*. LinkedIn. https://www.linkedin.com/pulse/ai-marketing-case-studies-discover-success-stories-scot-westwater-ag4ic/

Chapter 7
Artificial Intelligence and Service Marketing Innovation

Monica R.
Christ University, India

Aswin Varghese Soju
https://orcid.org/0009-0000-2676-6563
Christ University, India

Sathish Kumar B.
https://orcid.org/0000-0002-2292-842X
Christ University, India

ABSTRACT

The integration of artificial intelligence (AI) into service marketing in India is expected to significantly impact marketing strategies and economic dynamics. The emphasis on personalization, automation, predictive analytics, and chatbots will enhance customer engagement and brand loyalty, leading to increased sales and revenue. Automation of marketing workflows will streamline operations, improve efficiency, and foster business growth. AI's predictive analytics capabilities will help businesses make informed decisions about their marketing strategies, particularly in a diverse market like India. AI-driven chatbots will enhance customer satisfaction and engagement, contributing to positive brand perception and loyalty. However, there may be concerns about job displacement, particularly in routine tasks. The growth of AI-driven service marketing can contribute to the development of a technology-driven ecosystem in India, attracting investments, fostering entrepreneurship, and stimulating innovation.

DOI: 10.4018/979-8-3693-2153-9.ch007

WHAT IS SERVICE MARKETING?

Within the marketing domain, service marketing is a specialized area that concentrates on selling and marketing intangibles, such as advantages, experiences, and knowledge, as opposed to actual goods. Due to the intrinsic qualities of services, it requires a different set of tactics and considerations than typical product marketing. These include:

- Intangibility: Since services cannot be felt, tasted, or seen before being acquired, it is essential to concentrate on expressing their worth through narratives, case studies, and illustrations.
- Inseparability: Since the creation and consumption of services frequently occur concurrently, the relationship between the service provider and the client directly affects the quality of the service. Establishing confidence and providing a satisfying experience is crucial.
- Variability: Consistency and standardization are important components of service marketing because the quality of a service might change based on the provider, the time of day, and other circumstances.
- Perishability: Once a service is provided, it cannot be kept or returned, underscoring the significance of prompt delivery and effective service procedures (Nandini,2019).

NEED FOR INNOVATION IN SERVICE MARKETING

In marketing, innovation encompasses not just the use of new technologies but also the application of fresh, practical concepts. Innovation is crucial since it enhances your good or service. You can expand your market reach and boost revenue and sales by being innovative.

Innovation can impact different aspects of a business and take many different shapes. You can implement innovative concepts or technology to help your business differentiate itself from the competition. You may see increased sales, profit, and customer happiness after making minor adjustments. Depending on your demands and issues, think about incorporating design, manufacturing, and product innovation. By using creative campaigns and marketing tactics, you may identify the best way to reach and engage your target audience. Find out through research what features your product needs to improve the user experience. A positive customer experience will benefit both your clients and your company.

Innovations in services occur globally and in all industries. Naturally, this involves service providers, but service innovations can also be developed by businesses that are product-based. A service innovation modifies the customer experience to generate income for the business and value for the client. A business may see a rise in revenue through new service innovation if its current clients spend more, the company's reputation improves, they make recommendations, etc. A measurable aspect is product innovation. Enhancing a product's functioning or appearance by physical means is known as improvement. Innovation also adds value to services because it is an intangible good.

Both service-based and product-based businesses should value service innovation, although product-based businesses should prioritize it and service-based businesses frequently do not need it.

Understanding and meeting client demands is at the heart of service marketing's mission to build enduring relationships and, eventually, propel corporate success. There are several strategies involved in this:

- Building strong relationships with customers: Service marketing prioritizes customer interactions and experiences to build trust, loyalty, and positive word-of-mouth, which in turn secures recurring business and long-term value.
- Differentiating a service from rivals: To stand out in a crowded market, service marketing emphasizes the special features and advantages of a service. This could entail cutting-edge delivery strategies, excellent customer support, or specialized knowledge.
- Increasing reputation and brand awareness: In addition to bringing in new business, successful service marketing techniques build a favourable brand perception that fosters customer loyalty and increases market share.
- Promoting growth and profit for the organization (Leslie de Chernatony, 2010).

In the Fourth Industrial Revolution, artificial intelligence (AI)-driven service innovation—such as Microsoft's Sydney, Google's Bard, and OpenAI's ChatGPT—has emerged as one of the key factors influencing a company's ability to succeed. Studies that are currently available on the subject, however, reveal that these have been ad hoc in nature and have not provided a conceptual framework for the strategic management of AI-powered service innovation capability in dynamic marketplaces. As a result, this study synthesizes existing research, suggests a framework, and creates a plan to increase our understanding. The results show that three key factors influence the formation of AI-powered service innovation:

(1) AI-market capability relates to customer orientation, industry orientation, and cross-functional orientation;
(2) AI-infrastructure capability relates to data, business models, and ecosystem; and
(3) AI-management capability relates to AI-orientation, organizational learning, and AI ethics.

A framework for AI-powered service innovation capability: Review and agenda for future research (Akter et al., 2023).

EVOLUTION OF AI AND ITS IMPACT ON THE INDIAN ECONOMY

The evolution of Artificial Intelligence (AI) has been a long and complex journey, with its roots dating back to ancient times. The concept of AI was first introduced by Alan Turing in 1950, who proposed the Turing Test to determine a machine's ability to exhibit human-like intelligence. The 1956 Dartmouth Conference marked the birth of AI as a field, with early AI programs like the Logic Theorist and General Problem Solver. However, the enthusiasm for AI declined in the 1970s and 1980s due to challenges in symbolic AI and the complexity of real-world problems.

The resurgence of AI began in the 1990s with the advent of machine learning approaches, which allowed systems to learn from data and improve over time. Neural networks, inspired by the human brain structure, gained prominence, leading to breakthroughs in pattern recognition and speech processing. The development of the backpropagation algorithm for training neural networks was a pivotal moment in this era (Edem Gold,2023).

The 21st century saw an unprecedented acceleration in AI development, driven by big data convergence, increased computational power, and advanced algorithms. Machine learning, particularly deep learning, became the driving force behind AI's resurgence, with breakthroughs in computer vision, natural language processing, and speech recognition fueling applications like image recognition, language translation, and virtual assistants.

The concept of artificial general intelligence (AGI) has gained attention, with contemporary AI systems excelling in specialized domains such as image and speech recognition, language understanding, and autonomous decision-making. Artificial Intelligence (AI) is poised to drive economic growth in India, transforming various sectors and contributing to job creation. As India enters the fourth industrial revolution, AI is positioned as a key catalyst for this transformation. In industry and manufacturing, AI-powered automation is streamlining production processes, enhancing productivity, and reducing costs. This not only augments global competitiveness but also contributes to job creation by fostering a more efficient and dynamic manufacturing ecosystem.

In the services sector, AI is revolutionizing customer experiences, particularly in tech-driven domains like e-commerce, fintech, and customer support. Personalized recommendations, chatbots for instant assistance, and predictive analytics are enhancing customer engagement, and driving revenue growth. AI is playing a pivotal role in risk assessment, fraud detection, and the development of innovative financial products, strengthening the financial system's resilience and fostering investment and economic expansion.

The agricultural landscape in India is also experiencing the positive impact of AI, with precision agriculture optimized by AI-driven analytics and sensor technologies. AI-driven adaptive learning platforms cater to individual learning styles, providing personalized educational content and facilitating skill assessments. AI is also improving diagnostics, treatment planning, and patient care in healthcare, with advanced AI algorithms aiding in early disease detection and personalized treatment strategies. Telemedicine platforms powered by AI are expanding access to healthcare services, especially in remote areas, contributing to overall public health.

The startup ecosystem in India is witnessing a surge in AI-driven innovations, addressing diverse challenges and creating disruptive business models. However, challenges such as ethical considerations, data privacy, and job displacement need careful consideration. Responsible AI governance and policies that balance innovation with ethical considerations are crucial for ensuring sustainable and inclusive growth of AI in India. Upskilling the workforce to adapt to the evolving technological landscape is essential to mitigate job displacement risks and harness the full potential of AI as a catalyst for economic growth (Elysse Bell,2023).

AREAS OF SERVICE INNOVATION: DEN HERTOG'S MODEL

Pim den Hertog's 4-dimensional services innovation model, introduced in 2000, is a comprehensive framework for understanding service innovations. It identifies four key dimensions: New Service Concept, New Client Interface, New Delivery System, and Technology Options. These dimensions focus on the core service offering, customer interaction, delivery system, and technology options.

Human Resource (HR) Capability is crucial for successful implementation of service innovations, as it involves the skills, expertise, and competencies of the workforce. Organizational Capability focuses on the organization's ability to adapt and support service innovations, including aspects such as culture, structure, and leadership. Marketing & Distribution Capability is essential for successfully introducing and promoting service innovations, including strategies for communicating the value of new service concepts, reaching target audiences through innovative client interfaces, optimizing delivery system marketing, and leveraging technology options to enhance distribution channels.

To provide additional context, Den Hertog introduces three vital comparisons: To Existing & Competing Services, which examines how the new service innovation stacks up against existing services in the market and those offered by competitors. This helps organizations position their innovations strategically and identify unique selling propositions. To Actual & Potential Customer, it considers the reactions and preferences of both current and potential customers, aiding in gauging market acceptance and potential expansion of the service innovation. Lastly, to Service Workers, evaluating the impact of the innovation on the workforce is crucial. This model ensures that employees are equipped and empowered to contribute to the successful implementation of service innovations. In essence, Den Hertog's 4-dimensional services innovation model provides a comprehensive framework that goes beyond mere description, offering insights into the capabilities and comparisons crucial for successful service marketing innovation. This model guides organizations in navigating the complexities of the dynamic service landscape and fostering a culture of continuous innovation (Matthijs Janssen et al., 2015).

FOURTH INDUSTRIAL REVOLUTION

The Fourth Industrial Revolution (4IR) is a transformative phase in our lives, work, and interactions with technology. It is characterized by the rapid integration of cutting-edge technologies, such as artificial intelligence (AI), the Internet of Things (IoT), robotics, 3D printing, and advanced materials. These technologies are interconnected, creating a synergistic effect that amplifies their impact. Automation, a hallmark of the 4IR, is changing industries by leveraging connected devices and AI to streamline manufacturing processes, leading to increased efficiency and reduced costs. AI-powered data analytics enables businesses to make informed decisions, improving patient outcomes in healthcare.

The 4IR is not limited to the workplace; it shapes daily lives with smart homes equipped with IoT devices, autonomous vehicles, and advanced transportation systems. Education is also experiencing a transformation with adaptive learning platforms. However, with these advancements come challenges such as ethical considerations surrounding AI, data privacy concerns, and job displacement. The transformative power of the 4IR requires thoughtful and responsible governance to ensure its benefits are harnessed while mitigating potential risks.

In essence, the 4IR is a paradigm shift that is reshaping our world, blending digital, physical, and biological systems. Embracing this revolution means navigating the complexities of a rapidly changing landscape, where innovation is the currency, connectivity is the norm, and adaptability is the key to thriving in this era of unprecedented technological advancement.

(A. Bayode, J.A van der Poll & R.R Ramphal,2019)

ROLE OF ARTIFICIAL INTELLIGENCE

i. Fourth Industrial Revolution:

Artificial Intelligence (AI) is playing a pivotal role in the Fourth Industrial Revolution, transforming industries and economies worldwide. AI, including machine learning, natural language processing, and robotics, is driving unprecedented advancements in automation, connectivity, and data analytics. AI-driven machines are revolutionizing traditional manufacturing processes, leading to increased efficiency, reduced costs, and enhanced productivity. Smart factories use AI-driven technologies like the Internet of Things (IoT) and robotics to create interconnected systems that can autonomously operate, communicate, and adapt to changing conditions. AI is also driving data analytics, analyzing complex datasets to extract valuable insights for businesses. This capability is crucial in sectors such as finance, healthcare, and logistics, where AI algorithms can identify patterns, detect anomalies, and predict trends, facilitating more informed and strategic decision-making.

AI is also revolutionizing customer experiences and personalization, providing personalized recommendations, tailoring marketing strategies, and enhancing user interfaces. Virtual assistants and chatbots powered by AI offer seamless and efficient customer support, contributing to a more personalized and responsive service environment.

In healthcare, AI is driving innovations in diagnostics, treatment, and patient care. Advanced machine learning algorithms analyze medical data to assist in disease diagnosis and treatment planning, while AI-driven robotics enhance surgical precision and predictive analytics help identify potential health risks. AI also plays a crucial role in education and workforce development, with adaptive learning platforms using AI algorithms to tailor educational content to individual student needs and assist in skills assessment, matching individuals with training programs and employment opportunities that align with their capabilities and aspirations.

However, AI also poses challenges related to ethics, privacy, and workforce displacement. Ethical considerations demand careful scrutiny and responsible governance, while privacy concerns arise as AI systems collect and analyze vast amounts of personal data. Reskilling and upskilling initiatives are essential to ensure individuals can thrive in the evolving job market.

ii. Service marketing innovation:

Artificial Intelligence (AI) is revolutionizing service marketing by providing insights and personalized strategies. AI analyzes vast amounts of customer data to extract valuable insights into preferences, behaviours, and purchasing patterns, enabling businesses to create targeted content, recommendations, and promotions. AI-powered chatbots and virtual assistants provide instant and efficient customer support, improving customer engagement and satisfaction. AI-driven predictive analytics allows businesses to anticipate customer behaviours and market trends, enabling them to proactively adjust their strategies. Recommendation engines, which analyze customer behaviour and preferences, enhance cross-selling and upselling by providing personalized suggestions, leading to increased customer satisfaction and loyalty. Dynamic pricing optimization is enabled by AI algorithms, ensuring prices are adjusted in real time to optimize revenue and respond to changes in demand.

Sentiment analysis tools assess customer sentiments expressed in online reviews, social media, and other channels, helping businesses understand how customers perceive their services and adjust marketing strategies accordingly. AI technologies, such as Natural Language Processing (NLP), are used to generate personalized and targeted marketing content, ensuring that marketing messages are relevant and resonate with the audience.

Customer journey analysis helps businesses analyze the entire customer journey by examining touchpoints and interactions, optimizing the customer experience, identifying pain points, and delivering a more cohesive and personalized service. AI-driven AR applications enhance the customer experience by allowing virtual try-ons or experiences, increasing customer confidence and satisfaction. Marketing automation platforms streamline repetitive tasks, such as email campaigns and social media posting, by using AI to segment audiences, personalize content, and optimize the timing of marketing activities. As technology continues to evolve, businesses are likely to explore even more innovative ways to leverage AI for enhanced customer engagement and satisfaction.

RECENT OF INNOVATION IN SERVICE MARKETING

1. Augmented Reality (AR) in Retail Services:

Augmented Reality (AR) has become a game-changer in the retail industry, significantly enhancing the way customers interact with products and make purchase decisions. One of the prominent examples of AR in retail is the IKEA Place app. Launched by the Swedish furniture giant, this app allows users to virtually place IKEA furniture in their homes using their smartphones or tablets. By leveraging the device's camera and AR technology, customers can see how a specific piece of furniture fits into their living space in terms of size, color, and style.

The IKEA Place app addresses a common challenge in online furniture shopping—uncertainty about how a piece will look in a real-world setting. This innovative use of AR not only provides a virtual try-before-you-buy experience but also significantly reduces the likelihood of returns, enhancing customer satisfaction and confidence in their purchase decisions.

AR has also been applied in the fashion industry. For instance, brands like Gap and Converse have developed AR-powered apps that enable customers to virtually try on clothes and shoes. By superimposing digital images of clothing items onto the user's real-world environment, these apps offer a more engaging and personalized online shopping experience.

Another notable example is the use of AR in beauty and cosmetics. L'Oreal's Makeup Genius app, for instance, enables users to try on different makeup products virtually. By utilizing facial recognition technology, the app accurately maps the user's facial features, allowing them to experiment with various makeup looks in real time. This not only simplifies the product discovery process but also encourages users to explore and purchase new beauty products with confidence. In the automotive industry, AR is being employed to enhance the showroom experience. BMW's Augmented Reality Visualizer app, for instance, enables customers to visualize and customize their desired BMW model in real time. Users can explore different colour options, configurations, and features by simply pointing their mobile device at a physical space, such as a parking lot. This interactive and immersive experience contributes to a more informed and personalized decision-making process when purchasing a vehicle. AR is not limited to individual brands; it has also been adopted by online marketplaces. For example, Shopify, a popular e-commerce platform, has integrated AR functionalities into its platform, allowing merchants to showcase products in AR directly on their online stores. This democratization of AR technology enables a wide range of retailers to provide immersive product experiences to their customers, irrespective of their size or industry (Syed Shah Alam, 2021).

VIRTUAL REALITY (VR) IN TOURISM SERVICES

Virtual Reality (VR) has brought about a transformative shift in the tourism industry, offering immersive experiences that allow potential travellers to explore destinations virtually. Marriott Hotels, a global hospitality company, has embraced VR through its "VRoom Service" initiative, redefining the way guests engage with travel information. Marriott's VRoom Service enables hotel guests to experience virtual travel adventures from the comfort of their rooms. Using a VR headset provided by the hotel, guests can embark on virtual tours of popular destinations, such as Hawaii or London. This not only adds an element of entertainment to the hotel stay but also serves as a powerful tool for influencing travel decisions. The VR experience allows guests to virtually walk through iconic landmarks, experience local cultures, and visualize potential vacation spots. This immersive approach helps guests make more informed decisions about their next travel destination. It goes beyond traditional brochures or online travel guides, providing a firsthand, 360-degree view that sparks excitement and inspiration.

Beyond hotels, the tourism industry has witnessed the integration of VR in various aspects of the customer journey. Airlines, such as Qantas, have utilized VR to offer virtual tours of their cabins and destinations, allowing potential passengers to preview the in-flight experience and explore the sights they might encounter upon arrival. Destination marketing organizations have also embraced VR to showcase the unique attractions of their regions. For instance, Tourism Australia launched "Australia in 360," a VR experience that takes users on a virtual journey through the country's diverse landscapes and activities. This immersive content serves as a compelling promotional tool, enticing travelers to explore Australia in person.

In addition to pre-travel experiences, VR has found applications in post-travel memories. Hotels and travel agencies offer VR experiences that allow individuals to relive their vacations. For example, Thomas Cook, a travel agency, introduced VR postcards that enable customers to revisit their holiday destinations by inserting their smartphones into a VR headset. This innovation enhances the emotional connection customers have with their travel experiences, fostering brand loyalty. The cruise industry has also embraced VR technology to provide potential passengers with virtual ship tours. Carnival Cruise Line, for instance, offers a "Cruise VR" app that allows users to virtually explore the interiors and amenities of their cruise ships. This immersive preview helps individuals choose the right cruise experience based on their preferences and expectations (Shalini Talwar,2022).

CHATBOTS AND AI IN CUSTOMER SERVICE

Chatbots and Artificial Intelligence (AI) have become integral components of customer service strategies, transforming the way businesses interact with and support their customers. The implementation of AI-driven chatbots streamlines customer service processes, improves response times, and enhances overall customer satisfaction. Numerous companies across various industries have embraced this technology to provide efficient and personalized support. One compelling example of AI in customer service is Amazon's use of chatbots on its e-commerce platform. Amazon utilizes AI-powered chatbots to assist customers with a range of inquiries, including order tracking, product recommendations, and issue resolution. These chatbots leverage natural language processing (NLP) to understand and respond to customer queries, offering instant and accurate assistance. By automating routine tasks, Amazon ensures faster and more efficient customer interactions, freeing up human agents to focus on more complex issues.

Another notable example is the use of chatbots in the banking sector. Many financial institutions, such as Bank of America, have integrated AI-driven chatbots into their online platforms to provide customers with real-time support. These chatbots can answer queries related to account balances, transaction history, and even offer financial advice. The 24/7 availability of these virtual assistants ensures that customers can receive assistance at any time, contributing to a positive customer experience. In the telecommunications industry, companies like AT&T have adopted chatbots to handle customer queries and troubleshoot common issues. These AI-driven assistants can guide users through troubleshooting steps, provide information about billing inquiries, and offer support for service-related concerns. By leveraging chatbots, telecom companies can address customer needs promptly, reducing the reliance on traditional customer service channels and improving overall operational efficiency. The travel and hospitality sector has also embraced AI in customer service. For instance, airlines like KLM use AI chatbots to assist passengers with booking flights, checking-in, and providing travel-related information. These virtual assistants enhance the customer experience by offering personalized recommendations, handling reservation modifications, and addressing frequently asked questions, all within a chat interface. E-commerce platforms, beyond Amazon, often deploy AI chatbots to engage customers and guide them through the shopping process. Shopify, a popular e-commerce platform, enables businesses to integrate chatbots that can help customers find products, track orders, and provide information about promotions. This not only enhances the overall shopping experience but also contributes to increased sales and customer loyalty.

In addition to text-based chatbots, advancements in voice-activated AI have led to the integration of virtual assistants like Siri and Google Assistant in various customer service applications. These voice-activated AI systems enable users to perform tasks, seek information, and interact with devices using natural language commands, expanding the scope of AI-driven customer support. The integration of chatbots and AI in customer service, exemplified by Amazon, Bank of America, AT&T, KLM, and Shopify, showcases the versatility and impact of this technology across diverse industries. By automating routine tasks, providing instant responses, and offering personalized assistance, AI-driven customer service not only improves operational efficiency but also elevates the overall customer experience. As technology continues to evolve, businesses are likely to explore even more innovative ways to leverage AI for enhanced customer engagement and support (Adam, Wessel,2020).

SUBSCRIPTION-BASED SERVICES

Subscription-based services have revolutionized business models across various industries, providing consumers with convenient, flexible, and continuous access to a wide array of products and services. This innovative approach to pricing and consumption has become increasingly popular, reshaping the way companies deliver value to their customers. Examples abound, spanning entertainment, software, lifestyle, and beyond.

i. Streaming Services:

Perhaps the most well-known and widespread use of subscription-based services is in the streaming industry. Platforms like Netflix, Hulu, and Disney+ have fundamentally changed how people consume content. Instead of purchasing individual movies or shows, users subscribe to these services, gaining unlimited access to a vast library of entertainment content for a monthly fee. This model offers subscribers the flexibility to explore a diverse range of content without the commitment of purchasing each title individually.

ii. Music Subscription Services:

The music industry has also embraced the subscription model with services like Spotify, Apple Music, and Amazon Music. Users pay a monthly fee for unlimited access to an extensive catalogue of songs, albums, and playlists. This approach has shifted the industry away from individual song or album purchases, providing subscribers with the ability to discover and enjoy a broad spectrum of music without upfront costs.

iii. Software as a Service (SaaS):

In the realm of business and productivity, Software as a Service (SaaS) has gained prominence. Companies like Microsoft with Office 365, Adobe with Creative Cloud, and Salesforce with its CRM platform offer subscription-based models for their software solutions. This allows businesses and individuals to access the latest software updates, features, and support without the need for large upfront investments in software licenses.

iv. Meal Kit Subscriptions:

The food industry has witnessed the rise of subscription-based meal kit services such as Blue Apron and HelloFresh. Subscribers receive weekly deliveries of pre-portioned ingredients and recipes, allowing them to prepare restaurant-quality meals at home. This model caters to individuals seeking convenient and diverse meal options without the hassle of grocery shopping and meal planning.

v. Beauty and Personal Care Subscriptions:

Subscription services have extended to the beauty and personal care industry. Companies like Birchbox and Ipsy offer curated boxes of beauty products delivered to subscribers regularly. This model enables customers to explore and try new products, creating a personalized and convenient experience while eliminating the need to visit physical stores.

vi. Subscription Boxes for Hobbies:

Niche subscription boxes have emerged, catering to specific interests and hobbies. For example, Loot Crate delivers monthly boxes filled with collectables and merchandise related to gaming and pop culture. These subscriptions provide enthusiasts with a regular supply of curated items tailored to their passions.

vii. Fitness and Wellness Subscriptions:

With the growing emphasis on health and wellness, subscription-based services have entered the fitness industry. Platforms like Peloton offer subscription-based access to virtual fitness classes, allowing users to participate in live or on-demand workouts from the comfort of their homes. This model provides flexibility and diversity in fitness routines.

viii. Book Subscription Services:

Book lovers can now subscribe to services like Audible or Book of the Month, gaining access to a regular supply of audiobooks or curated book selections. These services offer convenience and variety, appealing to readers with different preferences.

BLOCKCHAIN IN FINANCIAL SERVICES

Blockchain technology has emerged as a transformative force in the financial services sector, offering increased security, transparency, and efficiency in various financial transactions. It serves as a decentralized and tamper-resistant ledger, enabling secure and trustless transactions. Several examples illustrate the diverse applications of blockchain in financial services.

The most well-known application of blockchain in finance is the creation of cryptocurrencies like Bitcoin and Ethereum. Bitcoin, introduced in 2009, operates on a decentralized blockchain, enabling peer-to-peer transactions without the need for intermediaries like banks. Ethereum, on the other hand, introduced smart contracts, self-executing contracts with the terms of the agreement directly written into code. The rise of decentralized finance (DeFi) platforms, built on blockchain networks like Ethereum, has further expanded the scope of financial services without traditional intermediaries.

Blockchain facilitates faster and more cost-effective cross-border payments and remittances. Ripple, a blockchain-based payment protocol, aims to streamline international transactions by providing a decentralized and efficient network for financial institutions. Ripple's technology reduces the time and cost associated with cross-border payments, making it an attractive solution for banks seeking to enhance their remittance services. Smart contracts, a key feature of blockchain technology, are self-executing contracts with predefined rules and conditions. They automate and enforce the terms of an agreement without the need for intermediaries. For example, in trade finance, a smart contract can automatically release payment when predefined conditions (such as successful delivery of goods) are met, reducing the risk of fraud and delays.

Blockchain is also used in supply chain finance to enhance transparency and traceability. By recording every transaction and movement of goods on a blockchain, participants in the supply chain can have real-time visibility into the provenance and status of products. This reduces the risk of fraud and ensures the authenticity of goods throughout the supply chain.

Blockchain offers solutions for secure and decentralized digital identity verification. Traditional identity verification processes often involve multiple intermediaries and are susceptible to data breaches. Blockchain-based identity verification allows individuals to control and share their identity information securely, enhancing privacy and reducing the risk of identity theft. Blockchain enables the tokenization of physical and financial assets, turning them into digital tokens that can be traded on blockchain platforms. This includes tokenized real estate, stocks, and even art. Security tokens issued on blockchain can represent ownership in traditional financial instruments, providing increased liquidity and accessibility to a broader range of investors. Several central banks are also exploring the use of blockchain technology to create their own digital currencies. A central bank digital currency (CBDC) is a digital form of a country's fiat currency. China's digital currency electronic payment (DCEP) project is one of the notable examples, where the People's Bank of China is experimenting with a digital yuan built on blockchain technology. Blockchain enhances security and reduces the risk of fraud in financial transactions. Its immutable and transparent nature makes it easier to trace and audit transactions, aiding in anti-money laundering (AML) compliance. Financial institutions can leverage blockchain to create a more secure and auditable record of transactions, reducing the risk of fraudulent activities (Mohd Javaid et. Al, 2022).

MOBILE PAYMENT SOLUTIONS

Mobile payment solutions have become a ubiquitous part of modern financial transactions, transforming the way people pay for goods and services. These solutions leverage the convenience of smartphones and mobile devices to enable quick, secure, and contactless transactions. Various mobile payment platforms have emerged, each offering unique features and catering to diverse consumer preferences. Mobile wallets are digital applications that allow users to store payment information, such as credit and debit card details, securely on their smartphones. Examples include Apple Pay, Google Pay, and Samsung Pay. Users can make payments at physical retail stores by tapping their smartphones on contactless terminals or online through in-app or web purchases. These wallets enhance security by using tokenization, where a unique token is generated for each transaction, minimizing the risk of exposing sensitive payment information. Peer-to-peer (P2P) payment apps enable users to send and receive money directly from their mobile devices. Venmo, owned by PayPal, is a popular example in the United States. It allows users to split bills, pay friends, and request payments with ease. The app often includes a social feed, adding a social component to financial transactions. In other regions, apps like Cash App and Paytm provide similar P2P payment functionalities. Traditional banks have embraced the shift towards mobile payments by developing their own mobile banking apps. These apps offer a range of services beyond basic payments, including account management, bill payments, fund transfers, and even mobile check deposits. Examples include Chase Mobile, Bank of America Mobile Banking, and HSBC Mobile Banking. Mobile banking apps provide customers with the flexibility to manage their finances on the go.

QR code payments have gained popularity as a simple and efficient mobile payment method. Apps like Alipay and WeChat Pay in China allow users to make payments by scanning QR codes at merchants' locations. The user's mobile device generates a unique QR code for the transaction, and the merchant's scanner reads and processes the payment. This method is widely used in various retail settings, including restaurants, shops, and transportation services.

Many mobile apps integrate payment functionalities directly, allowing users to make purchases within the app. This is common in e-commerce apps, where users can buy products or services without leaving the app. For example, the Amazon app allows customers to make purchases using stored payment information, streamlining the checkout process.

While not exclusively mobile, contactless card payments, often facilitated by near-field communication (NFC) technology, contribute to the broader landscape of mobile payments. Cards equipped with contactless technology, such as credit or debit cards, can be tapped or waved near a compatible terminal to complete a transaction. This method is widely adopted in various regions, and mobile wallets often support these contactless card payments.

In emerging markets, mobile payment platforms have played a crucial role in expanding financial inclusion. M-Pesa in Kenya is a notable example. M-Pesa allows users to deposit, withdraw, and transfer money using their mobile phones, even without access to traditional banking services. This has transformed the financial landscape in regions where traditional banking infrastructure may be limited.

With the rise of cryptocurrencies, mobile wallets dedicated to storing and managing digital assets have become prevalent. Apps like Coinbase and Trust Wallet allow users to securely store, send, and receive various cryptocurrencies directly from their mobile devices. These wallets contribute to the broader ecosystem of digital and decentralized currencies (Caitlin Simmons, 2023).

AI-ENHANCED EMAIL MARKETING

AI-enhanced email marketing is a revolutionary approach that uses artificial intelligence algorithms to analyze vast amounts of data, understand user behaviour, and dynamically tailor email content for individual recipients. This technology allows marketers to create highly personalized and contextually relevant email experiences, moving beyond traditional segmentation and rule-based campaigns. For example, in the fashion industry, AI can be used to analyze customers' browsing and purchase history, allowing retailers to curate personalized email campaigns that align with their preferences. AI-driven email marketing also optimizes the timing and frequency of email communication, allowing platforms to schedule email delivery at the optimal time for each recipient. This not only increases the likelihood of the email being noticed but also increases customer satisfaction.

A travel agency can use AI to analyze customer preferences, generate customized travel itineraries and recommendations, and automate the creation of personalized content. This streamlines the content creation process and ensures that customers receive tailored suggestions, increasing conversion rates and customer satisfaction. AI's natural language processing capabilities contribute to the refinement of email content, allowing companies to craft messaging that resonates with their target audience and addresses their specific needs and concerns. In the healthcare sector, AI can play a crucial role in patient engagement and communication, generating personalized health tips, appointment reminders, and educational content based on an individual's health history and preferences.

Hence, it is a powerful tool for businesses across various industries to elevate their engagement strategies. By harnessing AI's capabilities to understand, predict, and respond to individual user preferences, businesses can create email campaigns that are more effective in driving conversions and contributing to a more personalized and satisfying customer experience. As technology advances, the integration of AI in email marketing will likely become even more sophisticated, enabling marketers to forge deeper connections with their audience through hyper-personalized and contextually aware communication.

BENEFITS OF AI IN SERVICE MARKETING

Artificial Intelligence (AI) has revolutionized customer insights and personalization in service marketing innovation. With vast datasets, AI algorithms and machine learning techniques are used to analyze these data to discern nuanced patterns, behaviors, and preferences of consumers. This data-driven discernment is the foundation for crafting personalized marketing strategies, which transcend the conventional one-size-fits-all approach.

AI's ability to classify individuals into segments based on shared traits, propensities, and preferences underpins the delivery of targeted content, recommendations, and promotional endeavors. This results in a profound elevation in the relevance and resonance of marketing interactions, fostering individualized engagement for consumers. In the service marketing paradigm, AI serves as an indispensable conduit for the manifestation of personalized and targeted strategies.

The integration of AI-powered chatbots and virtual assistants represents a transformative stride in augmenting customer support mechanisms within the contemporary service marketing landscape. These automated entities operate tirelessly 24/7, handling routine inquiries, guiding customers through intricate processes, and offering personalized recommendations with calculated acumen. The salient advantage of chatbots lies in their capacity to contribute to the augmentation of customer engagement, resulting in reduced response times and enhanced customer satisfaction.

AI-driven predictive analytics marks a watershed moment in the orchestration of marketing strategies within the contemporary service marketing milieu. By harnessing the expansive vista of historical data, AI algorithms embark on a sophisticated journey of discerning patterns, extrapolating trends, and predicting future customer behaviors. This prescient acuity empowers marketers to proactively tailor their strategies to align with the ever-evolving dynamics of the market.

AI-driven recommendation engines emerge as paragons of precision in the landscape of service marketing innovation, wielding the analytical prowess of machine learning algorithms to decipher customer behavior and preferences. They orchestrate personalized recommendations, transcending the limitations of conventional approaches.

In service industries characterized by fluidity and variability, such as hospitality or transportation, the efficacy of dynamic pricing optimization cannot be overstated. AI, acting as the linchpin in this mechanism, facilitates an agile response to market dynamics, ensuring that pricing models remain attuned to the imperatives of competitiveness and profitability.

AI-driven sentiment analysis is a crucial tool in understanding and shaping customer perceptions in service marketing. With the proliferation of online reviews, social media interactions, and digital discourse, AI algorithms can discern the nuances of positive and negative sentiments expressed by customers. These insights serve as a compass for strategic decision-making, enabling businesses to harness positive sentiments for promotional activities, garnering testimonials, and fostering brand advocacy. Conversely, the identification of negative sentiments becomes a precursor to proactive service improvements, enabling businesses to address issues swiftly and ameliorate customer experiences.

The integration of AI, particularly Natural Language Processing (NLP), in content generation marks a paradigm shift in the art and science of service marketing. AI systems can comprehend, contextualize, and generate content that transcends generic overtures, establishing meaningful connections with consumers. The resonance of messages tailored to individual preferences contributes to heightened engagement and receptivity. By leveraging AI-driven content generation, businesses can curate narratives that not only reflect their brand ethos but also resonate intimately with the diverse preferences of their target audience.

Customer journey analysis is another transformative force in service marketing. AI algorithms delve into the journey, dissecting touchpoints, interactions, and feedback to discern patterns and pain points. This discernment becomes the bedrock for crafting strategies that elevate the customer experience from mere transactional encounters to a seamless and cohesive journey. AI facilitates this understanding by providing actionable insights that empower businesses to streamline processes, identify areas for improvement, and fortify customer touchpoints.

Augmented reality (AR) and virtual try-ons are transforming the era of immersive and interactive customer experiences. AR applications powered by AI algorithms enable virtual try-ons and experiences, enhancing customer confidence and satisfaction. This symbiotic marriage of AI and AR provides businesses with a powerful tool for not just marketing but actively engaging customers in an experiential journey.

Marketing automation is a linchpin in streamlining and optimizing repetitive tasks within the ambit of service marketing. AI-powered automation platforms undertake the mantle of these tasks, leveraging algorithms to segment audiences, personalize content, and optimize the timing of marketing endeavors. The crux of marketing automation lies in its capacity to liberate human resources from mundane tasks, allowing marketers to focus on strategy, creativity, and the cultivation of meaningful relationships with customers.

DRAWBACKS OF USING AI

AI in service marketing faces several challenges, including the lack of human touch, ethical concerns, privacy issues, overreliance on technology, initial implementation costs, complexity and learning curve, job displacement, limited creativity and intuition, vulnerability to malicious use, and dependence on data quality.

The absence of a genuine human touch in service marketing can lead to a sense of detachment, as human customer service representatives can respond to emotional nuances, adapt to unique situations, and provide a level of understanding that AI may struggle to emulate. Striking the right balance between automated efficiency and human connection is crucial to ensure a holistic and emotionally resonant service marketing experience.

Ethical considerations and bias are significant drawbacks in AI-driven service marketing. AI algorithms learn from historical data, which may inherently contain biases. Addressing these challenges requires ongoing vigilance, transparency, and the development of ethical guidelines to mitigate bias and ensure fair treatment across diverse customer demographics.

Privacy issues arise from the extensive use of AI in analyzing customer data. Businesses must implement robust data protection measures, transparent privacy policies, and communication strategies to assure customers that their information is handled responsibly and ethically.

Overreliance on technology poses a risk, as businesses may become so enamored with AI's capabilities that they neglect the indispensable role of human intuition, creativity, and emotional intelligence. Balancing the benefits of automation with the ethical responsibility to address workforce implications becomes a critical aspect of strategic planning for businesses embarking on AI adoption in service marketing.

The complexity associated with AI technologies introduces a learning curve for businesses seeking to implement them in service marketing. These systems often require specialized skills for proper implementation, management, and optimization. Finding qualified personnel who can navigate the intricacies of AI systems can be challenging.

The risk of job displacement arises from the automation of certain tasks through AI in service marketing, potentially impacting jobs associated with these functions. Proactive measures such as reskilling and upskilling initiatives become imperative to equip the workforce with the skills needed in an AI-driven marketing landscape.

AI systems are vulnerable to malicious use, including cyber-attacks, manipulative tactics, and exploitation. Businesses must implement robust cybersecurity measures, ethical guidelines, and continuous monitoring to safeguard against malicious activities.

Finally, the dependency on data quality is highly contingent on the efficacy of AI algorithms. In service marketing, where customer data is pivotal, the dependence on data quality becomes a critical consideration. To navigate these drawbacks, businesses must adopt a strategic and ethical approach to AI implementation in service marketing, emphasizing transparency, responsible use, and the ongoing evaluation of the impact on both customers and the workforce.

SCOPE OF AI INTEGRATION

AI integration in service marketing innovation offers businesses unprecedented opportunities to revolutionize customer experiences, streamline operations, and gain a competitive edge in the dynamic marketplace. Its ability to process vast amounts of data swiftly and derive actionable insights positions it as a pivotal tool in understanding customer behaviours, preferences, and trends. In the realm of personalized marketing, AI-driven algorithms enable businesses to tailor their offerings to individual customers, creating hyper-targeted campaigns that enhance engagement and conversion rates. Moreover, the integration of chatbots and virtual assistants powered by AI enhances customer service, providing real-time assistance, resolving queries, and offering personalized recommendations.

AI's impact extends beyond front-end customer interactions, permeating the entire customer journey. Predictive analytics, fueled by AI, empowers businesses to anticipate customer needs, optimize pricing strategies, and forecast market trends, leading to more informed decision-making. The use of AI in marketing automation ensures that communications are timely, relevant, and tailored to individual preferences, fostering a seamless and consistent customer experience across various touchpoints. In service innovation, AI plays a transformative role in augmenting existing services and introducing novel solutions. For example, AI-driven virtual try-ons and augmented reality applications enhance the online shopping experience, reducing uncertainty for customers and increasing satisfaction. In the healthcare sector, AI facilitates telemedicine and personalized health recommendations, improving overall patient outcomes. AI's impact on data analytics provides businesses with a deeper understanding of market trends, customer behavior, and competitor strategies. Machine learning algorithms can identify patterns and correlations that may not be apparent through traditional analytical methods, shaping marketing strategies, refining product offerings, and identifying untapped market segments. AI integration also optimizes resource allocation, cost management, and supply chain logistics, contributing to cost savings and agility in responding to market fluctuations and demands.

REFERENCES

Adam, M., & Wessel, M. (2020). AI-based chatbots in customer service and their effects on user compliance. SpringerLink. https://link.springer.com/article/10.1007/s12525-020-00414-7

Antunes, J. (2020, July 15). Artificial intelligence in marketing - a presentation of benefits and a framework for successful implementation. https://run.unl.pt/handle/10362/111603

Bayode, A., van der Poll, J. A., & Ramphal, R. R. (2019). 4th Industrial Revolution: Challenges and Opportunities in the South African Context. http://www.eares.org/siteadmin/upload/9179EAP1119285.pdf

Bell, E. (2023). General Intelligence (AGI): Definition, How It Works, and Examples. Investopedia. https://www.investopedia.com/artificial-general-intelligence-7563858#:~:text=Artificial%20general%20intelligence%20%28AGI%29%20is%20a%20theoretical%20pursuit,function%20only%20within%20a%20specific%20set%20of%20parameters%29

Flavián, C., & Casaló, L. V. (2021). Artificial intelligence in services: Current trends, benefits and challenges. *Service Industries Journal*, *41*(13–14), 853–859. doi:10.1080/02642069.2021.1989177

Frank, B. (2021). Artificial intelligence-enabled environmental sustainability of products Marketing benefits and their variation by consumer, location, and product types. *Journal of Cleaner Production*, *285*, 125242. doi:10.1016/j.jclepro.2020.125242

Gold, E. (2023). The History of Artificial Intelligence from the 1950s to Today, free code camp. https://www.freecodecamp.org/news/the-history-of-ai/

Gustafsson, A., Snyder, H., & Witell, L. (2020). Service Innovation: A new conceptualization and path forward. *Journal of Service Research*, *23*(2), 111–115. doi:10.1177/1094670520908929

Javaid. (2022). A review of Blockchain Technology applications for financial services. sciencedirect.com/science/article/pii/S2772485922000606#:~:text=Financial%20service%20providers%20find%20blockchain%20technology%20useful%20to,and%20transparency%2C%20and%20open%20up%20newer%20revenue%20opportunities.

Kunz, W. H., & Hogreve, J. (2011). Toward a deeper understanding of service marketing: The past, the present, and the future. *International Journal of Research in Marketing*, *28*(3), 231–247. doi:10.1016/j.ijresmar.2011.03.002

Leslie de Chernatony. (2010)/ Brand Management Through Narrowing the Gap Between Brand Identity and Brand Reputation/ Taylor and Francis Online. https://www.tandfonline.com/doi/citedby/10.1362/026725799784870432?scroll=top&needAccess=true

Lightfoot, H., & Gebauer, H. (2011b). Exploring the alignment between service strategy and service innovation. *Journal of Service Management*, *22*(5), 664–683. doi:10.1108/09564231111175004

Matthijs Janssen. (2015). Exploring a Multidimensional Approach to Service Innovation. SpringerLink. https://link.springer.com/chapter/10.1007/978-1-4471-6590-3_5

Mba, A. T. (2021, June 5). *Den Hertog services innovation model (4-dimensions, 2000)*. SolvInnov. https://solvinnov.com/den-hertog-model-for-describing-service-innovations/

Nandini, G. (2019). Features of Services: 8 Major Features of Service Marketing, economics discussion. https://www.economicsdiscussion.net/service-marketing/features-of-services-8-major-features-of-service-marketing/31597

Overgoor, G., Chica, M., Rand, W., & Weishampel, A. (2019). Letting the computers take over: Using AI to solve marketing problems. *California Management Review*, *61*(4), 156–185. doi:10.1177/0008125619859318

Purchase, S., & Voléry, T. (2020). Marketing innovation: A systematic review. *Journal of Marketing Management*, *36*(9–10), 763–793. doi:10.1080/0267257X.2020.1774631

Randhawa, K., & Scerri, M. (2015b). Service Innovation: A Review of the Literature. In Springer eBooks (pp. 27–51). doi:10.1007/978-1-4471-6590-3_2

Shahriar Akter. (2023). A framework for AI-powered service innovation capability: Review and agenda for future research. Science Direct. https://www.sciencedirect.com/science/article/abs/pii/S0166497223000792

Simmons, C. (2023). A Comprehensive Guide to Mobile Payment Technologies. Fintech Curated. https://fintechcurated.com/editorial/a-comprehensive-guide-to-mobile-payment-technologies/#:~:text=At%20its%20core%2C%20mobile%20payments%20leverage%20the%20power,mobile%20banking%20apps%2C%20and%20peer-to-peer%20%28P2P%29%20payment%20platforms

Syed Shah Alam. (2021). Factors Affecting Augmented Reality Adoption in the Retail Industry. Science Direct. https://www.sciencedirect.com/science/article/pii/S2199853122009118

Talwar, S. (2022). Digitalization and sustainability: virtual reality tourism in a post pandemic world. Taylor and Francis Online. https://www.tandfonline.com/doi/full/10.1080/09669582.2022.2029870

Chapter 8
Service Innovation Metamorphosis From Assimilation to Synthesis Approach for Building Disruptive Business Strategies

Sridhar Manohar
https://orcid.org/0000-0003-0173-3479
Chitkara Business School, Chitkara University, India

Ruchi Jain
https://orcid.org/0000-0001-5148-7654
Amity School of Business, Amity University, Noida, India

Ruchika Jeswal
Amity School of Business, Amity University, Noida, India

ABSTRACT

Existing theoretical and empirical researchers associated innovation with technological transformations and introduced radical/disruptive products and processes. However, considering the approaches and theories would be limited to manufacturing industries, innovation in service industries with non-technological aspects needs to be noticed. This study emphasises the need for a synthesis approach that could play a major role in building/enhancing service business models/frameworks. These frameworks need a stronger focus on using organizational, strategic, and marketing innovation typologies in formulating service business models resulting in low customer engagement and customer experience management. This chapter discusses various new business models that have evolved their features and benefits. Finally, this study concludes by emphasising the need for incorporating non-technical components when innovating in services and services-based firms.
DOI: 10.4018/979-8-3693-2153-9.ch008

1. INTRODUCTION TO SERVICE INNOVATION

Innovation is the initial use in production or the market, whereas an invention is a discovery or new existence, typically at the bench or lab (Roberts, 1988). Before Barras' (1986) study, researchers tended to use the term innovation concerning products, whereas service was viewed as a supporting component of the delivery process. Notably, innovation in services was approached similarly to innovation in a product where some exclusive characteristics of services made it difficult during implementation, which paved the way for the evolution of the concept of "Service Innovation". Service innovation has been gaining attention among researchers over the last three decades. Authors who previously thought of service innovation as akin to product innovation have had their ideas challenged by empirically based theories of service innovation. Studying and developing new approaches, strategies, theories, and measurements would help service firms develop exclusive service business models that could satisfy customer needs (Peixoto et al., 2023). However, it is not easy to analyze all the aspects of service innovation since it is a more comprehensive topic; thus, many researchers have attempted to study different branches of service innovation.

1.1. Service vs. Product innovation: A thorough analysis of research studies on innovation highlights three key distinctions between service and product innovation. They are (a) When it comes to service innovation, not only are services generated, but also the prerequisites for services (Mahavarpour et al., 2023), meaning that when customers want a service, both the production and delivery processes are involved. Since service innovation primarily relates to innovation in the delivery process, the company must integrate it with its current service industry-related business operations. This must be done when manufacturing items because R&D and production adhere to separate processes (Tatikonda & Zeithaml, 2001; Kampani & Jhamb, 2021). The front and back offices must integrate to address the disparity in goals and deadlines (An & Mikhaylov, 2024). In contrast, the front office is set up to meet customer requests, while the back office is organized to maximize productivity in the manufacturing industry (Menor et al., 2002). The third and most significant difference is in the investment and spending. Prior studies on innovation (Barras, 1986; Djellal & Gallouj, 2001) indicated that investment and spending are higher in manufacturing enterprises than in service sectors. The manufacturing firm spends more on R&D and manufacturing than developing new services. The benefits of products to consumers are also less than those of services, according to Atuahene-Gima (1996), and the rate of innovation in the service sector is far higher than that in production firms. DeBrentani and Cooper (1992) assert that when it comes to the generation of innovation, technology plays a lower role in service innovation than it does in product innovation.

Similarly, the differences can be experienced in the barriers to innovation, where the human recourse factor as a barrier is most prominent in services compared to products (Sirilli & Evangelista, 1998). Additional researchers, including Atuahene-Gima (1996) and Janz et al. (2001), contrasted the studies about product industries and service businesses. They found that certain characteristics of services, such as perishability, inseparability, and heterogeneity, completely differentiated them from products. This creates a need for business models/strategies that address the unique features of services for service industries by giving equal importance to technological and non-technological components. Further, contextual differentiation should be addressed (a) based on the industry and (b) based on the innovative concepts developed by the firm. Nevertheless, how is it measured? Drawbacks in existing business models: How can they be transformed/improved as per changing customer requirements? Can it be generalized to all service industries or subject to the individual industry? There remains a gap to be addressed.

1.2. New Service Development: Besides existing issues, authors who focused on service innovation could not clearly distinguish between service innovation and the new service development process. Both concepts were mostly addressed similarly by Johne and Storey (1998) and Alam (2002), leading to another confusion in the literature. Bettencourt (2010) states that most management teams must distinguish between service innovation and new service development. He further stated that service innovation only focuses on developing a new concept in service, whereas new service development occurs when it involves all the activities until commercialization. Booz et al. (1982) proposed an eight-step model for developing new services, popularized by Bowers in 1987. Create a long-term business plan, describe a new service, and generate ideas for selecting and developing new ideas. (iv) concept creation and assessment to identify potential new service ideas; (vii) market testing; (viii) commercialization; (vii) business analysis to assess the viability of the new service and project the profit; (vi) service creation and testing. Further clarification is urged between innovation and innovativeness, where innovation discusses the diffusion of new ideas through different channels into systems (Das, 2022). In contrast, innovativeness is the time of innovation adoption, and since it deals with a single innovation, the result obtained cannot be generalisable Subramanian & Nilakanta (1996). Understanding and focusing on this helps researchers and practitioners to incorporate it during the design of disruptive models/strategies.

1.3. Service Innovation and Performance: Many studies have used service innovation to determine firms' performance, like growth share profit, internal quality, and employee performance (Avlonitis et al., 2001; Van der Vegt & Janssen, 2003; Blazevic & Lievens, 2004). Limited studies considered service innovation to determine customer performance, such as customer satisfaction, repurchase, cross-buying, and loyalty (Price & Brodie 2001; Matching et al. 2004), and these concepts have to be taken care of in building holistic service innovation-based business models. The Early Mover Advantage idea (Lieberman & Montgomery 1988; Roberts & Amit 2003; Vashishth & Jhamb, 2021) and the Performance Gap theory, for example, both emphasize that while innovation is risky and success is not always guaranteed, it positively influences organizations' performance (Zaltman et al. 1973; Wischnevsky & Damanpour 2006).

Process performance and result performance, which includes financial and non-financial performance, are two categories under which a company's performance can be divided (Avlonitis et al. 2001; Song et al. 2009). Utilizing cutting-edge technology and non-technological elements to create new models or modify old models makes it easier to produce service performance, financial incentives, non-financial rewards, or market positioning (Wind and Mahajan 1997; Benner & Tushman 2003). Additional performances could be expanding markets, giving current clients more advantages, enhancing the worth of existing services, or completely developing a new service. Process performance is measured based on (a) criterion cost, (b) effectiveness of innovation, and (c) speed of innovation activity in the firm. The result performance is measured based on financial and non-financial performance. Considering the financial result performance, which is further classified as (1) business performance: measured based on (a) firm's turnover, (b) market share, (c) productivity, (d) exports, (e) profit for the firm and (f) return on investment equity and assets (2) organization performance, which is measured based on (a) sales per employee, (b) net profit per employee, (c) gross margin and (d) growth in employment and (3) innovation performance, which is measured based on (a) time and cost of innovation, (b) frequency of innovation, and (c) new or upgraded features in product/services. Focusing on non-financial results, performance can be classified as (1) internal non-financial result performance, such as employee satisfaction and involvement in the strategic or competitive advantage of the firm, and (2) external non-financial performance, like customer satisfaction, customer loyalty, service quality, and behavioral intention of the customer.

1.4. Service Innovation for Quality: McAdam and Armstrong (2001) have reported that innovation and quality are two key management terms adopted by private organizations and have achieved greater success. The authors stated that innovative products/services with good quality measures adopted by the firm lead to superior performance outcomes. Over a broad variety of business improvement initiatives, there is an inherent connection between innovation and quality. Over a broad variety of business improvement initiatives, there is an inherent connection between innovation and quality. Jain and Gupta (2004) also stated that a firm that provides innovation with high-quality services to its employees would likely achieve superior performance. The service profit chain frameworks by Heskett et al. (1997) have predicted firms' performance by improving both internal and external service quality. Other researchers adopted this framework to predict the firm's performance by improving internal and external service quality (Loveman 1998; Lau 2000). Return on the quality model also suggested that internal and external service quality improvement would improve the firm's performance (Rust et al. 1995; Heskett et al. 1997; Anderson & Mittal 2000). One of the key elements to improve service quality would be to bring frequent innovation within the firm. Since innovation entails offering clients a product or service distinct from the competition, it ought to enhance the customer experience. Therefore, attracting clients and satisfying them so they become loyal is the fundamental goal of innovation. (Zineldin 2000 and Oliver 1999) stated that satisfaction is a customer's reaction based on the difference between what they anticipate about the service/ product and what they receive in fulfilling their goal, desire or need. Thus, the ultimate goal for any firm must be building appropriate business models for profitable outcomes (Avlonitis et al. 2001 Gonzalez Mieres et al. 2012).

1.5. Service Innovation as Disruptive Business Strategy: The contemporary catastrophic events, including the COVID-19 pandemic, have significantly affected service providers. These incidents have significantly caused economic disruption, including changes in consumer behavior, work practices and government policies. According to the International Monetary Fund, the global financial crisis of 2009 had a real GDP year-on-year percentage change of -0.1% and the great lockdown that began in 2020 had a change of -3%. The total output loss during 2020-2021 from the pandemic crisis was approximately £9 trillion. The IMF has also stated that both advanced economies, emerging and developing economies, are in a state of recession. Despite these challenges, service providers are trying to resume normal operations because of the importance of economic stability and growth. Therefore, service providers are working to overcome the challenges, address significant changes and continuously provide value to customers and stakeholders while supporting communities and promoting social and environmental responsibility. Thus, endeavoring to adjust to new consumer behaviors and market conditions. The pandemic has accelerated the shift towards digital marketing channels, with more businesses focusing on online advertising, social media marketing and e-commerce. This has increased investment in digital marketing technologies and strategies like search engine optimization, SEO pay-per-click PPC advertising and email marketing.

Furthermore, with a rise in online shopping, a preference for contactless payment methods and a higher demand for health and safety products, the focus has shifted to more new consumer needs and preferences. Empowering the existing service framework with Technology tools like Artificial intelligence, Machine Learning techniques, Automation, Augmented and Virtual Reality, Robotics, Quantum computing, etc., can help service providers analyze and interpret large amounts of customer data, providing insights for improving service personalization. Non

Technological innovation is another important factor in structuring the entire service innovation, such as adjusting or enhancing organizational strategy choices and marketing initiatives. Technology and non-technological aspects of service innovation are combined holistically, with equal emphasis required and articulated using S-D Logic.

All marketing techniques and tactics that were based on products and other tangible goods—also referred to as "goods-dominant logic"—were attacked by Vargo and Morgan in 2005. They published S-D logic, which argued that the exchange of services, as opposed to only things, is what society, markets, and organizations are most concerned with. When it happens, one service is swapped out for another. Additionally, they emphasized how all markets are built on the exchange of services, all communities have service-based economies, and all firms are service enterprises. To focus on service-dominant logic, marketers must switch from G-D reasoning to S-D logic and redefine their fundamental methodologies, concepts, ideas, and strategies. In particular, according to innovation experts, service innovation research is equivalent to product innovation research (Vargo & Morgan) (2005).

Service innovation has been growing rapidly in the modern economy and is changing the way businesses deliver their services and interact with their customers (Freni, 2022). Over the past few years with this development, the consumer preferences, global reach and interconnectedness has also surged leading to a transformation in the traditional businesses (Gallouj et al., 2015). This rapid growth is reshaping businesses leading to an emergence of entirely new markets and innovative business models (Panigrahi et al., 2017). Geographical reach and industry growth are two important drivers of taking the innovation industry forward (Amoroso et al., 2023). An openness to expanding businesses through geographical segments opens up new markets and allows businesses to reach new customer bases, helping foster their unique needs. This expansion encourages businesses to stay updated by innovating continuously and gaining a competitive edge. Simultaneously, overall industry growth also creates opportunities for innovation and helps in expanding knowledge. With the expansion of industry and technology, come new ideas for development and scope for addressing challenges. However, alongside the potential benefits of growth in service innovation, there are numerous challenges that businesses must navigate. New solutions and business models are coming into emergence in order to address these issues. Feng & Sivakumar (2016) give empirical evidence that service innovation has an impact on innovation performance given the propensity of collaboration and shared economy for service firms. It has the potential of creating innovative and collaborative business models that turn out to be cost effective and of expected consumer quality. The gap between consumer expectations and actual delivery is also a major issue in an era where consumers are attracted towards personalized products. Organizations can foster consumer needs by integrating consumer ideas with internal knowledge of the firm (Tang & Lush, 2018). The model of open innovation serves as a sustainable trend providing external information to channelize into internal and organizational ideas.

There is a potential of driving innovation into the service industry to create opportunities and cost effective facilities for consumers through the model of gig economy. Gig economy involves individuals who provide services through digital platforms to other businesses (Cho & Cho, 2020), the biggest example being Uber that provides a platform for consumers and service providers. Such innovations are required to revolutionize the service sector for growth and creating competitive advantage.

This chapter embarks on an exploration of non-technological aspects of service innovation. By delving into the existing literature, there exists a need for stronger frameworks focusing on organizational, strategic and marketing service innovation models to enhance customer experience.

First section provides an overview of the different branches of service innovation starting with service vs. the product innovation. In this part distinctions between serve and product innovation are addressed. The next part of the introduction section comprises new service development that is used for generating and developing new ideas. Further it involves service innovation and performance. The literature reveals limited studies considering service innovation to determine customer performance, which gives a pathway for the next part of service innovation for quality. The last introductory part is of service innovation as disruptive business strategy. This section has the significance of investigation, highlighting the need for this study.

Next section outlines the research methodology to identify the articles relevant for the study. For refining the articles, SPAR-4-SLR was used as the primary method for further reviewing the existing literature to identify potential gaps in the literature. A broad classification of service innovation on the bases of degree of novelty and forms of innovation was presented in the third section with the next section being the different approaches to service innovation.

Section 5 identifies the barriers and enablers of service innovation that addresses the importance of technological and non-technological components to be competitive in the market. Growth of service innovation in terms of (i) geography and industry; and (ii) technological and non-technological innovation is discussed in section 6.

The next section interprets the importance and rise of service innovation which develops a pathway for emerging new business models based on collaboration, open innovation and gig economy. By reflecting the findings from existing literature, this section contributes to advancing knowledge in the field and suggests business models for future research. The conclusion section summarizes the findings presented in the chapter by highlighting the key insights and implications of the study. It also provides avenues for future research providing a closure to the study.

2. METHODOLOGY

The method used to identify the foundational and base articles related to service innovation, strategies, and potential future research areas is discussed in this section. The first step in gathering articles on innovation and service innovation was to access search engines and databases like EBSCO, Google Scholar, etc. For the researchable concept of "Service Innovation," a list of keywords was created, including terms like "Innovation," "services," "barriers," "factors," "product," "process," "process typologies," "organization," "innovation and performance," "dimensions," and "new service development," among others. The list of keywords was combined in any way that was conceivable to conduct the search.

All of the articles related to the keywords that were available were downloaded and separated based on their relationships. The content was gathered from a variety of Journal publishers, including Sage Publications, Scopus Elsevier, Emerald, Business Communication Quarterly, Routledge, Taylor & Francis, Oxford University Press, Wiley Online Library, Inderscience Publications, World Scientific Publishers, David Publications, Scientific Research, etc. All articles released between 1970 and 2023 were included in the search. Using the SPAR 4SLR framework for inclusion and exclusion criteria, a total of 380 articles were filtered, and by deleting the duplication, the final list was reduced to 247. Out of those, 84 of the articles dealt with service innovation approaches, and 73 of them dealt with typologies, dimensions, service innovation measurement, empirical studies involving outcome variables and service innovation, and conceptual studies involving the measurement of service innovation. According to Tranfield et al. (2003), a systematic review should be conducted by multiple reviewers. This study adhered to this recommendation, and the authors carefully analyzed the articles to identify any gaps in the literature.

3. CLASSIFICATION OF SERVICE INNOVATION

The two broad classifications of innovation measurement are the degree of novelty and forms of innovation (Table 1). Under degree of novelty, innovation is further classified into (a) disruptive innovation or sustaining innovation and (b) radical innovation or incremental innovation. According to Christensen et al. (2000),

Keyword String	TITLE-ABS-KEY (("Service Innovation*") AND ("Facilitators" OR "Barriers" OR "Factors") AND ("Product" OR "Process" OR "Strategies")) AND (" Business Models") (LIMIT-TO (PUBSTAGE, "final")) AND (LIMIT-TO (DOCTYPE, "ar") OR LIMIT-TO (DOCTYPE, "ch")) AND (LIMIT-TO (SUBJAREA, "BUSI") OR LIMIT-TO (SUBJAREA, "ECON")) AND (LIMIT-TO (LANGUAGE, "English")) AND (LIMIT-TO (SRCTYPE, "j"))

disruptive innovation is an innovation that creates a new market and new value network, that is, the innovation that improves the service or product that already does not exist in the market and is designed for the first time. Whereas sustaining innovation does not create a new innovative market, rather it improves the value of the existing one. Similarly, researchers classified measurement based on the degree of novelty as radical and incremental innovation (Ettlie et al. 1984; Tushman et al. 1985; Dewar and Dutton 1986; Orlikowski 1991). Radical innovation is nonlinear paradigmatic changes that depart from existing knowledge or practice. On the other hand, incremental is a linear cumulative change that implies a minor improvement or adjustment in existing knowledge or technology.

Product innovation, process innovation, marketing innovation, input innovation, and organizational innovation are the five key categories of service innovation (Gadrey et al., 1995; Tejada and Moreno, 2013). It majorly relies on market capability that encompasses the customer orientation (Akter et al., 2023). In relation to this, the authors need to consider some typologies, such as marketing innovation, input typology, and organization innovation, while measuring service innovation is the main issue identified. On the other hand, several authors added additional typologies to the current service innovation typologies, including administrative innovation, strategic typology, and technology innovation. The measurement elements in these typologies were mostly related to product innovation, whether typologies were included or excluded when measuring service innovation. Later arguments were made against the inclusion of technological innovation in the typologies that were developed to measure service innovation by authors such as Barras (1986), Edvardsson (1997), Sirilli and Evangelista (1998). This allowed academics to mix several product and

Table 1. Classification of service innovation

S.No.	Basis of Service Innovation	Service Innovation Nomenclature
1.	***Degree of novelty***	(i) Disruptive innovation
		(ii) Sustaining innovation
		(iii) Radical innovation
		(iv) Incremental innovation.
2.	***Forms of innovation***	(i) Product innovation,
		(ii) Process innovation,
		(iii) Marketing innovation,
		(iv) Input innovation,
		(v) Organizational innovation

Source: compiled from referred resources by authors

service innovation typologies to develop comprehensive business models (Gallouj and Weinstein 1997; Coombs and Miles 2000).

Miller and Friesen (1982) explored the measurement of service innovation by dimensions, and the dimensions considered were: (a) New product or service innovation; (b) Methods of production or provision of services; and (c) Risk taken by senior executives in search of unique and creative solutions. Hertog (2000) provided a four-dimensional model of service innovation that was similar to this, with the dimensions being (a) the service concept, (b) the client interface, (c) the service delivery system, and (d) technological options. Later, Avlonitis and colleagues (2001) highlighted several factors, such as (a) the Newness of the delivery process; (b) Adjustments to the service; (c) the Newness of the service to the market; and (d) the Newness of the service to the company. The work of Sidhu et al. (2007), which indicates the complexity of service and represents these complexities by three dimensions, including (a) Supply-side, (b) Customer-side, and (c) Geographical/Institutional, has recently been embraced by various studies. Customers-focused innovation, service-dominant innovation, conventional innovation, and collaboration-based innovation are a few dimensions listed by Nam and Lee (2010). Cheng and Krumwiede (2012) recently adopted a three-dimensional measurement, with the dimensions being (1) Types of innovation, (2) Radicalness of innovation, and (3) Frequency of innovation. Although researchers aimed to measure the same notion, it can be seen from the review on the measurement of service innovation by dimensions that they needed a consistent phrase for measuring dimensions, with the name of the dimension frequently changing from one author to another. The Hertog (2000) dimensions were widely adopted by several authors in the investigations (Miles 2008 and Lin 2012). It is also clear from the review that the dimensions were largely the same from one author to the next; only the terminology was different.

4. APPROACHES TO SERVICE INNOVATION

Coombs and Miles (2000) classified three schools of thought, primarily focusing on the author's approach towards innovation. The research findings of Griffin (1997), Sirilli and Evangelista (1998), and Hughes and Wood (2000) emphasized that there are many similarities between product innovation and service innovation. Thus, whether it is a new product or service, they contribute heavily to the concept of innovation, which is termed the "Assimilation approach" Gallouj and Weinstein (1997); Fitzsimmons and Fitzsimmons (2000), and Menor et al. (2002) criticized the studies related to the "Assimilation approach". They stated that there are differences between innovation in product and service firms. These differences are majorly based on the characteristics of services like intangibility, heterogeneity, perishability and simultaneity, which makes services unique. This school's contribution was termed as "*Demarcation approach*".

Coombs and Miles (2000) and Gallouj and Windrum (2009) stated that products and services are similar during innovation. Thus, there is no need for a completely separate approach, and there is a need to integrate both product-oriented and service-oriented approaches. This school of thought was termed the "Synthesis approach". Carlborg et al. (2013), who reviewed the evolution of service innovation literature, found that at the formation stage, service innovation was focused on the product and production process. Later in the maturity phase, literature was focused on the involvement of customers and in the final stage, during the multidimensional phase, researchers reviewed more on multidisciplinary research where service innovation is viewed as a multidimensional construct that includes product-related aspects, where the findings of Carlborg et al. (2013) is in line with the approaches proposed by Coombs and Miles (2000). Considering the authors' argument, building innovative business models or strategies in service by adopting product innovation components alone is difficult; hence, integrated, holistic models are essential.

5. BARRIERS AND FACILITATORS OF SERVICE INNOVATION

Understanding diverse considerations is necessary while developing a business model or service plan. The literature on innovation identified and categorised elements that serve as obstacles or enablers. Economic factors like risks to the economy, costs associated with innovation, and a lack of funding were categorised by Martikainen (2008). Internal factors like market information, organizational structure, and a need for more technical information were also included, as were other factors like ignorance of customers' attention to suppliers and rivals. Similar lists of human traits and monetary considerations for marketing management were made by Larsen and Lewis in 2007. However, Segarra-Blasco and Arauzo-Carod (2008) focused on financial and market expertise. Other factors mentioned by several authors include the characteristics of the global market, supplier and customer feedback, rival domestic market characteristics, strong project leaders' access to capital and human resources capabilities, taxation of new goods processes, and government tax (Foley & Gren 1995 Tidd et al. 1997 and Pihkala et al. 2002).

The significance of cutting-edge technologies was emphasized by authors (Moore & Benbasat, 1991, Verhagen & Dolen, 2009; Verma & Tandon, 2022), who concentrated on the review of technology considerations. According to certain writings (Galia & Legros 2004 Martikainen 2008 Segarra-Blasco & Arauzo-Carod 2008), a significant impediment to creativity is more technology knowledge. According to Hadjimanolis (1999), a barrier to creativity is difficulty locating technical information. A certain body of literature examined factors like governmental regulation. According to Allen et al. (1978) study, the three elements that make up the regulating factor are initiating, sustaining, and restructuring processes. Similarly, the government's decision to embrace innovation is positively influenced by providing information regarding innovations, financial support during development, and procedural development facilitation (Moon & Bretschneider 1997). Governmental standards and norms 1984 Piatier Innovation taxes imposed by the government (Foley & Gren 1995) Tidd and others, 1997 government strategies for market regulation protections for workers and consumers Environment of the government Hadjimanolis (1999) government taxation of goods and services Government-sponsored R&D and pollution-control demonstration initiatives, Pihkala et al. Some elements listed as obstacles to or enablers of the firm's innovation activity include Taylor et al. (2005). The review analysis of factors influencing/facilitating service innovation revealed that before beginning an innovation activity, service organizations must focus on these important elements, among which incorporating technology and non-technology components is necessary to be competitive in the market. These elements encourage innovation when they are concentrated.

6. GROWTH OF SERVICE INNOVATION

6.1. Geographic and Industry: The previous few decades have considerably increased service innovation. The main driver of innovation has been the industrial revolution. During that time, innovation spread around the globe. Since the first industrial revolution, innovation has been the primary force behind economic expansion. It mostly affected the various parts of Europe. The geographical patterns of development and income distribution have also been influenced by it. Every succeeding revolution had a unique topography. North America joined the elite group of wealthy nations during the Second Industrial Revolution, expanding the industrialized areas of Europe. ICT life sciences and biotechnologies, financial engineering, and advancements in transportation and logistics were all part of the third industrial revolution, which began around 1980. Innovation and economic growth extended throughout northeast Asia from Japan to the Republic of Korea and then to China. Beijing, Shenzhen, Tokyo, Seoul, and Beijing have all developed into megacities that influence the course of technological advancement.

The world's innovation could have been more evenly distributed and concentrated in some areas. Urban areas with emerging middle-income and high-income economies have seen the most innovation. These cities also turned out to be the centers for the growth of innovation ecosystems. The important areas were the Greater Boston Metropolitan region in Massachusetts and the US Southern portion of the San Francisco Bay Area in Northern California. The main topic of discussion is regional concentration within a process of global dispersion. The reality is that innovation activity in Western Europe and the United States is increasing mostly in urban regions. Still, it is also rapidly spreading and expanding to hubs outside the traditional cities. Innovation has always been a global phenomenon, but as demands mount, it is becoming to congregate and concentrate in certain, typically urban areas. According to figures from 2022, Switzerland has been awarded the most imaginative economy in the world for the 12th year in a row, followed by the United States, Sweden, the United Kingdom, and the Netherlands. China is approaching the top 10, while Turkey and India debuted in the top 40. (Global Innovation Index 2022).

6.2. Technological and Non-Technological Innovation: In particular, innovation helps businesses easily navigate crises amid the current global crisis. Technological innovations are often characterized by creating or utilizing new technologies, such as new technical knowledge and technological creations. Non-technological innovations can affect corporate operations without necessarily involving a change in technology or adopting new technology. Instead, they may focus only on implementing new organizational principles, business practices, or other immaterial methods. The growth of the service sector is influenced by several variables, including technological innovation, the need for change, and increased client expectations. Urbanization, changing lifestyles, and rising purchasing power have increased the need for services that can offer more comfort and quality. (Nair 2018). Online food delivery apps, online travel and tourist booking, and online education and learning are just a few examples of advances in the service industries.

7. EMERGING SERVICE BUSINESS MODELS

The versatile environment of services in the digital world leads to intense competition and randomness in businesses, creating a void between strategies for business and processes, resulting in the emergence of new business models Al-Debi et al. (2008). A business model is the approach adopted by the organization to earn revenue while achieving its objectives. It is the method by which an organization defines its money-making procedures by choosing a specific stake in the value chain (Rappa 2008). Business models are also propagated as edifices of value creation and value delivery and as the capture mechanism of an organization (Teece 2010, p. 172). The essential elements of business models are depicted in Table (2) below

Table 2. Essential elements of the Business model

Authors and Key Elements	Chesbrough and Rosenbloom (2002)	Morris et al. (2005)	Johnson et al. (2008)	Osterwalder and Pigneur (2010)	Kaplan (2012)
1.	Value proposition	Value proposition	Customer value proposition	Value proposition	Value creation
2.	Market segment	Customers	Key resources	Customer segments	Value delivery
3.	Value network	Internal processes	Key processes	Customer relationships	Value capture
4.	Value chain	External	Profit	Key partners	
5.		positioning	formula		
6.	Revenue generation	Economic model		Key resources	
7.	Cost structure	Personal factors		Channels	
8.	Profit potential			Key activities	
9.				Cost structure	
10.				Revenue streams	

Source: (Barbu et.al., 2018)

Further, the concept of Servitization shifted the focus of organizations from providing products to providing services, thus making Service-centric business models prevalent Baines et al. (2017). This extended to digital Servitization, where the business model must be innovated around digital services, and value creation is intrinsically done through these services. It made linear development processes redundant and shifted the focus on the role of customers in value creation Parida et al. (2019). Thus, germinating new business models based on collaboration, open innovation and the gig economy.

7.1. Collaboration/ Shared Economy: The changing world scenario has given center stage to collaborative or sharing economies (Belk, 2014). The conceptual foundations of "shared economy" are getting rooted deeply and have remodeled common ideas about ownership and consumption. Consumers understand the advantages of paying to access or share products rather than owning them temporarily (Matzler et al., 2015). It is an emerging form of business model propagating usage rather than ownership, banking upon the networks or communities of people with the support of an internet-based ecosystem. The concept gets implemented in the form of shared consumption (carpooling), shared lifestyles (coworking), shared finance (crowdfunding, alternative currencies), contributory output (digital manufacturing, DIY, 3D printers) etc. Such an economic system gives due attention to resources and remains productive without compromising resource needs (Gupta and Racherla,

2018), leading to sustainability. The sharing economy has enormous potential for creating innovative business models and sustainable consumption practices that may defy traditional businesses (Martin, 2016).

7.2. Open Innovation: Business Model Innovation strategies a company embraces are the validated concept of "absorptive capacity" (Cohen & Levithal 1989). The open system of innovation was propagated by Chesbrough (2003) as it leads to the accumulation of better ideas from external knowledge sources. The usual sources of Innovation for Business models can be competitors, customers, and inter-organizational networks. Organizations can bundle better value by integrating external ideas with internal knowledge. Three archetype processes for open innovation were identified, i.e., Outside-in, inside-out and coupled (Gassmen & Enkel 2004) Figure 1 below. Outside-in process realizes the difference in the presence of knowledge creation and innovation, encouraging the flow of information from outside to inside the company. At the same time, the company can strategically use external channels for commercializing its ideas through an inside-out process. The third-coupled process integrates the two and harnesses the benefits of both processes for innovation.

7.3. Gig Economy: The businesses are flexible and adopt a gig-economy business model where work is performed on demand. It is characterized by role-based positions filled by independent contractors and freelancers. The gig economy leverages digital platforms to connect these freelancers with their consumers as and when demanded (Harris, 2017). The employer can represent the main source or an extra source of income for the worker (Lepanjuuri et al., 2018, p. 12). The cynical views of this business model propagate- the erosion of customer relationships, deprivation of

Figure 1. Archetype process of open innovation (Gassmen & Enkel, 2004)

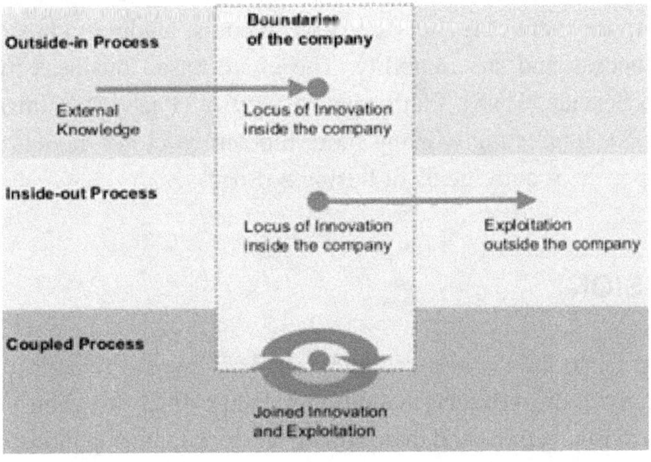

employee benefits, and minimalistic labor regulations resulting in lower costs to the businesses. Also, this business model allows its workers and consumers to co-create value in a more adaptable way with the possibility of a flexible lifestyle such as Airbnb, Uber, TaskRabbit or Upwork. It is characterized by choice to perform, autonomy due to the absence of supervisors and focus on the moment's needs (Ravenelle, 2019, pp. 5-6). Hence gaining popularity and being practiced worldwide with variations such as Uberization, Netflix model and cloud sharing.

7.3.1. Uberizations: In the gig economy, Uberization is the business model practised, transforming the market for services with the help of the latest technology, especially smartphones. In this business model, digital platforms or mobile apps replaced the middlemen required to connect talent to the right audience. Such platforms enabled comprehensive interaction between the provider and customer and ensured the minimum quality standards. The model got its name from Uber, creating a platform for people to hire and pay for rides. This uberization extended to any on-demand services such as food, stay, transportation, etc.

7.3.2. Netflix Model: The business model adopted by Netflix is an example of integrating the latest technology to fulfill customer expectations by disrupting established market structures. It redefined most of the value creation and value proposition elements by transforming DVD on rent to video streaming services. To retain customers and keep them interested, Netflix invests in new and exclusive content as its value proposition, thus reaching beyond pricing. Another innovative feature that catalyzes success is its recommendation system, which offers suggestions to users based on their consumption patterns. This data mining tool has taken Netflix to another level in terms of value creation and key resources as the basis for the core competencies of its business. It is pre-emptive by forecasting future growth and endowing high-scalability solutions in the gig economy.

7.3.3. Cloud Sharing: Cloud technology provides an exciting value proposition for businesses to outsource their Information technology ecosystem. It results in less cost and more avenues for service-based models, leading to business models' operational success and sustainability. The cloud-based business model can be Software as a Service (SaaS), Platform as a Service (PaaS), and Infrastructure as a Service (IaaS). Interestingly, many more innovative cloud models are evolving every day as per the requirements of business processes.

8. DISCUSSION

A crucial gap exists in existing research and frameworks related to innovation, particularly in the context of service industries. While much attention has been given to technological innovations and their impact on manufacturing industries, there's a significant need to recognize and address the unique challenges and opportunities for innovation within service sectors. Service industries often rely on non-technological aspects such as organizational structures, strategic planning, and marketing strategies to drive innovation. However, existing frameworks may not adequately capture the integration of both technological and non-technological components necessary for effective innovation in these sectors.

One key aspect that emerges is the importance of customer engagement and experience management in service innovation. Innovations in service industries must focus not only on product or process improvements but also on enhancing the overall customer experience. This includes addressing issues such as managing customer data, ensuring privacy and security, promoting sustainability, and adhering to ethical considerations. Service businesses must navigate complex challenges related to data management, privacy concerns, and sustainability while innovating their business models. The above chapter also touches upon the evolution of new business models within service industries for example Netflix model. These new models often incorporate features and benefits that go beyond traditional approaches, emphasizing the importance of adaptability and flexibility in today's dynamic business environment.

In conclusion, the discussion emphasizes the critical need for incorporating non-technical components into innovation strategies within service industries. By addressing the limitations of existing frameworks and adopting a more holistic approach that integrates technological and non-technological aspects, service-based firms can better position themselves for success in today's competitive marketplace.

9. FORECASTING FUTURE

The primary source of competitive advantage in the future is service innovation. Large businesses have adopted service as the catalyst for their organizations' expansion. Revolutionary new services have demonstrated how service innovation can drive economic growth in developing countries despite limited societal infrastructure or resources. Leading the way in the development of new IT-enabled service models is Salesforce.com, which offers customers software as a service rather than a licensed software product. IBM, a firm with a century-long history, changed its focus from primarily selling computer hardware and software to one that depends on service innovation for growth and competitive advantage (Spohrer and Maglio, 2010). Forecasting service innovation for the future with absolute certainty is impossible. However, some aspects like Artificial intelligence and automation would be increasingly integrated. Services would be increasingly tailored to an individual's preferences and needs. The subscription and sharing economy models are likely to grow further. In the future, industries like fashion and electronics will also offer subscription-based services and collaborative consumption options. The pace of change of service innovation would be rapid, and businesses need to stay adaptable and open to new technologies and trends to remain competitive.

10. CONCLUSION

Service innovations powered with tools like Artificial intelligence, Machine Learning, Augmented and Virtual Reality and Robotics, etc., offer unlimited disruptive business strategies for the firms to excel. Service innovation is viewed as a multidimensional construct and is now adopted by firms for value creation and value delivery. This "synthesis approach," based on both products and services, is an evolution over and above the earlier assimilation approach of service innovation and fueling new-age business models. The business frameworks based on the "shared economy" have transformed the general concept of ownership and pushed consumers to share the access products, thus leading to sustainability. On the same lines, the open innovation system leads to the pooling of better ideas from external knowledge sources. Firms with IT-based businesses vehemently use this idea as open source software and disrupt the monopoly of proprietary software worldwide. On the other hand, innovative business models used by Uber or Netflix represent the essence of the Gig economy, where work is performed based on the demand generated. It consists of autonomous contractors and freelancers networked with their target market through common digital platforms managed by companies like AirBnB or Swiggy. In a nutshell, all disruptions provide customers more power with more personalized strategies and incessant innovative approaches adopted by service firms.

REFERENCES

Aas, T. H., & Pedersen, P. E. (2011). The impact of service innovation on firm-level financial performance. *Service Industries Journal, 31*(13), 2071–2090. doi:10.1080/02642069.2010.503883

Ahuja, G., & Katila, R. (2001). Technological acquisitions and the innovation performance of acquiring firms: A longitudinal study. *Strategic Management Journal, 22*(3), 197–220. doi:10.1002/smj.157

Akter, S., Hossain, M. A., Sajib, S., Sultana, S., Rahman, M., Vrontis, D., & McCarthy, G. (2023). A framework for AI-powered service innovation capability: Review and agenda for future research. *Technovation*, *125*, 102768. doi:10.1016/j.technovation.2023.102768

Al-Debi, M. M., El-Haddadeh, R., & Avison, D. (2008). Defining the business model in the new world of digital business. *AMCIS 2008 Proceedings*, 300.

Alam, I. (2002). An exploratory investigation of user involvement in new service development. *Journal of the Academy of Marketing Science*, *30*(3), 250–261. doi:10.1177/0092070302303006

Allen, T. J., Utterback, J. M., Sirbu, M. A., Ashford, N. A., & Hollomon, J. H. (1978). Government influence on the process of innovation in Europe and Japan. *Research Policy*, *7*(2), 124–149. doi:10.1016/0048-7333(78)90002-1

Alpay, G., Bodur, M., Yilmaz, C., & Büyükbalci, P. (2012). How does innovativeness yield superior firm performance? The role of marketing effectiveness. *Innovation (North Sydney, N.S.W.)*, *14*(1), 107–128. doi:10.5172/impp.2012.14.1.107

Amoroso, S., Diodato, D., Hall, B. H., & Moncada-Paternò-Castello, P. (2023). Technological relatedness and industrial transformation: Introduction to the Special Issue. *The Journal of Technology Transfer*, *48*(2), 469–475. doi:10.1007/s10961-022-09941-1

An, J., & Mikhaylov, A. (2024). Technology-based forecasting approach for recognizing trade-off between time-to-market reduction and devising a scheduling process in open innovation management. *Journal of Open Innovation*, *10*(1), 100207. doi:10.1016/j.joitmc.2024.100207

Anderson, E. W., & Mittal, V. (2000). Strengthening the satisfaction-profit chain. *Journal of Service Research*, *3*(2), 107–120. doi:10.1177/109467050032001

Atuahene-Gima, K. (1996). Differential potency of factors affecting innovation performance in manufacturing and services firms in Australia. *Journal of Product Innovation Management*, *13*(1), 35–52. doi:10.1111/1540-5885.1310035

Avlonitis, G. J., Papastathaopoulou, P. G., & Gounaris, S. P. (2001). An empirically-based typology of product innovativeness for new financial services: Success and failure scenarios. *Journal of Product Innovation Management*, *18*(5), 324–342. doi:10.1111/1540-5885.1850324

Baines, T., Ziaee Bigdeli, A., Bustinza, O. F., Shi, V. G., Baldwin, J., & Ridgway, K. (2017). Servitization: Revisiting the state-of-the-art and research priorities. *International Journal of Operations & Production Management*, *37*(2), 256–278. doi:10.1108/IJOPM-06-2015-0312

Barbu, C. M., Bratu, R. Ş., & Sîrbu, E. M. (2018). Business models of the sharing economy. *Revista de Management Comparat International*, *19*(2), 154–166.

Barras, R. (1986). Towards a theory of innovation in services. *Research Policy*, *15*(4), 161–173. doi:10.1016/0048-7333(86)90012-0

Barrett, M., Davidson, E., Prabhu, J., & Vargo, S. L. (2015). Service innovation in the digital age. *Management Information Systems Quarterly*, *39*(1), 135–154. doi:10.25300/MISQ/2015/39:1.03

Belk, R. (2014). You are what you can access: Sharing and collaborative consumption online. *Journal of Business Research*, *67*(8), 1595–1600. doi:10.1016/j.jbusres.2013.10.001

Benner, M. J., & Tushman, M. L. (2003). Exploitation, exploration, and process management: The productivity dilemma revisited. *Academy of Management Review*, *28*(2), 238–256. doi:10.2307/30040711

Blazevic, V., & Lievens, A. (2004). Learning during the new financial service innovation process: Antecedents and performance effects. *Journal of Business Research*, *57*(4), 374–391. doi:10.1016/S0148-2963(02)00272-2

Booz, Allen, and Hamilton. (1982). *New Products for the 1980s*. Booz Allen Hamilton, Inc.

Bowers, M. R. (1987). Developing new services for hospitals: A suggested model. *Journal of Health Care Marketing*, *7*(2), 35–44. PMID:10301716

Carlborg, P., Kindström, D., & Kowalkowski, C. (2013). The evolution of service innovation research: A critical review and synthesis. *Service Industries Journal*, *34*(5), 1–26.

Cheng, C. C., & Krumwiede, D. (2012). The role of service innovation in the market orientation—New service performance linkage. *Technovation*, *32*(7), 487–497. doi:10.1016/j.technovation.2012.03.006

Chesbrough, H. W. (2003). *Open innovation: The new imperative for creating and profiting from technology*. Harvard Business Press.

Cho, W., & Cho, S. E. (2020). Entrepreneurial challenges in business model for the gig economy: Agendas for research and business development. *International Journal of Entrepreneurship*, *24*(1), 1–11.

Christensen, C. M., Bohmer, R., & Kenagy, J. (2000). Will disruptive innovations cure health care? *Harvard Business Review*, *78*(5), 102–112. PMID:11143147

Cohen, W. M., & Levinthal, D. A. (1989). Innovation and learning: The two faces of R & D. *Economic Journal (London)*, *99*(397), 569–596. doi:10.2307/2233763

Cooke, P., & Wills, D. (1999). Small firms, social capital and the enhancement of business performance through innovation programmes. *Small Business Economics*, *13*(3), 219–234. doi:10.1023/A:1008178808631

Coombs, R., & Miles, I. (2000). Innovation, measurement and services: the new problematique. In *Innovation Systems in the Service Economy, Kluwer Academic Publisher* (pp. 85–103). Springer, US. doi:10.1007/978-1-4615-4425-8_5

Das, B. (2022). Diffusion of innovations: Theoretical perspectives and empirical evidence. *African Journal of Science, Technology, Innovation and Development*, *14*(1), 94–103. doi:10.1080/20421338.2020.1814517

DeBrentani, U., & Cooper, R. G. (1992). Developing successful new financial services for businesses. *Industrial Marketing Management*, *21*(3), 231–241. doi:10.1016/0019-8501(92)90020-T

Dewar, R. D., & Dutton, J. E. (1986). The adoption of radical and incremental innovations: An empirical analysis. *Management Science*, *32*(11), 1422–1433. doi:10.1287/mnsc.32.11.1422

Djellal, F., & Gallouj, F. (2001). Patterns of innovation organization in service firms: Postal survey results and theoretical models. *Science & Public Policy*, *28*(1), 57–67. doi:10.3152/147154301781781688

Edvardsson, B. (1997). Quality in new service development: Key concepts and a frame of reference. *International Journal of Production Economics*, *52*(1), 31–46. doi:10.1016/S0925-5273(97)80765-7

Ettlie, J. E., Bridges, W. P., & O'keefe, R. D. (1984). Organization strategy and structural differences for radical versus incremental innovation. *Management Science*, *30*(6), 682–695. doi:10.1287/mnsc.30.6.682

Feng, C., & Sivakumar, K. (2016). The role of collaboration in service innovation across manufacturing and service sectors. *Service Science*, *8*(3), 263–281. doi:10.1287/serv.2016.0135

Fitzsimmons, J. A., & Fitzsimmons, M. J. (2000). *New Service Development: Creating Memorable Experiences*. Sage Publications. doi:10.4135/9781452205564

Flynn, L. R., & Goldsmith, R. E. (1993). A validation of the Goldsmith and Hofacker innovativeness scale. *Educational and Psychological Measurement, 53*(4), 1105–1116. doi:10.1177/0013164493053004023

Foley, P., & Gren, H. (1995).A successful High-Technology Company. In Small Business Success. The Small Business Research Trust, Paul Chapman Publishing.

Freni, G. (2022, May). Service Innovation: A Literature Review of Conceptual Perspectives. In *International Symposium: New Metropolitan Perspectives* (pp. 154–163). Springer International Publishing. doi:10.1007/978-3-031-06825-6_15

Gadrey, J., Gallouj, F., & Weinstein, O. (1995). New modes of innovation: How services benefit industry. *International Journal of Service Industry Management, 6*(3), 4–16. doi:10.1108/09564239510091321

Galia, F., & Legros, D. (2004). Complementarities between obstacles to innovation: Evidence from France. *Research Policy, 33*(8), 1185–1199. doi:10.1016/j.respol.2004.06.004

Gallouj, F., Weber, K. M., Stare, M., & Rubalcaba, L. (2015). The futures of the service economy in Europe: A foresight analysis. *Technological Forecasting and Social Change, 94*, 80–96. doi:10.1016/j.techfore.2014.06.009

Gallouj, F., & Weinstein, O. (1997). Innovation in services. *Research Policy, 26*(4), 537–556. doi:10.1016/S0048-7333(97)00030-9

Gallouj, F., & Windrum, P. (2009). Services and services innovation. *Journal of Evolutionary Economics, 19*(2), 141–148. doi:10.1007/s00191-008-0123-7

Gassmann, O., & Enkel, E. (2004, January). Towards a theory of Open Innovation: Three core process archetypes. 2004. *R&D Management Conference (RADMA).*

Gonzalez Mieres, C., Angel Lopez Sanchez, J., & Leticia Santos Vijande, M. (2012). Internal Marketing, Innovation and Performance in Business Services Firms: The Role of Organizational Unlearning. *International Journal of Management, 29*(4), 403–429.

Griffin, A. (1997). PDMA research on new product development practices: Updating trends and benchmarking best practices. *Journal of Product Innovation Management, 14*(6), 429–458. doi:10.1111/1540-5885.1460429

Gupta, S. K., & Racherla, U. S. (2018). Interdependence among dimensions of sustainability: Evidence from the Indian leather industry. *Management of Environmental Quality*, *29*(3), 406–415. doi:10.1108/MEQ-06-2017-0051

Hadjimanolis, A. (1999). Barriers to innovation for SMEs in a small less developed country (Cyprus). *Technovation*, *19*(9), 561–570. doi:10.1016/S0166-4972(99)00034-6

Hertog, P. D. (2000). Knowledge-intensive business services as co-producers of innovation. *International Journal of Innovation Management*, *4*(4), 491–528. doi:10.1142/S136391960000024X

Heskett, J. L., Sasser, W. E., & Schlesinger, L. A. (1997). *Service profit chain*. The Free Press. https://www.wipo.int/global_innovation_index/en/2022/

Hughes, A., & Wood, E. (2000). *Rethinking innovation comparisons between manufacturing and services: the experience of the CBR SME surveys in the UK*. Springer, US.

Istrate, E., & Harris, J. (2017). *The future of work: The rise of the gig economy*. National Association of Counties.

Jain, S. K., & Gupta, G. (2004). Measuring service quality: SERVQUAL vs. SERVPERF scales. *Vikalpa*, *29*(2), 25–37. doi:10.1177/0256090920040203

Janz, N., Ebling, G., Gottschalk, S., & Niggemann, H. (2001). The Mannheim innovation panels (MIP and MIP-S) of the Centre for European Economic Research (ZEW). *Schmollers Jahrbuch*, *121*(1), 123–129. doi:10.3790/schm.121.1.123

Johne, A., & Storey, C. (1998). New service development: A review of the literature and annotated bibliography. *European Journal of Marketing*, *32*(3/4), 184–251. doi:10.1108/03090569810204526

Kampani, N., & Jhamb, D. (2021). Examining the relationship among servicescape, perceived overall image and customer behavioural intentions in beauty salons: The moderating role of pleasure-arousal-dominance emotional state model. *International Journal of Services, Economics and Management*, *12*(2), 164–184.

Larsen, P., & Lewis, A. (2007). How award-winning SMEs manage the barriers to innovation. *Creativity and Innovation Management*, *16*(2), 142–151. doi:10.1111/j.1467-8691.2007.00428.x

Lau, R. S. (2000). Quality of work life and performance-An ad hoc investigation of two key elements in the service profit chain model. *International Journal of Service Industry Management*, *11*(5), 422–437. doi:10.1108/09564230010360164

Lepanjuuri, K., Wishart, R., & Cornick, P. (2018). *The characteristics of individuals in the gig economy* (Issue February). Retrieved August 12, 2023, from: https://www.gov.uk/government/ publications/gig-economy-research

Lieberman, M. B., & Montgomery, D. B. (1988). First-mover advantages. *Strategic Management Journal*, *9*(1), 41–58. doi:10.1002/smj.4250090706

Lin, L. (2012).The impact of service innovation on firm performance: evidence from the Chinese tourism sector, *The Service Industries Journal, 33*(15-16), 1-34.

Lin, M. C., Wang, C. C., Chen, M. S., & Chang, C. A. (2008). Using AHP and TOPSIS approaches in the customer-driven product design process. *Computers in Industry*, *59*(1), 17–31. doi:10.1016/j.compind.2007.05.013

Lovelock, C., & Gummesson, E. (2004). Whither services marketing? In search of a new paradigm and fresh perspectives. *Journal of Service Research*, *7*(1), 20–41. doi:10.1177/1094670504266131

Loveman, G. W. (1998). Employee satisfaction, customer loyalty, and financial performance an empirical examination of the service profit chain in retail banking. *Journal of Service Research*, *1*(1), 18–31. doi:10.1177/109467059800100103

Mahavarpour, N., Marvi, R., & Foroudi, P. (2023). A brief history of service innovation: The evolution of past, present, and future service innovation. *Journal of Business Research*, *160*, 113795. doi:10.1016/j.jbusres.2023.113795

Martikainen, M. (2008). Painoarvoa palveluiden Kehittamiselle, Elinkeinoelaman keskusliiton raportteja. Confederation of Finnish Industries.

Martin, C. J. (2016). The sharing economy: A pathway to sustainability or a nightmarish form of neoliberal capitalism? *Ecological Economics*, *121*, 149–159. doi:10.1016/j.ecolecon.2015.11.027

Matthing, J., Sandén, B., & Edvardsson, B. (2004). New service development: Learning from and with customers. *International Journal of Service Industry Management*, *15*(5), 479–498. doi:10.1108/09564230410564948

Matzler, K., Veider, V., Hautz, J., & Stadler, C. (2015). The impact of family ownership, management, and governance on innovation. *Journal of Product Innovation Management*, *32*(3), 319–333. doi:10.1111/jpim.12202

McAdam, R., & Armstrong, G. (2001). A symbiosis of quality and innovation in SMEs: A multiple case study analysis. *Managerial Auditing Journal*, *16*(7), 394–399. doi:10.1108/02686900110398296

Menor, L. J., Tatikonda, M. V., & Sampson, S. E. (2002). New Service Development: Areas for Exploitation and Exploration. *Journal of Operations Management*, *20*(2), 135–157. doi:10.1016/S0272-6963(01)00091-2

Miles, I. (2008). Patterns of innovation in service industries. *IBM Systems Journal*, *47*(1), 115–128. doi:10.1147/sj.471.0115

Miller, D., & Friesen, P. H. (1982). Innovation in conservative and entrepreneurial firms: Two models of strategic momentum. *Strategic Management Journal*, *3*(1), 1–25. doi:10.1002/smj.4250030102

Moon, M. J., & Bretschneider, S. (1997). Can state government actions affect innovation and its diffusion? An extended communication model and empirical test. *Technological Forecasting and Social Change*, *54*(1), 57–77. doi:10.1016/S0040-1625(96)00121-7

Moore, G. C., & Benbasat, I. (1991). Development of an instrument to measure the perceptions of adopting an information technology innovation. *Information Systems Research*, *2*(3), 192–222. doi:10.1287/isre.2.3.192

Nair, S. R. (2018). Analyzing the relationship between store attributes, satisfaction,patronage-intention and lifestyle in food and grocery store choice behavior. *International Journal of Retail & Distribution Management*, *46*(1), 70–89. doi:10.1108/IJRDM-06-2016-0102

Oliver, R. L. (1999). Whence consumer loyalty? *Journal of Marketing*, *63*(4_suppl1), 33–44. doi:10.1177/00222429990634s105

Orlikowski, W. J. (1991). Integrated information environment or matrix of control? The contradictory implications of information technology. *Accounting Management and Information Technologies*, *1*(1), 9–42. doi:10.1016/0959-8022(91)90011-3

Panigrahi, J. K., Tripathy, S., & Das, B. (2017). Thematic analysis of service innovation taxonomy within supply network, creating value for the system. *International Journal of Mechanical Engineering and Technology*, *8*(9), 57–69.

Parasuraman, A., Zeithaml, V. A., & Berry, L. L. (1985). A conceptual model of service quality and its implications for future research. *Journal of Marketing*, *49*(4), 41–50. doi:10.1177/002224298504900403

Parida, V., Sjödin, D., & Reim, W. (2019). Reviewing literature on digitalization, business model innovation, and sustainable industry: Past achievements and future promises. *Sustainability (Basel)*, *11*(2), 391. doi:10.3390/su11020391

Peixoto, M. R., Paula, F. D. O., & da Silva, J. F. (2023). Factors that influence service innovation: A systematic approach and a categorization proposal. *European Journal of Innovation Management*, *26*(5), 1189–1213. doi:10.1108/EJIM-05-2021-0268

Piatier, A. (1984). *Barriers to Innovation*. Frances Printer.

Pihkala, T., Linenpaa, H., & Vesalainen, L. (2002). Innovation Barriers amongst Clusters of European SMEs. *International Journal of Entrepreneurship and Innovation Management*, *2*(6), 520. doi:10.1504/IJEIM.2002.000499

Price, R., & Brodie, R. J. (2001). Transforming a Public Service Organization from Inside Out to Outside in The Case of Auckland City, New Zealand. *Journal of Service Research*, *4*(1), 50–59. doi:10.1177/109467050141005

Rappa, M. (2008). Business Models on the Web. https://digitalenterprise.org/models/models.html

Ravenelle, A. J. (2019). *Hustle and Gig*. University of California Press. doi:10.2307/j.ctvcwp0kc

Roberts, E. D. (1988). What we have learned-Managing invention and innovation. *Research Technology Management*, *1*(1), 11–29. doi:10.1080/08956308.1988.11670497

Roberts, P. W., & Amit, R. (2003). The dynamics of innovative activity and competitive advantage: The case of Australian retail banking, 1981 to 1995. *Organization Science*, *14*(2), 107–122. doi:10.1287/orsc.14.2.107.14990

Rust, R. T., Zahorik, A. J., & Keiningham, T. L. (1995). Return on quality (ROQ): Making service quality financially accountable. *Journal of Marketing*, *59*(2), 58–70. doi:10.1177/002224299505900205

Segarra-Blasco, A., & Arauzo-Carod, J. M. (2008). Sources of innovation and industry–university interaction: Evidence from Spanish firms. *Research Policy*, *37*(8), 1283–1295. doi:10.1016/j.respol.2008.05.003

Sidhu, J. S., Commandeur, H. R., & Volberda, H. W. (2007). The multifaceted nature of exploration and exploitation: Value of supply, demand, and spatial search for innovation. *Organization Science*, *18*(1), 20–38. doi:10.1287/orsc.1060.0212

Sirilli, G., & Evangelista, R. (1998). Technological innovation in services and manufacturing: Results from Italian surveys. *Research Policy*, *27*(9), 881–899. doi:10.1016/S0048-7333(98)00084-5

Song, L. Z., Song, M., & DiBenedetto, C. A. (2009). A staged service innovation model. *Decision Sciences*, *40*(3), 571–599. doi:10.1111/j.1540-5915.2009.00240.x

Spohrer, J., & Maglio, P. P. (2010). Toward a Science of Service Systems: Value and Symbols," in Subramanian, A. and S. Nilakanta (1996). Organizational innovativeness: exploring the relationship between organizational determinants of innovation, types of innovations, and measures of organizational performance. *Omega*, *24*(6), 631–647.

Tang, Z., & Lusch, R. F. (2018). Open Innovation: An SD Logic Perspective. In World Scientific Reference on Innovation: Volume 3: Open Innovation, Ecosystems and Entrepreneurship: Issues and Perspectives (pp. 13-35). doi:10.1142/9789813149083_0002

Tatikonda, M. V., & Zeithaml, V. A. (2001). Managing the new service development process: multi-disciplinary literature synthesis and directions for future research. In T. Boone & R. Ganeshan (Eds.), *New directions in supply-chain management* (pp. 200–233). AMACOM.

Taylor, M. R., Rubin, E. S., & Hounshell, D. A. (2005). Regulation as the mother of innovation: The case of SO2 control. *Law & Policy*, *27*(2), 348–378. doi:10.1111/j.1467-9930.2005.00203.x

Teece, D. J. (2010). Business models, business strategy and innovation. *Long Range Planning*, *43*(2/3), 172–194. doi:10.1016/j.lrp.2009.07.003

Tejada, P., & Moreno, P. (2013). Patterns of innovation in tourism 'Small and Medium-size Enterprises. *Service Industries Journal*, *33*(7-8), 749–758. doi:10.1080/02642069.2013.740469

Tidd, J., Bessant, J., & Pavitt, K. (1997). *Managing Innovation: Integrating Technological and Organizational Change* (Vol. 3). Wiley and Sons.

Tushman, M. L., Virany, B., & Romanelli, E. (1985). Executive succession, strategic reorientations, and organisation evolution: The minicomputer industry as a case in point. *Technology in Society*, *7*(2), 297–313. doi:10.1016/0160-791X(85)90031-4

Van der Vegt, G. S., & Janssen, O. (2003). The joint impact of interdependence and group diversity on innovation. *Journal of Management*, *29*(5), 729–751. doi:10.1016/S0149-2063_03_00033-3

Vargo, S. L., & Lusch, R. F. (2004). Evolving to a new dominant logic for marketing. *Journal of Marketing*, *68*(1), 1–17. doi:10.1509/jmkg.68.1.1.24036

Vargo, S. L., & Morgan, F. W. (2005). Services in society and academic thought: A historical analysis. *Journal of Macromarketing*, *25*(1), 42–53. doi:10.1177/0276146705275294

Vashishth, A., & Jhamb, D. (2021). Why should employers hire people with disabilities?–a review of benefits for the hospitality industry. *Revista Turismo & Desenvolvimento (Aveiro)*, (35), 9–21.

Verhagen, T., & Dolen, W. (2009). Online purchase intentions: A multi-channel store image perspective. *Information & Management*, *46*(2), 77–82. doi:10.1016/j.im.2008.12.001

Verma, B., & Tandon, U. (2022). Modelling barriers to wearable technologies in Indian context: validating the moderating role of technology literacy. Global Knowledge, Memory and Communication. doi:10.1108/GKMC-08-2022-0209

Voss, C. A. (1992). Measurement of Innovation and Design Performance in Services. *Design Management Journal*, *3*(1), 40–46. doi:10.1111/j.1948-7169.1992.tb00586.x

Wind, J., & Mahajan, V. (1997). Editorial: Issues and opportunities in new product development: an introduction to the special issue. *JMR, Journal of Marketing Research*, *34*(1), 1–12. doi:10.2307/3152060

Wischnevsky, J. D., & Damanpour, F. (2006). Organizational transformation and performance: An examination of three perspectives. *Journal of Managerial Issues*, *18*(1), 104–128.

Zaltman, G., Duncan, R., & Holbek, J. (1973). *Innovations and organizations*. Wiley.

Zineldin, M. (2000). Beyond relationship marketing: Technologicalship marketing. *Marketing Intelligence & Planning*, *18*(1), 9–23. doi:10.1108/02634500010308549

Chapter 9
The Convergence of Services and AI:
The Opportunities and Challenges With Special Reference to the Indian Market

Oindrila Chakraborty
J.D. Birla Institute, India

ABSTRACT

The chapter explores the far-reaching impact of AI on the Indian service sector, focusing on consumer attitudes and perceptions regarding the use of AI in service sectors. It addresses potential implications such as job displacement and workforce upskilling. The chapter explores AI adoption in the Indian market, its applications, benefits, challenges, and future possibilities. It also offers a glimpse of the ethical dilemmas and promising future of AI in the service industry. The data gathered through the qualitative survey would provide valuable insights into the attitudes and perceptions of Indian consumers on AI use in the Indian market along their difficulties and comfort zone about the use of AI in service sectors.

INTRODUCTION

In the ever-evolving landscape of the service sector, the integration of Artificial Intelligence (AI) has emerged as a transformative force. AI, a technological marvel that replicates human intelligence and decision-making processes, has made remarkable inroads into various service industries. From healthcare to finance, retail to customer support, AI is reshaping the way services are delivered,

DOI: 10.4018/979-8-3693-2153-9.ch009

optimizing processes, and enhancing customer experiences. In a world increasingly defined by automation and data-driven insights, the service sector finds itself at the forefront of a technological revolution. AI, with its ability to process vast amounts of data, identify patterns, and make real-time decisions, has become a linchpin in the pursuit of efficiency, personalization, and cost-effectiveness. Whether it's virtual assistants providing instant customer support, predictive analytics aiding in inventory management, or healthcare algorithms diagnosing diseases, AI is not just a tool but a driving force behind innovation. One of the key advantages of AI in the service sector is its capacity to streamline operations and enhance productivity. It can sift through data at speeds impossible for humans, leading to quicker and more accurate decision-making. As we venture further into the digital age, the symbiotic relationship between AI and the service sector will undoubtedly shape the way we interact with businesses and receive services. Moreover, AI-driven chatbots and virtual assistants offer customers a round-the-clock support system, improving response times and user satisfaction. In essence, AI is not merely a tool to reduce labour costs but a catalyst for delivering higher-quality services. It has taken the horizon of services to a multifarious level through diverse applications. For example, AI-powered chatbots are used for providing instant responses to customer inquiries and solve common issues through text or voice interactions; AI algorithms analyse customer data to make personalized product or content recommendations, enhancing the user experience; in industries like manufacturing and transportation, AI is used for predicting equipment maintenance needs, reducing downtime and improving efficiency; AI is employed to analyse social media and customer feedback to gauge public sentiment about products, services, or brands; AI systems can detect unusual patterns or transactions to prevent fraud in financial services, online marketplaces, and more; AI processes vast amounts of data to provide insights into market trends, consumer behaviour, and competitive intelligence; AI tools assist in generating content, from news articles to social media posts, often used in media and marketing services; AI-powered translation services, like Google Translate, offer real-time language translation to bridge communication gaps; AI is used as an aid to doctors in diagnosing medical conditions and interpreting medical images like X-rays and MRIs; AI-driven bots automate routine tasks in areas such as data entry, payroll, and invoice processing, streamlining operations; AI helps in providing recommendations for accommodations, travel routes, and personalizing travel experiences. AI-based platforms offer personalized learning paths and feedback to students, enhancing the education sector; AI analyses data to optimize inventory management, demand forecasting, and logistics, improving efficiency; AI is used in HR for resume screening, employee onboarding, and identifying potential talent within the organization; AI is used for menu optimization, food delivery logistics, and personalized customer recommendations. However, everything about the usage of AI is not that glorious.

The integration of AI in the service sector is not without its challenges. Concerns about data privacy, security, and the potential for job displacement remain. Striking the right balance between automation and maintaining a human touch is a continuous struggle, though AI is taking almost all spheres of service industry by storm. The challenges require careful consideration and ethical application of AI technologies.

BACKGROUND OF SERVICES MARKETING AND USE OF AI IN SERVICE SECTORS

Artificial intelligence (AI) has been steadily infiltrating the service sector for years, and its impact is only deepening. The integration of artificial intelligence (AI) in service sectors has been transformative, reshaping processes, enhancing customer experiences, and driving operational efficiency. This portion explores the landscape of AI applications in services, examining its historical trajectory, current trends, and future implications. Let's take a glimpse into the historical background of its use:

Early Exploration (1960s-1990s)

The initial foray of AI in services focused on automating basic tasks and replicating human expertise. Rule-based systems and chatbots emerged, handling straightforward inquiries and scheduling appointments (Melnik & Shah, 2003). Expert systems captured knowledge in specific domains, aiding decision-making in areas like medical diagnosis (Shortliffe, 1979). However, these early systems were limited in robustness. Some of these concepts are discussed in details below-

Simple Automation

The commencement of exploring AI based services dates back to basic usage. The earliest applications focused on automating basic tasks like scheduling appointments, routing calls, and generating basic reports. It started with the rudimentary chatbots and rule-based systems.

Expert Systems

AI captured human expertise in specific domains (e.g., medical diagnosis) to guide decision-making could be traced back as early usage. Though these systems were limited in scope and adaptability.

Predictive Analytics

Early forms of machine learning emerged, enabling basic data analysis and basic predictions like customer churn, fraud detection.

Rise of Modern AI (2000s-Present)

The dawn of the 21st century ushered in an era of advanced AI techniques, inflamed by increased computing power and vast data availability. Machine learning algorithms enabled predictive analytics, forecasting customer churn or identifying fraudulent activities (Brynjolfsson & McAfee, 2014). Natural language processing blossomed, leading to the development of sophisticated chatbots and virtual assistants capable of engaging in natural conversations and offering personalized customer service (Ghoosh, 2020). AI algorithms began informing complex decision-making, influencing pricing strategies, credit risk assessments, and even insurance claims processing (Chen & Moore, 2012).Some of these are discussed in details below-

Advancements in Computing Power and Data

Increased processing capabilities and vast data availability fueled the development of more sophisticated AI techniques like deep learning and natural language processing.

Personalization and Customization

AI enabled businesses to personalize customer experiences, tailor recommendations, and offer dynamic services based on individual needs and preferences.

Chatbots and Virtual Assistants

Conversational AI revolutionized customer service with chatbots that handle basic inquiries, schedule appointments, and even offer emotional support.

Automated Decision-Making

AI algorithms started informing pricing strategies, credit risk assessments, and even insurance claims processing.

Current Landscape of AI

The current landscape of AI in services is teeming with innovation.

Increased Automation

AI is automating ever-more complex tasks, including document analysis, medical image diagnosis, and financial forecasting, freeing human employees for higher-level cognitive work (Manyika et al., 2017).

Hyper-Personalization

AI continues to refine its ability to personalize experiences, predicting individual needs and desires in real-time across various service sectors. As already highlighted, AI's ability to personalize experiences is reaching new heights, predicting individual desire and transferring tailored services in real-time across various sectors based on those needs and desires (Sarker & Sarker, 2020).

Emergence of Robotic Process Automation (RPA)

Software robots mimic human actions to automate repetitive tasks, further streamlining operations and boosting efficiency.(Van der Auwermeulen et al., 2017).

Looking ahead, AI promises to transform services even further. Self-driving cars and drones could revolutionize delivery(Amazon Prime Air for last mile deliver-deploying AI-powered drones to deliver packages directly to customers' doorsteps; these drones can autonomously navigate predetermined routes, avoiding obstacles and adhering to safety regulations, Ford and Walmart have partnered to develop a fleet of self-driving delivery trucks; these trucks use AI to optimize routes, navigate traffic, and safely deliver goods to their destinations, DHL utilizes AI-powered drones equipped with LiDAR and machine vision technology to automate inventory counting and tracking; these drones can quickly scan shelves and identify discrepancies, improving accuracy and efficiency, Zipline operates a network of fixed-wing drones that can autonomously deliver critical medical supplies, such as vaccines and blood products, to remote villages and healthcare facilities.) while AI-powered medical diagnostics and treatment may reshape healthcare. Personalized education and entertainment tailored to individual preferences are also on the horizon.

MAIN FOCUS OF THE CHAPTER

Under the given circumstances, this chapter would explore the profound impact of AI on the service sector, shedding light on its applications, benefits, and the challenges it presents, as well as the exciting possibilities it holds for the future through analysing and discussing the trends. This chapter also, sets the stage for a comprehensive exploration of the diverse ways AI is being harnessed, the ethical questions it raises, and the exciting future it promises for the service industry. The chapter would also take the audience through a miniscule qualitative survey to capture the viewpoints of the Indian consumers regarding the use of AI in service sector and the mental positivity and uncertainty of the target consumers in Indian market. The chapter would explore essentially the answers for the following questions:

1. Are the Indian consumers well aware of need and use of AI in service sectors?
2. Is there any visible demographic variations(age, gender, education, Occupation etc.) in awareness and knowledge of AI in service sector?
3. What are the types of AI based services availed by Indian consumers?
4. What is the degree of dependence of Indian consumers on AI based Services?
5. Do they have trust on AI based services?
6. Are they satisfied with AI based services?
7. Is there any threat perception or fear psychosis or sense of uncertainty working in the mind of Indian consumers regarding AI generated or controlled services?

LITERATURE REVIEW ON ARTIFICIAL INTELLIGENCE IN SERVICE SECTORS

Literature wise also the use of AI in service sector has been quite in discussion. Chatbots and virtual assistants are increasingly being used to handle customer inquiries, provide technical support, and personalize customer interactions for long (Lemon & Cerpa, 2016). Also, AI algorithms are employed for targeted advertising, lead generation, and dynamic pricing to optimize marketing campaigns and improve sales conversions (Brynjolfsson, Hitt, & Kim, 2017).AI-powered systems are used for route optimization, predictive maintenance, and automated inventory management to streamline operations and reduce costs (Kearney, 2018).AI algorithms are utilized for fraud detection, credit risk assessment, and personalized financial advice, leading to greater efficiency and improved customer engagement (PWC, 2017). AI is revolutionizing healthcare through medical diagnosis, personalized treatment plans, and robotic surgery, offering greater accuracy and improved patient outcomes (Esteva et al., 2019). Madlberger (2023) found that AI is being used in a variety of ways in the service sector, including to improve customer service, personalize marketing, increase sales, and streamline operations. Bharadwaj et al. (2020) argued that AI is the next frontier for value creation in the service sector. Lee et al. (2022) provided a comprehensive review of the literature on AI in the service sector, highlighting the various ways in which AI is being used to improve customer service, personalize marketing, increase sales, and streamline operations.

DESIGN OF THE CHAPTER

The chapter would have two portions as already mentioned. The first portion would mainly deal with the contemporary literature review on the background and related aspects of use of AI in service sectors through a chronological data exploration. The second portion would deal with a miniscule survey with Indian target consumers for service sectors in the age range of eighteen to above fifty years to check the awareness, knowledge, frequency of usage, areas of usage and satisfaction level of the aforementioned class of respondents and their comfort level with the use of AI in service sector. There has been also an endeavour to seek the answers of whether there is any mental apprehensions working at the back of the mind of the respondents regarding fostering the AI in service sector or not, since this is comparatively an emerging trend in the service sectors. This study is based on qualitative analysis through a theme based pattern coding or category coding . The questionnaire used is a semi structured questionnaire which has been surveyed through online forms, WhatsApp messages, video and phone conferencing with some open ended and nominal response based dichotomous/ multiple choice questions. The sampling technique is purposive with the condition of the respondents to be familiar with the word AI, irrespective of the proper awareness or not. The figure 1 depicts the overall chapter design, while the tables (Table1, Table 2, Table 3 and Table 4) below provide detailed demographic profiling of respondents using various parameters, showcasing information on different segments such as age, gender, qualification. Occupation etc.

TRENDS OF USING AI IN SERVICE SECTORS

Sivaraman (2023) highlighted a few trends in the use of AI in the service sector- first is the increasing use of AI to automate tasks and streamline operations, secondly the growing adoption of AI to personalize customer experiences and finally, the more and more development of the new AI-powered products and services. A few of the emerging trends have been discussed below and have been summed up in figure 2 for ease of understanding.

Deeper Integration of AI

AI would become increasingly embedded in service platforms and processes, leading to more intelligent and autonomous services through AI powered chat bots and virtual assistance along with customers sentiment analysis via customer feedback and social media data to understand sentiment, identify trends, and improve customer

Figure 1. Showing the design of the chapter

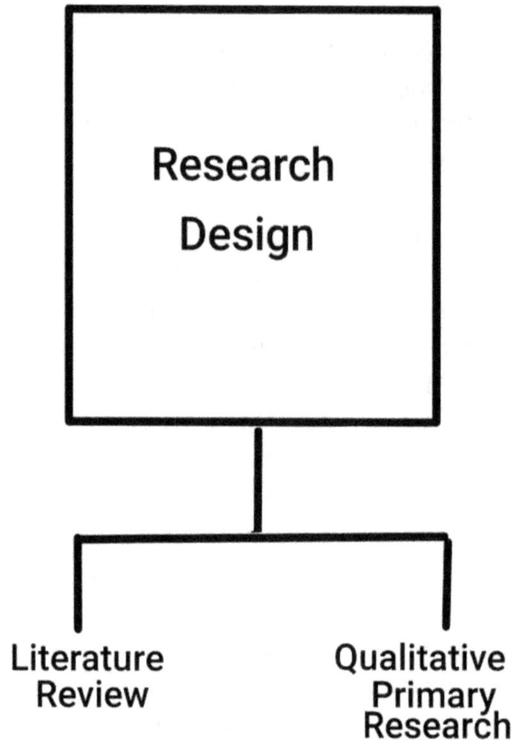

satisfaction. AI also analyses customer purchase history and browsing behaviour to recommend personalized products, increasing sales and customer engagement. There is a concept of Smart mirrors in retail industry to use AI for suggesting outfits based on body type, preferences, and occasion, enhancing the shopping experience. AI also adjusts hotel and airline prices based on real-time demand, competitor pricing, and customer data, optimizing revenue and attracting customers through dynamic pricing. In hospitality industry, use of Smart robots could handle tasks like room service, luggage delivery, and concierge services, providing a futuristic and efficient guest experience. In finance industry, AI analyses financial transactions to identify suspicious activity and prevent fraud, protecting both customers and businesses. The concept of Robo-advisors aka AI-powered platforms provide personalized investment advice and portfolio management, making financial services more accessible. In healthcare industry, Medical diagnosis has been possible through AI algorithms which analyse medical images and data to assist doctors in diagnosis, leading to faster and more accurate results. Also, Personalized treatment plans are possible

Table 1. Showing the respondents profiling age wise

Serial Number	Age Group (Years)	Number of Respondents
1	Lower than 20	58
2	20-30	66
3	31-40	62
4	41-50	58
5	above 50	47
Total		291

Table 2. Showing the respondents profiling qualification wise

Serial Number	Qualification	Number of Respondents
1	Undergraduate	156
2	Postgraduate	78
3	Researchers	45
4	Professional Degree holders	12
Total		291

as AI analyses patient data to recommend personalized treatment plans and predict potential health risks, improving patient outcomes.

Table 3. Showing the respondents profiling occupation wise

Serial Number	Occupation	Number of Respondents
1	Students	89
2	Employed	97
3	Professionals	63
4	Home makers	42
Total		291

Table 4. Showing the respondents profiling gender wise

Serial Number	Gender	Number of Respondents
1	Female	137
2	Male	154
Total		291

Rise of Human-AI Collaboration

Humans and AI would work together in a complementary manner, leveraging each other's strengths to deliver superior service experiences in days to come. Already it has been well in practice in some of the fields like Healthcare, Customer Service, Financial Services, Retail, Hospitality etc.

AI algorithms analyse medical scans and flag potential abnormalities for doctors to review in healthcare industry. This allows doctors to focus on complex cases while the AI handles routine screening. Surgical robots are again an extremely useful AI based tools. Surgeons collaborate with AI-powered robots for minimally invasive procedures. The robot assists with precision and stability, while the surgeon retains control and decision-making.

Robo-advisors with human oversight are also an excellent evidence of Human-AI collaboration in finance industry. AI-powered platforms provide personalized investment recommendations based on customer data. However, human financial advisors offer additional guidance and adjustments for specific needs and risk tolerance. Fraud detection teams in financial services are also enabled with AI tools. AI algorithms identify suspicious activity, but human analysts investigate and make final decisions about fraud prevention measures.

In retail industry, Personalized product recommendations is another manifestation of Human- AI interface. AI analyses past purchases and browsing behaviour to suggest relevant products. Human salespeople then use this information to offer additional recommendations and enhance the shopping experience. Smart inventory management in the similar manner efficiently helps to manage supply chain in seamless manner. AI predicts demand and optimizes inventory levels, while human managers ensure product availability and adjust strategies based on market conditions.

In hospitality industry, Concierge robots are again another set of wonderful invention. AI-powered robots provide basic information and services, while human staff handle complex requests and personalize guest interactions, creating a unique and memorable experience. Dynamic pricing is another initiative in the same pattern. AI algorithms suggest pricing based on demand and competitor analysis, but human managers fine-tune pricing strategies and consider additional factors like local events and special promotions.

These examples highlight the strengths of both humans and AI through the successful symbiosis. Humans offer creativity, empathy, and critical thinking, while AI excels at data analysis, automation, and pattern recognition. By working together, humans and AI can achieve greater efficiency, accuracy, and ultimately, a better service experience for customers. But effective AI-human collaboration requires trust, clear communication, and ongoing training for both humans and AI systems. The future of the service sector lies in the symbiotic relationship between humans and AI, where each partner leverages their unique strengths to provide superior service with a perfect synergy.

Personalization and Customization

AI will enable highly personalized and customized service offerings tailored to individual customer needs and preferences and revolutionizing the service sector through it. E-commerce giants like Amazon and Netflix are Leveraging AI to analyse the purchase history and browsing behaviour of their customers. Based on these insights, they recommend products or shows customers are likely to enjoy, increasing customer engagement and sales. AI algorithms consider factors like demand, seasonality, competitor pricing, and the travel history to personalize hotel rates for a specific customer. This ensures the customer gets the best deals while hotels optimize their revenue. Travel booking platforms use AI powered chatbots that understand the travel preferences and budget of a specific customer and can then suggest personalized itineraries, flights, and hotels, making trip planning smooth and efficient. Smart Home Customization is possible through AI assistants like Google Assistant and Amazon Alexa. They can learn the routines and preferences of target customers using the available data and search history. They can then adjust the thermostat, lighting, and music based on the real-time needs and schedule, creating a personalized and comfortable home environment. Healthcare Advancements like AI analysis of medical data and scans to generate personalized treatment plans and predict potential health risks. This allows doctors to tailor care to individual patients, leading to better outcomes. Besides, in financial sectors, Robo-advisors offer personalized investment advice based on the risk tolerance and financial goals of the customers. In academia, AI-powered tutoring systems adapt to each student's learning pace and style, offering individualized support. In manufacturing industry, AI can personalize product design and production based on customer preferences and real-time data.

AI powered Personalization and Customization has manifold benefits including enhanced customer experience, increased loyalty and engagement and improved efficiency and profitability. Personalized experiences foster deeper connections with brands and services. People feel valued and understood when services cater to their specific needs. Businesses can target resources and marketing efforts more effectively. The future of AI in the service sector lies in creating a seamless blend of personalization and human touch. By harnessing the power of AI responsibly, we can unlock a world of personalized services that cater to individual needs and preferences, making the service experience truly unique and delightful.

Focus on Explainability and Trust

Building trust in AI through explainable algorithms and ensuring responsible AI development will be crucial for wider adoption in the service sector. Like explainable AI in Loan Approval by Upstart. Upstart, the lending platform, uses AI to assess creditworthiness beyond traditional credit scores. They provide applicants with a clear breakdown of the factors influencing their loan decision, including salary history, employment stability, and alternative data sources. This transparency fosters trust and empowers borrowers to understand their credit profile. Some companies use AI-powered Chatbots with Transparency Buttons. Like KLM Royal Dutch Airlines equip their AI chatbots with "explain why" buttons. Clicking this button reveals the reasoning behind the chatbot's response, enabling users to understand the logic behind the AI's recommendations or actions. Algorithmic Auditing and Bias Detection are also supporting the explicability. Organizations like Fairness Intelligence conduct algorithmic audits to identify potential biases in AI systems. These audits help companies ensure their AI algorithms are fair and unbiased, mitigating discriminatory outcomes in areas like hiring, healthcare, and criminal justice. Human Oversight and Collaborative Decision-Making are again endorsing the same. Many companies employ a human-in-the-loop approach for AI-powered decisions in critical areas like healthcare diagnosis or financial trading. This ensures that humans review and approve AI recommendations before they are implemented, adding a layer of accountability and mitigating risks associated with solely relying on AI. Public Engagement and Education are also based Explainability and Trust. Companies like Google AI host Explainable AI conferences and workshops to educate the public about the principles and limitations of AI. This transparency builds trust by demystifying AI technology and fostering open dialogue about its responsible development and application. Beyond these examples, focusing on explainability and trust in AI also involves developing user-friendly interfaces that present AI reasoning and insights in a clear and understandable way, prioritizing data privacy and security to ensure that user data used for AI models is protected. Establishing ethical guidelines and frameworks for AI development and deployment in the service sector are also part of Explainability and Trust.

By prioritizing explainability and trust, companies can unlock the full potential of AI in the service sector while mitigating concerns and fostering a more responsible and sustainable future for human-AI collaboration.

ISSUES AND CHALLENGES OF USING AI IN SERVICE SECTORS

Job Displacement

Automation through AI raises concerns about job losses and the need for workforce retraining and upskilling (Brynjolfsson & McAfee, 2011). Though it also creates new opportunities for jobs requiring skills in AI development, data analysis, and human-computer interaction.

Ethical Considerations

Issues such as bias in AI algorithms, transparency, and accountability need to be addressed to ensure ethical and responsible use of AI in services.

Data Privacy and Security

Protecting customer data and ensuring privacy is crucial when implementing AI-powered services.

Technological Limitations

Current AI technologies have limitations in areas such as natural language understanding and common sense reasoning, which can hinder their effectiveness in certain service applications.

ETHICAL CONSIDERATIONS AND USE OF ARTIFICIAL INTELLIGENCE IN SERVICE SECTORS

Concerns about bias, transparency, and job displacement raise the need for responsible AI development and implementation in service industries. The rapid advancement of AI necessitates careful consideration of ethical implications. Concerns about bias, transparency, and job displacement require responsible development and implementation of AI in service sectors (Mittelstadt et al., 2019). Ensuring human-AI collaboration and addressing ethical concerns will be crucial for the sustainable and equitable growth of AI in services.

The future of AI in service sectors is brimming with possibilities. We can expect AI to power self-driving delivery services, diagnose diseases in real-time, and personalize education and entertainment like never before. However, navigating

Figure 2. Showing the emerging trends of AI usage in service sectors

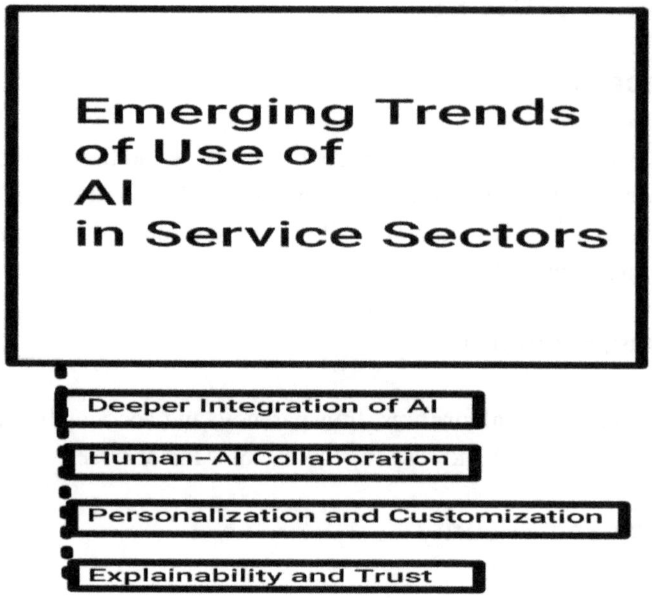

ethical concerns and ensuring human-AI collaboration will be crucial for responsible and sustainable growth.

DISCUSSION

The survey reveals a noticeable difference among various generations of respondents, with Generation Z and Millennials being identified as the most aware class of respondents undoubtedly, followed by Generation X and Baby Boomers, irrespective of their academic qualifications. The subtle differences found amongst different respondents with diverse academic qualification does not make it really a varied and significantly important differentiating factor amongst the respondents. Apparently, it seems to be more familiar with men though the difference in awareness may not be statistically significant, showing again extremely minute difference with the other gender. Nonetheless, the demographic variabilities are shown through Table 5, Table 6, Table 8, Table 9 and not tested through any statistical tools. Hence may not be conclusive in nature to draw a concrete inference . Also, the Table 7 based on the survey, shows that the City Dwellers are more distinctively aware of the AI usage in service sectors than Suburbanites because of obvious parochial differences and more of exposure to recent innovation of the civilization. Table 10 reveals that a major chunk of the respondents consider themselves as knowledgeable and confident to use it during any phase of availing the services. While enquired about the types of AI used for availing services the categories like Chatbot/Autobot, AI based Voice Assistants, e- commerce Recommendations / Personalised Recommendations, AI based Social Media Intelligence and Interferences are surfaced (Table 11) with difficulties like repetitive loop without understanding the actual problems while using autobots or chatbots, fear of data phishing while using voice assistants, fear of unnecessary biased and sponsored information while availing the website recommendations and disturbance while going through social media (Table 12). Table 13 reveals that most of the respondents are quite accustomed using AI while availing services in different sectors and majority of them are comfortable while using it (Table 14), although the level of comfort is not of great extent always (Table 15). The level of satisfaction is varied (Table 16), while a portion of respondents are dissatisfied with the AI based services as it lacks human handholding. Table 17 divulges that still most of the people prefers human-human interfaces foe service encounters due to mental uncertainty and other challenges (Table 18).

FUTURE RESEARCH DIRECTIONS

This study solely focuses on qualitative analysis and exploration of the topic, with no statistical analysis being conducted. As a result, it is unable to capture statistically significant variability. Therefore, further exploration of this study could benefit from the use of different statistical tools and tests, and could be subjected to hypotheses testing.

CONCLUSION

The service sector, long regarded as the domain of human interaction, is facing a seismic shift with the integration of Artificial Intelligence (AI). This potent cocktail is brewing a future of enhanced efficiency, personalized experiences, and data-driven decision-making, poised to redefine the very nature of service delivery. It has unleashed highest form of efficiency. AI automates repetitive tasks, streamlining workflows and freeing human capital for higher-value interactions. Chatbots handle basic queries, AI-powered scheduling optimizes resource allocation, and predictive maintenance minimizes downtime. The result? A leaner, more efficient service ecosystem. AI has amplified Personalization .AI analyzes customer data, learning preferences and anticipating needs. This unlocks hyper-personalized experiences, from tailored recommendations to proactive service solutions. Customers feel

Table 5. Showing the awareness of respondents based on age

Serial Number	Age Group (Years)	Number of Respondents	Aware	Percentage	Category
1	Lower than 20	58	49	84.48	Generation Z
2	20-30	66	62	93.94	Millennials
3	31-40	62	50	80.65	Generation X
4	41-50	58	37	63.79	
5	above 50	47	15	31.91	Baby Boomers
Total		291	213	73.20	Over all Awareness

Table 6. Showing the awareness of respondents based on gender

Serial Number	Gender	Number of Respondents	Aware	Percentage
1	Female	137	98	71.53
2	Male	154	115	74.68
Total		291	213	73.20

Table 7. Showing the awareness of respondents based on residential pattern

Serial Number		Number of Respondents	Aware	Percentage
1	City Dwellers	210	176	83.81
2	Suburbanites	81	37	45.68
Total		291	213	73.20

Table 8. Showing the awareness of respondents based on qualification

Serial Number	Qualification	Number of Respondents	Aware	Percentage
1	Undergraduate	156	121	77.56
2	Postgraduate	78	54	69.23
3	Researchers	45	31	68.89
4	Professional Degree holders	12	7	58.33
Total		291	213	73.20

valued and engaged, fostering loyalty and brand advocacy.AI has also built a Data-driven wisdom. AI's analytical prowess translates data into actionable insights. Businesses can forecast demand, optimize pricing, and identify profitable segments

Table 9. Showing the awareness of respondents based on occupation

Serial Number	Occupation	Number of Respondents	Aware	Percentage
1	Students	89	77	86.52
2	Employed	97	79	81.44
3	Professionals	63	51	80.95
4	Home makers	42	6	14.29
Total		291	213	73.20

Table 10. Showing the self-proclaimed knowledge of respondents

Serial Number	Self-Proclaimed Knowledgeable (Self-Assessment Report)	Number of Respondents	Percentage
1	Considers Knowledgeable	148	50.86
2	Does not Consider Knowledgeable	82	28.18
3	Not Confident	61	20.96
Total		291	100.00

Table 11. Showing the types of AI uses by respondents in service sectors

Serial Number	Types of AI (Category Coding)	Number of Respondents	Percentage
1	Autobots / Chatbots	206	70.79
2	AI Based Voice Assistants	198	68.04
3	e- commerce Recommendations / Personalised Recommendations	106	36.43
4	AI Based Social Media Intelligence and Interferences	89	30.58

Table 12. Showing the problems faced by respondents while using AI-based services

Serial Number	Types of AI (Category Coding)	Types of Problems Faced While Using	Number of Respondents	Percentage
1	Autobots / Chatbots	Caught in a loop	98	33.68
		Difficulty in understanding	79	27.15
		Restricted Information	29	9.97
2	AI Based Voice Assistants	Embarrassing	56	19.24
		Fear of data phishing	142	48.80
3	e- commerce Recommendations / Personalised Recommendations	Unnecessary Information/ Annoying	62	21.31
		Sponsored	44	15.12
4	AI Based Social Media Intelligence and Interferences	Disturbing	89	30.58

Table 13. Showing the frequency of usage of AI while availing services

Serial Number	Frequency of Using AI	Number of Respondents	Percentage
1	Rarely	34	11.68
2	Seldom	67	23.02
3	Very often	93	31.96
4	Unless this is the only option	19	6.53

Table 14. Showing the responses for being comfortable while using AI in services

Serial Number	Comfortable While Using AI in Services	Number of Respondents	Percentage
1	Yes	167	57.39
2	No	46	15.81
3	Unsure	78	26.80

Table 15. Showing the responses for the level of comfort while using AI in services

Serial Number	Level of Comfort While Availing AI in Services	Number of Respondents	Percentage
1	Extremely Comfortable	89	30.58
2	Comfortable	120	41.24
3	Unsure	82	28.18

Table 16. Showing the responses for the level of satisfaction while using AI in services

Serial Number	Level of Satisfaction While Availing AI in Services	Number of Respondents	Percentage
1	Extremely Satisfied	56	19.24
2	Satisfied	85	29.21
3	Unsure	54	18.56
4	Dissatisfied	82	28.18
5	Extremely Dissatisfied	14	4.81

Table 17. Showing the responses for the preferences of the interfaces

Serial Number	Preferences	Number of Respondents	Percentage
1	Human-Human Interface	159	54.64
2	Human-AI Interface	96	32.99
3	Depends on situation	36	12.37

Table 18. Showing the responses with the reasons of the preferences of the interfaces

Serial Number	Reasons for Preferences (Category Coding)	Number of Respondents	Percentage
1	Limited Information	96	32.99
2	Less of Flexibility	89	30.58
3	Fear Psychosis/ Mental Threat/Ethical Considerations	106	36.43

with unparalleled accuracy. This data-driven approach leads to smarter decisions, reduced risk, and sustained growth. The Human-AI symphony is truly showing excellence and overpowering any other collaboration do far. AI's true power lies in its synergy with human intelligence. Instead of replacing humans, AI augments their capabilities. Imagine an AI assistant guiding doctors towards accurate diagnoses, or a customer service agent empowered with real-time insights to resolve complex issues. The collaboration unlocks possibilities beyond the reach of human-only endeavours. However, this transformation isn't without its challenges. Ethical considerations, data privacy concerns, and the need for responsible AI development must be addressed. Upskilling human workforces and ensuring inclusivity are equally crucial. In conclusion, the use of AI in the service sector presents an opportunity for unparalleled growth and customer satisfaction. By embracing this transformative technology responsibly, we can unlock a future where service not only exceeds expectations but seamlessly adapts to individual needs, ushering in a new era of personalized, efficient, and intelligent care.

REFERENCES

Bharadwaj, S., Kohli, A. K., & El Sawy, O. A. (2020). Artificial Intelligence: Next Frontier for Value Creation. *Journal of Business Research, 119*, 428–439.

Brynjolfsson, E., Hitt, L., & Kim, H. (2017). Marketing in the Age of Artificial Intelligence. *Harvard Business Review*, *95*(7-8), 70–80.

Brynjolfsson, E., & McAfee, A. (2011). *Second Machine Age: Work, Prosperity, and Human Destiny*. W. W. Norton & Company.

Brynjolfsson, E., & McAfee, A. (2014). *The Second Machine Age: Work, Progress, and Prosperity in A Time of Brilliant Technologies*. W. W. Norton & Company.

Chen, H., & Moore, A. H. (2012). *Business Intelligence and Analytics: From Data to Knowledge*. John Wiley & Sons.

Esteva, A., Kuprel, B., Novoa, R. A., Quintano, J., & Andreu-Perez, P. (2019). Deep Learning-Based Computer Vision for Medical Image Analysis. *Journal of Medical Imaging (Bellingham, Wash.)*, *6*(4), 044503. PMID:32280727

Ghoosh, A. (2020). *Conversational AI in Customer Service: Transforming the Human-Computer interaction*. CRC Press.

Kearney. (2018). *Artificial Intelligence In The Healthcare Sector: Unleashing The Potential Of AI To Transform Healthcare*. Academic Press.

Lee, K., Kim, M., & Kim, W. (2022). Artificial Intelligence in the Service Sector: A Review of the Literature. *International Journal of Information Science and Management*, *17*(1), 1–27.

Lemon, K. N., & Cerpa, N. (2016). A Comparative Study of Conversational Systems. *Interacting with Computers*, *28*(4), 329–344.

Madlberger, M. (2023). Artificial Intelligence and Business Value: A Literature Review. *Journal of Management Information Systems*, *39*(3), 1012–1034.

Manyika, M., Chui, M., Mirembe, S., Ramaswamy, S., & Trabshaw, J. (2017). Jobs Lost, Jobs Gained: Workforce Transitions. In *A Time of Automation*. McKinsey Global Institute.

Melnik, G., & Shah, R. (2003). *Customer Relationships and Information Technology: Moving Beyond the CRM Debate*. Routledge.

Mittelstadt, B., Allo, P., Taddeo, M., & Wachter, S. (2019). *The Ethics of Algorithms: Fairness, Accountability, and Transparency*. Oxford University Press.

Sarker, S., & Sarker, M. (2020). *Service Innovation in the Digital Age: Leveraging Technology to Create Transformative Experiences*. Routledge.

Shortliffe, E. H. (1979). *MYCIN: A Computer Program For the Diagnosis of Infectious Diseases*. Elsevier.

Sivaraman, D. (2023). *AI in Service Industry: Trends and Opportunities*. McKinsey & Company.

Van der Auwermeulen, T., De Backer, M., Van Den Poel, D., & Snoeck, H. (2017). Potential Roles of Robotic Process Automation in Financial Services. *Journal of Financial Transformation*, *36*(2), 126–136.

KEY TERMS AND DEFINITIONS

Baby Boomers: Sometimes Baby Boomers are simply called Boomers, are the demographic cohort born between the mid-1940s and the mid-1960s (approximately 1946-1964). This generation, following the Silent Generation and preceding Generation X, witnessed and actively shaped a period of immense societal, cultural, and economic change in the West. Baby Boomers are often characterized by Optimism and Idealism, Work Ethic and Consumerism, Technological Adaptability, Political Engagement, Strong Sense of Community and Aging Challenges etc. Growing up in a period of relative prosperity and post-war optimism, many Boomers embraced ideas of individualism, social progress, and self-expression. They challenged traditional norms and actively pursued social justice movements for civil rights, feminism, and environmentalism. Boomers are known for their strong work ethic and dedication. They entered the workforce during a period of economic expansion and contributed significantly to its growth. This era also saw the rise of consumer culture, with Boomers fueling demand for new products and experiences. While not born into a digital world like later generations, Boomers readily embraced technological advancements as they emerged. They adapted to computers, the internet, and mobile technology, though their tech savviness may not rival younger generations. Boomers are a politically active generation. They participated in major protests and movements of the 1960s and 70s, shaped various political landscapes, and continue to hold significant voting power. Despite emphasizing individualism, Boomers also hold a strong sense of community. They formed tight bonds with their peers through shared experiences and cultural movements, creating a lasting collective identity. As Boomers reach retirement age, they face unique challenges related to social security, healthcare, and long-term care. Their sheer numbers and changing needs put pressure on societal systems and resources. Boomers' values and experiences often differ from those of younger generations. Understanding these differences is crucial for addressing intergenerational conflicts and fostering collaboration across generations. Beyond their direct contributions, Boomers left a lasting legacy on society. They challenged social norms, expanded economic opportunities, and championed individual expression, shaping the world we live in today.

City Dweller: It is a broad term encompassing anyone who lives in a city. However, depending on the context, it can carry specific connotations and nuances. It may mean simply the residents or inhabitants of a city. This is the most basic definition, simply outlining where someone lives. The sociological definition states Individuals shaped by the unique characteristics of urban environments. This definition acknowledges the impact of living in a densely populated, diverse, and constantly evolving space on people's social interactions, cultural experiences, and economic opportunities. It is to be remembered that City dweller is not a monolithic category. Within any city, there is immense diversity in terms of income, ethnicity, cultural background, and lifestyles. The definition can be subjective and context-dependent. The specific meaning of "city dweller" may vary depending on the discussion, research question, or social context. Urban experiences can vary greatly across different cities. The characteristics of a city dweller in a small town or village will differ significantly from those in a large metropolis. Overall, while "city dweller" provides a general label for people living in urban areas, understanding the various ways it can be defined and the limitations of the term is crucial for effective communication and analysis.

Generation X (Gen X): They are also known as the In-Betweeners. It is the demographic cohort sandwiched between the iconic Baby Boomers and the much-discussed Millennials. Their birth years generally fall between the mid-1960s and the early 1980s(though specific ranges can vary slightly). Gen X is characterized by being Independent and Resourceful, full of Pragmatism and Scepticism, Dark Humour and Sarcasm, Cynicism and Disillusionment, Strong Community Bonds Tech-Savvy with Boundaries, having Entrepreneurial Spirit and maintaining Work-Life Balance. Growing up in the shadow of the Boomers and witnessing economic uncertainty, Gen Xers developed a strong sense of independence and self-reliance. They are resourceful and adaptable, often embracing DIY solutions and carving their own paths. Witnessing the economic struggles of their parents and the idealism of the Boomers, Gen Xers tend to be more pragmatic and skeptical. They focus on practical solutions and are less swayed by grand narratives or hype.While comfortable with technology, Gen Xers often draw a line between the digital and real worlds. They value real-life interaction and prioritize human connection over constant online engagement. Gen Xers prioritize work-life balance and value personal time. They seek flexibility and meaning in their work, and are less likely to subscribe to the "hustle culture" mentality. Many Gen Xers are drawn to entrepreneurship and self-employment. Their resourcefulness and adaptability make them well-suited to navigating the uncertainties of starting their own ventures. Having witnessed societal shifts and economic challenges, Gen Xers often developed a dry sense of humor and sarcastic wit as a coping mechanism. They are not afraid to laugh at themselves or point out absurdities. Some Gen Xers exhibit a level of cynicism or disillusionment, born from witnessing their parents' struggles and experiencing economic instability. However, many have channeled this into activism and advocacy for positive change. Despite their independent nature, Gen Xers value strong community bonds. They cherish close friendships and prioritize real-life connections over superficial online interactions.

Generation Z (Gen Z): Refers to the demographic cohort succeeding Millennials and preceding Generation Alpha. While specific year ranges can vary slightly, most sources place their birth years between the mid-to-late 1990s and the early 2010s. Gen Z is characterized by traits like being Digital Natives, Socially Conscious, having

Entrepreneurial Spirit, Financially Cautious, Tech-Savvy, believer of Diversity and Inclusion and being pragmatic etc. as their significant qualities. Unlike previous generations who transitioned into a digital world, Gen Z grew up with the internet and mobile technology seamlessly integrated into their lives. They are comfortable navigating online platforms, utilizing social media, and consuming information digitally, Gen Z is known for its strong social conscience and activism. They are passionate about issues like climate change, racial and gender equality, and LGBTQ+ rights. They readily mobilize online and offline to advocate for change. Many Gen Zers are drawn to entrepreneurship and self-employment. They value flexibility, innovation, and making a positive impact through their work. The rise of the gig economy and online platforms has opened new avenues for their entrepreneurial spirit. Having witnessed the economic hardships faced by Millennials, Gen Z is generally more cautious about finances. They prioritize saving and making financially responsible decisions, often due to student loan debt and rising living costs. Gen Z is the most racially and ethnically diverse generation in history. They value inclusivity and challenge traditional norms around gender, sexual orientation, and identity. Gen Z is highly proficient in using technology for communication, entertainment, and learning. They readily adopt new trends and platforms, pushing the boundaries of what's possible in the digital world.Having grown up exposed to a constant flow of information, Gen Z is more skeptical and discerning about what they read or see online. They value authenticity and seek sources of information they can trust. They also take a practical approach to life, focusing on achievable goals and realistic solutions.

Millennials(Gen Y): They are also known as Generation Y, are the demographic cohort following Generation X and preceding Generation Z. Their precise birth years vary slightly, but most sources consider them to be born between the early 1980s and the mid-to-late 1990s. They are characterised by traits like being Tech-Savvy and Connected, Entrepreneurial and Creative, Financially Challenged, Socially Conscious and Inclusive, Ambitious and Purpose-Driven, Skeptical and Discerning etc. Coming of age during the rise of the internet and digital technology, Millennials are highly comfortable navigating online spaces, using social media, and consuming information digitally. They actively utilize technology for communication, entertainment, and information gathering.Millennials are often described as having a strong entrepreneurial spirit and valuing individual expression. They seek career flexibility, purpose, and a sense of making a difference through their work. This leads to a higher than average participation in freelance, self-employment, and creative industries. Many Millennials entered the workforce during the Great Recession, facing economic hardship and rising debt, particularly student loans. This has cultivated a generation that is generally more cautious and responsible with finances, seeking budget-conscious solutions and financial security. Millennials often exhibit strong social awareness and a commitment to social justice issues like environmentalism, LGBTQ+ rights, and racial and gender equality. They value diversity and inclusivity, challenging traditional norms and advocating for fair and equitable treatment for all. Despite facing challenges, Millennials are generally ambitious and goal-oriented. They crave meaningful work and experiences that contribute to a greater good. They emphasize personal growth, self-improvement, and making a positive impact on the world around them. Having grown up amidst information overload, Millennials tend to be skeptical and critical consumers of information. They place a high value on authenticity and reliability, often relying on trusted sources and personal experiences instead of readily accepting traditional narratives.

APPENDIX

Questionnaire for Awareness of AI in Service Sectors
The following questionnaire would be used only for academic purposes, no commercial utilisation would be allowed. Please feel free to respond, complete confidentiality would be maintained to avoid any complication.
Age: Lower than 20/20-30/31-40/41-50/Above 50
Education: Undergraduate / Postgraduate/ Researchers/Professional Degree Holders
Profession: Student /Employed/ Professional/Home makers/Others(please Specify-)
Please Give Answers to the Following Questions:

1. Are you aware of the term 'AI': Yes/ No
2. Do you consider yourself as enough knowledgeable about AI? Yes/ No/Not sure
3. Have you ever used AI for availing any service? Yes/ No
4. What types of AI have you used while availing services?.....
5. What kind of problems have you faced while using AI while availing services?....
6. What is the frequency of using AI while availing services? Rarely/Seldom/ Very often/Unless this is the only option
7. Are you comfortable using AI while availing services? Yes/ No/Unsure
8. What is your level of comfort while availing services with AI? Extremely Comfortable/Comfortable/Unsure
9. Are you satisfied with using AI in services? Extremely Satisfied/Satisfied/ Unsure/ Dissatisfied/ Extremely Dissatisfied
10. Between a Human-Human Interface and Human-AI Interface, which one would you prefer more? Human-Human Interface/Human-AI Interface/Depends on situation
11. Why is it so?....

Thank you

Compilation of References

Aaker, J., Fournier, S., & Brasel, S. A. (2004). When good brands do bad. *The Journal of Consumer Research, 31*(1), 1–16. doi:10.1086/383419

Aase, L., & Timimi, F. K. (2013). Health Care Social Media: Engagement and Health Care in the Digital Era. *Clinical Obstetrics and Gynecology, 56*(3), 471–476. doi:10.1097/GRF.0b013e31829d6058 PMID:23787711

Aas, T. H., & Pedersen, P. E. (2011). The impact of service innovation on firm-level financial performance. *Service Industries Journal, 31*(13), 2071–2090. doi:10.1080/02642069.2010.503883

Abdalla, M. C. E., & de Castilho, S. R. (2017). Analysis of Drug Adversiting Targeted to Health Professionals. *Revista de Direito Sanitário, 18*(1), 101–120. doi:10.11606/issn.2316-9044.v18i1p101-120

Abdullayeva, F. J. (2022). Internet of Things-based Healthcare System on Patient Demographic Data in Health 4.0. *CAAI Transactions on Intelligence Technology, 7*(4), 644–657. Advance online publication. doi:10.1049/cit2.12128

Abraham, M., Mitchelmore, S., Collins, S., Maness, J., Kistulinec, M., Khodabandeh, S., & Visser, J. (2017). *Profiting from personalization*. Boston Consulting Group.

Abusalma, A. (2021). The effect of implementing artificial intelligence on job performance in commercial banks of Jordan. *Management Science Letters, 11*(7), 2061–2070. doi:10.5267/j.msl.2021.3.003

Adam, M., & Wessel, M. (2020). AI-based chatbots in customer service and their effects on user compliance. SpringerLink. https://link.springer.com/article/10.1007/s12525-020-00414-7

Agaba, M. (2021). *Account-based Marketing in B2B-Marketing*. Academic Press.

Agência Nacional de Vigilância Sanitária (ANVISA). (2020, October 14). *Legislação de Propaganda. Ministério Da Saúde*. https://www.gov.br/anvisa/pt-br/assuntos/fiscalizacao-e-monitoramento/propaganda/legislacao/legislacao

Agersborg, C., Månsson, I., & Roth, E. (2020). *Brand Management and Artificial Intelligence-A World of Man Plus Machine-A qualitative study exploring how Artificial Intelligence can contribute to Brand Management in the B2C sector*. Academic Press.

Agrawal, A., Gans, J. S., & Goldfarb, A. (2019). Artificial intelligence: The ambiguous labor market impact of automating prediction. *The Journal of Economic Perspectives*, *33*(2), 31–50. doi:10.1257/jep.33.2.31

Ahern, D. K., Woods, S. S., Lightowler, M. C., Finley, S. W., & Houston, T. K. (2011). Promise of and Potential for Patient-Facing Technologies to Enable Meaningful Use. *American Journal of Preventive Medicine*, *40*(5, Supply 2), S162–S172. doi:10.1016/j.amepre.2011.01.005 PMID:21521591

Ahmad, K. A., Khujamatov, H., Akhmedov, N., Bajuri, M. Y., Ahmad, M. N., & Ahmadian, A. (2022). Emerging Trends and Evolutions for Smart City Healthcare Systems. *Sustainable Cities and Society*, *80*, 103695. doi:10.1016/j.scs.2022.103695

Ahn, J., Kim, J., & Sung, Y. (2022). The effect of gender stereotypes on artificial intelligence recommendations. *Journal of Business Research*, *141*, 50–59. doi:10.1016/j.jbusres.2021.12.007

Ahuja, G., & Katila, R. (2001). Technological acquisitions and the innovation performance of acquiring firms: A longitudinal study. *Strategic Management Journal*, *22*(3), 197–220. doi:10.1002/smj.157

Akhmetov, I., & Bubnov, R. V. (2015). Assessing Value of Innovative Molecular Diagnostic Tests in the Concept of Predictive, Preventive, and Personalized Medicine. *The EPMA Journal*, *6*(19), 19. Advance online publication. doi:10.1186/s13167-015-0041-3 PMID:26425215

Akter, S., Hossain, M. A., Sajib, S., Sultana, S., Rahman, M., Vrontis, D., & McCarthy, G. (2023). A framework for AI-powered service innovation capability: Review and agenda for future research. *Technovation*, *125*, 102768. doi:10.1016/j.technovation.2023.102768

Alam, I. (2002). An exploratory investigation of user involvement in new service development. *Journal of the Academy of Marketing Science*, *30*(3), 250–261. doi:10.1177/0092070302303006

Al-Debi, M. M., El-Haddadeh, R., & Avison, D. (2008). Defining the business model in the new world of digital business. *AMCIS 2008 Proceedings*, 300.

Alene, E. T. (2020). Determinants that influence the performance of women entrepreneurs in micro and small enterprises in Ethiopia. *Journal of Innovation and Entrepreneurship*, *9*(1), 1–20. doi:10.1186/s13731-020-00132-6

Alhawiti, K. M. (2015). Advances in artificial intelligence using speech recognition. *International Journal of Computer and Information Engineering*, *9*(6), 1432–1435.

Alkhaldi, O., McMillan, B., Maddah, N., & Ainsworth, J. (2023). Interventions Aimed at Enhancing Healthcare Providers' Behaviour towards the Prescription of Mobile Health Apps: A Systematic Review. *JMIR mHealth and uHealth*, *11*(e43561), e43561. Advance online publication. doi:10.2196/43561 PMID:36848202

Allen, T. J., Utterback, J. M., Sirbu, M. A., Ashford, N. A., & Hollomon, J. H. (1978). Government influence on the process of innovation in Europe and Japan. *Research Policy*, *7*(2), 124–149. doi:10.1016/0048-7333(78)90002-1

Allioui, H., & Mourdi, Y. (2023). Unleashing the potential of AI: Investigating cutting-edge technologies that are transforming businesses. *International Journal of Computer Engineering and Data Science*, *3*(2), 1–12.

Allison, L., Liu, Y., Murtinu, S., & Wei, Z. (2023). Gender and firm performance around the world: The roles of finance, technology and labor. *Journal of Business Research*, *154*, 113322. doi:10.1016/j.jbusres.2022.113322

Al-Makhaita, H. M., Sabra, A. A., & Hafez, A. S. (2014). Job performance among nurses working in two different health care levels, Eastern Saudi Arabia: A comparative study. *International Journal of Medical Science and Public Health*, *3*(7), 832–837. doi:10.5455/ijmsph.2014.240420142

Alpay, G., Bodur, M., Yilmaz, C., & Büyükbalci, P. (2012). How does innovativeness yield superior firm performance? The role of marketing effectiveness. *Innovation (North Sydney, N.S.W.)*, *14*(1), 107–128. doi:10.5172/impp.2012.14.1.107

Alqahtani, F., & Orji, R. (2020). Insights from user reviews to improve mental health apps. *Health Informatics Journal*, *26*(3), 2042–2066. doi:10.1177/1460458219896492 PMID:31920160

Ameen, N., Tarhini, A., Reppel, A., & Anand, A. (2021). Customer Experiences in the Age of Artificial Intelligence. *Computers in Human Behavior*, *114*(106548), 106548. Advance online publication. doi:10.1016/j.chb.2020.106548 PMID:32905175

Amoroso, S., Diodato, D., Hall, B. H., & Moncada-Paternò-Castello, P. (2023). Technological relatedness and industrial transformation: Introduction to the Special Issue. *The Journal of Technology Transfer*, *48*(2), 469–475. doi:10.1007/s10961-022-09941-1

Andersen, P., Archacki, R., De Bellefonds, N., & Ratajczak, D. (2017). How digital leaders are transforming B2B marketing. *BCG Insights*.

Anderson, E. W., & Mittal, V. (2000). Strengthening the satisfaction-profit chain. *Journal of Service Research*, *3*(2), 107–120. doi:10.1177/109467050032001

Anderson, S., Rayburn, S. W., & Sierra, J. J. (2019). Future Thinking: The Role of Marketing in Healthcare. *European Journal of Marketing*, *53*(8), 1521–1545. doi:10.1108/EJM-10-2017-0779

An, J., Kwak, H., Qureshi, H. M., & Weber, I. (2021). Precision Public Health Campaign: Delivering Persuasive Messages to Relevant Segments Through Targeted Advertisements on Social Media. *JMIR Formative Research*, *5*(9), e22313. doi:10.2196/22313 PMID:34559055

An, J., & Mikhaylov, A. (2024). Technology-based forecasting approach for recognizing trade-off between time-to-market reduction and devising a scheduling process in open innovation management. *Journal of Open Innovation*, *10*(1), 100207. doi:10.1016/j.joitmc.2024.100207

Antoja, G., Ribera, J., & Mur, J. (2019). ¿Cómo Financiar Las Apps de Salud? IESE Business School, University of Navarra.

Antunes, J. (2020, July 15). Artificial intelligence in marketing - a presentation of benefits and a framework for successful implementation. https://run.unl.pt/handle/10362/111603

Apotheker, J. (2023). *What Will Happen to Marketing in the Age of AI?* TED. https://www.ted.com/talks/jessica_apotheker_what_will_happen_to_marketing_in_the_age_of_ai

Araujo, T., Copulsky, J. R., Hayes, J. L., Kim, S. J., & Srivastava, J. (2020). Purchasing Exposure to Fostering Engagement: Brand–Consumer Experiences in the Emerging Computational Advertising Landscape. *Journal of Advertising*, *49*(4), 428–445. doi:10.1080/00913367.2020.1795756

Arni, P., & Laddha, S. (2017). Adoption of Digital Marketing in Health Industry. *Journal of Management*, *13*(1), 38–53.

Arredondo, A. (2014). Type 2 Diabetes and Health Care Costs in Latin America: Exploring the Need for Greater Preventive Medicine. *BMC Medicine*, *12*(136), 136. Advance online publication. doi:10.1186/s12916-014-0136-z PMID:25266304

Atuahene-Gima, K. (1996). Differential potency of factors affecting innovation performance in manufacturing and services firms in Australia. *Journal of Product Innovation Management*, *13*(1), 35–52. doi:10.1111/1540-5885.1310035

Auerswald, M., & Moshagen, M. (2019). How to determine the number of factors to retain in exploratory factor analysis: A comparison of extraction methods under realistic conditions. *Psychological Methods*, *24*(4), 468–491. doi:10.1037/met0000200 PMID:30667242

Autoridade Nacional de Medicamento e Produtos de Saúde. (2023, March 20). *O INFARMED.* Serviço Nacional de Saúde. https://www.infarmed.pt/web/infarmed/apresentacao

Avlonitis, G. J., Papastathaopoulou, P. G., & Gounaris, S. P. (2001). An empirically-based typology of product innovativeness for new financial services: Success and failure scenarios. *Journal of Product Innovation Management*, *18*(5), 324–342. doi:10.1111/1540-5885.1850324

Aydin, G., & Silahtaroglu, G. (2021). Insights Into Mobile Health Application Market Via a Content Analysis of Marketplace Data With Machine Learning. *PLoS One*, *16*(1), 1–22. doi:10.1371/journal.pone.0244302 PMID:33406100

Babatunde, A. O., Shobanke, H. A., Akinade, A. A., Michael, A. J., Osadare, M., Akanbi, O. K., Favour, O. C., & Adebisi, Y. A. (2021). Enhancing Preventive Medicine Over Curative Medicine: Role of Telemedicine. *Public Health in Practice (Oxford, England)*, *2*, 100130. doi:10.1016/j.puhip.2021.100130 PMID:36101617

Bacon, A. (2021). Strategic account-based marketing: How to tame this beast. In *B2B Marketing: A Guidebook for the Classroom to the Boardroom* (pp. 419–435). Springer International Publishing. doi:10.1007/978-3-030-54292-4_17

Bag, S., Dhamija, P., Singh, R. K., Rahman, M. S., & Sreedharan, V. R. (2023). Big Data Analytics and Artificial Intelligence Technologies Based Collaborative Platform Empowering Absorptive Capacity in Health Care Supply Chain: An Empirical Study. *Journal of Business Research, 154*, 113315. . doi:10.1016/j.jbusres.2022.113315

Bagozzi, R. P., & Yi, Y. (1988). On the Evaluation of Structural Equation Models. *Journal of the Academy of Marketing Science*, *16*(1), 74–94. doi:10.1007/BF02723327

Baines, T., Ziaee Bigdeli, A., Bustinza, O. F., Shi, V. G., Baldwin, J., & Ridgway, K. (2017). Servitization: Revisiting the state-of-the-art and research priorities. *International Journal of Operations & Production Management, 37*(2), 256–278. doi:10.1108/IJOPM-06-2015-0312

Balapour, A., Reychav, I., Sabherwal, R., & Azuri, J. (2019). Mobile Technology Identity and Self-Efficacy: Implications for the Adoption of Clinically Supported Mobile Health Apps. *International Journal of Information Management, 49*, 58–68. doi:10.1016/j.ijinfomgt.2019.03.005

Banjo, H., & Olufemi, O. (2014). Demographic Variables and Job Performance: Any Link? (A Case of Insurance Salesmen). *Acta Universitatis Danubius. Economica, 10*(4), 19–30.

Barbu, C. M., Bratu, R. Ş., & Sîrbu, E. M. (2018). Business models of the sharing economy. *Revista de Management Comparat International, 19*(2), 154–166.

Barnard, A., & Parker, C. (2012). *Campaign it!: Achieving success through communication.* Kogan Page Publishers.

Barras, R. (1986). Towards a theory of innovation in services. *Research Policy, 15*(4), 161–173. doi:10.1016/0048-7333(86)90012-0

Barrett, M., Davidson, E., Prabhu, J., & Vargo, S. L. (2015). Service innovation in the digital age. *Management Information Systems Quarterly, 39*(1), 135–154. doi:10.25300/MISQ/2015/39:1.03

Bayode, A., van der Poll, J. A., & Ramphal, R. R. (2019). 4th Industrial Revolution: Challenges and Opportunities in the South African Context. http://www.eares.org/siteadmin/upload/9179EAP1119285.pdf

Belk, R. (2014). You are what you can access: Sharing and collaborative consumption online. *Journal of Business Research, 67*(8), 1595–1600. doi:10.1016/j.jbusres.2013.10.001

Bell, E. (2023). General Intelligence (AGI): Definition, How It Works, and Examples. Investopedia. https://www.investopedia.com/artificial-general-intelligence-7563858#:~:text=Artificial%20general%20intelligence%20%28AGI%29%20is%20a%20theoretical%20pursuit,function%20only%20within%20a%20specific%20set%20of%20parameters%29

Bell, E., Bryman, A., & Harley, B. (2022). *Business research methods* (6th ed.). Oxford University Press. doi:10.1093/hebz/9780198869443.001.0001

Belliger, A., & Krieger, D. J. (2018). The Digital Transformation of Healthcare. In K. North, O. Haas, & R. Maier (Eds.), *Progress in IS Knowledge Management in Digital Change New Findings and Practical Cases* (pp. 311–326). Springer. https://doi.org/https://doi.org/10.1007/978-3-319-73546-7_19

Benko, A., & Lányi, C. S. (2009). History of artificial intelligence. In *Encyclopedia of Information Science and Technology* (2nd ed., pp. 1759–1762). IGI Global. doi:10.4018/978-1-60566-026-4.ch276

Benner, M. J., & Tushman, M. L. (2003). Exploitation, exploration, and process management: The productivity dilemma revisited. *Academy of Management Review*, *28*(2), 238–256. doi:10.2307/30040711

Bentler, P. M., & Bonett, D. G. (1980). Significance tests and goodness of fit in the analysis of covariance structures. *Psychological Bulletin*, *88*(3), 588–606. doi:10.1037/0033-2909.88.3.588

Berkowitz, E. N. (2021). Essentials of Health Care Marketing (5o edição). J. & B. Learning.

Bharadwaj, S., Kohli, A. K., & El Sawy, O. A. (2020). Artificial Intelligence: Next Frontier for Value Creation. *Journal of Business Research*, *119*, 428–439.

Bhayani, S., & Vachhani, N. V. (2014). Internet Marketing vs Traditional Marketing: A Comparative Analysis. *FIIB Business Review*, *3*(3), 53–63. doi:10.1177/2455265820140309

Blandford, A. E. (2013). *Semi-structured qualitative studies*. Interaction Design Foundation.

Blazevic, V., & Lievens, A. (2004). Learning during the new financial service innovation process: Antecedents and performance effects. *Journal of Business Research*, *57*(4), 374–391. doi:10.1016/S0148-2963(02)00272-2

Bollen, K. A. (1990). Overall Fit in Covariance Structure Models: Two Types of Sample Size Effects. *Psychological Bulletin*, *107*(2), 256–259. doi:10.1037/0033-2909.107.2.256

Bondaronek, P., Alkhaldi, G., Slee, A., Hamilton, F. L., & Murray, E. (2018). Quality of publicly available physical activity apps: Review and content analysis. *JMIR mHealth and uHealth*, *6*(3), 1–17. doi:10.2196/mhealth.9069 PMID:29563080

Boniolo, F., Dorigatti, E., Ohnmacht, A. J., Saur, D., Schubert, B., & Menden, M. P. (2021). Artificial Intelligence in Early Drug Discovery Enabling Precision Medicine. *Expert Opinion on Drug Discovery*, *16*(9), 991–1007. doi:10.1080/17460441.2021.1918096 PMID:34075855

Bonoma, T. V. (1985). Case research in marketing: Opportunities, problems, and a process. *JMR, Journal of Marketing Research*, *22*(2), 199–208. doi:10.1177/002224378502200209

Booz, Allen, and Hamilton. (1982). *New Products for the 1980s*. Booz Allen Hamilton, Inc.

Bowers, M. R. (1987). Developing new services for hospitals: A suggested model. *Journal of Health Care Marketing*, *7*(2), 35–44. PMID:10301716

Box, D., & Pottas, D. (2013). Improving Information Security Behaviour in the Healthcare Context. *Procedia Technology*, *9*, 1093–1103. doi:10.1016/j.protcy.2013.12.122

Bozic, K., Pierce, R., & Herndon, J. (2004). Health Care Technology Assessment: Basic Principles and Clinical Applications. *The Journal of Bone and Joint Surgery. American Volume*, *86*(6), 1305–1314. doi:10.2106/00004623-200406000-00028 PMID:15173308

Brooks, R. A. (1991). Intelligence without representation. *Artificial Intelligence*, *47*(1-3), 139–159. doi:10.1016/0004-3702(91)90053-M

Brougham, D., & Haar, J. (2018). Smart technology, artificial intelligence, robotics, and algorithms (STARA): Employees' perceptions of our future workplace. *Journal of Management & Organization*, *24*(2), 239–257. doi:10.1017/jmo.2016.55

Bryman, A. (2016). *Social research methods* (5th ed.). Oxford University Press.

Brynjolfsson, E., Hitt, L., & Kim, H. (2017). Marketing in the Age of Artificial Intelligence. *Harvard Business Review*, *95*(7-8), 70–80.

Brynjolfsson, E., & McAfee, A. (2011). *Second Machine Age: Work, Prosperity, and Human Destiny*. W. W. Norton & Company.

Brynjolfsson, E., & McAfee, A. (2014). *The Second Machine Age: Work, Progress, and Prosperity in A Time of Brilliant Technologies*. W. W. Norton & Company.

Brynjolfsson, E., & McAfee, A. (2014). *The second machine age: Work, progress, and prosperity in a time of brilliant technologies*. WW Norton & Company.

Buhalis, D., & Leung, R. (2018). Smart hospitality—Interconnectivity and interoperability towards an ecosystem. *International Journal of Hospitality Management*, *71*, 41–50. doi:10.1016/j.ijhm.2017.11.011

Burgess, B., Schwartz, J., & Leavitt, R. (2018). Raising the Game with ABM: 2018 ABM Benchmark Study. October). The Companies That Will Grow Your Revenue. In Lighting Design and Application: L.D. and A, 50.

Burgess, B., & Munn, D. (2021). *A Practitioner's Guide to Account-Based Marketing: Accelerating Growth in Strategic Accounts*. Kogan Page Publishers.

Burgess, B., & Shercliff, T. (2022). *Account-based Growth: Unlocking Sustainable Value Through Extraordinary Customer Focus*. Kogan Page Publishers.

Butler, M. G., & Callahan, C. M. (2014). Human resource outsourcing: Market and operating performance effects of administrative HR functions. *Journal of Business Research*, *67*(2), 218–224. doi:10.1016/j.jbusres.2012.09.026

Calder, B. J., Malthouse, E. C., & Schaedel, U. (2009). Engagement with Online Media and Advertising Effectiveness. *Journal of Interactive Marketing*. https://www.researchgate.net/publication/237046588_Engagement_with_Online_Media_and_Advertising_Effectiveness

Çalışkan, A., & Köroğlu, E. Ö. (2022). Job performance, Task performance, Contextual performance: Development and validation of a new scale. *Uluslararası İktisadi ve İdari Bilimler Dergisi*, *8*(2), 180–201. doi:10.29131/uiibd.1201880

Carlborg, P., Kindström, D., & Kowalkowski, C. (2013). The evolution of service innovation research: A critical review and synthesis. *Service Industries Journal*, *34*(5), 1–26.

Carter, E. (2023). *200+ Senior Marketers Dish on How They Use AI.* WebFX. https://www.webfx.com/blog/marketing/how-marketing-leaders-use-ai/

Cassell, C., & Symon, G. (Eds.). (2004). *Essential guide to qualitative methods in organizational research*. Sage publications. doi:10.4135/9781446280119

Cellan-Jones, R. (2014). *Stephen Hawking warns artificial intelligence could end mankind*. BBC Interview, online at Retrieved from https://www.bbc.com/news/technology-30290540

Chaffey, D. (2023). *RACE marketing model*. Dr Dave Chaffey: Digital Insights. https://www.davechaffey.com/digital-marketing-glossary/race-marketing-planning-model/

Chakraborty, D., & Paul, J. (2023). Healthcare Apps' Purchase Intention: A Consumption Values Perspective. *Technovation, 120*(102481). Advance online publication. doi:10.1016/j.technovation.2022.102481

Chakravorty, T., Jha, K., & Barthwal, S. (2018). Digital Technologies as Enablers of Care Quality and Performance: A Conceptual Review of Hospital Supply Chain Network. *The IUP Journal of Supply Chain Management, 15*(3).

Chang, V., Ganatra, M. A., Hall, K., Golightly, L., & Xu, Q. A. (2022). An Assessment of Machine Learning Models and Algorithms for Early Prediction and Diagnosis of Diabetes Using Health Indicators. *Healthcare Analytics*, *2*, 100118. doi:10.1016/j.health.2022.100118

Chatterjee, S., Chaudhuri, R., Vrontis, D., Thrassou, A., & Ghosh, S. K. (2021). Adoption of artificial intelligence-integrated CRM systems in agile organizations in India. *Technological Forecasting and Social Change*, *168*, 120783. doi:10.1016/j.techfore.2021.120783

Chaturvedi, R., & Verma, S. (2023b). Opportunities and challenges of AI-driven customer service. *Artificial Intelligence in Customer Service: The next Frontier for Personalized Engagement*, 33–71.

Chaturvedi, R., & Verma, S. (2023a). Opportunities and Challenges of AI-Driven Customer Service. In J. N. Sheth, V. Jain, E. Mogaji, & A. Ambika (Eds.), *Artificial Intelligence in Customer Service: The Next Frontier for Personalized Engagement* (pp. 33–71). Springer International Publishing. doi:10.1007/978-3-031-33898-4_3

Cheng, C. C., & Krumwiede, D. (2012). The role of service innovation in the market orientation New service performance linkage. *Technovation*, *32*(7), 487–497. doi:10.1016/j.technovation.2012.03.006

Cheng, X., Lin, X., Shen, X. L., Zarifis, A., & Mou, J. (2022). The dark sides of AI. *Electronic Markets*, *32*(1), 11–15. doi:10.1007/s12525-022-00531-5 PMID:35600917

Chen, H., & Moore, A. H. (2012). *Business Intelligence and Analytics: From Data to Knowledge*. John Wiley & Sons.

Chesbrough, H. W. (2003). *Open innovation: The new imperative for creating and profiting from technology*. Harvard Business Press.

Chintalapati, S., & Pandey, S. K. (2022). Artificial intelligence in marketing: A systematic literature review. *International Journal of Market Research*, *64*(1), 38–68. doi:10.1177/14707853211018428

Cho, W., & Cho, S. E. (2020). Entrepreneurial challenges in business model for the gig economy: Agendas for research and business development. *International Journal of Entrepreneurship, 24*(1), 1–11.

Christensen, C. M., Bohmer, R., & Kenagy, J. (2000). Will disruptive innovations cure health care? *Harvard Business Review, 78*(5), 102–112. PMID:11143147

Coffey, A. (2014). Analysing documents. In U. Flick (Ed.), *The SAGE handbook of qualitative data analysis* (pp. 367–380). SAGE Publications. doi:10.4135/9781446282243.n25

Cohen, W. M., & Levinthal, D. A. (1989). Innovation and learning: The two faces of R & D. *Economic Journal (London), 99*(397), 569–596. doi:10.2307/2233763

Çolak, O. (2023). The impact of artificial intelligence on thc employment structure of the tourism industry: An interview with ChatGPT. *İktisadi İdari ve Siyasal Araştırmalar Dergisi, 8*(22), 919-939.

Comissão Europeia. (2014). *Livro Verde Sobre a Saúde Móvel.* SWD(2014) 135 final.

Confessore, N. (2018). *Cambridge Analytica and Facebook: The Scandal and the Fallout So Far.* The New York Times. https://www.nytimes.com/2018/04/04/us/politics/cambridge-analytica-scandal-fallout.html

Cooke, P., & Wills, D. (1999). Small firms, social capital and the enhancement of business performance through innovation programmes. *Small Business Economics, 13*(3), 219–234. doi:10.1023/A:1008178808631

Coombs, R., & Miles, I. (2000). Innovation, measurement and services: the new problematique. In *Innovation Systems in the Service Economy, Kluwer Academic Publisher* (pp. 85–103). Springer, US. doi:10.1007/978-1-4615-4425-8_5

Cooper, C. L. (1984). Work organization and occupational stress. *Automation, Work Organization and Occupational Stress*, 151-176.

Corbin, C. L., Kelley, S. W., & Schwartz, R. W. (2001). Concepts in Service Marketing for Healthcare Professionals. *American Journal of Surgery, 181*(1), 1–7. doi:10.1016/S0002-9610(00)00535-3 PMID:11248166

Crespo, C. F., Ferreira, A. G., & Cardoso, R. M. (2023). The influence of storytelling on the consumer–brand relationship experience. *Journal of Marketing Analytics, 11*(1), 41–56. doi:10.1057/s41270-021-00149-0

Creswell, J. W., & Báez, J. C. (2020). *30 essential skills for the qualitative researcher.* Sage Publications.

Crié, D., & Chebat, J.-C. (2013). Health Marketing: Toward an Integrative Perspective. *Journal of Business Research, 66*(1), 123–126. doi:10.1016/j.jbusres.2012.09.002

Cun, Y., Bengio, Y., & Hinton, G. (2015). Deep learning. *Nature, 521*(7553), 436-444.

Cunha, C. R. (2023). Do conhecimento tácito ao conhecimento baseado em IA Insights: Uma reengenharia em curso? *RISTI (Porto)*, *51*(51), 1–4. doi:10.17013/risti.51.1-4

Das, B. (2022). Diffusion of innovations: Theoretical perspectives and empirical evidence. *African Journal of Science, Technology, Innovation and Development*, *14*(1), 94–103. doi:10.1080/20421338.2020.1814517

Davenport, T., Guha, A., Grewal, D., & Bressgott, T. (2020). How artificial intelligence will change the future of marketing. *Journal of the Academy of Marketing Science*, *48*(1), 24–42. doi:10.1007/s11747-019-00696-0

de Oliveira, M. O. R., Heldt, R., Silveira, C. S., & Luce, F. B. (2023). Brand equity chain and brand equity measurement approaches. In Marketing Intelligence and Planning (Vol. 41, Issue 4, pp. 442–456). Emerald Publishing. doi:10.1108/MIP-06-2022-0222

DeBrentani, U., & Cooper, R. G. (1992). Developing successful new financial services for businesses. *Industrial Marketing Management*, *21*(3), 231–241. doi:10.1016/0019-8501(92)90020-T

Decreto-Lei n.o 238/2015 do Ministério da Saúde, Diário da República: I série, n.o 201 8953 (2015). https://dre.pt/dre/detalhe/decreto-lei/238-2015-70686132?_ts=1679316560455

Decrop, A. (1999). Triangulation in qualitative tourism research. *Tourism Management*, *20*(1), 157–161. doi:10.1016/S0261-5177(98)00102-2

del Castillo, J. A. G., López-Sanchez, C., Tur-Viñes, V., del Castillo-López, Á. G., & Soler, I. R. (2017). A Publicidade Comercial e a Publicidade Social no Contexto da Saúde. In D. Caldevilla (Ed.), *Linguagens e Persuasão: Novas Criações Narrativas* (pp. 159–168). Media XXI., https://www.researchgate.net/publication/313528191_A_publicidade_comercial_e_a_publicidade_social_no_contexto_da_saude

Delgadillo, J., & Atzil-Slonim, D. (2022). Artificial Intelligence, Machine Learning and Mental Health. In *Encyclopedia of Mental Health (3a Edição)*. Elsevier. doi:10.1016/B978-0-323-91497-0.00177-6

Demiris, G., Iribarren, S. J., Sward, K., Lee, S., & Yang, R. (2019). Patient Generated Health Data Use in Clinical Practice: A Systematic Review. *Nursing Outlook*, *67*(4), 311–330. doi:10.1016/j.outlook.2019.04.005 PMID:31277895

Denning, S. (2005). *The leader's guide to storytelling: Mastering the art and discipline of business narrative*. John Wiley & Sons.

Dennison, L., Morrison, L., Conway, G., & Yardley, L. (2013). Opportunities and Challenges for Smartphone Applications in Supporting Health Behavior Change: Qualitative study. *Journal of Medical Internet Research*, *15*(4), e86. doi:10.2196/jmir.2583 PMID:23598614

Denny, R. M. (2006). Pushing the boundaries of ethnography in the practice of market research. Handbook of qualitative research methods in marketing, 430.

Denzin, N. K., & Lincoln, Y. S. (Eds.). (2011). *The Sage handbook of qualitative research.* Sage Publications.

Dewanti, H. E., & Artaya, I. P. (2019, February). The Influence of Training, Work Experience, and Competence on Employee Performance at Surabaya Husada Utama Hospital. In *Journal of World Conference (JWC)* (Vol. 1, No. 1, pp. 93-101). Doi:10.29138/prd.v1i1.27

Dewar, R. D., & Dutton, J. E. (1986). The adoption of radical and incremental innovations: An empirical analysis. *Management Science*, *32*(11), 1422–1433. doi:10.1287/mnsc.32.11.1422

Dicuonzo, G., Donofrio, F., Fusco, A., & Shini, M. (2023). Healthcare System: Moving Forward with Artificial Intelligence. *Technovation*, *120*, 102510. doi:10.1016/j.technovation.2022.102510

Djellal, F., & Gallouj, F. (2001). Patterns of innovation organization in service firms: Postal survey results and theoretical models. *Science & Public Policy*, *28*(1), 57–67. doi:10.3152/147154301781781688

Dormehl, L. (2018). *Replaced by robots: 10 jobs that could be hit hard by the AI revolution.* Retrieved from https://www.digitaltrends.com/cool-tech/examples-of-robots-replacing-jobs/

Dresma. (2022). *5 Ways Amazon Uses AI in eCommerce to Drive Sales*. https://dresma.ai/5-ways-amazon-uses-ai-in-ecommerce-to-drive-sales/

Duan, Y., Edwards, J. S., & Dwivedi, Y. K. (2019). Artificial intelligence for decision making in the era of Big Data–evolution, challenges and research agenda. *International Journal of Information Management*, *48*, 63–71. doi:10.1016/j.ijinfomgt.2019.01.021

Dyer, W. G. Jr, & Wilkins, A. L. (1991). Better stories, not better constructs, to generate better theory: A rejoinder to Eisenhardt. *Academy of Management Review*, *16*(3), 613–619. doi:10.2307/258920

Edvardsson, B. (1997). Quality in new service development: Key concepts and a frame of reference. *International Journal of Production Economics*, *52*(1), 31–46. doi:10.1016/S0925-5273(97)80765-7

Edwards, J. S., Duan, Y., & Robins, P. C. (2000). An analysis of expert systems for business decision making at different levels and in different roles. *European Journal of Information Systems*, *9*(1), 36–46. doi:10.1057/palgrave.ejis.3000344

Eisenhardt, K. M. (1989). Building theories from case study research. *Academy of Management Review*, *14*(4), 532–550. doi:10.2307/258557

Elfil, M., & Negida, A. (2017). *Sampling methods in Clinical Research; an Educational Review.* Shahid Beheshti University of Medical Sciences. https://www.ncbi.nlm.nih.gov/pmc/articles/PMC5325924/

Elhager, S. (2023). *Role of AI in Advertising.* AiHello. https://www.aihello.com/resources/blog/role-of-ai-in-advertising/

Elish, M. C., & Boyd, D. (2018). Situating methods in the magic of Big Data and AI. *Communication Monographs*, *85*(1), 57–80. doi:10.1080/03637751.2017.1375130

Ellington, L. (2014). Technology: impact on the practice of storytelling. In *Handbook of Research on Education and Technology in a Changing Society* (pp. 104–115). IGI Global. doi:10.4018/978-1-4666-6046-5.ch008

Esteva, A., Kuprel, B., Novoa, R. A., Quintano, J., & Andreu-Perez, P. (2019). Deep Learning-Based Computer Vision for Medical Image Analysis. *Journal of Medical Imaging (Bellingham, Wash.)*, *6*(4), 044503. PMID:32280727

Ettlie, J. E., Bridges, W. P., & O'keefe, R. D. (1984). Organization strategy and structural differences for radical versus incremental innovation. *Management Science*, *30*(6), 682–695. doi:10.1287/mnsc.30.6.682

Feng, C., & Sivakumar, K. (2016). The role of collaboration in service innovation across manufacturing and service sectors. *Service Science*, *8*(3), 263–281. doi:10.1287/serv.2016.0135

Fertonani, H. P., de Pires, D. E. P., Biff, D., & Scherer, M. D. dos A. (2015). The Health Care Model: Concepts and Challenges for Primary Health Care in Brazil. *Ciencia & Saude Coletiva*, *20*(6), 1869–1878. doi:10.1590/1413-81232015206.13272014 PMID:26060965

Findlay, P., Lindsay, C., McQuarrie, J., Bennie, M., Corcoran, E. D., & Van Der Meer, R. (2017). Employer choice and job quality: Workplace innovation, work redesign, and employee perceptions of job quality in a complex health-care setting. *Work and Occupations*, *44*(1), 113–136. doi:10.1177/0730888416678038

Fitzsimmons, J. A., & Fitzsimmons, M. J. (2000). *New Service Development: Creating Memorable Experiences*. Sage Publications. doi:10.4135/9781452205564

Flavián, C., & Casaló, L. V. (2021). Artificial intelligence in services: Current trends, benefits and challenges. *Service Industries Journal*, *41*(13–14), 853–859. doi:10.1080/02642069.2021.1989177

Flynn, L. R., & Goldsmith, R. E. (1993). A validation of the Goldsmith and Hofacker innovativeness scale. *Educational and Psychological Measurement*, *53*(4), 1105–1116. doi:10.1177/0013164493053004023

Foley, P., & Gren, H. (1995).A successful High-Technology Company. In Small Business Success. The Small Business Research Trust, Paul Chapman Publishing.

Frank, B. (2021). Artificial intelligence-enabled environmental sustainability of products Marketing benefits and their variation by consumer, location, and product types. *Journal of Cleaner Production*, *285*, 125242. doi:10.1016/j.jclepro.2020.125242

Freni, G. (2022, May). Service Innovation: A Literature Review of Conceptual Perspectives. In *International Symposium: New Metropolitan Perspectives* (pp. 154–163). Springer International Publishing. doi:10.1007/978-3-031-06825-6_15

Frey, C. B., & Osborne, M. A. (2017). The future of employment: How susceptible are jobs to computerisation? *Technological Forecasting and Social Change, 114*, 254–280. doi:10.1016/j.techfore.2016.08.019

Gabbatt, A. (2011). IBM computer Watson wins Jeopardy clash. *The Guardian, 17.*

Gadrey, J., Gallouj, F., & Weinstein, O. (1995). New modes of innovation: How services benefit industry. *International Journal of Service Industry Management, 6*(3), 4–16. doi:10.1108/09564239510091321

Galia, F., & Legros, D. (2004). Complementarities between obstacles to innovation: Evidence from France. *Research Policy, 33*(8), 1185–1199. doi:10.1016/j.respol.2004.06.004

Gallouj, F., Weber, K. M., Stare, M., & Rubalcaba, L. (2015). The futures of the service economy in Europe: A foresight analysis. *Technological Forecasting and Social Change, 94*, 80–96. doi:10.1016/j.techfore.2014.06.009

Gallouj, F., & Weinstein, O. (1997). Innovation in services. *Research Policy, 26*(4), 537–556. doi:10.1016/S0048-7333(97)00030-9

Gallouj, F., & Windrum, P. (2009). Services and services innovation. *Journal of Evolutionary Economics, 19*(2), 141–148. doi:10.1007/s00191-008-0123-7

Gao, B., Wang, Y., Xie, H., Hu, Y., & Hu, Y. (2023). Artificial Intelligence in Advertising: Advancements, challenges, and ethical considerations in targeting, personalization, content creation, and ad optimization. *SAGE Open, 13*(4). doi:10.1177/21582440231210759

García-Madurga, M. Á., & Grilló-Méndez, A. J. (2023). Artificial Intelligence in the Tourism Industry: An Overview of Reviews. *Administrative Sciences, 13*(8), 172. doi:10.3390/admsci13080172

Gassmann, O., & Enkel, E. (2004, January). Towards a theory of Open Innovation: Three core process archetypes. 2004. *R&D Management Conference (RADMA).*

Gennatas, E. D., & Chen, J. H. (2021). Artificial Intelligence in Medicine: Past, Present, and Future. In L. Xing, M. L. Giger, & J. K. Min (Eds.), *Artificial Intelligence in Medicine: Technical Basis and Clinical Applications* (pp. 3–18). Academic Press. doi:10.1016/B978-0-12-821259-2.00001-6

Ghoosh, A. (2020). *Conversational AI in Customer Service: Transforming the Human-Computer interaction.* CRC Press.

Godey, B., Manthiou, A., Pederzoli, D., Rokka, J., Aiello, G., Donvito, R., & Singh, R. (2016). Social media marketing efforts of luxury brands: Influence on brand equity and consumer behavior. *Journal of Business Research, 69*(12), 5833–5841. doi:10.1016/j.jbusres.2016.04.181

Gold, E. (2023). The History of Artificial Intelligence from the 1950s to Today, free code camp. https://www.freecodecamp.org/news/the-history-of-ai/

Goldberg, L. (2018). *A brief history of artificial intelligence in advertising*. Econsultancy. https://econsultancy.com/a-brief-history-of-artificial-intelligence-in-advertising/

Golec, C., Isaacson, P., & Fewless, J. (2019). *Account-based marketing: how to target and engage the companies that will grow your revenue*. John Wiley & Sons.

Gonzalez Mieres, C., Angel Lopez Sanchez, J., & Leticia Santos Vijande, M. (2012). Internal Marketing, Innovation and Performance in Business Services Firms: The Role of Organizational Unlearning. *International Journal of Management*, *29*(4), 403–429.

Goodson, L., & Phillimore, J. (2004). The inquiry paradigm in qualitative tourism research. In *Qualitative research in tourism* (pp. 48–63). Routledge. doi:10.4324/9780203642986

Gordon, T. (2023). *The Impact of AI on Marketing: Opportunities and Challenges*. https://www.linkedin.com/pulse/impact-ai-marketing-opportunities-challenges-tracewell-trace-gordon/

Goulding, C. (2002). Grounded theory: A practical guide for management, business and market researchers. *Grounded Theory*, 1-186.

Grashof, N., & Kopka, A. (2023). Artificial intelligence and radical innovation: An opportunity for all companies? *Small Business Economics*, *61*(2), 771–797. doi:10.1007/s11187-022-00698-3

Griffin, A. (1997). PDMA research on new product development practices: Updating trends and benchmarking best practices. *Journal of Product Innovation Management*, *14*(6), 429–458. doi:10.1111/1540-5885.1460429

Gummesson, E. (2005). Qualitative research in marketing: Road-map for a wilderness of complexity and unpredictability. *European Journal of Marketing*, *39*(3/4), 309–327. doi:10.1108/03090560510581791

Gupta, S. K., & Racherla, U. S. (2018). Interdependence among dimensions of sustainability: Evidence from the Indian leather industry. *Management of Environmental Quality*, *29*(3), 406–415. doi:10.1108/MEQ-06-2017-0051

Gustafsson, J. (2017) *Single case studies vs. multiple case studies: A comparative study*. Academic Press.

Gustafsson, A., Snyder, H., & Witell, L. (2020). Service Innovation: A new conceptualization and path forward. *Journal of Service Research*, *23*(2), 111–115. doi:10.1177/1094670520908929

Hadjimanolis, A. (1999). Barriers to innovation for SMEs in a small less developed country (Cyprus). *Technovation*, *19*(9), 561–570. doi:10.1016/S0166-4972(99)00034-6

Hair, J. F. J., Black, W. C., Babin, B. J., & Anderson, R. E. (2010). *Multivariate Data Analysis. A global perspective* (7th ed.). Prentice Hall.

Hair, J. F. Jr, Ringle, C. M., & Sarstedt, M. (2013). Partial least squares structural equation modeling: Rigorous applications, better results and higher acceptance. *Long Range Planning*, *46*(1-2), 1–12. doi:10.1016/j.lrp.2013.01.001

Hajipour, V., Hekmat, S., & Amini, M. (2023). A value-oriented Artificial Intelligence-as-a-Service business plan using integrated tools and services. *Decision Analytics Journal, 8*, 100302. https://doi.org/https://doi.org/10.1016/j.dajour.2023.100302

Haleem, A., Javaid, M., Qadri, M. A., Singh, R. P., & Suman, R. (2022). Artificial intelligence (A.I.) applications for marketing: A literature-based study. *International Journal of Intelligent Networks*.

Haleem, A., Javaid, M., Qadri, M. A., Singh, R. P., & Suman, R. (2022). Artificial Intelligence (AI) Applications for Marketing: A Literature-Based Study. *International Journal of Intelligent Networks*, *3*, 119–132. doi:10.1016/j.ijin.2022.08.005

Hanlon, A., & Jones, K. (2023). Ethical concerns about social media privacy policies: Do users have the ability to comprehend their consent actions? *Journal of Strategic Marketing*, 1–18. doi:10.1080/0965254X.2023.2232817

Hardesty, L. (2019). *The history of Amazon's recommendation algorithm.* Amazon science. https://www.amazon.science/the-history-of-amazons-recommendation-algorithm

Hartley, J. (2004). What is a case study? *Essential guide to qualitative methods in organizational research*, 323-333.

Hashmi, A. R., Amirah, N. A., & Yusof, Y. (2020). Mediating effect of integrated systems on the relationship between supply chain management practices and public healthcare performance: Structural Equation Modeling. *International Journal of Management and Sustainability*, *9*(3), 148–160. doi:10.18488/journal.11.2020.93.148.160

Hathaliya, J. J., & Tanwar, S. (2020). An Exhaustive Survey on Security and Privacy Issues in Healthcare 4.0. *Computer Communications*, *153*, 311–335. doi:10.1016/j.comcom.2020.02.018

He, A.-Z., & Zhang, Y. (2023). AI-powered touch points in the customer journey: A systematic literature review and research agenda. *Journal of Research in Interactive Marketing*, *17*(4), 620–639. doi:10.1108/JRIM-03-2022-0082

Heding, T., Knudtzen, C. F., & Bjerre, M. (2020). *Brand management: Mastering research, theory and practice*. Routledge. doi:10.4324/9780367172596

He, H., & Harris, L. (2020). The impact of Covid-19 pandemic on corporate social responsibility and marketing philosophy. *Journal of Business Research*, *116*, 176–182. doi:10.1016/j.jbusres.2020.05.030 PMID:32457556

Hertog, P. D. (2000). Knowledge-intensive business services as co-producers of innovation. *International Journal of Innovation Management*, *4*(4), 491–528. doi:10.1142/S136391960000024X

Heskett, J. L., Sasser, W. E., & Schlesinger, L. A. (1997). *Service profit chain*. The Free Press. https://www.wipo.int/global_innovation_index/en/2022/

He, Y., Tang, J., Liu, D., Tang, S., Liu, Q., & Li, D. (2021). Innovation System of Preventive Medicine Based on Big Data Technology. *6th International Conference on Smart Grid and Electrical Automation*, 506–509. 10.1109/ICSGEA53208.2021.00120

Hoque, A. S. M. M., & Awang, Z. (2019). Does gender difference play moderating role in the relationship between entrepreneurial marketing and Bangladeshi SME performance? *Accounting*, *5*(1), 35–52. doi:10.5267/j.ac.2018.6.001

Ho, S. P. S., & Chow, M. Y. C. (2023). The role of artificial intelligence in consumers' brand preference for retail banks in Hong Kong. *Journal of Financial Services Marketing*. Advance online publication. doi:10.1057/s41264-022-00207-3

Huang, M. H., & Rust, R. T. (2021). Engaged to a robot? The role of AI in service. *Journal of Service Research*, *24*(1), 30–41. doi:10.1177/1094670520902266

Huang, M.-H., & Rust, R. T. (2021). A strategic framework for artificial intelligence in marketing. *Journal of the Academy of Marketing Science*, *49*(1), 30–50. doi:10.1007/s11747-020-00749-9

Hughes, A., & Wood, E. (2000). *Rethinking innovation comparisons between manufacturing and services: the experience of the CBR SME surveys in the UK*. Springer, US.

Hunter, J. E., & Hunter, R. F. (1984). Validity and utility of alternative predictors of job performance. *Psychological Bulletin*, *96*(1), 72–98. doi:10.1037/0033-2909.96.1.72

Igbaria, M., & Shayo, C. (1997). The impact of race and gender differences on job performance evaluations and career success. *Equal Opportunities International*, *16*(8), 12–23. doi:10.1108/eb010703

International Business Machines. (n.d.). *What is healthcare technology?* Retrieved September 6, 2022, from https://www.ibm.com/topics/healthcare-technology

ISO 10668. (2010). *ISO 10668:2010 - Brand valuation-Requirements for monetary brand valuation*. www.iso.org

Israfilzade, K., & Guliyeva, N. (2023). The Cross-Generational Impacts of Digital Remarketing: An Examination of Purchasing Behaviours among Generation Z and Generation Y. *Futurity Economics & Law*, *3*(2), 73-94. http://www.futurity-econlaw.com/index.php/FEL/article/view/109

Istrate, E., & Harris, J. (2017). *The future of work: The rise of the gig economy*. National Association of Counties.

Jackson, K., & Bazeley, P. (2019). *Qualitative data analysis with NVivo* (3rd ed.). Sage publications.

Jain, S. K., & Gupta, G. (2004). Measuring service quality: SERVQUAL vs. SERVPERF scales. *Vikalpa*, *29*(2), 25–37. doi:10.1177/0256090920040203

Janz, N., Ebling, G., Gottschalk, S., & Niggemann, H. (2001). The Mannheim innovation panels (MIP and MIP-S) of the Centre for European Economic Research (ZEW). *Schmollers Jahrbuch*, *121*(1), 123–129. doi:10.3790/schm.121.1.123

Jarek, K., & Mazurek, G. (2019). Marketing and Artificial Intelligence. *Central European Business Review, 8*(2).

Jarrahi, M. H. (2018). Artificial intelligence and the future of work: Human-AI symbiosis in organizational decision making. *Business Horizons, 61*(4), 577–586. doi:10.1016/j.bushor.2018.03.007

Javaid. (2022). A review of Blockchain Technology applications for financial services. sciencedirect.com/science/article/pii/S2772485922000606#:~:text=Financial%20service%20providers%20find%20blockchain%20technology%20useful%20to,and%20transparency%2C%20and%20open%20up%20newer%20revenue%20opportunities.

Jebara, T. (2018). *Netflix Research: Machine Learning.* https://research.netflix.com/research-area/machine-learning

Jia, N., Luo, X., Fang, Z., & Liao, C. (2023). *When and how artificial intelligence augments employee creativity. Academy of Management Journal.* doi:10.5465/amj.2022.0426

Jiang, Y., Ding, X., Liu, D., Gui, X., Zhang, W., & Zhang, W. (2022). Designing Intelligent Self-Checkup Based Technologies for Everyday Healthy Living. *International Journal of Human-Computer Studies, 166*, 102866. doi:10.1016/j.ijhcs.2022.102866

Joecks, J., Pull, K., & Vetter, K. (2013). Gender diversity in the boardroom and firm performance: What exactly constitutes a "critical mass?" *Journal of Business Ethics, 118*(1), 61–72. doi:10.1007/s10551-012-1553-6

Johne, A., & Storey, C. (1998). New service development: A review of the literature and annotated bibliography. *European Journal of Marketing, 32*(3/4), 184–251. doi:10.1108/03090569810204526

Jöreskog, K. G., & Sörbom, D. (1993). *LISREL 8: Structural equation modeling with the SIMPLIS command language.* Scientific Software International.

Jöreskog, K. G. (1969). A general approach to confirmatory maximum likelihood factor analysis. *Psychometrika, 34*(2), 183–202. doi:10.1007/BF02289343

Júnior, Í. M. B. A., & Ianotti, G. de C. (2010). Ética e Medicina Preditiva. *Revista Brasileira de Saúde Materno Infantil, 10*(SUPPL. 2), S377–S382. doi:10.1590/S1519-38292010000600016

Kabanoff, B., Waldersee, R., & Cohen, M. (1995). Espoused values and organizational change themes. *Academy of Management Journal, 38*(4), 1075–1104. doi:10.2307/256621

Kahtalian, M. (2000). Marketing de Serviços. *Colecção Gestão Empresarial*, 19–29.

Kaiser, H. F. (1974). An index of factorial simplicity. *Psychometrika, 39*(1), 31-36. doi:10.1007/BF02291575

Kaiser, H. F. (1958). The varimax criterion for analytic rotation in factor analysis. *Psychometrika, 23*(3), 187–200. doi:10.1007/BF02289233

Kaiser, H. F. (1960). The application of electronic computers to factor analysis. *Educational and Psychological Measurement, 20*(1), 141–151. doi:10.1177/001316446002000116

Kampani, N., & Jhamb, D. (2021). Examining the relationship among servicescape, perceived overall image and customer behavioural intentions in beauty salons: The moderating role of pleasure-arousal-dominance emotional state model. *International Journal of Services, Economics and Management, 12*(2), 164–184.

Kanter, R. M. (1977). Men and women of the corporation: New edition. Basic Books.

Kapferer, J.-N. (2008). *The new strategic brand management: Creating and sustaining brand equity long term.* Kogan Page Publishers.

Kaplan, A., & Haenlein, M. (2019). Siri, Siri, in my hand: Who's the fairest in the land? On the interpretations, illustrations, and implications of artificial intelligence. *Business Horizons, 62*(1), 15–25. doi:10.1016/j.bushor.2018.08.004

Kargl, D. (2022*). Methbot – How the King of Fraud made $3 million per day with advertising fraud.* Fraud0. https://www.fraud0.com/resources/methbot/

Kaur, J., Verma, R., Alharbe, N. R., Agrawal, A., & Khan, R. A. (2021). Importance of Fog Computing in Healthcare 4.0. In *Signals and Communication Technology* (pp. 79–101). Springer Science and Business Media Deutschland GmbH. doi:10.1007/978-3-030-46197-3_4

Kearney. (2018). *Artificial Intelligence In The Healthcare Sector: Unleashing The Potential Of AI To Transform Healthcare.* Academic Press.

Keller, K. L., & Kotler, P. (2012). Administração de Marketing (14a Edição). Prentice Hall.

Keller, K. L., & Kotler, P. (2013). Administração de marketing. In *Pearson Education do Brasil L.tda (14a edição, Issue edição).* Prentice Hall.

Keller, K. L., & Lehmann, D. R. (2003). How do brands create value? *Marketing Management, 12*(3), 26.

Khan, S., Rasheed, R., Rashid, A., Abbas, Q., & Mahboob, F. (2022). The effect of demographic characteristics on job performance: An empirical study from Pakistan. *The Journal of Asian Finance. Economics and Business, 9*(2), 283–294. doi:10.13106/jafeb.2022.vol9.no2.0283

Khan, W. A., & Vieito, J. P. (2013). CEO gender and firm performance. *Journal of Economics and Business, 67*, 55–66. doi:10.1016/j.jeconbus.2013.01.003

Kiefer, K., Heileman, M., & Pett, T. L. (2022). Does gender still matter? An examination of small business performance. *Small Business Economics, 58*(1), 141–167. doi:10.1007/s11187-020-00403-2

Kietzmann, J., Paschen, J., & Treen, E. (2018). Artificial intelligence in advertising: How marketers can leverage artificial intelligence along the consumer journey. *Journal of Advertising Research, 58*(3), 263–267. doi:10.2501/JAR-2018-035

Kim, H., & Park, M. (2024). When digital celebrity talks to you: How human-like virtual influencers satisfy consumer's experience through social presence on social media endorsements. *Journal of Retailing and Consumer Services*, *76*, 103581. doi:10.1016/j.jretconser.2023.103581

Kim, S. Y. (2011). Prediction of hotel bankruptcy using support vector machine, artificial neural network, logistic regression, and multivariate discriminant analysis. *Service Industries Journal*, *31*(3), 441–468. doi:10.1080/02642060802712848

Kline, R. B. (1998). *Structural equation modeling*. Guilford.

Koch, C. (2016). How the computer beat the go player. *Scientific American Mind*, *27*(4), 20–23. doi:10.1038/scientificamericanmind0716-20

Kofman, A., & Tobin, A. (2019). *Facebook Ads Can Still Discriminate Against Women and Older Workers, Despite a Civil Rights Settlement.* ProPublica. https://www.propublica.org/article/facebook-ads-can-still-discriminate-against-women-and-older-workers-despite-a-civil-rights-settlement

Kononenko, O. (2021). Theoretical Aspects of the Organization Brand Management. *Innovative Technologies and Scientific Solutions for Industries*, *1*(15), 76–82. doi:10.30837/ITSSI.2021.15.076

Koo, B., Curtis, C., & Ryan, B. (2021). Examining the impact of artificial intelligence on hotel employees through job insecurity perspectives. *International Journal of Hospitality Management*, *95*, 102763. doi:10.1016/j.ijhm.2020.102763

Kotler, P., & Armstrong, G. (2015). Princípios de Marketing (S. Afonso, S. Nascimento, V. Souza, A. Mendes, & M. Guimarães, Eds.; 15a Edição). Pearson Education.

Kreiswirth, M. (2000). Merely telling stories? Narrative and knowledge in the human sciences. *Poetics Today*, *21*(2), 293–318. doi:10.1215/03335372-21-2-293

Krippendorff, K. (2018). *Content analysis: An introduction to its methodology*. Sage Publications.

Krishen, A. S., Dwivedi, Y. K., Bindu, N., & Kumar, K. S. (2021). A Broad Overview of Interactive Digital Marketing: A Bibliometric Network Analysis. *Journal of Business Research*, *131*, 183–195. doi:10.1016/j.jbusres.2021.03.061

Krishnan, G., & Selvam, G. (2019). Factors Influencing the Download of Mobile Health Apps: Content Review-Led Regression Analysis. *Health Policy and Technology*, *8*(4), 356–364. doi:10.1016/j.hlpt.2019.09.001

Krueger, R. A., & Casey, M. A. (2014). *Focus groups: A practical guide for applied research*. Sage publications.

Kulkov, I., Tsvetkova, A., & Ivanova-Gongne, M. (2023). Identifying Institutional Barriers When Implementing New Technologies in the Healthcare Industry. *European Journal of Innovation Management*, *26*(4), 909–932. doi:10.1108/EJIM-02-2021-0093

Kumar, P., Tomar, P. K., Bharti, S., Naredla, S., Ibrahim, R. K., & Alazzam, M. B. (2023). Maximizing the Potential of Artificial Intelligence in Digital Marketing. In *2023 3rd International Conference on Advance Computing and Innovative Technologies in Engineering (ICACITE)* (pp. 2736-2741). IEEE. 10.1109/ICACITE57410.2023.10183113

Kumar, V., Dixit, A., Javalgi, R. G., & Dass, M. (2016). Research framework, strategies, and applications of intelligent agent technologies (IATs) in marketing. *Journal of the Academy of Marketing Science*, *44*(1), 24–45. doi:10.1007/s11747-015-0426-9

Kumar, V., Rajan, B., Venkatesan, R., & Lecinski, J. (2019). Understanding the role of artificial intelligence in personalized engagement marketing. *California Management Review*, *61*(4), 135–155. doi:10.1177/0008125619859317

Kunz, W. H., & Hogreve, J. (2011). Toward a deeper understanding of service marketing: The past, the present, and the future. *International Journal of Research in Marketing*, *28*(3), 231–247. doi:10.1016/j.ijresmar.2011.03.002

Kuziemsky, C., & Vimarlund, V. (2018). Multi-Sided Markets for Transforming Healthcare Service Delivery. *Studies in Health Technology and Informatics*, *626–630*. Advance online publication. doi:10.3233/978-1-61499-852-5-626 PMID:29678036

Lagan, S., Sandler, L., & Torous, J. (2021). Evaluating Evaluation Frameworks: A Scoping Review of Frameworks for Assessing Health Apps. *BMJ Open*, *11*(3, e047001), e047001. Advance online publication. doi:10.1136/bmjopen-2020-047001 PMID:33741674

Larivière, B., Bowen, D., Andreassen, T. W., Kunz, W., Sirianni, N. J., Voss, C., Wunderlich, N. V., & De Keyser, A. (2017). "Service Encounter 2.0": An investigation into the roles of technology, employees and customers. *Journal of Business Research*, *79*(C), 238–246. doi:10.1016/j.jbusres.2017.03.008

Larsen, P., & Lewis, A. (2007). How award-winning SMEs manage the barriers to innovation. *Creativity and Innovation Management*, *16*(2), 142–151. doi:10.1111/j.1467-8691.2007.00428.x

Laskowski, N., & Tucci, L. (2023). *Artificial intelligence (AI)*. Enterprise AI. https://www.techtarget.com/searchenterpriseai/definition/AI-Artificial-Intelligence

Lau, R. S. (2000). Quality of work life and performance-An ad hoc investigation of two key elements in the service profit chain model. *International Journal of Service Industry Management*, *11*(5), 422–437. doi:10.1108/09564230010360164

Lebcir, R., Hill, T., Atun, R., & Cubric, M. (2021). Stakeholders' Views on the Organisational Factors Affecting Application of Artificial Intelligence in Healthcare: A Scoping Review Protocol. *BMJ Open*, *11*(3, e044074), e044074. Advance online publication. doi:10.1136/bmjopen-2020-044074 PMID:33753441

Lee, D. (2019). A Model for Designing Healthcare Service Based on the Patient Experience. *International Journal of Healthcare Management*, *12*(3), 180–188. doi:10.1080/20479700.2017.1359956

Lee, K., Kim, M., & Kim, W. (2022). Artificial Intelligence in the Service Sector: A Review of the Literature. *International Journal of Information Science and Management*, *17*(1), 1–27.

Lee, M. C. M., Scheepers, H., Lui, A. K. H., & Ngai, E. W. T. (2023). The implementation of artificial intelligence in organizations: A systematic literature review. *Information & Management*, *60*(5), 103816. doi:10.1016/j.im.2023.103816

Lee, W., Schwartz, N., Bansal, A., Khor, S., Hammarlund, N., Basu, A., & Devine, B. (2023). A Scoping Review of the Use of Machine Learning in Health Economics and Outcomes Research: Part 1—Data From Wearable Devices. *Value in Health*, *26*(2), 292–299. doi:10.1016/j.jval.2022.08.005 PMID:36115806

Lemon, K. N., & Cerpa, N. (2016). A Comparative Study of Conversational Systems. *Interacting with Computers*, *28*(4), 329–344.

Lepanjuuri, K., Wishart, R., & Cornick, P. (2018). *The characteristics of individuals in the gig economy* (Issue February). Retrieved August 12, 2023, from: https://www.gov.uk/government/publications/gig-economy-research

Leslie de Chernatony. (2010)/ Brand Management Through Narrowing the Gap Between Brand Identity and Brand Reputation/ Taylor and Francis Online. https://www.tandfonline.com/doi/citedby/10.1362/026725799784870432?scroll=top&needAccess=true

Li, X., Rong, K., & Shi, X. (2024). Situating artificial intelligence in organization: A human-machine relationship perspective? A commentary on Kemp's (2023) paper "competitive advantages through artificial intelligence: Toward a theory of situated AI." *Journal of Digital Economy*. https://doi.org/https://doi.org/10.1016/j.jdec.2024.01.001

Li, C. Y., & Zhang, J. T. (2023). Chatbots or me? Consumers' switching between human agents and conversational agents. *Journal of Retailing and Consumer Services*, *72*, 103264. doi:10.1016/j.jretconser.2023.103264

Lieberman, M. B., & Montgomery, D. B. (1988). First-mover advantages. *Strategic Management Journal*, *9*(1), 41–58. doi:10.1002/smj.4250090706

Lifshitz, A. (2014). La Medicina Curativa y La Medicina Preventiva: Alcances y Limitaciones. *Medicina Interna de México*, *30*(1), 64–72.

Lightfoot, H., & Gebauer, H. (2011b). Exploring the alignment between service strategy and service innovation. *Journal of Service Management*, *22*(5), 664–683. doi:10.1108/09564231111175004

Li, J., Bonn, M. A., & Ye, B. H. (2019). Hotel employee's artificial intelligence and robotics awareness and its impact on turnover intention: The moderating roles of perceived organizational support and competitive psychological climate. *Tourism Management*, *73*, 172–18. doi:10.1016/j.tourman.2019.02.006

Li, J., & Carayon, P. (2021). Health Care 4.0: A Vision for Smart and Connected Health Care. *IISE Transactions on Healthcare Systems Engineering*, *11*(3), 171–180. doi:10.1080/24725579.2021.1884627 PMID:34497970

Lin, L. (2012).The impact of service innovation on firm performance: evidence from the Chinese tourism sector, *The Service Industries Journal, 33*(15-16), 1-34.

Lin, M. C., Wang, C. C., Chen, M. S., & Chang, C. A. (2008). Using AHP and TOPSIS approaches in the customer-driven product design process. *Computers in Industry, 59*(1), 17–31. doi:10.1016/j.compind.2007.05.013

Liu, N., Li, S., Du, Y., Torralba, A., & Tenenbaum, J. B. (2022, October). Compositional visual generation with composable diffusion models. In *European Conference on Computer Vision* (pp. 423-439). Cham: Springer Nature Switzerland. 10.1007/978-3-031-19790-1_26

Liu, X., Faes, L., Kale, A. U., Wagner, S. K., Fu, D. J., Bruynseels, A., Mahendiran, T., Moraes, G., Shamdas, M., Kern, C., Ledsam, J. R., Schmid, M. K., Balaskas, K., Topol, E. J., Bachmann, L. M., Keane, P. A., & Denniston, A. K. (2019). A Comparison of Deep Learning Performance Against Health-Care Professionals in Detecting Diseases from Medical Imaging: A Systematic Review and Meta-Analysis. *The Lancet. Digital Health, 1*(6), e271–e297. doi:10.1016/S2589-7500(19)30123-2 PMID:33323251

Lovelock, C., & Gummesson, E. (2004). Whither services marketing? In search of a new paradigm and fresh perspectives. *Journal of Service Research, 7*(1), 20–41. doi:10.1177/1094670504266131

Loveman, G. W. (1998). Employee satisfaction, customer loyalty, and financial performance an empirical examination of the service profit chain in retail banking. *Journal of Service Research, 1*(1), 18–31. doi:10.1177/109467059800100103

Lubis, A., Purike, E., Stiadi, M., Judijanto, L., & Tobing, F. (2023). The Triad of Marketing Success: Product Innovation, Customer Engagement, and Market Penetration. *International Journal of Economic Literature, 1*(3), 245–257.

Mackey, J. D., Roth, P. L., Van Iddekinge, C. H., & McFarland, L. A. (2019). A meta-analysis of gender proportionality effects on job performance. *Group & Organization Management, 44*(3), 578–610. doi:10.1177/1059601117730519

Madlberger, M. (2023). Artificial Intelligence and Business Value: A Literature Review. *Journal of Management Information Systems, 39*(3), 1012–1034.

Mahavarpour, N., Marvi, R., & Foroudi, P. (2023). A brief history of service innovation: The evolution of past, present, and future service innovation. *Journal of Business Research, 160*, 113795. doi:10.1016/j.jbusres.2023.113795

Mailchimp. (2023a). *Digital Marketing. Mailchimp.* https://mailchimp.com/pt-br/marketing-glossary/digital-marketing/

Mailchimp. (2023b). *O Que é Marketing de Relacionamento com o Cliente*. Mailchimp. https://mailchimp.com/pt-br/resources/customer-relationship-marketing/

Malviya, B., Othman, B., Saxena, K., & Almashaqbeh, H. A. (2022). An Empirical Analysis in Measuring the Impact of Artificial Intelligence for Better Marketing Communication to the End-Users Effectively in the Digital Era. In *2022 2nd International Conference on Advance Computing and Innovative Technologies in Engineering (ICACITE)* (pp. 2374-2378). IEEE.

Manyika, M., Chui, M., Mirembe, S., Ramaswamy, S., & Trabshaw, J. (2017). Jobs Lost, Jobs Gained: Workforce Transitions. In *A Time of Automation*. McKinsey Global Institute.

Marketing Accountability Standards Board. (2023a). *Health Care Marketing*. The Universal Marketing Dictionary. https://marketing-dictionary.org/h/health-care-marketing/

Marketing Accountability Standards Board. (2023b). *Marketing*. The Universal Marketing Dictionary. https://marketing-dictionary.org/m/marketing/

Marmolejo-Ramos, F., Workman, T., Walker, C., Lenihan, D., Moulds, S., Correa, J. C., & Sonna, B. (2022). AI-powered narrative building for facilitating public participation and engagement. *Discover Artificial Intelligence*, *2*(1), 7. doi:10.1007/s44163-022-00023-7

Martikainen, M. (2008). Painoarvoa palveluiden Kehittamiselle, Elinkeinoelaman keskusliiton raportteja. Confederation of Finnish Industries.

Martin, C. J. (2016). The sharing economy: A pathway to sustainability or a nightmarish form of neoliberal capitalism? *Ecological Economics*, *121*, 149–159. doi:10.1016/j.ecolecon.2015.11.027

Mason, J. (2017). Qualitative researching. Qualitative researching, 1-288.

Matthijs Janssen. (2015). Exploring a Multidimensional Approach to Service Innovation. SpringerLink. https://link.springer.com/chapter/10.1007/978-1-4471-6590-3_5

Matthing, J., Sandén, B., & Edvardsson, B. (2004). New service development: Learning from and with customers. *International Journal of Service Industry Management*, *15*(5), 479–498. doi:10.1108/09564230410564948

Matzler, K., Veider, V., Hautz, J., & Stadler, C. (2015). The impact of family ownership, management, and governance on innovation. *Journal of Product Innovation Management*, *32*(3), 319–333. doi:10.1111/jpim.12202

Mba, A. T. (2021, June 5). *Den Hertog services innovation model (4-dimensions, 2000)*. SolvInnov. https://solvinnov.com/den-hertog-model-for-describing-service-innovations/

McAdam, R., & Armstrong, G. (2001). A symbiosis of quality and innovation in SMEs: A multiple case study analysis. *Managerial Auditing Journal*, *16*(7), 394–399. doi:10.1108/02686900110398296

McDaniel, M. A., Schmidt, F. L., & Hunter, J. E. (1988). Job experience correlates of job performance. *The Journal of Applied Psychology*, *73*(2), 327–330. doi:10.1037/0021-9010.73.2.327 PMID:21261409

McLean, G., Osei-Frimpong, K., & Barhorst, J. (2021). Alexa, do voice assistants influence consumer brand engagement? – Examining the role of AI powered voice assistants in influencing consumer brand engagement. *Journal of Business Research, 124*, 312–328. doi:10.1016/j.jbusres.2020.11.045

Melnik, G., & Shah, R. (2003). *Customer Relationships and Information Technology: Moving Beyond the CRM Debate*. Routledge.

Menor, L. J., Tatikonda, M. V., & Sampson, S. E. (2002). New Service Development: Areas for Exploitation and Exploration. *Journal of Operations Management, 20*(2), 135–157. doi:10.1016/S0272-6963(01)00091-2

Michelini, L., & Fiorentino, D. (2012). New business models for creating shared value. *Social Responsibility Journal, 8*(4), 561–577. doi:10.1108/17471111211272129

Mikalef, P., & Gupta, M. (2021). Artificial intelligence capability: Conceptualization, measurement calibration, and empirical study on its impact on organizational creativity and firm performance. *Information & Management, 58*(3), 103434. doi:10.1016/j.im.2021.103434

Mikalef, P., Islam, N., Parida, V., Singh, H., & Altwaijry, N. (2023). Artificial intelligence (AI) competencies for organizational performance: A B2B marketing capabilities perspective. *Journal of Business Research, 164*, 113998. doi:10.1016/j.jbusres.2023.113998

Miles, I. (2008). Patterns of innovation in service industries. *IBM Systems Journal, 47*(1), 115–128. doi:10.1147/sj.471.0115

Miles, M. B., & Huberman, A. M. (1994). *Qualitative data analysis: An expanded sourcebook.* Sage Publications.

Miller, D., & Friesen, P. H. (1982). Innovation in conservative and entrepreneurial firms: Two models of strategic momentum. *Strategic Management Journal, 3*(1), 1–25. doi:10.1002/smj.4250030102

Miller, S. M. (2018). AI: Augmentation, more so than automation. *Asian Management Insights, 5*(1), 1–20.

Mills, E. C., Savage, E., Lieder, J., & Chiu, E. S. (2020). Telemedicine and the COVID-19 Pandemic: Are We Ready to Go Live? *Advances in Skin & Wound Care, 33*(8), 410–417. doi:10.1097/01.ASW.0000669916.01793.93 PMID:32701252

Mirza, F., Norris, T., & Stockdale, R. (2008). Mobile Technologies and the Holistic Management of Chronic Diseases. *Health Informatics Journal, 14*(4), 309–321. doi:10.1177/1460458208096559 PMID:19008280

Mittelstadt, B., Allo, P., Taddeo, M., & Wachter, S. (2019). *The Ethics of Algorithms: Fairness, Accountability, and Transparency*. Oxford University Press.

Mohammadi, V., & Minaei, S. (2019). Artificial intelligence in the production process. In *Engineering tools in the beverage industry* (pp. 27–63). Woodhead Publishing. doi:10.1016/B978-0-12-815258-4.00002-0

Moin, S. M. A., & Moin, S. M. A. (2020). Conclusion: The Future of Storytelling. *Brand Storytelling in the Digital Age: Theories, Practice and Application*, 89-96.

Mondal, T., Jayadeva, S. M., Pani, R., Subramanian, M. P. A., & Sumana, B. K. (2022). E Marketing Strategy in Health Care Using IoT and Machine Learning. *Materials Today: Proceedings*, *56*, 2087–2091. doi:10.1016/j.matpr.2021.11.417

Moon, M. J., & Bretschneider, S. (1997). Can state government actions affect innovation and its diffusion? An extended communication model and empirical test. *Technological Forecasting and Social Change*, *54*(1), 57–77. doi:10.1016/S0040-1625(96)00121-7

Moore, G. C., & Benbasat, I. (1991). Development of an instrument to measure the perceptions of adopting an information technology innovation. *Information Systems Research*, *2*(3), 192–222. doi:10.1287/isre.2.3.192

Mullen, A., Marcos Cuevas, J., & Theoharakis, V. (n.d.). *The anatomy of account-based marketing-a conceptualisation of strategic dimensions*. American Marketing Association.

Musaiqer, H. H., & Hamdan, A. (2023). The Role of Artificial Intelligence in Brand Building: A Review. In R. El Khoury & N. Nasrallah (Eds.), *Emerging Trends and Innovation in Business and Finance* (pp. 307–318). Springer Nature Singapore. doi:10.1007/978-981-99-6101-6_22

Nabavieh, A. (2023). *Navigating the Future: Visual and Voice Search Optimization in 2024*. https://www.linkedin.com/pulse/navigating-future-visual-voice-search-optimization-2024-ali-nabavieh-ezfvc/

Nair, S. R. (2018). Analyzing the relationship between store attributes, satisfaction,patronage-intention and lifestyle in food and grocery store choice behavior. *International Journal of Retail & Distribution Management*, *46*(1), 70–89. doi:10.1108/IJRDM-06-2016-0102

Nam, K., Dutt, C. S., Chathoth, P., Daghfous, A., & Khan, M. S. (2021). The adoption of artificial intelligence and robotics in the hotel industry: Prospects and challenges. *Electronic Markets*, *31*(3), 553–574. doi:10.1007/s12525-020-00442-3

Nandini, G. (2019). Features of Services: 8 Major Features of Service Marketing, economics discussion. https://www.economicsdiscussion.net/service-marketing/features-of-services-8-major-features-of-service-marketing/31597

Neuendorf, K. A. (2017). *The content analysis guidebook*. Sage Publications. doi:10.4135/9781071802878

Ng, T. W., & Feldman, D. C. (2010). The relationships of age with job attitudes: A meta-analysis. *Personnel Psychology*, *63*(3), 677–718. doi:10.1111/j.1744-6570.2010.01184.x

Nunes, A., Limpo, T., & Castro, S. L. (2019). Acceptance of Mobile Health Applications: Examining Key Determinants and Moderators. *Frontiers in Psychology, 10*(2791), 2791. Advance online publication. doi:10.3389/fpsyg.2019.02791 PMID:31920836

Nunez, A. (2023). *AI in Advertising: Everything You Need to Leverage an Industry-Level Transformation.* Podium. https://www.podium.com/article/ai-in-advertising/

O'Connor, G. E., & Myrden, S., Alkire, L., Lee, K., Köcher, S., Kandampully, J., & Williams, J. D. (2021). Digital Health Experience: A Regulatory Focus Perspective. *Journal of Interactive Marketing, 56*, 121–136. doi:10.1016/j.intmar.2021.07.002

Olan, F., Ogiemwonyi Arakpogun, E., Suklan, J., Nakpodia, F., Damij, N., & Jayawickrama, U. (2022). Artificial intelligence and knowledge sharing: Contributing factors to organizational performance. *Journal of Business Research, 145*, 605–615. doi:10.1016/j.jbusres.2022.03.008

Oldenburg, B., Taylor, C. B., O'Neil, A., Cocker, F., & Cameron, L. D. (2015). Using New Technologies to Improve the Prevention and Management of Chronic Conditions in Populations. *Annual Review of Public Health, 36*(1), 483–505. doi:10.1146/annurev-publhealth-031914-122848 PMID:25581147

Oliver, R. L. (1999). Whence consumer loyalty? *Journal of Marketing, 63*(4_suppl1), 33–44. doi:10.1177/00222429990634s105

Orlikowski, W. J. (1991). Integrated information environment or matrix of control? The contradictory implications of information technology. *Accounting Management and Information Technologies, 1*(1), 9–42. doi:10.1016/0959-8022(91)90011-3

Overgoor, G., Chica, M., Rand, W., & Weishampel, A. (2019). Letting the computers take over: Using AI to solve marketing problems. *California Management Review, 61*(4), 156–185. doi:10.1177/0008125619859318

Pagliari, C., Sloan, D., Gregor, P., Sullivan, F., Detmer, D., Kahan, J. P., Oortwijn, W., & MacGillivray, S. (2005). What is eHealth (4): A Scoping Exercise to Map the Field. *Journal of Medical Internet Research, 7*(1), e9. doi:10.2196/jmir.7.1.e9 PMID:15829481

Panigrahi, J. K., Tripathy, S., & Das, B. (2017). Thematic analysis of service innovation taxonomy within supply network, creating value for the system. *International Journal of Mechanical Engineering and Technology, 8*(9), 57–69.

Pappas, A., Fumagalli, E., Rouziou, M., & Bolander, W. (2023). More than Machines: The Role of the Future Retail Salesperson in Enhancing the Customer Experience. *Journal of Retailing, 99*(4), 518–531. doi:10.1016/j.jretai.2023.10.004

Parasuraman, A., Zeithaml, V. A., & Berry, L. L. (1985). A conceptual model of service quality and its implications for future research. *Journal of Marketing, 49*(4), 41–50. doi:10.1177/002224298504900403

Parida, V., Sjödin, D., & Reim, W. (2019). Reviewing literature on digitalization, business model innovation, and sustainable industry: Past achievements and future promises. *Sustainability (Basel), 11*(2), 391. doi:10.3390/su11020391

Park, G., Kim, Y., Park, K., & Agarwal, A. (2016). Patient-Centric Quality Assessment Framework for Healthcare Services. *Technological Forecasting and Social Change, 113*(Part B), 468–474. . doi:10.1016/j.techfore.2016.07.012

Patel, P., & Thakkar, A. (2020). The upsurge of deep learning for computer vision applications. *Iranian Journal of Electrical and Computer Engineering, 10*(1), 538. doi:10.11591/ijece.v10i1.pp538-548

Peixoto, M. R., Paula, F. D. O., & da Silva, J. F. (2023). Factors that influence service innovation: A systematic approach and a categorization proposal. *European Journal of Innovation Management, 26*(5), 1189–1213. doi:10.1108/EJIM-05-2021-0268

Peng, W., Kanthawala, S., Yuan, S., & Hussain, S. A. (2016). A Qualitative Study of User Perceptions of Mobile Health Apps. *BMC Public Health, 16*(1158), 1158. Advance online publication. doi:10.1186/s12889-016-3808-0 PMID:27842533

Perez-Vega, R., Kaartemo, V., Lages, C. R., Razavi, N. B., & Männistö, J. (2021). Reshaping the contexts of online customer engagement behavior via artificial intelligence: A conceptual framework. *Journal of Business Research, 129*, 902–910. doi:10.1016/j.jbusres.2020.11.002

Piatier, A. (1984). *Barriers to Innovation*. Frances Printer.

Pihkala, T., Linenpaa, H., & Vesalainen, L. (2002). Innovation Barriers amongst Clusters of European SMEs. *International Journal of Entrepreneurship and Innovation Management, 2*(6), 520. doi:10.1504/IJEIM.2002.000499

Pisco, L., & Biscaia, J. L. (2001). Qualidade de Cuidados de Saúde Primários. *Revista Portuguesa de Saude Publica, 2*, 43–51. https://doi.org/hdl.handle.net/10362/101394

Polkinghorne, D. E. (1995). Narrative configuration in qualitative analysis. *International Journal of Qualitative Studies in Education : QSE, 8*(1), 5–23. doi:10.1080/0951839950080103

Post Digital. (2023). *Marketing de Relacionamento na Área da Saúde: O Guia Completo*. Post Digital.

Prentice, C. (2019). *Emotional intelligence and marketing*. World Scientific Publishing Co. Pte, Ltd. doi:10.1142/11363

Prentice, C., Dominique Lopes, S., & Wang, X. (2020). Emotional intelligence or artificial intelligence–an employee perspective. *Journal of Hospitality Marketing & Management, 29*(4), 377–403. doi:10.1080/19368623.2019.1647124

Price, R., & Brodie, R. J. (2001). Transforming a Public Service Organization from Inside Out to Outside in The Case of Auckland City, New Zealand. *Journal of Service Research, 4*(1), 50–59. doi:10.1177/109467050141005

Purcărea, T. V. (2016). Creating the Ideal Patient Experience. *Journal of Medicine and Life*, *9*(4), 380–385. doi:10.22336/jml.2016.0411 PMID:27928442

Purchase, S., & Voléry, T. (2020). Marketing innovation: A systematic review. *Journal of Marketing Management*, *36*(9–10), 763–793. doi:10.1080/0267257X.2020.1774631

Qudsi, I. E. (2023). AI-Powered Influencer Marketing: Opportunities and Challenges. *Forbes*. https://www.forbes.com/sites/forbesagencycouncil/2023/06/27/ai-powered-influencer-marketing-opportunities-and-challenges/?sh=5f8a4f2359e6

Quiñones, M. A., Ford, J. K., & Teachout, M. S. (1995). The relationship between work experience and job performance: A conceptual and meta-analytic review. *Personnel Psychology*, *48*(4), 887–910. doi:10.1111/j.1744-6570.1995.tb01785.x

Radu, G., Solomon, M., Gheorghe, C. M., Hostiuc, M., Bulescu, I. A., & Purcarea, V. L. (2017). The Adaptation of Health Care Marketing to the Digital Era. *Journal of Medicine and Life*, *10*(1), 44–46. http://www.ncbi.nlm.nih.gov/pubmed/28255375%0Ahttp://www.pubmedcentral.nih.gov/articlerender.fcgi?artid=PMC5304370 PMID:28255375

Rahman, M. S., Bag, S., Hossain, M. A., Abdel Fattah, F. A. M., Gani, M. O., & Rana, N. P. (2023). The new wave of AI-powered luxury brands online shopping experience: The role of digital multisensory cues and customers' engagement. *Journal of Retailing and Consumer Services*, *72*, 103273. doi:10.1016/j.jretconser.2023.103273

Randhawa, K., & Scerri, M. (2015b). Service Innovation: A Review of the Literature. In Springer eBooks (pp. 27–51). doi:10.1007/978-1-4471-6590-3_2

Rappa, M. (2008). Business Models on the Web. https://digitalenterprise.org/models/models.html

Ratnawati, E., Sukidjo, S., & Efendi, R. (2020). The Effect of Work Motivation and Work Experience on Employee Performance. *International Journal of Multicultural and Multireligious Understanding*, *7*(8), 109–116. doi:10.18415/ijmmu.v7i8.1809

Rautela, S. (2021, March). Social Media for New Product Launch: A Study of Social Media Platforms Across the RACE Planning Framework. *International Journal of Interactive Mobile Technologies*, *15*(5), 187. doi:10.3991/ijim.v15i05.18147

Ravenelle, A. J. (2019). *Hustle and Gig*. University of California Press. doi:10.2307/j.ctvcwp0kc

Rawashdeh, A. (2023). The consequences of artificial intelligence: an investigation into the impact of AI on job displacement in accounting. *Journal of Science and Technology Policy Management*. doi:10.1108/JSTPM-02-2023-0030

Rawlinson, K. (2015). Microsoft's Bill Gates insists AI is a threat. *BBC News*.

Razzak, M. I., Imran, M., & Xu, G. (2020). Big Data Analytics for Preventive Medicine. *Neural Computing & Applications*, *32*(9), 4417–4451. doi:10.1007/s00521-019-04095-y PMID:32205918

Richards, L. (2020). Handling qualitative data: A practical guide. *Handling Qualitative Data*, 1-336.

Riege, A. M. (2003). Validity and reliability tests in case study research: A literature review with "hands-on" applications for each research phase. *Qualitative Market Research, 6*(2), 75–86. doi:10.1108/13522750310470055

Roberts, E. D. (1988). What we have learned-Managing invention and innovation. *Research Technology Management, 1*(1), 11–29. doi:10.1080/08956308.1988.11670497

Roberts, P. W., & Amit, R. (2003). The dynamics of innovative activity and competitive advantage: The case of Australian retail banking, 1981 to 1995. *Organization Science, 14*(2), 107–122. doi:10.1287/orsc.14.2.107.14990

Robson, C. (2002). *Real-world research: A resource for social scientists and practitioner-researchers* (2nd ed.). Blackwell Publishers.

Russell, S. (2016). *Artificial Intelligence: A Modern Approach, eBook* (Global Edition). Pearson Education, Limited.

Rust, R. T., Zahorik, A. J., & Keiningham, T. L. (1995). Return on quality (ROQ): Making service quality financially accountable. *Journal of Marketing, 59*(2), 58–70. doi:10.1177/002224299505900205

Rydstedt, L. W., Johansson, G., & Evans, G. W. (1998). A longitudinal study of workload, health and well-being among male and female urban bus drivers. *Journal of Occupational and Organizational Psychology, 71*(1), 35–45. doi:10.1111/j.2044-8325.1998.tb00661.x

Samuel, Y., George, J., & Samuel, J. (2020). Beyond stem, how can women engage big data, analytics, robotics and artificial intelligence? an exploratory analysis of confidence and educational factors in the emerging technology waves influencing the role of, and impact upon, women. *arXiv preprint arXiv:2003.11746.*

Sandrin, V. (2021). *The Struggle between Human-centredness and Intelligent Technologies: a Critical Discussion on the Use of Customer Data in Marketing Practice-A Survey Analysis of the RIR Clusters in Veneto*. Academic Press.

Santos, P., Sá, L., Couto, L., & Hespanhol, A. (2017). Health Literacy as a Key for Effective Preventive Medicine. *Cogent Social Sciences, 3*(1), 1407522. doi:10.1080/23311886.2017.1407522

SAP SE. (2024, January 15). *O que é IA generativa?* Https://Www.Sap.Com/Brazil/Products/Artificial-Intelligence/What-Is-Generative-Ai.Html

Sarker, S., & Sarker, M. (2020). *Service Innovation in the Digital Age: Leveraging Technology to Create Transformative Experiences*. Routledge.

Sato, M. K. de S. (2002). A Propaganda e a Publicidade de Medicamentos e a Informação ao Consumidor. *Publicidade de Medicamentos e Informação Ao Público, 3*(3), 89–115. http://www.revistas.usp.br/rdisan/article/view/83839/86720

Schell, C. (1992). The value of the case study as a research strategy. Manchester Business School, 2(1), 1-15.

Schmidt, F. L., Hunter, J. E., Outerbridge, A. N., & Goff, S. (1988). Joint relation of experience and ability with job performance: Test of three hypotheses. *The Journal of Applied Psychology*, *73*(1), 46–57. doi:10.1037/0021-9010.73.1.46

Schnurr, H.-P., Aronsky, D., & Wenke, D. (2018). Medicine 4.0 - Interplay of Intelligent Systems and Medical Experts. In K. North, O. Haas, & R. Maier (Eds.), *Knowledge Management in Digital Change - New Findings and Practical Cases* (pp. 51–63). Springer. doi:10.1007/978-3-319-73546-7_3

Scholz, S., & Teetz, L. (2022). Smart Health via mHealth? Potentials of Mobile Health Apps for Improving Prevention and Adherence of Breast Cancer Patients. *Digital Health*, *8*, 1–12. doi:10.1177/20552076221074127 PMID:35096411

Segarra-Blasco, A., & Arauzo-Carod, J. M. (2008). Sources of innovation and industry–university interaction: Evidence from Spanish firms. *Research Policy*, *37*(8), 1283–1295. doi:10.1016/j.respol.2008.05.003

Sestino, A., Prete, M. I., Piper, L., & Guido, G. (2023). The future of online marketing strategies and digital tools: New challenges and contributions to RACE framework. *International Journal of Electronic Trade*, *1*(1), 4–27. doi:10.1504/IJETRADE.2023.133310

Shahriar Akter. (2023). A framework for AI-powered service innovation capability: Review and agenda for future research. Science Direct. https://www.sciencedirect.com/science/article/abs/pii/S0166497223000792

Shahzad, M. F., Xu, S., Naveed, W., Nusrat, S., & Zahid, I. (2023). Investigating the impact of artificial intelligence on human resource functions in the health sector of China: A mediated moderation model. *Heliyon*, *9*(11), e21818. doi:10.1016/j.heliyon.2023.e21818 PMID:38034787

Shaw, J., Rudzicz, F., Jamieson, T., & Goldfarb, A. (2019). Artificial intelligence and the implementation challenge. *Journal of Medical Internet Research*, *21*(7), e13659. https://preprints.jmir.org/preprint/13659. doi:10.2196/13659 PMID:31293245

Shirom, A., Shechter Gilboa, S., Fried, Y., & Cooper, C. L. (2008). Gender, age and tenure as moderators of work-related stressors' relationships with job performance: A meta-analysis. *Human Relations*, *61*(10), 1371–1398. doi:10.1177/0018726708095708

Shivajirao, S. K. D. M. P., & Verma, R. (2022). Examining the Impact of Storytelling in Content Marketing on Consumer Engagement and Brand Loyalty. *African Diaspora Journal of Mathematics, 25*(6), 121-130.

Shortliffe, E. H. (1979). *MYCIN: A Computer Program For the Diagnosis of Infectious Diseases*. Elsevier.

Sidhu, J. S., Commandeur, H. R., & Volberda, H. W. (2007). The multifaceted nature of exploration and exploitation: Value of supply, demand, and spatial search for innovation. *Organization Science*, *18*(1), 20–38. doi:10.1287/orsc.1060.0212

Silva, B. M. C., Rodrigues, J. J. P. C., Díez, I. de la T., López-Coronado, M., & Saleem, K. (2015). Mobile-Health: A Review of Current State in 2015. *Journal of Biomedical Informatics*, *56*, 265–272. doi:10.1016/j.jbi.2015.06.003 PMID:26071682

Silver, C., & Lewins, A. (2007). *Using software in qualitative research: A step-by-step guide*. Sage.

Silverman, D. (2013). *Doing qualitative research* (4th ed.).

Simmons, C. (2023). A Comprehensive Guide to Mobile Payment Technologies. Fintech Curated. https://fintechcurated.com/editorial/a-comprehensive-guide-to-mobile-payment-technologies/#:~:text=At%20its%20core%2C%20mobile%20payments%20leverage%20the%20power,mobile%20banking%20apps%2C%20and%20peer-to-peer%20%28P2P%29%20payment%20platforms

Sirilli, G., & Evangelista, R. (1998). Technological innovation in services and manufacturing: Results from Italian surveys. *Research Policy*, *27*(9), 881–899. doi:10.1016/S0048-7333(98)00084-5

Sivaraman, D. (2023). *AI in Service Industry: Trends and Opportunities*. McKinsey & Company.

Song, L. Z., Song, M., & DiBenedetto, C. A. (2009). A staged service innovation model. *Decision Sciences*, *40*(3), 571–599. doi:10.1111/j.1540-5915.2009.00240.x

Sony, M., Antony, J., & McDermott, O. (2022). The Impact of Healthcare 4.0 on the Healthcare Service Quality: A Systematic Literature Review. *Hospital Topics*, 1–17. doi:10.1080/00185868.2022.2048220 PMID:35324390

Souiden, N., Ladhari, R., & Chiadmi, N. E. (2017). Destination personality and destination image. *Journal of Hospitality and Tourism Management*, *32*, 54–70. doi:10.1016/j.jhtm.2017.04.003

Spanos, M. (2021). Brand storytelling in the age of artificial intelligence. *Journal of Brand Strategy*, *10*(1), 6–13.

Spencer, M. K. (2018, April 27). *Will AI replace humans?* Retrieved from https://medium.com/futuresin/will-ai-replace-humans-42c19c114cb8

Spohrer, J., & Maglio, P. P. (2010). Toward a Science of Service Systems: Value and Symbols," in Subramanian, A. and S. Nilakanta (1996).Organizational innovativeness: exploring the relationship between organizational determinants of innovation, types of innovations, and measures of organizational performance. *Omega*, *24*(6), 631–647.

Stake, R. E. (2005). Qualitative case studies. In N. K. Denzin & Y. S. Lincoln (Eds.), *The SAGE handbook of qualitative research* (3rd ed., pp. 443–466). SAGE Publications.

Stake, R. E. (2013). *Multiple case study analysis*. Guilford press.

Statista. (2023). *Global programmatic advertising spending from 2017 to 2028*. https://www.statista.com/statistics/275806/programmatic-spending-worldwide/

Stephen, D. A., Nordin, A., Nilsson, J., & Persenius, M. (2022). Using mHealth Applications for Self-Care – An Integrative Review on Perceptions Among Adults with Type 1 Diabetes. *BMC Endocrine Disorders*, *22*(138), 138. Advance online publication. doi:10.1186/s12902-022-01039-x PMID:35614419

Stolle, S. (August 25, 2022). *Qualitative Research – Advantages & Disadvantages.* Bachelor Print. https://www.bachelorprint.com/methodology/qualitative-research/

Stoyanov, S. R., Hides, L., Kavanagh, D. J., & Wilson, H. (2016). Development and Validation of the User Version of the Mobile Application Rating Scale (uMARS). *JMIR mHealth and uHealth*, *4*(2), e72. doi:10.2196/mhealth.5849 PMID:27287964

Sujith, A. V. L. N., Sajja, G. S., Mahalakshmi, V., Nuhmani, S., & Prasanalakshmi, B. (2022). Systematic Review of Smart Health Monitoring Using Deep Learning and Artificial Intelligence. *Neuroscience Informatics (Online)*, *2*(3), 100028. doi:10.1016/j.neuri.2021.100028

Sullivan, D. (2015). *FAQ: All about the new Google RankBrain algorithm.* Academic Press.

Sullivan, Y., & Fosso Wamba, S. (2024). Artificial intelligence and adaptive response to market changes: A strategy to enhance firm performance and innovation. *Journal of Business Research*, *174*, 114500. doi:10.1016/j.jbusres.2024.114500

Swaminathan, V., Sorescu, A., Steenkamp, J. B. E. M., O'Guinn, T. C. G., & Schmitt, B. (2020). Branding in a Hyperconnected World: Refocusing Theories and Rethinking Boundaries. *Journal of Marketing*, *84*(2), 24–46. doi:10.1177/0022242919899905

Syed Shah Alam. (2021). Factors Affecting Augmented Reality Adoption in the Retail Industry. Science Direct. https://www.sciencedirect.com/science/article/pii/S2199853122009118

Tahoun, N. (2020). *The utilization of artificial intelligence in online advertising and its perceived effectiveness.* Academic Press.

Tallia, S., Zulsibtain, M. A., Ali, R., & Hafeez, M. H. (2018). Strategic Marketing of Health Care Services : A Systematic Review. *International Journal of Management and Applied Science*, *4*(12), 23–28.

Talwar, S. (2022). Digitalization and sustainability: virtual reality tourism in a post pandemic world. Taylor and Francis Online. https://www.tandfonline.com/doi/full/10.1080/09669582.2022.2029870

Tang, Z., & Lusch, R. F. (2018). Open Innovation: An SD Logic Perspective. In World Scientific Reference on Innovation: Volume 3: Open Innovation, Ecosystems and Entrepreneurship: Issues and Perspectives (pp. 13-35). doi:10.1142/9789813149083_0002

Tang, X. (2020). The Role of Artificial Intelligence in Medical Imaging Research. *BJR Open*, *2*(1), 20190031. Advance online publication. doi:10.1259/bjro.20190031 PMID:33178962

Tasheva, Z., & Karpovich, V. (2024). Supercharge human potential through ai to increase productivity the workforce in the companies. *American Journal of Applied Science and Technology*, *4*(02), 24–29. doi:10.37547/ajast/Volume04Issue02-05

Tatikonda, M. V., & Zeithaml, V. A. (2001). Managing the new service development process: multi-disciplinary literature synthesis and directions for future research. In T. Boone & R. Ganeshan (Eds.), *New directions in supply-chain management* (pp. 200–233). AMACOM.

Taylor, H. (2017). *B2B marketing strategy: differentiate, develop and deliver lasting customer engagement*. Kogan Page Publishers.

Taylor, M. R., Rubin, E. S., & Hounshell, D. A. (2005). Regulation as the mother of innovation: The case of SO2 control. *Law & Policy*, *27*(2), 348–378. doi:10.1111/j.1467-9930.2005.00203.x

Teece, D. J. (2010). Business models, business strategy and innovation. *Long Range Planning*, *43*(2/3), 172–194. doi:10.1016/j.lrp.2009.07.003

Tejada, P., & Moreno, P. (2013). Patterns of innovation in tourism 'Small and Medium-size Enterprises. *Service Industries Journal*, *33*(7-8), 749–758. doi:10.1080/02642069.2013.740469

Tellis, W. (1997). Introduction to case study. *The qualitative report*, *3*(2), 1–14.

Terkola, R., Antoñanzas, F., & Postma, M. (2017). Economic Evaluation of Personalized Medicine: A Call for Real-World Data. *The European Journal of Health Economics*, *18*(9), 1065–1067. doi:10.1007/s10198-017-0890-x PMID:28382502

Thakur, C. K. (2023) *The future of AI in marketing - what to expect in the next 5 years?* https://www.linkedin.com/pulse/future-ai-marketing-what-expect-next-5-years-a-i-marketing-/

Theodoridis, P. K., & Gkikas, D. C. (2019). How artificial intelligence affects digital marketing. In Strategic Innovative Marketing and Tourism: 7th ICSIMAT, Athenian Riviera, Greece, 2018 (pp. 1319-1327). Springer International Publishing. doi:10.1007/978-3-030-12453-3_151

Thompson, M. (n.d.). *Ikea's new augmented reality app lets you try out furniture in your home*. The Spaces. https://thespaces.com/ikea-place-app/

Tidd, J., Bessant, J., & Pavitt, K. (1997). *Managing Innovation: Integrating Technological and Organizational Change* (Vol. 3). Wiley and Sons.

Tight, M. (2019). Documentary research in the social sciences. *Documentary Research in the Social Sciences*, 1-232.

Timimi, F. K. (2013). The Shape of Digital Engagement: Health Care and Social Media. *The Journal of Ambulatory Care Management*, *36*(3), 187–192. doi:10.1097/JAC.0b013e3182965512 PMID:23748265

Topol, E. J. (2019). High-Performance Medicine: The Convergence of Human and Artificial Intelligence. *Nature Medicine*, *25*(1), 44–56. doi:10.1038/s41591-018-0300-7 PMID:30617339

Torres, C. (2009). A Bíblia do Marketing Digital: Tudo o Que Você Queria Saber do Marketing e Não Tinha a Quem Perguntar. Novatec Editora.

Toumia, O., & Zouari, F. (2024a). Artificial Intelligence and Venture Capital Decision-Making. In R. Sharma, K. Mehta, & P. Yu (Eds.), *Fostering Innovation in Venture Capital and Startup Ecosystems*. IGI Global. doi:10.4018/979-8-3693-1326-8.ch002

Toumia, O., & Zouari, F. (2024b). Effect of Artificial Intelligence Awareness on Job Performance with Employee Experience as a Mediating Variable. In O. Meçik (Ed.), *Reskilling the Workforce for Technological Advancement* (pp. 141–161). IGI Global. doi:10.4018/979-8-3693-0612-3.ch007

Tracy, S. J. (2019). *Qualitative research methods: Collecting evidence, crafting analysis, communicating impact*. John Wiley & Sons.

Travers, M. (2001). Qualitative research through case studies. *Qualitative research through case studies*, 1-208.

Trawnih, A., Al-Masaeed, S., Alsoud, M., & Alkufahy, A. (2022). Understanding artificial intelligence experience: A customer perspective. *International Journal of Data and Network Science*, *6*(4), 1471–1484. doi:10.5267/j.ijdns.2022.5.004

Tuomi, I. (2019). *The Impact of Artificial Intelligence on Learning, Teaching, and Education: Policies for the Future. JRC Science for Policy Report*. European Commission. doi:10.2760/12297

Tushman, M. L., Virany, B., & Romanelli, E. (1985). Executive succession, strategic reorientations, and organisation evolution: The minicomputer industry as a case in point. *Technology in Society*, *7*(2), 297–313. doi:10.1016/0160-791X(85)90031-4

Unilever. (2021). *Act 2 Unstereotype makes end-to-end inclusive marketing a priority*. https://www.unilever.com/news/news-search/2021/act-2-unstereotype-makes-inclusive-marketing-a-priority/

Upadhyay, S., & McCormick, K. (2018). *The Revenue Acceleration Rules: Supercharge Sales and Marketing Through Artificial Intelligence, Predictive Technologies and Account-Based Strategies*. John Wiley & Sons.

Vajre, S. (2016). *Account-based marketing for dummies*. John Wiley & Sons.

Valenti, A., Srinivasan, S., Yildirim, G., & Pauwels, K. (2023). Direct mail to prospects and email to current customers? Modeling and field-testing multichannel marketing. *Journal of the Academy of Marketing Science*, 1–20. doi:10.1007/s11747-023-00962-2

Van der Auwermeulen, T., De Backer, M., Van Den Poel, D., & Snoeck, H. (2017). Potential Roles of Robotic Process Automation in Financial Services. *Journal of Financial Transformation*, *36*(2), 126–136.

Van der Vegt, G. S., & Janssen, O. (2003). The joint impact of interdependence and group diversity on innovation. *Journal of Management*, *29*(5), 729–751. doi:10.1016/S0149-2063_03_00033-3

Van Doorn, J., Lemon, K. N., Mittal, V., Pick, D., Pirner, P., & Verhoef, P. C. (2010). Customer Engagement Behavior: Theoretical Foundations and Research Directions. *Journal of Service Research, 13*(3), 253–266. doi:10.1177/1094670510375599

Vargo, S. L., & Lusch, R. F. (2004). Evolving to a new dominant logic for marketing. *Journal of Marketing, 68*(1), 1–17. doi:10.1509/jmkg.68.1.1.24036

Vargo, S. L., & Morgan, F. W. (2005). Services in society and academic thought: A historical analysis. *Journal of Macromarketing, 25*(1), 42–53. doi:10.1177/0276146705275294

Vashishth, A., & Jhamb, D. (2021). Why should employers hire people with disabilities?–a review of benefits for the hospitality industry. *Revista Turismo & Desenvolvimento (Aveiro)*, (35), 9–21.

Verghese, A., Shah, N. H., & Harrington, R. A. (2018). What This Computer Needs Is a Physician: Humanism and Artificial Intelligence. *Journal of the American Medical Association, 319*(1), 19–20. doi:10.1001/jama.2017.19198 PMID:29261830

Verhagen, T., & Dolen, W. (2009). Online purchase intentions: A multi-channel store image perspective. *Information & Management, 46*(2), 77–82. doi:10.1016/j.im.2008.12.001

Verma, B., & Tandon, U. (2022). Modelling barriers to wearable technologies in Indian context: validating the moderating role of technology literacy. Global Knowledge, Memory and Communication. doi:10.1108/GKMC-08-2022-0209

Vial, G. (2019). Understanding Digital Transformation: A Review and a Research Agenda. *The Journal of Strategic Information Systems, 28*(2), 118–144. doi:10.1016/j.jsis.2019.01.003

Vidrih, M., & Mayahi, S. (2023). Generative AI-Driven Storytelling: A New Era for Marketing. *arXiv preprint arXiv:2309.09048.*

Vimarlund, V. (2017). The Future of Two-Sided E-Health Markets. In V. Vimarlund (Ed.), *E-Health Two-Sided Markets: Implementation and Business Models* (pp. 189–195). Elsevier Inc. doi:10.1016/B978-0-12-805250-1.00020-4

Vincent, V. U. (2021). Integrating intuition and artificial intelligence in organizational decision-making. *Business Horizons, 64*(4), 425–438. doi:10.1016/j.bushor.2021.02.008

Vlačić, B., Corbo, L., Silva, S. C., & Dabić, M. (2021). The evolving role of artificial intelligence in marketing: A review and research agenda. *Journal of Business Research, 128*, 187–203. doi:10.1016/j.jbusres.2021.01.055

Voss, C. A. (1992). Measurement of Innovation and Design Performance in Services. *Design Management Journal, 3*(1), 40–46. doi:10.1111/j.1948-7169.1992.tb00586.x

Vrontis, D., Christofi, M., Pereira, V., Tarba, S., Makrides, A., & Trichina, E. (2022). Artificial intelligence, robotics, advanced technologies and human resource management: A systematic review. *International Journal of Human Resource Management, 33*(6), 1237–1266. doi:10.1080/09585192.2020.1871398

Wang, C. L. (2021). New frontiers and future directions in interactive marketing: Inaugural Editorial. *Journal of Research in Interactive Marketing*, *15*(1), 1–9. doi:10.1108/JRIM-03-2021-270

WebbM. (2019). The impact of artificial intelligence on the labor market. *Available at* SSRN 3482150. doi:10.2139/ssrn.3482150

Westwater, S. (2023). *AI Marketing Case Studies – Discover Success Stories and Cutting-Edge Strategies*. LinkedIn. https://www.linkedin.com/pulse/ai-marketing-case-studies-discover-success-stories-scot-westwater-ag4ic/

Wijayati, D. T., Rahman, Z., Rahman, M. F. W., Arifah, I. D. C., & Kautsar, A. (2022). A study of artificial intelligence on employee performance and work engagement: The moderating role of change leadership. *International Journal of Manpower*, *43*(2), 486–512. doi:10.1108/IJM-07-2021-0423

Wilson, H. J., & Daugherty, P. R. (2018). Collaborative intelligence: Humans and AI are joining forces. *Harvard Business Review*, *96*(4), 114–123.

Wind, J., & Mahajan, V. (1997). Editorial: Issues and opportunities in new product development: an introduction to the special issue. *JMR, Journal of Marketing Research*, *34*(1), 1–12. doi:10.2307/3152060

Wischnevsky, J. D., & Damanpour, F. (2006). Organizational transformation and performance: An examination of three perspectives. *Journal of Managerial Issues*, *18*(1), 104–128.

World Health Organization. (2010). *Telemedicine - Opportunities and Developments in Member States : Report on the Second Global Survey on eHealth*. World Health Organization.

Wu, M., & Chen, L. (2015, November). Image recognition based on deep learning. In *2015 Chinese automation congress (CAC)* (pp. 542-546). IEEE.

Yetgin, M. A., & Toumia, O. (2023). *Perceptions of Employees of Technology Emerging With Generative Pre-Trained Transformer-3 in Organizations*. Gazi Kitabevi.

Yin, R. K. (2003). Designing case studies. *Qualitative Research Methods*, *5*(14), 359-386.

Yin, R. K. (1984). *Case Study Research: Design and Methods*. Sage Publications.

Yin, R. K. (2011). *Applications of case study research*. Sage Publications.

Younus, A. M. (2021). Utilization Of Artificial Intelligence (Ann) In Project Management Services: A Proposed Model of Application. *Central Asian Journal of Theoretical and Applied Science*, *2*(10), 121–131.

Yu, G., & Schwartz, Z. (2006). Forecasting short time-series tourism demand with artificial intelligence models. *Journal of Travel Research*, *45*(2), 194–203. doi:10.1177/0047287506291594

Zainal, Z. (2007). Case study as a research method. *Jurnal kemanusiaan*, *5*(1).

Zaltman, G., Duncan, R., & Holbek, J. (1973). *Innovations and organizations*. Wiley.

Zeba, G., Dabić, M., Čičak, M., Daim, T., & Yalcin, H. (2021). Technology mining: Artificial intelligence in manufacturing. *Technological Forecasting and Social Change*, *171*, 120971. doi:10.1016/j.techfore.2021.120971

Zel, S., & Kongar, E. (2020, September). Transforming digital employee experience with artificial intelligence. In *2020 IEEE/ITU International Conference on Artificial Intelligence for Good (AI4G)* (pp. 176-179). IEEE. 10.1109/AI4G50087.2020.9311088

Zhang, R., Yao, X., Ye, L., & Chen, M. (2022). Students' adaptive deep learning path and teaching strategy of contemporary ceramic art under the background of Internet+. *Frontiers in Psychology*, *13*, 938840. doi:10.3389/fpsyg.2022.938840 PMID:36118465

Zineldin, M. (2000). Beyond relationship marketing: Technologicalship marketing. *Marketing Intelligence & Planning*, *18*(1), 9–23. doi:10.1108/02634500010308549

Zinkhan, G. M. (2002). Relationship Marketing: Theory and Implementation. *Journal of Market - Focused Management, 5*, 83–89. . doi:10.1023/A:1014031025271

Złotowski, J., Yogeeswaran, K., & Bartneck, C. (2017). Can we control it? Autonomous robots threaten human identity, uniqueness, safety, and resources. *International Journal of Human-Computer Studies*, *100*, 48–54. doi:10.1016/j.ijhcs.2016.12.008

Zouari, F. (2019). Neural network based adaptive backstepping dynamic surface control of drug dosage regimens in cancer treatment. *Neurocomputing*, *366*, 248–263. doi:10.1016/j.neucom.2019.07.096

Related References

To continue our tradition of advancing information science and technology research, we have compiled a list of recommended IGI Global readings. These references will provide additional information and guidance to further enrich your knowledge and assist you with your own research and future publications.

Abdul Razak, R., & Mansor, N. A. (2021). Instagram Influencers in Social Media-Induced Tourism: Rethinking Tourist Trust Towards Tourism Destination. In M. Dinis, L. Bonixe, S. Lamy, & Z. Breda (Eds.), *Impact of New Media in Tourism* (pp. 135-144). IGI Global. https://doi.org/10.4018/978-1-7998-7095-1.ch009

Abir, T., & Khan, M. Y. (2022). Importance of ICT Advancement and Culture of Adaptation in the Tourism and Hospitality Industry for Developing Countries. In C. Ramos, S. Quinteiro, & A. Gonçalves (Eds.), *ICT as Innovator Between Tourism and Culture* (pp. 30–41). IGI Global. https://doi.org/10.4018/978-1-7998-8165-0.ch003

Abir, T., & Khan, M. Y. (2022). Importance of ICT Advancement and Culture of Adaptation in the Tourism and Hospitality Industry for Developing Countries. In C. Ramos, S. Quinteiro, & A. Gonçalves (Eds.), *ICT as Innovator Between Tourism and Culture* (pp. 30–41). IGI Global. https://doi.org/10.4018/978-1-7998-8165-0.ch003

Abtahi, M. S., Behboudi, L., & Hasanabad, H. M. (2017). Factors Affecting Internet Advertising Adoption in Ad Agencies. *International Journal of Innovation in the Digital Economy*, *8*(4), 18–29. doi:10.4018/IJIDE.2017100102

Afenyo-Agbe, E., & Mensah, I. (2022). Principles, Benefits, and Barriers to Community-Based Tourism: Implications for Management. In I. Mensah & E. Afenyo-Agbe (Eds.), *Prospects and Challenges of Community-Based Tourism and Changing Demographics* (pp. 1–29). IGI Global. doi:10.4018/978-1-7998-7335-8.ch001

Agbo, V. M. (2022). Distributive Justice Issues in Community-Based Tourism. In I. Mensah & E. Afenyo-Agbe (Eds.), *Prospects and Challenges of Community-Based Tourism and Changing Demographics* (pp. 107–129). IGI Global. https://doi.org/10.4018/978-1-7998-7335-8.ch005

Agrawal, S. (2017). The Impact of Emerging Technologies and Social Media on Different Business(es): Marketing and Management. In O. Rishi & A. Sharma (Eds.), *Maximizing Business Performance and Efficiency Through Intelligent Systems* (pp. 37–49). Hershey, PA: IGI Global. doi:10.4018/978-1-5225-2234-8.ch002

Ahmad, A., & Johari, S. (2022). Georgetown as a Gastronomy Tourism Destination: Visitor Awareness Towards Revisit Intention of Nasi Kandar Restaurant. In M. Valeri (Ed.), *New Governance and Management in Touristic Destinations* (pp. 71–83). IGI Global. https://doi.org/10.4018/978-1-6684-3889-3.ch005

Alkhatib, G., & Bayouq, S. T. (2021). A TAM-Based Model of Technological Factors Affecting Use of E-Tourism. *International Journal of Tourism and Hospitality Management in the Digital Age*, *5*(2), 50–67. https://doi.org/10.4018/IJTHMDA.20210701.oa1

Altinay Ozdemir, M. (2021). Virtual Reality (VR) and Augmented Reality (AR) Technologies for Accessibility and Marketing in the Tourism Industry. In C. Eusébio, L. Teixeira, & M. Carneiro (Eds.), *ICT Tools and Applications for Accessible Tourism* (pp. 277-301). IGI Global. https://doi.org/10.4018/978-1-7998-6428-8.ch013

Anantharaman, R. N., Rajeswari, K. S., Angusamy, A., & Kuppusamy, J. (2017). Role of Self-Efficacy and Collective Efficacy as Moderators of Occupational Stress Among Software Development Professionals. *International Journal of Human Capital and Information Technology Professionals*, *8*(2), 45–58. doi:10.4018/IJHCITP.2017040103

Aninze, F., El-Gohary, H., & Hussain, J. (2018). The Role of Microfinance to Empower Women: The Case of Developing Countries. *International Journal of Customer Relationship Marketing and Management*, *9*(1), 54–78. doi:10.4018/IJCRMM.2018010104

Antosova, G., Sabogal-Salamanca, M., & Krizova, E. (2021). Human Capital in Tourism: A Practical Model of Endogenous and Exogenous Territorial Tourism Planning in Bahía Solano, Colombia. In V. Costa, A. Moura, & M. Mira (Eds.), *Handbook of Research on Human Capital and People Management in the Tourism Industry* (pp. 282–302). IGI Global. https://doi.org/10.4018/978-1-7998-4318-4.ch014

Arsenijević, O. M., Orčić, D., & Kastratović, E. (2017). Development of an Optimization Tool for Intangibles in SMEs: A Case Study from Serbia with a Pilot Research in the Prestige by Milka Company. In M. Vemić (Ed.), *Optimal Management Strategies in Small and Medium Enterprises* (pp. 320–347). Hershey, PA: IGI Global. doi:10.4018/978-1-5225-1949-2.ch015

Aryanto, V. D., Wismantoro, Y., & Widyatmoko, K. (2018). Implementing Eco-Innovation by Utilizing the Internet to Enhance Firm's Marketing Performance: Study of Green Batik Small and Medium Enterprises in Indonesia. *International Journal of E-Business Research, 14*(1), 21–36. doi:10.4018/IJEBR.2018010102

Asero, V., & Billi, S. (2022). New Perspective of Networking in the DMO Model. In M. Valeri (Ed.), *New Governance and Management in Touristic Destinations* (pp. 105–118). IGI Global. https://doi.org/10.4018/978-1-6684-3889-3.ch007

Atiku, S. O., & Fields, Z. (2017). Multicultural Orientations for 21st Century Global Leadership. In N. Baporikar (Ed.), *Management Education for Global Leadership* (pp. 28–51). Hershey, PA: IGI Global. doi:10.4018/978-1-5225-1013-0.ch002

Atiku, S. O., & Fields, Z. (2018). Organisational Learning Dimensions and Talent Retention Strategies for the Service Industries. In N. Baporikar (Ed.), *Global Practices in Knowledge Management for Societal and Organizational Development* (pp. 358–381). Hershey, PA: IGI Global. doi:10.4018/978-1-5225-3009-1.ch017

Atsa'am, D. D., & Kuset Bodur, E. (2021). Pattern Mining on How Organizational Tenure Affects the Psychological Capital of Employees Within the Hospitality and Tourism Industry: Linking Employees' Organizational Tenure With PsyCap. *International Journal of Tourism and Hospitality Management in the Digital Age, 5*(2), 17–28. https://doi.org/10.4018/IJTHMDA.2021070102

Ávila, L., & Teixeira, L. (2018). The Main Concepts Behind the Dematerialization of Business Processes. In M. Khosrow-Pour, D.B.A. (Ed.), Encyclopedia of Information Science and Technology, Fourth Edition (pp. 888-898). Hershey, PA: IGI Global. https://doi.org/ doi:10.4018/978-1-5225-2255-3.ch076

Ayorekire, J., Mugizi, F., Obua, J., & Ampaire, G. (2022). Community-Based Tourism and Local People's Perceptions Towards Conservation: The Case of Queen Elizabeth Conservation Area, Uganda. In I. Mensah & E. Afenyo-Agbe (Eds.), *Prospects and Challenges of Community-Based Tourism and Changing Demographics* (pp. 56–82). IGI Global. https://doi.org/10.4018/978-1-7998-7335-8.ch003

Baleiro, R. (2022). Tourist Literature and the Architecture of Travel in Olga Tokarczuk and Patti Smith. In R. Baleiro & R. Pereira (Eds.), *Global Perspectives on Literary Tourism and Film-Induced Tourism* (pp. 202-216). IGI Global. https://doi.org/10.4018/978-1-7998-8262-6.ch011

Barat, S. (2021). Looking at the Future of Medical Tourism in Asia. *International Journal of Tourism and Hospitality Management in the Digital Age*, *5*(1), 19–33. https://doi.org/10.4018/IJTHMDA.2021010102

Barbosa, C. A., Magalhães, M., & Nunes, M. R. (2021). Travel Instagramability: A Way of Choosing a Destination? In M. Dinis, L. Bonixe, S. Lamy, & Z. Breda (Eds.), *Impact of New Media in Tourism* (pp. 173-190). IGI Global. https://doi.org/10.4018/978-1-7998-7095-1.ch011

Bari, M. W., & Khan, Q. (2021). Pakistan as a Destination of Religious Tourism. In E. Alaverdov & M. Bari (Eds.), *Global Development of Religious Tourism* (pp. 1-10). IGI Global. https://doi.org/10.4018/978-1-7998-5792-1.ch001

Bartens, Y., Chunpir, H. I., Schulte, F., & Voß, S. (2017). Business/IT Alignment in Two-Sided Markets: A COBIT 5 Analysis for Media Streaming Business Models. In S. De Haes & W. Van Grembergen (Eds.), *Strategic IT Governance and Alignment in Business Settings* (pp. 82–111). Hershey, PA: IGI Global. doi:10.4018/978-1-5225-0861-8.ch004

Bashayreh, A. M. (2018). Organizational Culture and Organizational Performance. In W. Lee & F. Sabetzadeh (Eds.), *Contemporary Knowledge and Systems Science* (pp. 50–69). Hershey, PA: IGI Global. doi:10.4018/978-1-5225-5655-8.ch003

Bechthold, L., Lude, M., & Prügl, R. (2021). Crisis Favors the Prepared Firm: How Organizational Ambidexterity Relates to Perceptions of Organizational Resilience. In A. Zehrer, G. Glowka, K. Schwaiger, & V. Ranacher-Lackner (Eds.), *Resiliency Models and Addressing Future Risks for Family Firms in the Tourism Industry* (pp. 178–205). IGI Global. https://doi.org/10.4018/978-1-7998-7352-5.ch008

Bedford, D. A. (2018). Sustainable Knowledge Management Strategies: Aligning Business Capabilities and Knowledge Management Goals. In N. Baporikar (Ed.), *Global Practices in Knowledge Management for Societal and Organizational Development* (pp. 46–73). Hershey, PA: IGI Global. doi:10.4018/978-1-5225-3009-1.ch003

Bekjanov, D., & Matyusupov, B. (2021). Influence of Innovative Processes in the Competitiveness of Tourist Destination. In J. Soares (Ed.), *Innovation and Entrepreneurial Opportunities in Community Tourism* (pp. 243–263). IGI Global. https://doi.org/10.4018/978-1-7998-4855-4.ch014

Bharwani, S., & Musunuri, D. (2018). Reflection as a Process From Theory to Practice. In M. Khosrow-Pour, D.B.A. (Ed.), Encyclopedia of Information Science and Technology, Fourth Edition (pp. 1529-1539). Hershey, PA: IGI Global. doi:10.4018/978-1-5225-2255-3.ch132

Bhatt, G. D., Wang, Z., & Rodger, J. A. (2017). Information Systems Capabilities and Their Effects on Competitive Advantages: A Study of Chinese Companies. *Information Resources Management Journal, 30*(3), 41–57. doi:10.4018/IRMJ.2017070103

Bhushan, M., & Yadav, A. (2017). Concept of Cloud Computing in ESB. In R. Bhadoria, N. Chaudhari, G. Tomar, & S. Singh (Eds.), *Exploring Enterprise Service Bus in the Service-Oriented Architecture Paradigm* (pp. 116–127). Hershey, PA: IGI Global. doi:10.4018/978-1-5225-2157-0.ch008

Bhushan, S. (2017). System Dynamics Base-Model of Humanitarian Supply Chain (HSCM) in Disaster Prone Eco-Communities of India: A Discussion on Simulation and Scenario Results. *International Journal of System Dynamics Applications, 6*(3), 20–37. doi:10.4018/IJSDA.2017070102

Binder, D., & Miller, J. W. (2021). A Generations' Perspective on Employer Branding in Tourism. In V. Costa, A. Moura, & M. Mira (Eds.), *Handbook of Research on Human Capital and People Management in the Tourism Industry* (pp. 152–174). IGI Global. https://doi.org/10.4018/978-1-7998-4318-4.ch008

Birch Freeman, A. A., Mensah, I., & Antwi, K. B. (2022). Smiling vs. Frowning Faces: Community Participation for Sustainable Tourism in Ghanaian Communities. In I. Mensah & E. Afenyo-Agbe (Eds.), *Prospects and Challenges of Community-Based Tourism and Changing Demographics* (pp. 83–106). IGI Global. https://doi.org/10.4018/978-1-7998-7335-8.ch004

Biswas, A., & De, A. K. (2017). On Development of a Fuzzy Stochastic Programming Model with Its Application to Business Management. In S. Trivedi, S. Dey, A. Kumar, & T. Panda (Eds.), *Handbook of Research on Advanced Data Mining Techniques and Applications for Business Intelligence* (pp. 353–378). Hershey, PA: IGI Global. doi:10.4018/978-1-5225-2031-3.ch021

Boragnio, A., & Faracce Macia, C. (2021). "Taking Care of Yourself at Home": Use of E-Commerce About Food and Care During the COVID-19 Pandemic in the City of Buenos Aires. In M. Korstanje (Ed.), *Socio-Economic Effects and Recovery Efforts for the Rental Industry: Post-COVID-19 Strategies* (pp. 45–71). IGI Global. https://doi.org/10.4018/978-1-7998-7287-0.ch003

Borges, V. D. (2021). Happiness: The Basis for Public Policy in Tourism. In A. Perinotto, V. Mayer, & J. Soares (Eds.), *Rebuilding and Restructuring the Tourism Industry: Infusion of Happiness and Quality of Life* (pp. 1–25). IGI Global. https://doi.org/10.4018/978-1-7998-7239-9.ch001

Bücker, J., & Ernste, K. (2018). Use of Brand Heroes in Strategic Reputation Management: The Case of Bacardi, Adidas, and Daimler. In A. Erdemir (Ed.), *Reputation Management Techniques in Public Relations* (pp. 126–150). Hershey, PA: IGI Global. doi:10.4018/978-1-5225-3619-2.ch007

Buluk Eşitti, B. (2021). COVID-19 and Alternative Tourism: New Destinations and New Tourism Products. In M. Demir, A. Dalgıç, & F. Ergen (Eds.), *Handbook of Research on the Impacts and Implications of COVID-19 on the Tourism Industry* (pp. 786–805). IGI Global. https://doi.org/10.4018/978-1-7998-8231-2.ch038

Bureš, V. (2018). Industry 4.0 From the Systems Engineering Perspective: Alternative Holistic Framework Development. In R. Brunet-Thornton & F. Martinez (Eds.), *Analyzing the Impacts of Industry 4.0 in Modern Business Environments* (pp. 199–223). Hershey, PA: IGI Global. doi:10.4018/978-1-5225-3468-6.ch011

Buzady, Z. (2017). Resolving the Magic Cube of Effective Case Teaching: Benchmarking Case Teaching Practices in Emerging Markets – Insights from the Central European University Business School, Hungary. In D. Latusek (Ed.), *Case Studies as a Teaching Tool in Management Education* (pp. 79–103). Hershey, PA: IGI Global. doi:10.4018/978-1-5225-0770-3.ch005

Camillo, A. (2021). *Legal Matters, Risk Management, and Risk Prevention: From Forming a Business to Legal Representation*. IGI Global. doi:10.4018/978-1-7998-4342-9.ch004

Căpusneanu, S., & Topor, D. I. (2018). Business Ethics and Cost Management in SMEs: Theories of Business Ethics and Cost Management Ethos. In I. Oncioiu (Ed.), *Ethics and Decision-Making for Sustainable Business Practices* (pp. 109–127). Hershey, PA: IGI Global. doi:10.4018/978-1-5225-3773-1.ch007

Chan, R. L., Mo, P. L., & Moon, K. K. (2018). Strategic and Tactical Measures in Managing Enterprise Risks: A Study of the Textile and Apparel Industry. In K. Strang, M. Korstanje, & N. Vajjhala (Eds.), *Research, Practices, and Innovations in Global Risk and Contingency Management* (pp. 1–19). Hershey, PA: IGI Global. doi:10.4018/978-1-5225-4754-9.ch001

Charlier, S. D., Burke-Smalley, L. A., & Fisher, S. L. (2018). Undergraduate Programs in the U.S: A Contextual and Content-Based Analysis. In J. Mendy (Ed.), *Teaching Human Resources and Organizational Behavior at the College Level* (pp. 26–57). Hershey, PA: IGI Global. doi:10.4018/978-1-5225-2820-3.ch002

Chumillas, J., Güell, M., & Quer, P. (2022). The Use of ICT in Tourist and Educational Literary Routes: The Role of the Guide. In C. Ramos, S. Quinteiro, & A. Gonçalves (Eds.), *ICT as Innovator Between Tourism and Culture* (pp. 15–29). IGI Global. https://doi.org/10.4018/978-1-7998-8165-0.ch002

Dahlberg, T., Kivijärvi, H., & Saarinen, T. (2017). IT Investment Consistency and Other Factors Influencing the Success of IT Performance. In S. De Haes & W. Van Grembergen (Eds.), *Strategic IT Governance and Alignment in Business Settings* (pp. 176–208). Hershey, PA: IGI Global. doi:10.4018/978-1-5225-0861-8.ch007

Damnjanović, A. M. (2017). Knowledge Management Optimization through IT and E-Business Utilization: A Qualitative Study on Serbian SMEs. In M. Vemić (Ed.), *Optimal Management Strategies in Small and Medium Enterprises* (pp. 249–267). Hershey, PA: IGI Global. doi:10.4018/978-1-5225-1949-2.ch012

Daneshpour, H. (2017). Integrating Sustainable Development into Project Portfolio Management through Application of Open Innovation. In M. Vemić (Ed.), *Optimal Management Strategies in Small and Medium Enterprises* (pp. 370–387). Hershey, PA: IGI Global. doi:10.4018/978-1-5225-1949-2.ch017

Daniel, A. D., & Reis de Castro, V. (2018). Entrepreneurship Education: How to Measure the Impact on Nascent Entrepreneurs. In A. Carrizo Moreira, J. Guilherme Leitão Dantas, & F. Manuel Valente (Eds.), *Nascent Entrepreneurship and Successful New Venture Creation* (pp. 85–110). Hershey, PA: IGI Global. doi:10.4018/978-1-5225-2936-1.ch004

David, R., Swami, B. N., & Tangirala, S. (2018). Ethics Impact on Knowledge Management in Organizational Development: A Case Study. In N. Baporikar (Ed.), *Global Practices in Knowledge Management for Societal and Organizational Development* (pp. 19–45). Hershey, PA: IGI Global. doi:10.4018/978-1-5225-3009-1.ch002

De Uña-Álvarez, E., & Villarino-Pérez, M. (2022). Fostering Ecocultural Resources, Identity, and Tourism in Inland Territories (Galicia, NW Spain). In G. Fernandes (Ed.), *Challenges and New Opportunities for Tourism in Inland Territories: Ecocultural Resources and Sustainable Initiatives* (pp. 1-16). IGI Global. https://doi.org/10.4018/978-1-7998-7339-6.ch001

Delias, P., & Lakiotaki, K. (2018). Discovering Process Horizontal Boundaries to Facilitate Process Comprehension. *International Journal of Operations Research and Information Systems*, *9*(2), 1–31. doi:10.4018/IJORIS.2018040101

Denholm, J., & Lee-Davies, L. (2018). Success Factors for Games in Business and Project Management. In *Enhancing Education and Training Initiatives Through Serious Games* (pp. 34–68). Hershey, PA: IGI Global. doi:10.4018/978-1-5225-3689-5.ch002

Deshpande, M. (2017). Best Practices in Management Institutions for Global Leadership: Policy Aspects. In N. Baporikar (Ed.), *Management Education for Global Leadership* (pp. 1–27). Hershey, PA: IGI Global. doi:10.4018/978-1-5225-1013-0.ch001

Deshpande, M. (2018). Policy Perspectives for SMEs Knowledge Management. In N. Baporikar (Ed.), *Knowledge Integration Strategies for Entrepreneurship and Sustainability* (pp. 23–46). Hershey, PA: IGI Global. doi:10.4018/978-1-5225-5115-7.ch002

Dezdar, S. (2017). ERP Implementation Projects in Asian Countries: A Comparative Study on Iran and China. *International Journal of Information Technology Project Management*, *8*(3), 52–68. doi:10.4018/IJITPM.2017070104

Domingos, D., Respício, A., & Martinho, R. (2017). Reliability of IoT-Aware BPMN Healthcare Processes. In C. Reis & M. Maximiano (Eds.), *Internet of Things and Advanced Application in Healthcare* (pp. 214–248). Hershey, PA: IGI Global. doi:10.4018/978-1-5225-1820-4.ch008

Dosumu, O., Hussain, J., & El-Gohary, H. (2017). An Exploratory Study of the Impact of Government Policies on the Development of Small and Medium Enterprises in Developing Countries: The Case of Nigeria. *International Journal of Customer Relationship Marketing and Management*, *8*(4), 51–62. doi:10.4018/IJCRMM.2017100104

Durst, S., Bruns, G., & Edvardsson, I. R. (2017). Retaining Knowledge in Smaller Building and Construction Firms. *International Journal of Knowledge and Systems Science*, *8*(3), 1–12. doi:10.4018/IJKSS.2017070101

Edvardsson, I. R., & Durst, S. (2017). Outsourcing, Knowledge, and Learning: A Critical Review. *International Journal of Knowledge-Based Organizations*, *7*(2), 13–26. doi:10.4018/IJKBO.2017040102

Edwards, J. S. (2018). Integrating Knowledge Management and Business Processes. In M. Khosrow-Pour, D.B.A. (Ed.), Encyclopedia of Information Science and Technology, Fourth Edition (pp. 5046-5055). Hershey, PA: IGI Global. doi:10.4018/978-1-5225-2255-3.ch437

Eichelberger, S., & Peters, M. (2021). Family Firm Management in Turbulent Times: Opportunities for Responsible Tourism. In A. Zehrer, G. Glowka, K. Schwaiger, & V. Ranacher-Lackner (Eds.), *Resiliency Models and Addressing Future Risks for Family Firms in the Tourism Industry* (pp. 103–124). IGI Global. https://doi.org/10.4018/978-1-7998-7352-5.ch005

Eide, D., Hjalager, A., & Hansen, M. (2022). Innovative Certifications in Adventure Tourism: Attributes and Diffusion. In R. Augusto Costa, F. Brandão, Z. Breda, & C. Costa (Eds.), *Planning and Managing the Experience Economy in Tourism* (pp. 161-175). IGI Global. https://doi.org/10.4018/978-1-7998-8775-1.ch009

Ejiogu, A. O. (2018). Economics of Farm Management. In *Agricultural Finance and Opportunities for Investment and Expansion* (pp. 56–72). Hershey, PA: IGI Global. doi:10.4018/978-1-5225-3059-6.ch003

Ekanem, I., & Abiade, G. E. (2018). Factors Influencing the Use of E-Commerce by Small Enterprises in Nigeria. *International Journal of ICT Research in Africa and the Middle East*, *7*(1), 37–53. doi:10.4018/IJICTRAME.2018010103

Ekanem, I., & Alrossais, L. A. (2017). Succession Challenges Facing Family Businesses in Saudi Arabia. In P. Zgheib (Ed.), *Entrepreneurship and Business Innovation in the Middle East* (pp. 122–146). Hershey, PA: IGI Global. doi:10.4018/978-1-5225-2066-5.ch007

El Faquih, L., & Fredj, M. (2017). Ontology-Based Framework for Quality in Configurable Process Models. *Journal of Electronic Commerce in Organizations*, *15*(2), 48–60. doi:10.4018/JECO.2017040104

Faisal, M. N., & Talib, F. (2017). Building Ambidextrous Supply Chains in SMEs: How to Tackle the Barriers? *International Journal of Information Systems and Supply Chain Management*, *10*(4), 80–100. doi:10.4018/IJISSCM.2017100105

Fernandes, T. M., Gomes, J., & Romão, M. (2017). Investments in E-Government: A Benefit Management Case Study. *International Journal of Electronic Government Research*, *13*(3), 1–17. doi:10.4018/IJEGR.2017070101

Figueira, L. M., Honrado, G. R., & Dionísio, M. S. (2021). Human Capital Management in the Tourism Industry in Portugal. In V. Costa, A. Moura, & M. Mira (Eds.), *Handbook of Research on Human Capital and People Management in the Tourism Industry* (pp. 1–19). IGI Global. doi:10.4018/978-1-7998-4318-4.ch001

Gao, S. S., Oreal, S., & Zhang, J. (2018). Contemporary Financial Risk Management Perceptions and Practices of Small-Sized Chinese Businesses. In I. Management Association (Ed.), Global Business Expansion: Concepts, Methodologies, Tools, and Applications (pp. 917-931). Hershey, PA: IGI Global. doi:10.4018/978-1-5225-5481-3.ch041

Garg, R., & Berning, S. C. (2017). Indigenous Chinese Management Philosophies: Key Concepts and Relevance for Modern Chinese Firms. In B. Christiansen & G. Koc (Eds.), *Transcontinental Strategies for Industrial Development and Economic Growth* (pp. 43–57). Hershey, PA: IGI Global. doi:10.4018/978-1-5225-2160-0.ch003

Gencer, Y. G. (2017). Supply Chain Management in Retailing Business. In U. Akkucuk (Ed.), *Ethics and Sustainability in Global Supply Chain Management* (pp. 197–210). Hershey, PA: IGI Global. doi:10.4018/978-1-5225-2036-8.ch011

Gera, R., Arora, S., & Malik, S. (2021). Emotional Labor in the Tourism Industry: Strategies, Antecedents, and Outcomes. In V. Costa, A. Moura, & M. Mira (Eds.), *Handbook of Research on Human Capital and People Management in the Tourism Industry* (pp. 73–91). IGI Global. https://doi.org/10.4018/978-1-7998-4318-4.ch004

Giacosa, E. (2018). The Increasing of the Regional Development Thanks to the Luxury Business Innovation. In L. Carvalho (Ed.), *Handbook of Research on Entrepreneurial Ecosystems and Social Dynamics in a Globalized World* (pp. 260–273). Hershey, PA: IGI Global. doi:10.4018/978-1-5225-3525-6.ch011

Glowka, G., Tusch, M., & Zehrer, A. (2021). The Risk Perception of Family Business Owner-Manager in the Tourism Industry: A Qualitative Comparison of the Intra-Firm Senior and Junior Generation. In A. Zehrer, G. Glowka, K. Schwaiger, & V. Ranacher-Lackner (Eds.), *Resiliency Models and Addressing Future Risks for Family Firms in the Tourism Industry* (pp. 126–153). IGI Global. https://doi.org/10.4018/978-1-7998-7352-5.ch006

Glykas, M., & George, J. (2017). Quality and Process Management Systems in the UAE Maritime Industry. *International Journal of Productivity Management and Assessment Technologies*, *5*(1), 20–39. doi:10.4018/IJPMAT.2017010102

Glykas, M., Valiris, G., Kokkinaki, A., & Koutsoukou, Z. (2018). Banking Business Process Management Implementation. *International Journal of Productivity Management and Assessment Technologies*, *6*(1), 50–69. doi:10.4018/IJPMAT.2018010104

Gomes, J., & Romão, M. (2017). The Balanced Scorecard: Keeping Updated and Aligned with Today's Business Trends. *International Journal of Productivity Management and Assessment Technologies*, *5*(2), 1–15. doi:10.4018/IJPMAT.2017070101

Gomes, J., & Romão, M. (2017). Aligning Information Systems and Technology with Benefit Management and Balanced Scorecard. In S. De Haes & W. Van Grembergen (Eds.), *Strategic IT Governance and Alignment in Business Settings* (pp. 112–131). Hershey, PA: IGI Global. doi:10.4018/978-1-5225-0861-8.ch005

Goyal, A. (2021). Communicating and Building Destination Brands With New Media. In M. Dinis, L. Bonixe, S. Lamy, & Z. Breda (Eds.), *Impact of New Media in Tourism* (pp. 1-20). IGI Global. https://doi.org/10.4018/978-1-7998-7095-1.ch001

Grefen, P., & Turetken, O. (2017). Advanced Business Process Management in Networked E-Business Scenarios. *International Journal of E-Business Research*, *13*(4), 70–104. doi:10.4018/IJEBR.2017100105

Guasca, M., Van Broeck, A. M., & Vanneste, D. (2021). Tourism and the Social Reintegration of Colombian Ex-Combatants. In J. da Silva, Z. Breda, & F. Carbone (Eds.), *Role and Impact of Tourism in Peacebuilding and Conflict Transformation* (pp. 66-86). IGI Global. https://doi.org/10.4018/978-1-7998-5053-3.ch005

Haider, A., & Saetang, S. (2017). Strategic IT Alignment in Service Sector. In S. Rozenes & Y. Cohen (Eds.), *Handbook of Research on Strategic Alliances and Value Co-Creation in the Service Industry* (pp. 231–258). Hershey, PA: IGI Global. doi:10.4018/978-1-5225-2084-9.ch012

Hajilari, A. B., Ghadaksaz, M., & Fasghandis, G. S. (2017). Assessing Organizational Readiness for Implementing ERP System Using Fuzzy Expert System Approach. *International Journal of Enterprise Information Systems*, *13*(1), 67–85. doi:10.4018/IJEIS.2017010105

Haldorai, A., Ramu, A., & Murugan, S. (2018). Social Aware Cognitive Radio Networks: Effectiveness of Social Networks as a Strategic Tool for Organizational Business Management. In H. Bansal, G. Shrivastava, G. Nguyen, & L. Stanciu (Eds.), *Social Network Analytics for Contemporary Business Organizations* (pp. 188–202). Hershey, PA: IGI Global. doi:10.4018/978-1-5225-5097-6.ch010

Hall, O. P. Jr. (2017). Social Media Driven Management Education. *International Journal of Knowledge-Based Organizations*, *7*(2), 43–59. doi:10.4018/IJKBO.2017040104

Hanifah, H., Halim, H. A., Ahmad, N. H., & Vafaei-Zadeh, A. (2017). Innovation Culture as a Mediator Between Specific Human Capital and Innovation Performance Among Bumiputera SMEs in Malaysia. In N. Ahmad, T. Ramayah, H. Halim, & S. Rahman (Eds.), *Handbook of Research on Small and Medium Enterprises in Developing Countries* (pp. 261–279). Hershey, PA: IGI Global. doi:10.4018/978-1-5225-2165-5.ch012

Hartlieb, S., & Silvius, G. (2017). Handling Uncertainty in Project Management and Business Development: Similarities and Differences. In Y. Raydugin (Ed.), *Handbook of Research on Leveraging Risk and Uncertainties for Effective Project Management* (pp. 337–362). Hershey, PA: IGI Global. doi:10.4018/978-1-5225-1790-0.ch016

Hass, K. B. (2017). Living on the Edge: Managing Project Complexity. In Y. Raydugin (Ed.), *Handbook of Research on Leveraging Risk and Uncertainties for Effective Project Management* (pp. 177–201). Hershey, PA: IGI Global. doi:10.4018/978-1-5225-1790-0.ch009

Hawking, P., & Carmine Sellitto, C. (2017). Developing an Effective Strategy for Organizational Business Intelligence. In M. Tavana (Ed.), *Enterprise Information Systems and the Digitalization of Business Functions* (pp. 222–237). Hershey, PA: IGI Global. doi:10.4018/978-1-5225-2382-6.ch010

Hawking, P., & Sellitto, C. (2017). A Fast-Moving Consumer Goods Company and Business Intelligence Strategy Development. *International Journal of Enterprise Information Systems*, *13*(2), 22–33. doi:10.4018/IJEIS.2017040102

Hawking, P., & Sellitto, C. (2017). Business Intelligence Strategy: Two Case Studies. *International Journal of Business Intelligence Research*, *8*(2), 17–30. doi:10.4018/IJBIR.2017070102

Hee, W. J., Jalleh, G., Lai, H., & Lin, C. (2017). E-Commerce and IT Projects: Evaluation and Management Issues in Australian and Taiwanese Hospitals. *International Journal of Public Health Management and Ethics*, *2*(1), 69–90. doi:10.4018/IJPHME.2017010104

Hernandez, A. A. (2018). Exploring the Factors to Green IT Adoption of SMEs in the Philippines. *Journal of Cases on Information Technology*, *20*(2), 49–66. doi:10.4018/JCIT.2018040104

Hollman, A., Bickford, S., & Hollman, T. (2017). Cyber InSecurity: A Post-Mortem Attempt to Assess Cyber Problems from IT and Business Management Perspectives. *Journal of Cases on Information Technology, 19*(3), 42–70. doi:10.4018/JCIT.2017070104

Ibrahim, F., & Zainin, N. M. (2021). Exploring the Technological Impacts: The Case of Museums in Brunei Darussalam. *International Journal of Tourism and Hospitality Management in the Digital Age, 5*(1), 1–18. https://doi.org/10.4018/IJTHMDA.2021010101

Igbinakhase, I. (2017). Responsible and Sustainable Management Practices in Developing and Developed Business Environments. In Z. Fields (Ed.), *Collective Creativity for Responsible and Sustainable Business Practice* (pp. 180–207). Hershey, PA: IGI Global. doi:10.4018/978-1-5225-1823-5.ch010

Iwata, J. J., & Hoskins, R. G. (2017). Managing Indigenous Knowledge in Tanzania: A Business Perspective. In P. Jain & N. Mnjama (Eds.), *Managing Knowledge Resources and Records in Modern Organizations* (pp. 198–214). Hershey, PA: IGI Global. doi:10.4018/978-1-5225-1965-2.ch012

Jain, P. (2017). Ethical and Legal Issues in Knowledge Management Life-Cycle in Business. In P. Jain & N. Mnjama (Eds.), *Managing Knowledge Resources and Records in Modern Organizations* (pp. 82–101). Hershey, PA: IGI Global. doi:10.4018/978-1-5225-1965-2.ch006

James, S., & Hauli, E. (2017). Holistic Management Education at Tanzanian Rural Development Planning Institute. In N. Baporikar (Ed.), *Management Education for Global Leadership* (pp. 112–136). Hershey, PA: IGI Global. doi:10.4018/978-1-5225-1013-0.ch006

Janošková, M., Csikósová, A., & Čulková, K. (2018). Measurement of Company Performance as Part of Its Strategic Management. In R. Leon (Ed.), *Managerial Strategies for Business Sustainability During Turbulent Times* (pp. 309–335). Hershey, PA: IGI Global. doi:10.4018/978-1-5225-2716-9.ch017

Jean-Vasile, A., & Alecu, A. (2017). Theoretical and Practical Approaches in Understanding the Influences of Cost-Productivity-Profit Trinomial in Contemporary Enterprises. In A. Jean Vasile & D. Nicolò (Eds.), *Sustainable Entrepreneurship and Investments in the Green Economy* (pp. 28–62). Hershey, PA: IGI Global. doi:10.4018/978-1-5225-2075-7.ch002

Joia, L. A., & Correia, J. C. (2018). CIO Competencies From the IT Professional Perspective: Insights From Brazil. *Journal of Global Information Management, 26*(2), 74–103. doi:10.4018/JGIM.2018040104

Juma, A., & Mzera, N. (2017). Knowledge Management and Records Management and Competitive Advantage in Business. In P. Jain & N. Mnjama (Eds.), *Managing Knowledge Resources and Records in Modern Organizations* (pp. 15–28). Hershey, PA: IGI Global. doi:10.4018/978-1-5225-1965-2.ch002

K., I., & A, V. (2018). Monitoring and Auditing in the Cloud. In K. Munir (Ed.), *Cloud Computing Technologies for Green Enterprises* (pp. 318-350). Hershey, PA: IGI Global. https://doi.org/ doi:10.4018/978-1-5225-3038-1.ch013

Kabra, G., Ghosh, V., & Ramesh, A. (2018). Enterprise Integrated Business Process Management and Business Intelligence Framework for Business Process Sustainability. In A. Paul, D. Bhattacharyya, & S. Anand (Eds.), *Green Initiatives for Business Sustainability and Value Creation* (pp. 228–238). Hershey, PA: IGI Global. doi:10.4018/978-1-5225-2662-9.ch010

Kaoud, M. (2017). Investigation of Customer Knowledge Management: A Case Study Research. *International Journal of Service Science, Management, Engineering, and Technology*, *8*(2), 12–22. doi:10.4018/IJSSMET.2017040102

Katuu, S. (2018). A Comparative Assessment of Enterprise Content Management Maturity Models. In N. Gwangwava & M. Mutingi (Eds.), *E-Manufacturing and E-Service Strategies in Contemporary Organizations* (pp. 93–118). Hershey, PA: IGI Global. doi:10.4018/978-1-5225-3628-4.ch005

Khan, M. Y., & Abir, T. (2022). The Role of Social Media Marketing in the Tourism and Hospitality Industry: A Conceptual Study on Bangladesh. In C. Ramos, S. Quinteiro, & A. Gonçalves (Eds.), *ICT as Innovator Between Tourism and Culture* (pp. 213–229). IGI Global. https://doi.org/10.4018/978-1-7998-8165-0.ch013

Kinnunen, S., Ylä-Kujala, A., Marttonen-Arola, S., Kärri, T., & Baglee, D. (2018). Internet of Things in Asset Management: Insights from Industrial Professionals and Academia. *International Journal of Service Science, Management, Engineering, and Technology*, *9*(2), 104–119. doi:10.4018/IJSSMET.2018040105

Klein, A. Z., Sabino de Freitas, A., Machado, L., Freitas, J. C. Jr, Graziola, P. G. Jr, & Schlemmer, E. (2017). Virtual Worlds Applications for Management Education. In L. Tomei (Ed.), *Exploring the New Era of Technology-Infused Education* (pp. 279–299). Hershey, PA: IGI Global. doi:10.4018/978-1-5225-1709-2.ch017

Kővári, E., Saleh, M., & Steinbachné Hajmásy, G. (2022). The Impact of Corporate Digital Responsibility (CDR) on Internal Stakeholders' Satisfaction in Hungarian Upscale Hotels. In M. Valeri (Ed.), *New Governance and Management in Touristic Destinations* (pp. 35–51). IGI Global. https://doi.org/10.4018/978-1-6684-3889-3.ch003

Kożuch, B., & Jabłoński, A. (2017). Adopting the Concept of Business Models in Public Management. In M. Lewandowski & B. Kożuch (Eds.), *Public Sector Entrepreneurship and the Integration of Innovative Business Models* (pp. 10–46). Hershey, PA: IGI Global. doi:10.4018/978-1-5225-2215-7.ch002

Kumar, J., Adhikary, A., & Jha, A. (2017). Small Active Investors' Perceptions and Preferences Towards Tax Saving Mutual Fund Schemes in Eastern India: An Empirical Note. *International Journal of Asian Business and Information Management*, *8*(2), 35–45. doi:10.4018/IJABIM.2017040103

Latusi, S., & Fissore, M. (2021). Pilgrimage Routes to Happiness: Comparing the Camino de Santiago and Via Francigena. In A. Perinotto, V. Mayer, & J. Soares (Eds.), *Rebuilding and Restructuring the Tourism Industry: Infusion of Happiness and Quality of Life* (pp. 157–182). IGI Global. https://doi.org/10.4018/978-1-7998-7239-9.ch008

Lavassani, K. M., & Movahedi, B. (2017). Applications Driven Information Systems: Beyond Networks toward Business Ecosystems. *International Journal of Innovation in the Digital Economy*, *8*(1), 61–75. doi:10.4018/IJIDE.2017010104

Lazzareschi, V. H., & Brito, M. S. (2017). Strategic Information Management: Proposal of Business Project Model. In G. Jamil, A. Soares, & C. Pessoa (Eds.), *Handbook of Research on Information Management for Effective Logistics and Supply Chains* (pp. 59–88). Hershey, PA: IGI Global. doi:10.4018/978-1-5225-0973-8.ch004

Lechuga Sancho, M. P., & Martín Navarro, A. (2022). Evolution of the Literature on Social Responsibility in the Tourism Sector: A Systematic Literature Review. In G. Fernandes (Ed.), *Challenges and New Opportunities for Tourism in Inland Territories: Ecocultural Resources and Sustainable Initiatives* (pp. 169–186). IGI Global. https://doi.org/10.4018/978-1-7998-7339-6.ch010

Lederer, M., Kurz, M., & Lazarov, P. (2017). Usage and Suitability of Methods for Strategic Business Process Initiatives: A Multi Case Study Research. *International Journal of Productivity Management and Assessment Technologies*, *5*(1), 40–51. doi:10.4018/IJPMAT.2017010103

Lee, I. (2017). A Social Enterprise Business Model and a Case Study of Pacific Community Ventures (PCV). In V. Potocan, M. Üngan, & Z. Nedelko (Eds.), *Handbook of Research on Managerial Solutions in Non-Profit Organizations* (pp. 182–204). Hershey, PA: IGI Global. doi:10.4018/978-1-5225-0731-4.ch009

Leon, L. A., Seal, K. C., Przasnyski, Z. H., & Wiedenman, I. (2017). Skills and Competencies Required for Jobs in Business Analytics: A Content Analysis of Job Advertisements Using Text Mining. *International Journal of Business Intelligence Research, 8*(1), 1–25. doi:10.4018/IJBIR.2017010101

Levy, C. L., & Elias, N. I. (2017). SOHO Users' Perceptions of Reliability and Continuity of Cloud-Based Services. In M. Moore (Ed.), *Cybersecurity Breaches and Issues Surrounding Online Threat Protection* (pp. 248–287). Hershey, PA: IGI Global. doi:10.4018/978-1-5225-1941-6.ch011

Levy, M. (2018). Change Management Serving Knowledge Management and Organizational Development: Reflections and Review. In N. Baporikar (Ed.), *Global Practices in Knowledge Management for Societal and Organizational Development* (pp. 256–270). Hershey, PA: IGI Global. doi:10.4018/978-1-5225-3009-1.ch012

Lewandowski, M. (2017). Public Organizations and Business Model Innovation: The Role of Public Service Design. In M. Lewandowski & B. Kożuch (Eds.), *Public Sector Entrepreneurship and the Integration of Innovative Business Models* (pp. 47–72). Hershey, PA: IGI Global. doi:10.4018/978-1-5225-2215-7.ch003

Lhannaoui, H., Kabbaj, M. I., & Bakkoury, Z. (2017). A Survey of Risk-Aware Business Process Modelling. *International Journal of Risk and Contingency Management, 6*(3), 14–26. doi:10.4018/IJRCM.2017070102

Li, J., Sun, W., Jiang, W., Yang, H., & Zhang, L. (2017). How the Nature of Exogenous Shocks and Crises Impact Company Performance?: The Effects of Industry Characteristics. *International Journal of Risk and Contingency Management, 6*(4), 40–55. doi:10.4018/IJRCM.2017100103

Lopez-Fernandez, M., Perez-Perez, M., Serrano-Bedia, A., & Cobo-Gonzalez, A. (2021). Small and Medium Tourism Enterprise Survival in Times of Crisis: "El Capricho de Gaudí. In D. Toubes & N. Araújo-Vila (Eds.), *Risk, Crisis, and Disaster Management in Small and Medium-Sized Tourism Enterprises* (pp. 103–129). IGI Global. doi:10.4018/978-1-7998-6996-2.ch005

Mahajan, A., Maidullah, S., & Hossain, M. R. (2022). Experience Toward Smart Tour Guide Apps in Travelling: An Analysis of Users' Reviews on Audio Odigos and Trip My Way. In R. Augusto Costa, F. Brandão, Z. Breda, & C. Costa (Eds.), *Planning and Managing the Experience Economy in Tourism* (pp. 255-273). IGI Global. https://doi.org/10.4018/978-1-7998-8775-1.ch014

Malega, P. (2017). Small and Medium Enterprises in the Slovak Republic: Status and Competitiveness of SMEs in the Global Markets and Possibilities of Optimization. In M. Vemić (Ed.), *Optimal Management Strategies in Small and Medium Enterprises* (pp. 102–124). Hershey, PA: IGI Global. doi:10.4018/978-1-5225-1949-2.ch006

Malewska, K. M. (2017). Intuition in Decision-Making on the Example of a Non-Profit Organization. In V. Potocan, M. Üngan, & Z. Nedelko (Eds.), *Handbook of Research on Managerial Solutions in Non-Profit Organizations* (pp. 378–399). Hershey, PA: IGI Global. doi:10.4018/978-1-5225-0731-4.ch018

Maroofi, F. (2017). Entrepreneurial Orientation and Organizational Learning Ability Analysis for Innovation and Firm Performance. In N. Baporikar (Ed.), *Innovation and Shifting Perspectives in Management Education* (pp. 144–165). Hershey, PA: IGI Global. doi:10.4018/978-1-5225-1019-2.ch007

Marques, M., Moleiro, D., Brito, T. M., & Marques, T. (2021). Customer Relationship Management as an Important Relationship Marketing Tool: The Case of the Hospitality Industry in Estoril Coast. In M. Dinis, L. Bonixe, S. Lamy, & Z. Breda (Eds.), Impact of New Media in Tourism (pp. 39-56). IGI Global. https://doi.org/doi:10.4018/978-1-7998-7095-1.ch003

Martins, P. V., & Zacarias, M. (2017). A Web-based Tool for Business Process Improvement. *International Journal of Web Portals*, *9*(2), 68–84. doi:10.4018/IJWP.2017070104

Matthies, B., & Coners, A. (2017). Exploring the Conceptual Nature of e-Business Projects. *Journal of Electronic Commerce in Organizations*, *15*(3), 33–63. doi:10.4018/JECO.2017070103

Mayer, V. F., Fraga, C. C., & Silva, L. C. (2021). Contributions of Neurosciences to Studies of Well-Being in Tourism. In A. Perinotto, V. Mayer, & J. Soares (Eds.), *Rebuilding and Restructuring the Tourism Industry: Infusion of Happiness and Quality of Life* (pp. 108–128). IGI Global. https://doi.org/10.4018/978-1-7998-7239-9.ch006

McKee, J. (2018). Architecture as a Tool to Solve Business Planning Problems. In M. Khosrow-Pour, D.B.A. (Ed.), Encyclopedia of Information Science and Technology, Fourth Edition (pp. 573-586). Hershey, PA: IGI Global. doi:10.4018/978-1-5225-2255-3.ch050

McMurray, A. J., Cross, J., & Caponecchia, C. (2018). The Risk Management Profession in Australia: Business Continuity Plan Practices. In N. Bajgoric (Ed.), *Always-On Enterprise Information Systems for Modern Organizations* (pp. 112–129). Hershey, PA: IGI Global. doi:10.4018/978-1-5225-3704-5.ch006

Meddah, I. H., & Belkadi, K. (2018). Mining Patterns Using Business Process Management. In R. Hamou (Ed.), *Handbook of Research on Biomimicry in Information Retrieval and Knowledge Management* (pp. 78–89). Hershey, PA: IGI Global. doi:10.4018/978-1-5225-3004-6.ch005

Melian, A. G., & Camprubí, R. (2021). The Accessibility of Museum Websites: The Case of Barcelona. In C. Eusébio, L. Teixeira, & M. Carneiro (Eds.), *ICT Tools and Applications for Accessible Tourism* (pp. 234–255). IGI Global. https://doi.org/10.4018/978-1-7998-6428-8.ch011

Mendes, L. (2017). TQM and Knowledge Management: An Integrated Approach Towards Tacit Knowledge Management. In D. Jaziri-Bouagina & G. Jamil (Eds.), *Handbook of Research on Tacit Knowledge Management for Organizational Success* (pp. 236–263). Hershey, PA: IGI Global. doi:10.4018/978-1-5225-2394-9.ch009

Menezes, V. D., & Cavagnaro, E. (2021). Communicating Sustainable Initiatives in the Hotel Industry: The Case of the Hotel Jakarta Amsterdam. In F. Brandão, Z. Breda, R. Costa, & C. Costa (Eds.), *Handbook of Research on the Role of Tourism in Achieving Sustainable Development Goals* (pp. 224-234). IGI Global. https://doi.org/10.4018/978-1-7998-5691-7.ch013

Menezes, V. D., & Cavagnaro, E. (2021). Communicating Sustainable Initiatives in the Hotel Industry: The Case of the Hotel Jakarta Amsterdam. In F. Brandão, Z. Breda, R. Costa, & C. Costa (Eds.), *Handbook of Research on the Role of Tourism in Achieving Sustainable Development Goals* (pp. 224-234). IGI Global. https://doi.org/10.4018/978-1-7998-5691-7.ch013

Mitas, O., Bastiaansen, M., & Boode, W. (2022). If You're Happy, I'm Happy: Emotion Contagion at a Tourist Information Center. In R. Augusto Costa, F. Brandão, Z. Breda, & C. Costa (Eds.), *Planning and Managing the Experience Economy in Tourism* (pp. 122-140). IGI Global. https://doi.org/10.4018/978-1-7998-8775-1.ch007

Mnjama, N. M. (2017). Preservation of Recorded Information in Public and Private Sector Organizations. In P. Jain & N. Mnjama (Eds.), *Managing Knowledge Resources and Records in Modern Organizations* (pp. 149–167). Hershey, PA: IGI Global. doi:10.4018/978-1-5225-1965-2.ch009

Mokoqama, M., & Fields, Z. (2017). Principles of Responsible Management Education (PRME): Call for Responsible Management Education. In Z. Fields (Ed.), *Collective Creativity for Responsible and Sustainable Business Practice* (pp. 229–241). Hershey, PA: IGI Global. doi:10.4018/978-1-5225-1823-5.ch012

Monteiro, A., Lopes, S., & Carbone, F. (2021). Academic Mobility: Bridging Tourism and Peace Education. In J. da Silva, Z. Breda, & F. Carbone (Eds.), *Role and Impact of Tourism in Peacebuilding and Conflict Transformation* (pp. 275-301). IGI Global. https://doi.org/10.4018/978-1-7998-5053-3.ch016

Muniapan, B. (2017). Philosophy and Management: The Relevance of Vedanta in Management. In P. Ordóñez de Pablos (Ed.), *Managerial Strategies and Solutions for Business Success in Asia* (pp. 124–139). Hershey, PA: IGI Global. doi:10.4018/978-1-5225-1886-0.ch007

Murad, S. E., & Dowaji, S. (2017). Using Value-Based Approach for Managing Cloud-Based Services. In A. Turuk, B. Sahoo, & S. Addya (Eds.), *Resource Management and Efficiency in Cloud Computing Environments* (pp. 33–60). Hershey, PA: IGI Global. doi:10.4018/978-1-5225-1721-4.ch002

Mutahar, A. M., Daud, N. M., Thurasamy, R., Isaac, O., & Abdulsalam, R. (2018). The Mediating of Perceived Usefulness and Perceived Ease of Use: The Case of Mobile Banking in Yemen. *International Journal of Technology Diffusion*, *9*(2), 21–40. doi:10.4018/IJTD.2018040102

Naidoo, V. (2017). E-Learning and Management Education at African Universities. In N. Baporikar (Ed.), *Management Education for Global Leadership* (pp. 181–201). Hershey, PA: IGI Global. doi:10.4018/978-1-5225-1013-0.ch009

Naidoo, V., & Igbinakhase, I. (2018). Opportunities and Challenges of Knowledge Retention in SMEs. In N. Baporikar (Ed.), *Knowledge Integration Strategies for Entrepreneurship and Sustainability* (pp. 70–94). Hershey, PA: IGI Global. doi:10.4018/978-1-5225-5115-7.ch004

Naumov, N., & Costandachi, G. (2021). Creativity and Entrepreneurship: Gastronomic Tourism in Mexico. In J. Soares (Ed.), *Innovation and Entrepreneurial Opportunities in Community Tourism* (pp. 90-108). IGI Global. https://doi.org/10.4018/978-1-7998-4855-4.ch006

Nayak, S., & Prabhu, N. (2017). Paradigm Shift in Management Education: Need for a Cross Functional Perspective. In N. Baporikar (Ed.), *Management Education for Global Leadership* (pp. 241–255). Hershey, PA: IGI Global. doi:10.4018/978-1-5225-1013-0.ch012

Nedelko, Z., & Potocan, V. (2017). Management Solutions in Non-Profit Organizations: Case of Slovenia. In V. Potocan, M. Üngan, & Z. Nedelko (Eds.), *Handbook of Research on Managerial Solutions in Non-Profit Organizations* (pp. 1–22). Hershey, PA: IGI Global. doi:10.4018/978-1-5225-0731-4.ch001

Nedelko, Z., & Potocan, V. (2017). Priority of Management Tools Utilization among Managers: International Comparison. In V. Wang (Ed.), *Encyclopedia of Strategic Leadership and Management* (pp. 1083–1094). Hershey, PA: IGI Global. doi:10.4018/978-1-5225-1049-9.ch075

Nedelko, Z., Raudeliūnienė, J., & Črešnar, R. (2018). Knowledge Dynamics in Supply Chain Management. In N. Baporikar (Ed.), *Knowledge Integration Strategies for Entrepreneurship and Sustainability* (pp. 150–166). Hershey, PA: IGI Global. doi:10.4018/978-1-5225-5115-7.ch008

Nguyen, H. T., & Hipsher, S. A. (2018). Innovation and Creativity Used by Private Sector Firms in a Resources-Constrained Environment. In S. Hipsher (Ed.), *Examining the Private Sector's Role in Wealth Creation and Poverty Reduction* (pp. 219–238). Hershey, PA: IGI Global. doi:10.4018/978-1-5225-3117-3.ch010

Obicci, P. A. (2017). Risk Sharing in a Partnership. In *Risk Management Strategies in Public-Private Partnerships* (pp. 115–152). Hershey, PA: IGI Global. doi:10.4018/978-1-5225-2503-5.ch004

Obidallah, W. J., & Raahemi, B. (2017). Managing Changes in Service Oriented Virtual Organizations: A Structural and Procedural Framework to Facilitate the Process of Change. *Journal of Electronic Commerce in Organizations, 15*(1), 59–83. doi:10.4018/JECO.2017010104

Ojo, O. (2017). Impact of Innovation on the Entrepreneurial Success in Selected Business Enterprises in South-West Nigeria. *International Journal of Innovation in the Digital Economy, 8*(2), 29–38. doi:10.4018/IJIDE.2017040103

Okdinawati, L., Simatupang, T. M., & Sunitiyoso, Y. (2017). Multi-Agent Reinforcement Learning for Value Co-Creation of Collaborative Transportation Management (CTM). *International Journal of Information Systems and Supply Chain Management, 10*(3), 84–95. doi:10.4018/IJISSCM.2017070105

Olivera, V. A., & Carrillo, I. M. (2021). Organizational Culture: A Key Element for the Development of Mexican Micro and Small Tourist Companies. In J. Soares (Ed.), *Innovation and Entrepreneurial Opportunities in Community Tourism* (pp. 227–242). IGI Global. doi:10.4018/978-1-7998-4855-4.ch013

Ossorio, M. (2022). Corporate Museum Experiences in Enogastronomic Tourism. In R. Augusto Costa, F. Brandão, Z. Breda, & C. Costa (Eds.), Planning and Managing the Experience Economy in Tourism (pp. 107-121). IGI Global. https://doi.org/doi:10.4018/978-1-7998-8775-1.ch006

Ossorio, M. (2022). Enogastronomic Tourism in Times of Pandemic. In G. Fernandes (Ed.), *Challenges and New Opportunities for Tourism in Inland Territories: Ecocultural Resources and Sustainable Initiatives* (pp. 241–255). IGI Global. https://doi.org/10.4018/978-1-7998-7339-6.ch014

Özekici, Y. K. (2022). ICT as an Acculturative Agent and Its Role in the Tourism Context: Introduction, Acculturation Theory, Progress of the Acculturation Theory in Extant Literature. In C. Ramos, S. Quinteiro, & A. Gonçalves (Eds.), *ICT as Innovator Between Tourism and Culture* (pp. 42–66). IGI Global. https://doi.org/10.4018/978-1-7998-8165-0.ch004

Pal, K. (2018). Building High Quality Big Data-Based Applications in Supply Chains. In A. Kumar & S. Saurav (Eds.), *Supply Chain Management Strategies and Risk Assessment in Retail Environments* (pp. 1–24). Hershey, PA: IGI Global. doi:10.4018/978-1-5225-3056-5.ch001

Palos-Sanchez, P. R., & Correia, M. B. (2018). Perspectives of the Adoption of Cloud Computing in the Tourism Sector. In J. Rodrigues, C. Ramos, P. Cardoso, & C. Henriques (Eds.), *Handbook of Research on Technological Developments for Cultural Heritage and eTourism Applications* (pp. 377–400). Hershey, PA: IGI Global. doi:10.4018/978-1-5225-2927-9.ch018

Papadopoulou, G. (2021). Promoting Gender Equality and Women Empowerment in the Tourism Sector. In F. Brandão, Z. Breda, R. Costa, & C. Costa (Eds.), Handbook of Research on the Role of Tourism in Achieving Sustainable Development Goals (pp. 152-174). IGI Global. https://doi.org/ doi:10.4018/978-1-7998-5691-7.ch009

Papp-Váry, Á. F., & Tóth, T. Z. (2022). Analysis of Budapest as a Film Tourism Destination. In R. Baleiro & R. Pereira (Eds.), *Global Perspectives on Literary Tourism and Film-Induced Tourism* (pp. 257-279). IGI Global. https://doi.org/10.4018/978-1-7998-8262-6.ch014

Patiño, B. E. (2017). New Generation Management by Convergence and Individual Identity: A Systemic and Human-Oriented Approach. In N. Baporikar (Ed.), *Innovation and Shifting Perspectives in Management Education* (pp. 119–143). Hershey, PA: IGI Global. doi:10.4018/978-1-5225-1019-2.ch006

Patro, C. S. (2021). Digital Tourism: Influence of E-Marketing Technology. In M. Dinis, L. Bonixe, S. Lamy, & Z. Breda (Eds.), *Impact of New Media in Tourism* (pp. 234-254). IGI Global. https://doi.org/10.4018/978-1-7998-7095-1.ch014

Pawliczek, A., & Rössler, M. (2017). Knowledge of Management Tools and Systems in SMEs: Knowledge Transfer in Management. In A. Bencsik (Ed.), *Knowledge Management Initiatives and Strategies in Small and Medium Enterprises* (pp. 180–203). Hershey, PA: IGI Global. doi:10.4018/978-1-5225-1642-2.ch009

Pejic-Bach, M., Omazic, M. A., Aleksic, A., & Zoroja, J. (2018). Knowledge-Based Decision Making: A Multi-Case Analysis. In R. Leon (Ed.), *Managerial Strategies for Business Sustainability During Turbulent Times* (pp. 160–184). Hershey, PA: IGI Global. doi:10.4018/978-1-5225-2716-9.ch009

Perano, M., Hysa, X., & Calabrese, M. (2018). Strategic Planning, Cultural Context, and Business Continuity Management: Business Cases in the City of Shkoder. In A. Presenza & L. Sheehan (Eds.), *Geopolitics and Strategic Management in the Global Economy* (pp. 57–77). Hershey, PA: IGI Global. doi:10.4018/978-1-5225-2673-5.ch004

Pereira, R., Mira da Silva, M., & Lapão, L. V. (2017). IT Governance Maturity Patterns in Portuguese Healthcare. In S. De Haes & W. Van Grembergen (Eds.), *Strategic IT Governance and Alignment in Business Settings* (pp. 24–52). Hershey, PA: IGI Global. doi:10.4018/978-1-5225-0861-8.ch002

Pérez-Uribe, R. I., Torres, D. A., Jurado, S. P., & Prada, D. M. (2018). Cloud Tools for the Development of Project Management in SMEs. In R. Perez-Uribe, C. Salcedo-Perez, & D. Ocampo-Guzman (Eds.), *Handbook of Research on Intrapreneurship and Organizational Sustainability in SMEs* (pp. 95–120). Hershey, PA: IGI Global. doi:10.4018/978-1-5225-3543-0.ch005

Petrisor, I., & Cozmiuc, D. (2017). Global Supply Chain Management Organization at Siemens in the Advent of Industry 4.0. In L. Saglietto & C. Cezanne (Eds.), *Global Intermediation and Logistics Service Providers* (pp. 123–142). Hershey, PA: IGI Global. doi:10.4018/978-1-5225-2133-4.ch007

Pierce, J. M., Velliaris, D. M., & Edwards, J. (2017). A Living Case Study: A Journey Not a Destination. In N. Silton (Ed.), *Exploring the Benefits of Creativity in Education, Media, and the Arts* (pp. 158–178). Hershey, PA: IGI Global. doi:10.4018/978-1-5225-0504-4.ch008

Pipia, S., & Pipia, S. (2021). Challenges of Religious Tourism in the Conflict Region: An Example of Jerusalem. In E. Alaverdov & M. Bari (Eds.), *Global Development of Religious Tourism* (pp. 135-148). IGI Global. https://doi.org/10.4018/978-1-7998-5792-1.ch009

Poulaki, P., Kritikos, A., Vasilakis, N., & Valeri, M. (2022). The Contribution of Female Creativity to the Development of Gastronomic Tourism in Greece: The Case of the Island of Naxos in the South Aegean Region. In M. Valeri (Ed.), *New Governance and Management in Touristic Destinations* (pp. 246–258). IGI Global. https://doi.org/10.4018/978-1-6684-3889-3.ch015

Radosavljevic, M., & Andjelkovic, A. (2017). Multi-Criteria Decision Making Approach for Choosing Business Process for the Improvement: Upgrading of the Six Sigma Methodology. In J. Stanković, P. Delias, S. Marinković, & S. Rochhia (Eds.), *Tools and Techniques for Economic Decision Analysis* (pp. 225–247). Hershey, PA: IGI Global. doi:10.4018/978-1-5225-0959-2.ch011

Radovic, V. M. (2017). Corporate Sustainability and Responsibility and Disaster Risk Reduction: A Serbian Overview. In M. Camilleri (Ed.), *CSR 2.0 and the New Era of Corporate Citizenship* (pp. 147–164). Hershey, PA: IGI Global. doi:10.4018/978-1-5225-1842-6.ch008

Raghunath, K. M., Devi, S. L., & Patro, C. S. (2018). Impact of Risk Assessment Models on Risk Factors: A Holistic Outlook. In K. Strang, M. Korstanje, & N. Vajjhala (Eds.), *Research, Practices, and Innovations in Global Risk and Contingency Management* (pp. 134–153). Hershey, PA: IGI Global. doi:10.4018/978-1-5225-4754-9.ch008

Raman, A., & Goyal, D. P. (2017). Extending IMPLEMENT Framework for Enterprise Information Systems Implementation to Information System Innovation. In M. Tavana (Ed.), *Enterprise Information Systems and the Digitalization of Business Functions* (pp. 137–177). Hershey, PA: IGI Global. doi:10.4018/978-1-5225-2382-6.ch007

Rao, Y., & Zhang, Y. (2017). The Construction and Development of Academic Library Digital Special Subject Databases. In L. Ruan, Q. Zhu, & Y. Ye (Eds.), *Academic Library Development and Administration in China* (pp. 163–183). Hershey, PA: IGI Global. doi:10.4018/978-1-5225-0550-1.ch010

Ravasan, A. Z., Mohammadi, M. M., & Hamidi, H. (2018). An Investigation Into the Critical Success Factors of Implementing Information Technology Service Management Frameworks. In K. Jakobs (Ed.), *Corporate and Global Standardization Initiatives in Contemporary Society* (pp. 200–218). Hershey, PA: IGI Global. doi:10.4018/978-1-5225-5320-5.ch009

Rezaie, S., Mirabedini, S. J., & Abtahi, A. (2018). Designing a Model for Implementation of Business Intelligence in the Banking Industry. *International Journal of Enterprise Information Systems*, *14*(1), 77–103. doi:10.4018/IJEIS.2018010105

Richards, V., Matthews, N., Williams, O. J., & Khan, Z. (2021). The Challenges of Accessible Tourism Information Systems for Tourists With Vision Impairment: Sensory Communications Beyond the Screen. In C. Eusébio, L. Teixeira, & M. Carneiro (Eds.), *ICT Tools and Applications for Accessible Tourism* (pp. 26–54). IGI Global. https://doi.org/10.4018/978-1-7998-6428-8.ch002

Rodrigues de Souza Neto, V., & Marques, O. (2021). Rural Tourism Fostering Welfare Through Sustainable Development: A Conceptual Approach. In A. Perinotto, V. Mayer, & J. Soares (Eds.), *Rebuilding and Restructuring the Tourism Industry: Infusion of Happiness and Quality of Life* (pp. 38–57). IGI Global. https://doi.org/10.4018/978-1-7998-7239-9.ch003

Romano, L., Grimaldi, R., & Colasuonno, F. S. (2017). Demand Management as a Success Factor in Project Portfolio Management. In L. Romano (Ed.), *Project Portfolio Management Strategies for Effective Organizational Operations* (pp. 202–219). Hershey, PA: IGI Global. doi:10.4018/978-1-5225-2151-8.ch008

Rubio-Escuderos, L., & García-Andreu, H. (2021). Competitiveness Factors of Accessible Tourism E-Travel Agencies. In C. Eusébio, L. Teixeira, & M. Carneiro (Eds.), *ICT Tools and Applications for Accessible Tourism* (pp. 196–217). IGI Global. https://doi.org/10.4018/978-1-7998-6428-8.ch009

Rucci, A. C., Porto, N., Darcy, S., & Becka, L. (2021). Smart and Accessible Cities?: Not Always – The Case for Accessible Tourism Initiatives in Buenos Aries and Sydney. In C. Eusébio, L. Teixeira, & M. Carneiro (Eds.), *ICT Tools and Applications for Accessible Tourism* (pp. 115–145). IGI Global. https://doi.org/10.4018/978-1-7998-6428-8.ch006

Ruhi, U. (2018). Towards an Interdisciplinary Socio-Technical Definition of Virtual Communities. In M. Khosrow-Pour, D.B.A. (Ed.), Encyclopedia of Information Science and Technology, Fourth Edition (pp. 4278-4295). Hershey, PA: IGI Global. doi:10.4018/978-1-5225-2255-3.ch371

Ryan, L., Catena, M., Ros, P., & Stephens, S. (2021). Designing Entrepreneurial Ecosystems to Support Resource Management in the Tourism Industry. In V. Costa, A. Moura, & M. Mira (Eds.), *Handbook of Research on Human Capital and People Management in the Tourism Industry* (pp. 265–281). IGI Global. https://doi.org/10.4018/978-1-7998-4318-4.ch013

Sabuncu, I. (2021). Understanding Tourist Perceptions and Expectations During Pandemic Through Social Media Big Data. In M. Demir, A. Dalgıç, & F. Ergen (Eds.), *Handbook of Research on the Impacts and Implications of COVID-19 on the Tourism Industry* (pp. 330–350). IGI Global. https://doi.org/10.4018/978-1-7998-8231-2.ch016

Safari, M. R., & Jiang, Q. (2018). The Theory and Practice of IT Governance Maturity and Strategies Alignment: Evidence From Banking Industry. *Journal of Global Information Management*, *26*(2), 127–146. doi:10.4018/JGIM.2018040106

Sahoo, J., Pati, B., & Mohanty, B. (2017). Knowledge Management as an Academic Discipline: An Assessment. In B. Gunjal (Ed.), *Managing Knowledge and Scholarly Assets in Academic Libraries* (pp. 99–126). Hershey, PA: IGI Global. doi:10.4018/978-1-5225-1741-2.ch005

Saini, D. (2017). Relevance of Teaching Values and Ethics in Management Education. In N. Baporikar (Ed.), *Management Education for Global Leadership* (pp. 90–111). Hershey, PA: IGI Global. doi:10.4018/978-1-5225-1013-0.ch005

Sambhanthan, A. (2017). Assessing and Benchmarking Sustainability in Organisations: An Integrated Conceptual Model. *International Journal of Systems and Service-Oriented Engineering*, *7*(4), 22–43. doi:10.4018/IJSSOE.2017100102

Sambhanthan, A., & Potdar, V. (2017). A Study of the Parameters Impacting Sustainability in Information Technology Organizations. *International Journal of Knowledge-Based Organizations*, *7*(3), 27–39. doi:10.4018/IJKBO.2017070103

Sánchez-Fernández, M. D., & Manríquez, M. R. (2018). The Entrepreneurial Spirit Based on Social Values: The Digital Generation. In P. Isaias & L. Carvalho (Eds.), *User Innovation and the Entrepreneurship Phenomenon in the Digital Economy* (pp. 173–193). Hershey, PA: IGI Global. doi:10.4018/978-1-5225-2826-5.ch009

Sanchez-Ruiz, L., & Blanco, B. (2017). Process Management for SMEs: Barriers, Enablers, and Benefits. In M. Vemić (Ed.), *Optimal Management Strategies in Small and Medium Enterprises* (pp. 293–319). Hershey, PA: IGI Global. doi:10.4018/978-1-5225-1949-2.ch014

Sanz, L. F., Gómez-Pérez, J., & Castillo-Martinez, A. (2018). Analysis of the European ICT Competence Frameworks. In V. Ahuja & S. Rathore (Eds.), *Multidisciplinary Perspectives on Human Capital and Information Technology Professionals* (pp. 225–245). Hershey, PA: IGI Global. doi:10.4018/978-1-5225-5297-0.ch012

Sarvepalli, A., & Godin, J. (2017). Business Process Management in the Classroom. *Journal of Cases on Information Technology, 19*(2), 17–28. doi:10.4018/JCIT.2017040102

Saxena, G. G., & Saxena, A. (2021). Host Community Role in Medical Tourism Development. In M. Singh & S. Kumaran (Eds.), *Growth of the Medical Tourism Industry and Its Impact on Society: Emerging Research and Opportunities* (pp. 105–127). IGI Global. https://doi.org/10.4018/978-1-7998-3427-4.ch006

Saygili, E. E., Ozturkoglu, Y., & Kocakulah, M. C. (2017). End Users' Perceptions of Critical Success Factors in ERP Applications. *International Journal of Enterprise Information Systems, 13*(4), 58–75. doi:10.4018/IJEIS.2017100104

Saygili, E. E., & Saygili, A. T. (2017). Contemporary Issues in Enterprise Information Systems: A Critical Review of CSFs in ERP Implementations. In M. Tavana (Ed.), *Enterprise Information Systems and the Digitalization of Business Functions* (pp. 120–136). Hershey, PA: IGI Global. doi:10.4018/978-1-5225-2382-6.ch006

Schwaiger, K. M., & Zehrer, A. (2021). The COVID-19 Pandemic and Organizational Resilience in Hospitality Family Firms: A Qualitative Approach. In A. Zehrer, G. Glowka, K. Schwaiger, & V. Ranacher-Lackner (Eds.), *Resiliency Models and Addressing Future Risks for Family Firms in the Tourism Industry* (pp. 32–49). IGI Global. https://doi.org/10.4018/978-1-7998-7352-5.ch002

Scott, N., & Campos, A. C. (2022). Cognitive Science of Tourism Experiences. In R. Augusto Costa, F. Brandão, Z. Breda, & C. Costa (Eds.), Planning and Managing the Experience Economy in Tourism (pp. 1-21). IGI Global. https://doi.org/ doi:10.4018/978-1-7998-8775-1.ch001

Seidenstricker, S., & Antonino, A. (2018). Business Model Innovation-Oriented Technology Management for Emergent Technologies. In M. Khosrow-Pour, D.B.A. (Ed.), Encyclopedia of Information Science and Technology, Fourth Edition (pp. 4560-4569). Hershey, PA: IGI Global. doi:10.4018/978-1-5225-2255-3.ch396

Selvi, M. S. (2021). Changes in Tourism Sales and Marketing Post COVID-19. In M. Demir, A. Dalgıç, & F. Ergen (Eds.), *Handbook of Research on the Impacts and Implications of COVID-19 on the Tourism Industry* (pp. 437–460). IGI Global. doi:10.4018/978-1-7998-8231-2.ch021

Senaratne, S., & Gunarathne, A. D. (2017). Excellence Perspective for Management Education from a Global Accountants' Hub in Asia. In N. Baporikar (Ed.), *Management Education for Global Leadership* (pp. 158–180). Hershey, PA: IGI Global. doi:10.4018/978-1-5225-1013-0.ch008

Sensuse, D. I., & Cahyaningsih, E. (2018). Knowledge Management Models: A Summative Review. *International Journal of Information Systems in the Service Sector, 10*(1), 71–100. doi:10.4018/IJISSS.2018010105

Seth, M., Goyal, D., & Kiran, R. (2017). Diminution of Impediments in Implementation of Supply Chain Management Information System for Enhancing its Effectiveness in Indian Automobile Industry. *Journal of Global Information Management, 25*(3), 1–20. doi:10.4018/JGIM.2017070101

Seyal, A. H., & Rahman, M. N. (2017). Investigating Impact of Inter-Organizational Factors in Measuring ERP Systems Success: Bruneian Perspectives. In M. Tavana (Ed.), *Enterprise Information Systems and the Digitalization of Business Functions* (pp. 178–204). Hershey, PA: IGI Global. doi:10.4018/978-1-5225-2382-6.ch008

Shaqrah, A. A. (2018). Analyzing Business Intelligence Systems Based on 7s Model of McKinsey. *International Journal of Business Intelligence Research, 9*(1), 53–63. doi:10.4018/IJBIR.2018010104

Sharma, A. J. (2017). Enhancing Sustainability through Experiential Learning in Management Education. In N. Baporikar (Ed.), *Management Education for Global Leadership* (pp. 256–274). Hershey, PA: IGI Global. doi:10.4018/978-1-5225-1013-0.ch013

Shetty, K. P. (2017). Responsible Global Leadership: Ethical Challenges in Management Education. In N. Baporikar (Ed.), *Innovation and Shifting Perspectives in Management Education* (pp. 194–223). Hershey, PA: IGI Global. doi:10.4018/978-1-5225-1019-2.ch009

Sinthupundaja, J., & Kohda, Y. (2017). Effects of Corporate Social Responsibility and Creating Shared Value on Sustainability. *International Journal of Sustainable Entrepreneurship and Corporate Social Responsibility, 2*(1), 27–38. doi:10.4018/IJSECSR.2017010103

Škarica, I., & Hrgović, A. V. (2018). Implementation of Total Quality Management Principles in Public Health Institutes in the Republic of Croatia. *International Journal of Productivity Management and Assessment Technologies, 6*(1), 1–16. doi:10.4018/IJPMAT.2018010101

Skokic, V. (2021). How Small Hotel Owners Practice Resilience: Longitudinal Study Among Small Family Hotels in Croatia. In A. Zehrer, G. Glowka, K. Schwaiger, & V. Ranacher-Lackner (Eds.), *Resiliency Models and Addressing Future Risks for Family Firms in the Tourism Industry* (pp. 50–73). IGI Global. doi:10.4018/978-1-7998-7352-5.ch003

Smuts, H., Kotzé, P., Van der Merwe, A., & Loock, M. (2017). Framework for Managing Shared Knowledge in an Information Systems Outsourcing Context. *International Journal of Knowledge Management, 13*(4), 1–30. doi:10.4018/IJKM.2017100101

Sousa, M. J., Cruz, R., Dias, I., & Caracol, C. (2017). Information Management Systems in the Supply Chain. In G. Jamil, A. Soares, & C. Pessoa (Eds.), *Handbook of Research on Information Management for Effective Logistics and Supply Chains* (pp. 469–485). Hershey, PA: IGI Global. doi:10.4018/978-1-5225-0973-8.ch025

Spremic, M., Turulja, L., & Bajgoric, N. (2018). Two Approaches in Assessing Business Continuity Management Attitudes in the Organizational Context. In N. Bajgoric (Ed.), *Always-On Enterprise Information Systems for Modern Organizations* (pp. 159–183). Hershey, PA: IGI Global. doi:10.4018/978-1-5225-3704-5.ch008

Steenkamp, A. L. (2018). Some Insights in Computer Science and Information Technology. In *Examining the Changing Role of Supervision in Doctoral Research Projects: Emerging Research and Opportunities* (pp. 113–133). Hershey, PA: IGI Global. doi:10.4018/978-1-5225-2610-0.ch005

Stipanović, C., Rudan, E., & Zubović, V. (2022). Reaching the New Tourist Through Creativity: Sustainable Development Challenges in Croatian Coastal Towns. In M. Valeri (Ed.), *New Governance and Management in Touristic Destinations* (pp. 231–245). IGI Global. https://doi.org/10.4018/978-1-6684-3889-3.ch014

Tabach, A., & Croteau, A. (2017). Configurations of Information Technology Governance Practices and Business Unit Performance. *International Journal of IT/Business Alignment and Governance, 8*(2), 1–27. doi:10.4018/IJITBAG.2017070101

Talaue, G. M., & Iqbal, T. (2017). Assessment of e-Business Mode of Selected Private Universities in the Philippines and Pakistan. *International Journal of Online Marketing, 7*(4), 63–77. doi:10.4018/IJOM.2017100105

Tam, G. C. (2017). Project Manager Sustainability Competence. In *Managerial Strategies and Green Solutions for Project Sustainability* (pp. 178–207). Hershey, PA: IGI Global. doi:10.4018/978-1-5225-2371-0.ch008

Tambo, T. (2018). Fashion Retail Innovation: About Context, Antecedents, and Outcome in Technological Change Projects. In I. Management Association (Ed.), Fashion and Textiles: Breakthroughs in Research and Practice (pp. 233-260). Hershey, PA: IGI Global. https://doi.org/ doi:10.4018/978-1-5225-3432-7.ch010

Tantau, A. D., & Frăţilă, L. C. (2018). Information and Management System for Renewable Energy Business. In *Entrepreneurship and Business Development in the Renewable Energy Sector* (pp. 200–244). Hershey, PA: IGI Global. doi:10.4018/978-1-5225-3625-3.ch006

Teixeira, N., Pardal, P. N., & Rafael, B. G. (2018). Internationalization, Financial Performance, and Organizational Challenges: A Success Case in Portugal. In L. Carvalho (Ed.), *Handbook of Research on Entrepreneurial Ecosystems and Social Dynamics in a Globalized World* (pp. 379–423). Hershey, PA: IGI Global. doi:10.4018/978-1-5225-3525-6.ch017

Teixeira, P., Teixeira, L., Eusébio, C., Silva, S., & Teixeira, A. (2021). The Impact of ICTs on Accessible Tourism: Evidence Based on a Systematic Literature Review. In C. Eusébio, L. Teixeira, & M. Carneiro (Eds.), *ICT Tools and Applications for Accessible Tourism* (pp. 1–25). IGI Global. doi:10.4018/978-1-7998-6428-8.ch001

Trad, A., & Kalpić, D. (2018). The Business Transformation Framework, Agile Project and Change Management. In M. Khosrow-Pour, D.B.A. (Ed.), Encyclopedia of Information Science and Technology, Fourth Edition (pp. 620-635). Hershey, PA: IGI Global. https://doi.org/ doi:10.4018/978-1-5225-2255-3.ch054

Trad, A., & Kalpić, D. (2018). The Business Transformation and Enterprise Architecture Framework: The Financial Engineering E-Risk Management and E-Law Integration. In B. Sergi, F. Fidanoski, M. Ziolo, & V. Naumovski (Eds.), *Regaining Global Stability After the Financial Crisis* (pp. 46–65). Hershey, PA: IGI Global. doi:10.4018/978-1-5225-4026-7.ch003

Trengereid, V. (2022). Conditions of Network Engagement: The Quest for a Common Good. In R. Augusto Costa, F. Brandão, Z. Breda, & C. Costa (Eds.), *Planning and Managing the Experience Economy in Tourism* (pp. 69-84). IGI Global. https://doi.org/10.4018/978-1-7998-8775-1.ch004

Turulja, L., & Bajgoric, N. (2018). Business Continuity and Information Systems: A Systematic Literature Review. In N. Bajgoric (Ed.), *Always-On Enterprise Information Systems for Modern Organizations* (pp. 60–87). Hershey, PA: IGI Global. doi:10.4018/978-1-5225-3704-5.ch004

Vargas-Hernández, J. G. (2017). Professional Integrity in Business Management Education. In N. Baporikar (Ed.), *Management Education for Global Leadership* (pp. 70–89). Hershey, PA: IGI Global. doi:10.4018/978-1-5225-1013-0.ch004

Varnacı Uzun, F. (2021). The Destination Preferences of Foreign Tourists During the COVID-19 Pandemic and Attitudes Towards: Marmaris, Turkey. In M. Demir, A. Dalgıç, & F. Ergen (Eds.), *Handbook of Research on the Impacts and Implications of COVID-19 on the Tourism Industry* (pp. 285–306). IGI Global. https://doi.org/10.4018/978-1-7998-8231-2.ch014

Vasista, T. G., & AlAbdullatif, A. M. (2017). Role of Electronic Customer Relationship Management in Demand Chain Management: A Predictive Analytic Approach. *International Journal of Information Systems and Supply Chain Management, 10*(1), 53–67. doi:10.4018/IJISSCM.2017010104

Vieru, D., & Bourdeau, S. (2017). Survival in the Digital Era: A Digital Competence-Based Multi-Case Study in the Canadian SME Clothing Industry. *International Journal of Social and Organizational Dynamics in IT, 6*(1), 17–34. doi:10.4018/IJSODIT.2017010102

Vijayan, G., & Kamarulzaman, N. H. (2017). An Introduction to Sustainable Supply Chain Management and Business Implications. In M. Khan, M. Hussain, & M. Ajmal (Eds.), *Green Supply Chain Management for Sustainable Business Practice* (pp. 27–50). Hershey, PA: IGI Global. doi:10.4018/978-1-5225-0635-5.ch002

Vlachvei, A., & Notta, O. (2017). Firm Competitiveness: Theories, Evidence, and Measurement. In A. Vlachvei, O. Notta, K. Karantininis, & N. Tsounis (Eds.), *Factors Affecting Firm Competitiveness and Performance in the Modern Business World* (pp. 1–42). Hershey, PA: IGI Global. doi:10.4018/978-1-5225-0843-4.ch001

Wang, C., Schofield, M., Li, X., & Ou, X. (2017). Do Chinese Students in Public and Private Higher Education Institutes Perform at Different Level in One of the Leadership Skills: Critical Thinking?: An Exploratory Comparison. In V. Wang (Ed.), *Encyclopedia of Strategic Leadership and Management* (pp. 160–181). Hershey, PA: IGI Global. doi:10.4018/978-1-5225-1049-9.ch013

Wang, J. (2017). Multi-Agent based Production Management Decision System Modelling for the Textile Enterprise. *Journal of Global Information Management, 25*(4), 1–15. doi:10.4018/JGIM.2017100101

Wiedemann, A., & Gewald, H. (2017). Examining Cross-Domain Alignment: The Correlation of Business Strategy, IT Management, and IT Business Value. *International Journal of IT/Business Alignment and Governance, 8*(1), 17–31. doi:10.4018/IJITBAG.2017010102

Wolf, R., & Thiel, M. (2018). Advancing Global Business Ethics in China: Reducing Poverty Through Human and Social Welfare. In S. Hipsher (Ed.), *Examining the Private Sector's Role in Wealth Creation and Poverty Reduction* (pp. 67–84). Hershey, PA: IGI Global. doi:10.4018/978-1-5225-3117-3.ch004

Yablonsky, S. (2018). Innovation Platforms: Data and Analytics Platforms. In *Multi-Sided Platforms (MSPs) and Sharing Strategies in the Digital Economy: Emerging Research and Opportunities* (pp. 72–95). Hershey, PA: IGI Global. doi:10.4018/978-1-5225-5457-8.ch003

Yaşar, B. (2021). The Impact of COVID-19 on Volatility of Tourism Stocks: Evidence From BIST Tourism Index. In M. Demir, A. Dalgıç, & F. Ergen (Eds.), *Handbook of Research on the Impacts and Implications of COVID-19 on the Tourism Industry* (pp. 23–44). IGI Global. https://doi.org/10.4018/978-1-7998-8231-2.ch002

Yusoff, A., Ahmad, N. H., & Halim, H. A. (2017). Agropreneurship among Gen Y in Malaysia: The Role of Academic Institutions. In N. Ahmad, T. Ramayah, H. Halim, & S. Rahman (Eds.), *Handbook of Research on Small and Medium Enterprises in Developing Countries* (pp. 23–47). Hershey, PA: IGI Global. doi:10.4018/978-1-5225-2165-5.ch002

Zacher, D., & Pechlaner, H. (2021). Resilience as an Opportunity Approach: Challenges and Perspectives for Private Sector Participation on a Community Level. In A. Zehrer, G. Glowka, K. Schwaiger, & V. Ranacher-Lackner (Eds.), *Resiliency Models and Addressing Future Risks for Family Firms in the Tourism Industry* (pp. 75–102). IGI Global. https://doi.org/10.4018/978-1-7998-7352-5.ch004

Zanin, F., Comuzzi, E., & Costantini, A. (2018). The Effect of Business Strategy and Stock Market Listing on the Use of Risk Assessment Tools. In *Management Control Systems in Complex Settings: Emerging Research and Opportunities* (pp. 145–168). Hershey, PA: IGI Global. doi:10.4018/978-1-5225-3987-2.ch007

Zgheib, P. W. (2017). Corporate Innovation and Intrapreneurship in the Middle East. In P. Zgheib (Ed.), *Entrepreneurship and Business Innovation in the Middle East* (pp. 37–56). Hershey, PA: IGI Global. doi:10.4018/978-1-5225-2066-5.ch003

About the Contributors

Ricardo Correia, with an academic career started in 2003, is Associated Professor at the Polytechnic Institute of Bragança (Portugal), where he is the head of the Master programme in Tourism Marketing, and visiting Professor at ISM University of Management and Economics (Lithuania). Ricardo has served as an external consultant in programs such as the European Union Agris Program and Interreg and as consultant for Deloitte & Touche. We should also emphasize his regular participation in research programs, conferences and international scientific meetings, as well as the publication of several chapters in books and articles in international journals.

* * *

Sathish Kumar B., a distinguished Master of Commerce teacher, brings expertise and passion to the classroom with dynamic teaching style and extensive research contribute to an enriching educational experience.

Monika Belhaj obtained her Doctor of Philosophy degree from the University of Tasmania, Australia, with a specialization in Management and Commerce. With a rich teaching background, she has covered various subjects, such as Project Management, Creative Leadership and Management. Furthermore, she has actively contributed to several research projects, serving as both a research developer and implementer.

Oindrila Chakraborty is a gold medalist in her MBA programme from University of Calcutta. She has 15 years of teaching experience in management education. She has completed her PhD from University of Calcutta and has several publications to furnish in National and International Journals of high repute.

Rta Fontes is a dedicated Ph.D. student specializing in Tourism at Aveiro University. With a passion for exploring the fascinating world of travel and leisure, she has delved deep into the realm of tourism behavior and spatiotemporal tracking. Ruta's academic journey has been marked by a commitment to research excellence, with numerous publications including papers and book chapters.

João Pedro Gomes is an assistant professor at the Instituto Politécnico de Bragança (Portugal), where he teaches computer networks and programming. He is also the coordinator of the Computer Resource Center and the coordinator of the Higher Professional Technical Course in Informatics. He is interested in IoT and artificial intelligence, among other areas of research.

Rchika Jeswal is currently working as Associate Professor in Amity School of Business, Amity University Noida. She has a rich teaching experience of over 20 years. She did her Ph D from Aligarh Muslim University and MBA from Lucknow University. Her research interests' areas are in the field of Customer Relationship Management, Sustainability, Entrepreneurship and the newer trends of Marketing. She has several research papers to her credit. She is a part of the review board of various indexed journals and book publishing house. She has been associated with many conferences and FDPs of premium institutes. Her forte lies in grooming the future of young minds. She has been instrumental in shaping the careers of several students of BBA over her entire career stint. Her forte lies in teaching, tutoring and mentoring students.

Sridhar Manohar currently working In Doctoral Research Center, Chitkara University, completed his doctorate in the area of Services Marketing from VIT Business School, VIT University. He has a Bachelor of Technology and Dual Masters in Business Administration and Organization Psychology. Dr. Sridhar further certified with FDP at IIM-A. He is expertise in Service Marketing, Innovation and Entrepreneurship, Scale Development Process and Multivariate Analytics and interests in teaching Business Analytics, Innovation and Entrepreneurship, Research Methodology and Marketing Management. He has published around 20 research papers that includes Scopus listed and ABDC ranked International Journals like – Society and Business Review, Benchmarking An International Journal, Electronics Market, Corporate Reputation Review, International Journal of Services and Operations Management, International journal of Business Excellence and presented papers and ideas in numerous international conferences.

Mnica R. is a Master of Commerce student with a strong passion for finance and business strategy, combining theoretical knowledge with practical insights. Strong analytical skills, effective communication, and continuous learning contribute to academic community, aiming to make impactful contributions in finance and strategic management.

Carlos Rompante Cunha is PhD in Computer Science from the University of Trás-Os-Montes e Alto Douro, Portugal. He is an Adjunct Professor in the Department of Informatics and Mathematics, EsACT-IPB. He is/was research member for 4 research projects and is currently co-adviser of 1 PhD student. He published +100 papers in international journals and conferences. He is also member of several International Journals and Conference' Scientific Committees for which frequently review papers. For several years, he was director of the Informatics and Communications BSc, and Coordinator of the Department of Informatics and Mathematics, EsACT-IPB. He was also coordinator of the EsACT-IPB Computer Resources Center. He is currently vice-dean of EsACT-IPB. Teaching Fields: Programming Languages and Distributed Systems. Research topics: Pervasive and Mobile Computing, Distributed Systems, IoT, and Machine Learning.

Aswin Soju is a dedicated Master of Commerce student with a passion for finance and business strategy. Known for academic excellence, this individual combines theoretical knowledge with practical insights gained through internships and extracurricular activities. Strong analytical skills, effective communication, and a commitment to continuous learning define their approach. Engaged in research projects, they contribute to the academic community. Adept at collaborating in diverse teams, they bring a proactive mindset to problem-solving. Eager to leverage their skills in the dynamic world of commerce, this M.Com student aspires to make impactful contributions in the realms of finance and strategic management.

Bruno Barbosa Sousa is Adjunct Professor of Marketing at Polytechnic Institute of Cávado and Ave (IPCA), Portugal and PhD in Marketing and Strategy in Universidade do Minho, Portugal. Head of Masters Program - Tourism Management and Marketing Tourism (IPCA); CiTUR – Center for Tourism Research, Development and Innovation and UNIAG research member. He has published in the Journal of Enterprising Communities, Tourism Management Perspectives, Current Issues in Tourism, Journal of Organizational Change Management, World Review of Entrepreneurship, Management and Sust. Development, among others. https://orcid.org/0000-0002-8588-2422.aac5d92a-6e64-4f88-8f01-362429bd4dc7

Oumeima Toumia is an assistant at IHEC of Sousse. She earned her Ph.D. in management (Business administration) from the Higher Institute of Management of Sousse. Her teaching experience was acquired through her position as an assistant from 2016 until 2023. She published papers in high-ranked journals and participated in has known international conferences. Her research interests include status quo, venture capital, digital transformation, artificial intelligence, firm performance, COVID-19, etc.

Cláudia Veloso is a PhD in Social Sciences (Economics and Management). She is Professor of Management (Marketing and Finances) at ESTGA - University of Aveiro. She is a researcher at GOVCOPP. She was a Member of the Board of the Centro Hospitalar do Nordeste (ULSNE) and Technical Adviser of the Ministry of Health of Portugal. She participated in 4 R&D projects, published more than 70 publications in peer-reviewed journals, book chapters and proceedings, and won 7 scientific awards.

Dominyka Venciute is the Director of Business Management and Analytics Programme and International Marketing and Management Programme at ISM University of Management and Economics. Her teaching subjects include Marketing Principles and Integrated Marketing Communications. Currently Dominyka is involved in post-doctoral studies where she is analyzing the role that leader and employee personal branding has on organizational outcomes. Her other research interests include entrepreneurship, social media marketing, personal branding and employer branding.

Farouk Zouari was born in Tunis, Tunisia, on August 27, 1980. He received his Engineer degree in Electrical Engineering, his magister degree in Automatic and Signal Processing, and his PhD degree in Electrical, Electronics, and Computer Engineering from the National Engineering School of Tunis, University of Tunis El Manar, Tunisia, in 2004, 2005 and 2014, respectively. He is currently a researcher at Laboratoire de Recherche en Automatique (LARA), École Nationale d'Ingénieurs de Tunis, Université de Tunis El Manar. His current research interests include artificial intelligence, adaptive control, chaos synchronization, financial systems and fractional-order plants.

Index

www.ingramcontent.com/pod-product-compliance
Lightning Source LLC
LaVergne TN
LVHW081331300926
849161LV00008B/1948
* 9 7 9 8 3 6 9 3 2 1 5 3 9 *